Computers
in Music
Education

Computers in Music Education

AMPLIFYING MUSICALITY

Andrew R. Brown

Queensland University of Technology
Brisbane, Australia

 Routledge
Taylor & Francis Group
New York   London

Routledge is an imprint of the
Taylor & Francis Group, an informa business

Routledge
Taylor & Francis Group
270 Madison Avenue
New York, NY 10016

Routledge
Taylor & Francis Group
2 Park Square
Milton Park, Abingdon
Oxon OX14 4RN

Printed in the United States of America on acid-free paper
10 9 8 7 6 5 4 3 2 1

International Standard Book Number-10: 0-415-97851-3 (Softcover) 0-415-97850-5 (Hardcover)
International Standard Book Number-13: 978-0-415-97851-4 (Softcover) 978-0-415-97850-7 (Hardcover)

Library of Congress Cataloging-in-Publication Data

Brown, Andrew R.
    Computers in music education : amplifying musicality / Andrew R. Brown.
        p. cm.
    Includes bibliographical references and index.
    ISBN 978-0-415-97851-4 -- ISBN 978-0-415-97850-7
    1. Music--Instruction and study--Technological innovations. 2. Computer music--Instruction and study. 3. Music and technology. I. Title.

MT1.B789 2007
780.7--dc22
                                                                                    2006100586

**Visit the Taylor & Francis Web site at
http://www.taylorandfrancis.com**

**and the Routledge Web site at
http://www.routledge.com**

Contents

Figures   xvii
Preface   xxi

SECTION I CONTEXT   **1**

1   Ways of making music with technology   **3**
       Changing technologies   4
       Changing minds   4
       The computer as a musical tool   6
       The computer as a musical medium   8
       The computer as a musical instrument   10
       Learning to use the computer for music making   12
       Conclusion   13
       Chapter summary   14
       Notes   15

2   Philosophical considerations   **17**
       Amplification   17
       Invisibility   18
       Context   20
       Metaphor   20
       Musicianship   22
       Scaffolding   22
       Intention   23
       Engagement   24

CONTENTS

	Meaning	26
	Conclusion	27
	Chapter summary	29
	Notes	29

3 A brief history of music technology — **31**

	Pre-electronic technologies	31
	Automated music	32
	Electronic musical technologies	34
	Layers of persistence	37
	Conclusion	38
	Chapter summary	39
	Notes	40

SECTION II PRODUCTION — **41**

4 Audio recording — **43**

	Sampling	43
	Audio file formats	45
	Manipulating samples	46
	Cutting and pasting	46
	Pitch shifting	46
	Filtering and equalization	47
	Amplitude envelopes	47
	Delays and reverb	47
	Hard disk recording	48
	Signal flow	48
	Recording mediums	49
	Tape	50
	Cassette	50
	Reel to reel	50
	DAT	50
	Disk	51
	Hard disk	51
	Mini disc	51
	Compact disc	51
	DVD	51
	Memory card	52
	Recording production techniques	52
	Clarity	52

Tone 52

Balance 53

Spatialization 53

Effects 53

Educational applications of digital recording technologies 54

Music production 54

Recorded portfolios 54

Reflection 55

Assessment 55

Conclusion 56

Chapter summary 58

Notes 58

5   Music publishing **59**

Notation as a representation 59

Learning with computer-based music notation 60

What to look for in a music notation system 63

Print quality 63

Input methods 63

Rhythmic transcription and rendering 64

Staves and articulations 64

Transformation and shifting 65

Text and drawing 65

Playback and audio rendering 65

Priorities for music publishing hardware 66

Conclusion 67

Chapter summary 69

Notes 70

6   MIDI sequencing **71**

Sequencer history 72

Modern sequencers 72

Track view 74

Phrase editor 74

Note editors 74

Waveform view 75

Loops 75

Making music with sequencers 76

Arranging 76

Composing 77

CONTENTS

	Production	77
	Analysis	78
	Performance	78
	Conclusion	79
	Chapter summary	81
	Notes	81

7	**Algorithmic music**	**83**
	Introducing algorithmic composition	84
	Uses of algorithmic composition	85
	Inside algorithmic processes	87
	Rule-based	87
	Probabilistic	87
	Connectionist	88
	Evolutionist	89
	Using commercial systems	90
	Exploring further	90
	Software for algorithmic composition	90
	Simple applications	90
	Environments	91
	Languages	91
	Sequencers with some algorithmic features	91
	Conclusion	91
	Chapter summary	93
	Notes	93

8	**Sound synthesis**	**95**
	Oscillator synthesis	97
	Additive synthesis	97
	Subtractive synthesis	98
	Ring modulation	99
	Frequency modulation	99
	Waveshaping	100
	Digital synthesis directions	101
	Granular synthesis	101
	Physical modeling	102
	Experimenting with sound synthesis	103
	Plugins and hosts	103
	Synthesis toolkits	104
	Signal generators	104

Useful links   105
Dedicated plugin hosts   105
   Synthesis toolkits (graphical)   105
   Synthesis toolkits (textual)   105
   Sound editors with tone generators 105
Conclusion   106
Chapter summary   107

SECTION III PRESENTATION   **109**

9   Synthesizer performance   **111**
What is a synthesizer?   112
Choosing a synthesizer for educational use   113
   Sound quality and quantity   113
   Ability to edit and create sounds   113
   Types of performance controllers   114
   Connections   114
Educational applications of synthesizers   114
   Individual work   114
   Class ensembles   114
   Composition   115
The synthesizer for solo performance   115
   Performance skills   115
Synthesizer ensemble performance   116
   Synthesizer-only ensembles   116
   Mixed electroacoustic ensembles   116
Interactive performance   117
Instrumental teaching of synthesizer performance   117
Conclusion   118
Chapter summary   119
Notes   120

10 Live electronic music   **121**
Introduction   121
History   122
   Early instruments   122
   New directions   123
   Experimentalists   124
   Connecting with rock music   124
   Dance music   125

CONTENTS

Equipment 126
    Hardware synthesizers 126
    Samplers 126
    Drum machines 127
    Turntables and mixers 127
    Software 127
    Controllers 128
    Headphones 129
Performance practices 129
Learning to make live electronic music 130
Conclusion 130
Chapter summary 132
Notes 132

11 Interactive computer music **133**
The interactive experience 134
Computer listening and response 135
Human input 136
Performance partnerships 138
Remote control 139
Useful links 139
    Dedicated applications 140
    Software environments 140
    Multimedia tools 140
    Auto-accompaniment software 140
Conclusion 141
Chapter summary 142
Notes 143

12 Digitizing and visualizing music **145**
Introduction 145
Audio formats 147
    PCM audio 147
    MP3 files 147
    AAC 148
    Ogg vorbis 148
    FLAC 148
Audio visualizations 149
    Oscilloscope 149
    Waveform display 150

Spectrum analyzer	150
Spectrogram	151
MIDI representation	152
MIDI visualization	153
Textual representation	153
Music fonts	154
Graphical representations	155
Graphic formats	155
Video formats	156
Presenting	156
Word processor	156
Digital slide show	157
HTML	157
PDF	158
Podcasts	158
CDs	158
DVDs	158
Using digital presentations for teaching and learning	159
Chapter summary	160
Notes	161

13 Music for visual narrative   **163**

Sound and image	163
Video	166
Structure	166
Synchronization	167
Theater	167
Sound design	168
Audio spatialization	168
Music	168
Dance	169
Collaboration	169
Gesture	170
Experimentation	170
Exhibition	171
Sonification of digital images	171
Mood	172
Temporality	172
Presentation	172

CONTENTS

	Conclusion	173
	Chapter summary	175
	Notes	175

14 Rich media environments **177**

Digital media	179
Forms of interactive media	179
Virtual reality simulations	179
Rich media documents	180
Sources of audio content	182
The musical challenge of interactivity	183
Skills of the sound designer	184
Rich media curriculum documents	184
Useful links	185
Document creation tools	185
Interactive systems	185
Media creation tools	185
Examples	186
Conclusion	186
Chapter summary	188
Notes	188

15 Music distribution in the age of the Internet **189**

Playing music on the Internet	190
Stakeholders and issues	190
Ownership	191
Access	192
Distributing music over the Internet	193
Physical distribution	193
File distribution	194
Internet radio	196
Music commentary on the Internet	197
Promoting music on the Internet	198
Useful Links	200
Music sales and promotion	200
Music promotion	200
Music information	200
Rights and commerce	200
RSS tools	200
Conclusion	201

Chapter summary		202
Note		203

SECTION IV REFLECTION   **205**

16   **Computers and music research**   **207**
The place of research in the music curriculum		207
Opportunities on the Internet		208
Searching		208
Convergence of media		209
Forms: online data collection		209
Cooperative projects		210
Access		211
Internet surfing tips		211
Discerning "good" information		211
Censorship		212
Copyright		213
Referencing		214
Sound on the Internet		214
Reporting research as multimedia documents		215
Narrative versus hypertext		215
Music production skills		216
Empowerment over knowledge		216
Conclusion		217
Chapter summary		218
Notes		219

17   **Music and sound analysis**   **221**
Strategies for music analysis		221
Data reduction		222
Pattern matching		222
Statistical analysis		222
Metaphoric description		223
Computer assisted analysis		224
Score analysis		225
Audio analysis		228
Conclusion		229
Chapter summary		231
Notes		231

CONTENTS

18 Aural and musicianship training   **233**

Software features   235
Interactivity   236
Access   237
Music representations   238
  Genre and styles   238
  Teaching considerations   239
Useful links   241
  Aural training   242
  Musicianship   242
Conclusion   243
Chapter summary   244
Notes   245

19 Assessment   **247**

What to assess   247
Computers in assessment   249
Production and response   249
Communications   251
Information management   252
Ownership and access   253
Automated assessment   254
Reporting   254
Useful links   255
  Tools for assessing   255
  Tools for reporting   256
Conclusion   256
Chapter summary   257
Notes   258

20 Administration   **259**

Document preparation   259
  Word processing   260
  Graphic design programs   261
  Desktop publishing   261
Presentation programs   262
Audiovisual documents   262
Information management   262
  Spreadsheet   263
  Database   264

Web sites   265
Learning management systems   266
Planning and scheduling   266
Data management   267
Useful links   267
    Documentation and presentation   268
    Information management   268
    Scheduling   269
Conclusion   269
Chapter summary   271

SECTION V IMPLEMENTATION   **273**

21   **Setting up a computer music system**   **275**
Task identification   275
Choosing equipment   276
Digital musical appliances   278
Selecting between alternatives   279
Ancillary equipment   280
Physical set up   280
Location and access   282
Ergonomics   283
Security   283
Maintenance   284
Conclusion   284
Chapter summary   285
Notes   286

22   **Distance education and e-learning**   **287**
E-learning technologies   288
Learning at a distance   289
E-learning design   290
Conclusion   291
Chapter summary   293
Notes   293

23   **Integrating new technologies**   **295**
Understanding and knowledge   296
Skills and techniques   296
Integration prompting change   297

CONTENTS

Change as evolution   298
Change as addition   298
Updating curriculum and pedagogy   299
A meaningful engagement with music   299
Teacher as helper   302
Organizing space and time   302
Hardware options   302
Connectivity   303
Ownership   304
Storage and housing   305
Funding   305
Training and professional development   306
Conclusion   306
Chapter summary   308
Notes   308

24   Possible futures for computers in music education   311
Equipment   312
Connectivity   313
Data mining   314
Information sharing   314
Stylistic diversity and syncretism   315
Legal frameworks   315
Live computational processes   316
Sonic expression   316
Notes   317

GLOSSARY   319
REFERENCES   323
Webography   323
Books and Articles   328
INDEX   331

Figures

1.1   A rich media document can combine text, video, and audio materials.   5
1.2   Metaphors for understanding computers as music-making devices.   6
1.3   Sound is converted to and from binary numbers for representation in a computer.   8
2.1   The modes of engagement ordered from most objective to most subjective.   25
3.1   The Minimoog synthesizer.   35
3.2   The Yamaha DX7 synthesizer.   36
4.1   Digitizing audio.   45
4.2   Audio signal flow in a simple hard disk recording system.   49
5.1   Publishing systems focus on CPN notation but some support TAB or the use of graphic symbols.   60
5.2   An example of a music handout prepared in the Sibelius program.   61
6.1   The main window of Apple's GarageBand software.   73
6.2   Sequencer track view.   74
6.3   Sequencer phrase editor.   74
6.4   Sequencer note editor.   75
6.5   Waveform view.   75
6.6   Sequencer loop example.   75
6.7   Navigating a musical phrase library.   76
7.1   A pentatonic melody algorithm written in the Scheme language for the Impromptu environment.   82
7.2   A pentatonic melody algorithm written in the Max/MSP visual programming environment.   84
7.3   A Markov matrix showing the probabilities of pitch sequences.   88
8.1   A tuned sound (e.g., a flute) has regularity that is heard as a pitch.   96
8.2   A untuned sound (e.g., a cymbal) is irregular and has no sense of pitch.   96
8.3   The amplitude envelope is visible when its waveform is displayed.   96
8.4   A sawtooth waveform has repeating ramp-like oscillations.   97
8.5   The outputs of two or more oscillators can be combined in additive synthesis.   98
8.6   In subtractive synthesis, oscillator output is passed through a filter.   98

8.7   The quickly varying output of the first oscillator modulates the
       amplitude of the second.   99
8.8   In simple frequency modulation, the output from the first oscillator is
       offset then used as the frequency input to the next oscillator.   100
8.9   Each cycle of the oscillator waveform is distorted by the
       waveshaping function.   101
8.10   Grains are very small bits of audio that can be assembled for
       playback at different densities.   102
9.1   The architecture of a typical synthesizer.   112
10.1   Ableton Live features a matrix of musical loops that can be varied
       in real-time.   128
11.1   The interface for M, an interactive MIDI-based software application.   138
12.1   A simple waveform displayed in a software oscilloscope.   149
12.2   A stereo waveform.   150
12.3   A twenty-band spectrum analyzer.   151
12.4   A spectrogram with corresponding waveform view.   152
12.5   MIDI data viewed on a piano roll display.   153
12.6   A melodic fragment in the abc music notation language.   154
12.7   Mixing music and standard fonts in a document.   154
13.1   Sequencers such as Apple's GarageBand can be used to create
       music for videos.   165
13.2   A still image from one of Toshio Iwai's Electroplankton games.   171
14.1   Rich media documents incorporate multiple types of media on one page. 178
14.2   Sibelius Notes uses the ability to embed scores that can be played
       to bring worksheets to life.   181
15.1   ccMixter, a site with music available for remixing under creative
       commons licenses.   192
15.2   The iTunes music store.   195
15.3   The front page of ArtistLaunch.com, a music promotion service.   199
16.1   A portion of Wikipedia's entry on J. S. Bach.   208
16.2   An example of an online music survey created as a blog.   210
16.3   A mind-map or flow-chart can be directly converted to a hypertext
       document, maintaining the richness of interconnections between
       information.   216
17.1   A pitch histogram of the first movement from Beethoven's First
       Symphony in C major, Op. 21.   223
17.2   An overview of Stravinsky's *The Rite of Spring* in a sequencer
       piano-roll display.   225
17.3   Arc Diagram view shows the links between repeated sections.   226
17.4   Music data in a spreadsheet.   228
17.5   Pitch contours are evident in a sonogram with a logarithmic
       frequency scale.   229
18.1   A melodic dictation window in Auralia.   234
18.2   Music learning games such as Mozart can be played by students on
       a PDA or phone.   237
18.3   A screen from the Music Sense application from the BBC's Music
       Essentials Web site.   241
19.1   Assessment criteria based on Keith Swanwick's dimensions.   250
19.2   The home page of the Moodle CMS system.   252

19.3   An example student report in Smart School Report Writer.   255
20.1   Assessment calculations in the spreadsheet.   263
20.2   Graph of the assessment data.   264
20.3   A section from a database table of an instrument inventory.   265
20.4   A Gantt chart displaying the timing and dependencies of project tasks.   267
21.1   A decision-making process for choosing music technologies.   276
21.2   Some options for computer set-ups in educational institutions.   281
23.1   Meaningful engagement.   300

Preface

This book explores the use of the computer for educational activities that lead to enhanced music making and the development of musical intelligence. It is a practical and philosophical guide for teachers, trainee teachers, and interested parents in the use of the computer for music education, and provides valuable information on specific topics for students and musicians generally. The material covers topics ranging in sophistication from musical games for young children, through audio recording and musicianship applications for the middle school, to analytical, algorithmic and interactive music activities suitable for senior students. The broad range of included material reflects the fact that a meaningful music education involves experiencing music making, reflecting upon that experience, and sharing music within a community. The book outlines how computers can play a role in facilitating and enhancing musical experiences and understandings and is applicable across all facets of music education.

This book is not a step-by-step guide to software usage that would replace an equipment manual, nor does it provide prescriptive lesson plans that would (more than likely) suit only a small range of educational circumstances. Instead, it paints a broad picture of the role the computer can play in areas including music publishing, sound recording, music distribution in the age of the Internet, music and sound analysis, and educational administration (to name a few of the topics covered). Each chapter outlines the ways in which computers can contribute to music education in a particular way, discusses relevant software applications including their strengths and weakness, and provides advice on effective usage and teaching strategies. Each chapter includes reflection questions, teaching tips, and suggested activities for teachers, as well as a chapter summary. An extensive list of Internet sites is provided at the end of the book to allow the reader to follow up any of the resources mentioned in the text. In addition, references to all citations and opportunities for further investigation are provided for the curious reader.

A number of conceptual frameworks are outlined in the earlier chapters to provide a context for the book's practical discussions. These frameworks are provided to support effective understanding of the role of the computer in music education programs. In particular, a dominant theme is understanding the computer as a musical instrument and, as a result, that its place in the music education program can be as integrated as that of any other musical instrument. A more detailed examination of the role of musical instruments, particularly the computer, shows that they can act as a tool, medium, or instrument. The computer can be a tool but its function is more than utilitarian, it can be a medium for musical investigation but its influence is not only on data, and it can be an instrument for expression where it participates in producing both music and musical intelligence. A second conceptual framework important to this book is the notion of a student's meaningful engagement with music making. Through this lens, types of musical activities and experiences are characterized as providing different modes of engagement that lead to particular types of learning, and also different aspects of musical meaning are identified that have an impact on students' enjoyment and motivation. This book outlines how the computer provides opportunities for meaningful engagement that can lead to a balanced and effective music education program.

The majority of the book focuses on providing practical advice and background information across the areas of typical computer music usage. These areas are music production, presentation, reflection, and implementation. The chapters on music production provide information on how the computer is used to produce music as scores and audio recordings. They examine the way a computer supports arranging, recording, song writing, remixing, record production, and so on. The chapters on music presentation are concerned with the use of the computer in live performance and in the preparation and display of documents, Web pages and so on. The chapters on reflection outline how computers can assist musical understanding through study and investigation. Topics include music research and analysis, how the computer can support musicianship and aural training activities, and how it can be used for assessment and administrative tasks. The chapters on implementation discuss the ways in which computers can be integrated into existing music education programs, including the pragmatics of funding, purchasing and accessing computing resources. A glossary of terms is provided to assist with understanding and clarifying the text. Words listed in the glossary are printed in bold the first time they appear in the book.

It is appropriate at the beginning of any book to acknowledge those who have influenced and assisted with its creation. There have been numerous colleagues and students who have informed my understanding of both music education and computers and their assistance and tolerance are much appreciated. In particular, I would like to acknowledge Steve Dillon and Kevin Purcell, two long-time collaborators in the use of music technologies in education, whose input and contribution to the ideas in this book are at times direct and always indirect. Most importantly, I would like to thank Lenore Keough who as partner and part-time editor has supported and guided the development of this work.

Music making is an experience derived from an aesthetic involvement with creative activities around sound production and representation. The computer is a capable sound-making device and an efficient manipulator of musical symbols, thus its appropriateness for music making seems clear. This book explores the possibilities of computer-assisted music making within a learning context, and reveals ways in which the computer can be an instrument for amplifying musicality.

Andrew R. Brown

Section I

CONTEXT

Chapter 1

Ways of making music with technology

Although sound recording technologies (in particular the tape recorder) have been the biggest technological change effecting music education in the past one hundred years, digital technologies, in the form of computer devices based on a **binary** number system, are the most visible technological change with which we are currently engaged, and the full impact of their influence is yet to be understood. In order to understand how digital technologies can best serve music education we need to be clear about the ways in which technologies interact with activities and thinking. This will assist educators to design technological environments that help the student develop musical intelligence through wise choices of curriculum content, engaging activities, the selection of appropriate technologies, and the fostering of a culture of creativity.

Our music education history is littered with changing technologies and the future seems equally full of new technological developments, as speculated on in chapter 24. As a part of maintaining the quality and relevance of music curricular, it is important to understand the way technological change effects students' musical understanding. Changes in understanding can best arise through growth and development activated by working with a variety of technological resources, from paper and pencil to turntable and computer.

The impact of technologies in turning musical ideas into musical realities depends as much on attitudes as it does on equipment. To assist in developing a productive approach toward music technologies this chapter outlines three approaches to music technologies and explores the possibilities of each of these relationships. In particular, the ways in which the computer can be viewed as a tool, medium, or musical instrument are described. When approached in these ways, computer music technologies can assist to transform abstract ideas into organized sound, thus amplifying a student's musicality.

The unique ways in which computers can process sound and musical symbols can lead to experiences that expose new ways of thinking and acting. We can, in fact, change our minds by changing technologies and/or our relationship with them. In this chapter we will discuss the importance of understanding this influential partnership with technology.

Technologies available to the music educator include printed documents, musical instruments, mechanical tools (such as metronomes), electronic and digital audio devices, MIDI sequencers, computers, printers, telephones, Internet communications, and the like. Clearly then, books are a technology, trumpets are a technology, and computers of all stripes are technologies, and although the focus of this book is on the computer, parallels between older and newer technologies will be continually drawn as a method of illuminating the pathway to positive partnerships with music technologies. The computer, like other technologies, can assist the musician in a variety of ways, it can help them develop musical skills, it can create and transform music and sound, and it can help them to express and communicate the music inside them.

Changing technologies

The use of music technologies for capturing and presenting student activities has resulted in changing curricular in the area of delivery, activities, and assessment. Students are now able to produce audio, video, and multimedia items. These advances have resulted in changing the minds of teachers about best music educational practice. Videoing or Webcasting a performance rather than holding central examinations is a case in point. The ability for students to produce presentations as audio recordings rather than only as text creates opportunities for integrated sound examples and enables equity for verbally orientated students to express themselves (Figure 1.1). In a computing environment these media formats can be integrated digitally and links between them established; for example, in a media-rich report a student could draw upon examples of sequenced and live versions of her arrangement to illustrate the changes in timbral expectations and results.

The introduction of the computer into the music program requires changes in the curriculum in terms of areas for skill development and considerations of authorship, an expansion of the range of activities that are seen as "musical," for example, being a DJ or record producer, and revised criteria for critical evaluation of music in digital media forms, and the provision of adequate infrastructure for creation, storage, review, and feedback in these forms.

Changing minds

While changes in technological resources can make a significant difference to the ways a music curriculum manifests itself, changing minds requires a more pervasive shift than mere substitution of resources. Changing minds is about changing metaphors. As we vary the way we represent musical knowledge by changing technologies, there emerge two important implications:

1. Musical knowledge can be represented through different media, as in the case of music notation being represented on paper or on computer screen.
2. Musical knowledge can be broadened when represented through different metaphors, as in the difference between computer audio software as a linear

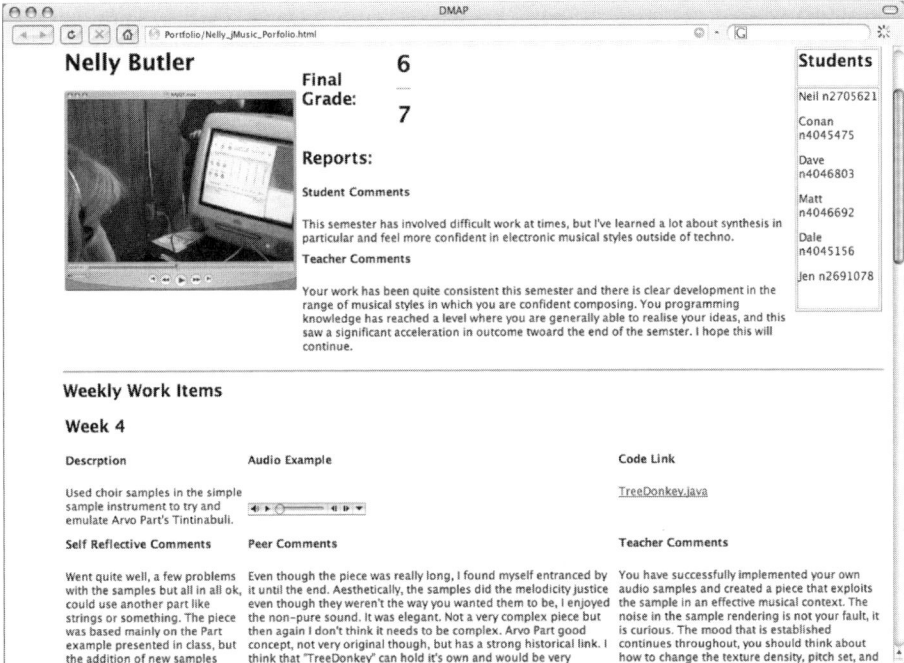

Figure 1.1 A rich media document can combine text, video, and audio materials.

"tape recorder" or as an "instrument" that responds dynamically to performance gestures.

Sonic context is also important to musical cognition. A sound may be considered relationally as part of a **soundscape** with a structural function[1] or discretely as a sound object described by its physical characteristics including time **envelope** and spectral **morphology**, in the manner pioneered by **musique concrète** composers.[2] The interaction of the music student with the variety of descriptions of music that are inherent in different technologies will, if reflected upon, expand the student's musical understanding and, in turn, reconstitute their self-conception as a music maker.

The substitution of media, although significant in itself, may not lead to significant changes in thinking if they employ the same metaphors. The value of changing technologies without shifting metaphors can include improved efficiency, financial savings, and increased integration of media systems; as is the case with substituting manuscript paper for music publishing software. But these substitutions may simply be expensive efficiency gains, and may not necessarily result in improved musical understanding or skill.

Changes in metaphor, however, frequently result in significant changes in thinking; in new potentialities for understanding the world of music (Figure 1.2). These changes occur with technological change to varying degrees, but are often transparent and little considered.[3] For example, the shift from class music performances on recorder to electronic piano has obvious changes including a shift from monophonic thinking to polyphonic and homophonic, physicality vertical pitch

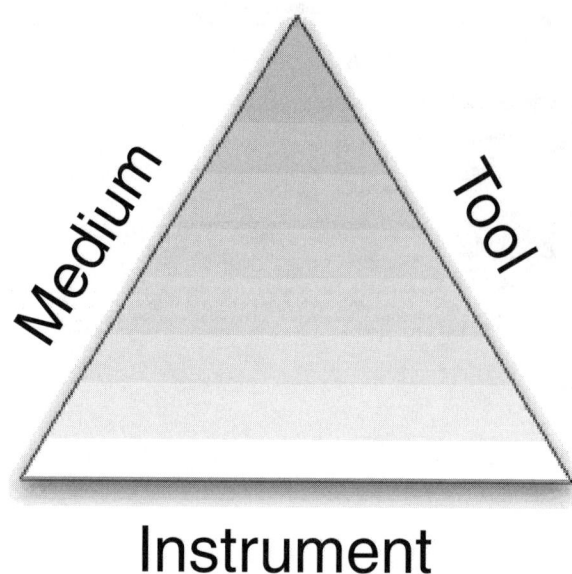

Figure 1.2 Metaphors for understanding computers as music-making devices.

orientation to horizontal, and abstract octave shift to concrete octave differences. These changes are significant, however, the change from electronic piano to laptop computer performance has even greater implications (at least possibilities) including a shift from a pitch and time focus to a timbre, time and space focus, from a one-to-one correspondence between gesture and sound-event to a one-to-many possibility (using complex sounds, arpeggiators, and algorithmic performance options), the ability to determine sonic parameters beyond percussive note onset, and significant changes in repertoire possibilities—particularly in contemporary music genres—and the associated cultural resonances of the new genres. Curriculum designers should be vigilant in their consideration of the metaphoric shifts they implement when they introduce technological change because it is these shifts that result in the most significant changes in the minds of students.

Three metaphorical perspectives that inform the use of the computer for music making are the computer as musical tool, the computer as a musical medium, and the computer as a musical instrument. The computer is, to varying degrees, each of these things and more. By seeing the computer from these perspectives, a broader range of musical applications emerge than from any one perspective alone. When viewed as a tool, the computer is seen as a device to be controlled, when understood as a medium it becomes a vehicle for exploring musical possibilities and, when approached as an instrument, it can be a conduit for musical expression.

The computer as a musical tool

The computer can be used as a musical tool and, like other tools, the computer can make jobs easier, tasks more efficient, and the previously impossible possible. Tools amplify skills, by providing leverage and extension. Just as an audio **amplifier** can make music louder, a computer can be a musicianship amplifier enhancing musical skills and increasing musical intelligence. Tools can be quite utilitarian; that is, employed simply to get a job done. For example, the piano can act as a tool for ear training where musical features such as intervals, chords, or rhythms are played for identification. There need not be any attempt at musical expressiveness in such tasks. The computer can similarly be used as a tool for aural training, with software such as Auralia or MacGammit providing drill and practice exercises.

Technologies, when used as tools, have been characterized by media theorist Marshall McLuhan as *extending* human capacity.[4] For example, a person can extend their reach for hunting by using a spear, travel faster and further by using a bicycle or airplane, see further by using a telescope, and hear more clearly by using an audio amplifier. Tools can extend intellectual abilities too, not just physical ones, so we can do math faster with calculators, express our ideas more clearly with languages, and understand weather patterns more thoroughly using computer simulations.

Musical tools can range from simple physical devices, such as a tuning fork, to a complex device such as an electronic tuner, to symbolic tools such as common practice notation, and to intellectual tools such as metrical rhythmic grouping. For example, the list of physical musical tools includes, horns, quills, metronomes, music stands, and player pianos. Intellectual musical tools include, the harmonic series, music notation, rules of species counterpoint, and **Fourier transforms**.

The piano has long been used as a tool for composition, where the composer sits at the piano with manuscript and pencil in hand using the piano to test ideas, confirm note choices, and playback compositional fragments. The computer, with a keyboard **controller** attached, can mimic this compositional practice using music publishing programs such as Finale and Sibelius and using a mouse instead of a pencil. The computer provides a rich canvas of tools for composition that go beyond imitation of manuscript. In particular, MIDI sequencers provide the ability to layer parts and hear them back with a variety of imitative acoustic or synthetic sounds. In this way a sound picture can be painted and modified. Importantly, the computer can be used recursively as a tool to develop other tools that extend your musical reach. For example, it can be used to sequence backing music for instrumental practice. Such backing music can easily be recorded at different speeds and in different keys to provide a variety of play-along accompaniments. When using a tool there is an expectation that you have a task clearly in mind. For example, in order to paint a house, a painter chooses different tools that he knows will be required for that specific house, he may choose brushes, rollers, a spray gun, ladders, and so on depending upon the circumstances. Music software tools also have different strengths and weaknesses that influence their appropriateness for the musical job at hand. It is important for a musician to understand their computer music tools, or tool kit, and how best these can work in conjunction with one another.

When relating to the computer as a musical tool (or tool kit), it is important to know what the dimensions of the musical job are and to be familiar with the features of each software and hardware tool. With these understandings the musician will be able to select the correct tools for the task at hand, and maximize their musical potential. When using the computer as musical tool, a person acts as a director of proceedings, controlling the computer to efficiently achieve their musical goals. This tool-use relationship with the computer is a common one, and so it should be quite clear how the computer, when used as a tool, can be a valuable musical assistant. The way in which the computer is a musical medium is a little less obvious.

The computer as a musical medium

All musical equipment is made of some material. As the music passes through this material it can be affected by its properties. For example, sound in the piano begins as vibrations in the strings, when they are struck by the hammers, which is then transferred to the wooden soundboard. The quality of the piano sound depends somewhat upon the type of steel used in the strings and the firmness of the hammers and, to a larger extent, on the properties of the soundboard. The type of wood and the construction have an impact upon the sound quality of the piano. Therefore, steel and wood are the media of the piano, and they are important in providing its characteristic sound and constraining its design. Another example of a musical medium is manuscript paper used for writing common practice notation. The properties of paper are well understood, and these include being two dimensional, able to "store" writing, accessible at any point at any time, easily transportable, and somewhat fragile. In the early twentieth century, the magnetic tape recorder emerged as a new medium capable of capturing and storing sound. This sound recording property revolutionized music making and distribution in that century. Computers are different from any previous music technology device because they are based on numbers; they use a digital medium (Figure 1.3).

The properties of mediums can have a dramatic effect on the musical potential of objects that are made from that medium, which is why the introduction of a new medium is so significant for music making, and therefore music education. For example, the use of brass for making trumpets provided more flexibility over trumpets made from animal horns or wood; the light weight, flexibility, and small cost of paper enabled the wide distribution of written music; and the introduction of electronic oscillators and filters enabled the creation of a new timbral pallet to augment those from acoustic sound sources. Digital devices, such as the computer, have a number of unique features, which will be expanded upon below, in particular they can simulate or model existing and imagined systems, they can repeat and copy data without loss of quality, and in the case of the modern computer that can do these tasks with incredible speed. Since the 1950s, musicians, from Risset and Xenakis to Eno and Eminem, have been exploring the musical potential of digital machines, and the journey has only just begun.

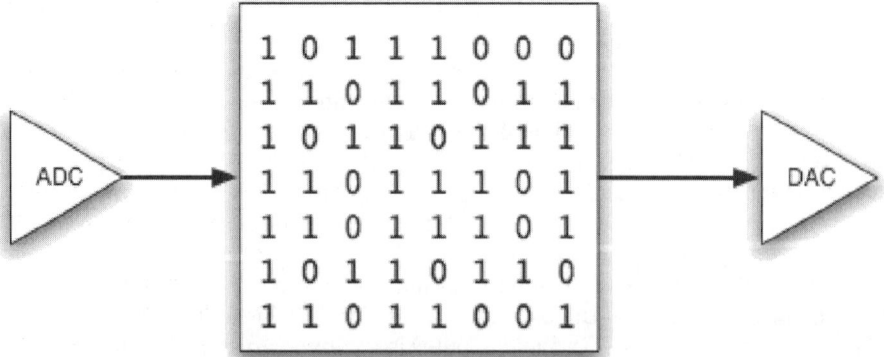

Figure 1.3   Sound in converted to and from binary numbers for representation in a computer.

Mediums are used to hold or communicate ideas or actions; these need to be translated into an appropriate form for transmission by the medium. At each stage of transferring information between mediums, there is a process of translation. For instance, the sound in the piano gets its energy from the force applied to the keyboard, the sound looses energy moving from the string to the soundboard and the design of the bridge, as the point of transfer, is critical to the tone of the piano. Also, writing music as notation on paper involves a translation from sound, or imagination, to a musical symbol system. Through this translation process, McLuhan argues, media become metaphors that translate experience into new forms.[5] A computer, like any other medium, effects the information (sound or music) that is stored in it or passes through it. The medium is not neutral; it has an effect on the music. When we are aware of this transforming nature of a medium, we can either compensate for it or utilize it. Only when we ignore it, or deny it, we risk the transformational change taking us by surprise or undermining our true intention.

Another property of a medium is persistence. When music is written on paper it becomes permanent, it takes on the life-span of the medium; as long as the paper survives so can the music. When writing music as common practice notation not all of the music's qualities are captured in full. Rhythm values are **quantized** to the closest rhythmic value (quaver, semiquaver, etc.), pitch is quantized to the closest semitone, and dynamics are reduced to general statements such as mezzo forte and crescendo. The medium of musical manuscript and the conventions of notation influence what aspects of the music are preserved and which are discarded. The computer usage expert Alan Kay made the point that the computer as a medium adds more to the representation than simply storing and recording.

> In a book you can print a score, and that's good. But on a computer, you not only can print the score, but you can start moving things around and experimenting with whole sets of musical languages. I've used the term "metamedia" to describe the computer, and what I mean is that it is a holder of all the media you can think of, as well as ones you haven't thought of yet. The computer allows you to capture important ideas, whatever the form of their expression, and convey them in a way that will help other people understand them, and maybe even add to them. [6]

If a computer is a medium, or even a meta-medium, what is the nature of that medium? It may appear that because the computer is made of metal and silicon that these are its media. However, unlike the piano, music or sound exists inside the computer's memory rather than in the physical structure of the computer. It may appear that electricity is the medium of the computer and, indeed, data is shifted to and from the computer as electricity; without electricity today's computers would not operate. However, it is more convincing to argue that electricity is simply a convenient power source and the computer might operate as well (or better) powered by light or organic matter; as is the case in some research laboratories. Whatever the power source, the computer, in its essence, is a digital device that uses numbers as its medium. Music is represented as numbers inside the computer, and when musical data is processed by software it is the numbers that are adjusted. As well, changes (addition, subtraction, and so on) do not degrade the numbers, so the data inside the computer is robust and persistent. As a consequence, the computer can simulate any number of musical possibilities in a nondestructive way allowing the musician to try different ideas and explore a vast range of musical possibilities.

How does the digital medium affect the music? A digital representation of music has particular characteristics that include the quantized nature of musical attributes such as loudness, pitch, and so on. In practice, the resolution of modern computers is so high that quantization is unproblematic, but there are occasions where it has an effect; for example, in aliasing of **waveforms** with spectra above the Nyquist **frequency**. The digital nature of the computer makes many processes easier than they would be in analogue form, such as time stretching, and some processes are fundamentally different, such as filtering. Like other media, digital sounds and processes can have their own flavor or color, and an awareness of the characteristic nature of the digital medium is important is establishing an effective relationship with the computer as a musical medium.

When using the computer as musical medium, the musician acts as an explorer. The possibilities of musical and sound transformations afforded by the computer can be depicted as a vast landscape. The computer as medium represents that terrain and various software applications or computational functions are vehicles for the musician to explore that terrain. The destination of this navigation around musical space is not always predetermined however musicians that are aesthetically attuned are able to notice the interesting discoveries that are available and the skilled musicians are able to exploit these discoveries to expressive ends. Musical explorations of previous mediums including wood, paper, and electrical current have taken centuries and new possibilities continue to be found. The brief history of musical exploration of digital systems has resulted in various electroacoutsic, rock, and electronic dance music genres and it is the children in our education systems today who will be the pioneers of the new musical possibilities of digital systems.

The computer as a musical instrument

Musical instruments such as the piano and guitar can be more than convenient tools or useful mediums. When played well these instruments become a means for musical expression, a vehicle for communicating musical ideas, and a clear and articulate musical voice. A close bond is ideally established between a performer and their instrument, and it is possible to have this relationship with the computer also. Any musical instrument, including the computer, amplifies your musical abilities. As Alan Kay suggests,

> You don't need technology to learn science and math. You just absolutely don't need it. What you need to have are the right conditions. In music, if you've got the right conditions and you've got music happening, then the instruments amplify what you've got like mad. The best thing a teacher can do is to set up the best conditions for each kid to learn. Once you have that, then the computer can help immeasurably.[7]

The metaphor of the computer as a musical instrument is the most powerful one in assisting the music educator to decide how best to use the computer. When presented with a decision about how to best utilize computing resources, or what the musical uses of the computer might be, we simply need to ask what we would do if it were a clarinet, piano, recorder, or xylophone about which we were speaking. This approach will usually yield an appropriate answer. Conversely, when it arises that a musical instrument is a useful resource for a music education activity, the computer should be considered a viable option.

The most common situation in which musical equipment becomes an instrument is in live performance. Playing the piano is generally associated with performance in real-time, and computer-based musical instruments are increasingly being played in real-time. For example, laptop computers are increasingly used in performance by live electronic musicians even in preference to keyboard synthesizers, groove boxes, and turntables. One thing that changes in computer performances is that the gestural relationship with sound is sometime less direct. In acoustic instrument performance the musician's gestures are translated into sonic results. Many instruments have a one-to-one gesture-to-sound relationship, including the press of the piano or synthesizer key, the turn of the **filter** cutoff dial, or the slide of the finger of the guitar fret board; each translate gesture into a direct audible result. Many electronic and computer-based instruments have a one-to-many gesture-to-sound relationship when a mouse gesture or parameter movement changes the complexity of a rhythmic part, or the timbre and volume of an entire ensemble of musical voices.

While performance is the most obvious use of the computer as an instrument, it is also possible to use the computer as an instrument in non-real-time where it acts as an ideas amplifier more than as a gesture amplifier. Most musical tasks involve a degree of real-time manipulation or improvisation and some preparation of musical materials, so it is possible to consider performance and composition as two ends of a continuum of improvisation. The computer music composer Paul Lansky[8] described his compositional processes as "improvisation in really slow time," which underscores the similarity between performance and composition experiences under the right circumstances. Those conditions are assisted by the design of software and hardware but are predominantly about the attitude and skills the musician brings to the partnership. In particular, being articulate in the representation system in use, and being willing to have their musicality leveraged and, at times, redirected by interaction with the computer. Using the computer as an instrument is, then, as much of an attitude as it is an activity.

Underlying such performability is a fluency and familiarity with the instrument that enables direct expression with little need for conscious reflection. The demands of real-time expression require this familiarity, like the ability to speak fluently without a conscious effort. Fluency in language is not limited to speech but can be present in writing tasks as well. In the same way, the instrument relationship with a computer can exist in composition as well as in performance; but both require an intense involvement that emerges from familiarity through practice. The instrument-player relationship becomes possible when you are musically articulate and fluent in the language of the computer. Often in this situation computer musicians can express themselves more clearly with the computer than with any other instrument. Their familiarity with the computer means that they think about music in digital terms and in the language of their software environment. Just as a pianist plays the piano or the orchestral composer writes directly to manuscript, the computer musician collaborates with the computer without translation. Engagement with the computer as an instrument is characterized by intuitive action, which becomes automatic through practice, just like riding a bicycle.

When using the computer as an instrument the musician generally acts as a player, responding intuitively rather than following a deliberate and conscious plan.

The use of the computer as musical instrument is often improvisational in character, even if the result is fixed at the end of the process. Importantly, the player accepts any influence of the instrument on their music as an inherent aspect of the music making. A relationship with the computer as musical instrument is more about partnering than controlling. The partnering is, at its best, bidirectional, the musician and the instrument both influence each other and the music.

As a musician begins to work closely with an instrument, even the computer, they begin to understand the musical world from the perspective of that instrument. The visual layout of the piano keyboard is a good example, where it provides a useful way of conceiving pitch as a stepped series of frequencies from low on the left to high on the right. These understandings, inherited from the instrument, can be so deeply ingrained that it is hard to see them as influences at all. The computer scientist and educationist Seymor Papert emphasized this point in his writings, noting that the "computer presence [can] contribute to mental processes not only instrumentally but in more essential, conceptual ways, influencing how people think even when they are far removed from the physical contact with a computer."[9]

The level of interaction whereby the musician's ways of thinking are directed, to a degree, by the computer and its way of working occur most deeply when the musician is engaged with the music such that the instrument appears transparent to the process. And, as Papert points out, this influence stays with the musician even beyond their contact with the instrument. It is clear that the instrument-player partnership involves a deep level of interaction, understanding and trust and this relationship is possible with the computer as much as for any other instrument.

Learning to use the computer for music making

The computer can be an excellent musical assistant if you understand the different ways in which you can work with it as a tool, medium, or instrument. However, like all equipment, the computer is a rather unintelligent assistant relying on us to make best use of it. As with the carpenter's chisel, the computer as a tool can make tasks easier if you develop the skills to handle it well. As with the potter's clay, the computer as a medium can be used to mould and shape your musical ideas, but to get the best results you must become aware of the possibilities and limitations of the medium. As with the saxophone, the computer as instrument can lead to fluent musical expressiveness once the workings of the instrument become so familiar as to be intuitive.

Despite a potentially close relationship, at the end of the day the computer is simply equipment, and relating to equipment is an uneven partnership where the musician's skill level and attitude make a bigger difference than instrument design or construction. For example, a better piano will make some improvement to the sound of piano music, and a faster or more fully featured computer or software package will also make some improvement to music made with it, however, in both cases a better-skilled musician will make a much more significant difference.

Of course, equipment can break; especially computers in their currently primitive stage of development. An experienced guitarist knows that strings and leads can break, and plans for this by carrying spares and replacing them regularly. An experienced computer musician knows that computers can crash and that files can become corrupted, and plans for this by saving regularly and maintaining backups of data. Learning to use the computer for music making is best approached like learning any other musical instrument and, like other musical instruments, it can be rewarding but requires regular and focused practice. The computer provides some immediate possibilities for music making with little effort, but to realize the full expressive potential the musician needs to develop their skills and understandings. By embracing a positive attitude toward the computer as a musical partner, musicians can develop a positive and deep relationship with music from which they will gain much insight and enjoyment.

Conclusion

As music educators change the nature of the technological environment in which they and their students operate to include more computer-based activities, new understandings become possible, and some older ones may be hidden. The computer can play the role of musicianship amplifier by being considered broadly as a tool, medium and instrument. To maximize learning from computer-based musical experiences, educators need to consciously contextualize technological changes and music-making activities for their students and provide adequate reflective opportunities.

Using digital technologies we can let expressions, reflections and outcomes be sonic, visual or textual, all in the one medium. Communicating the curriculum message can be rich with meaning and concrete examples, and music that is abstract or visually represented can become sound. The computer is a new instrument for making and presenting music in new ways, and its use can change experiences and ways of knowing. We can, in fact, change minds and change music by changing technologies and the way we use them.

Reflection questions

1. What are the metaphorical perspectives from which computers are viewed as music equipment?
2. What is the role of the teacher in changing technologies in a learning environment?
3. Which is more critical to effective music making with technology, attitudes, or equipment?
4. In what ways can a computer assist a musician?
5. To what degree are technological skills, musical skills?
6. What are the dominant metaphors used in computer music technologies?
7. Name some computer-based musical tools, and describe how their usage is tool-like?
8. Which musical mediums are commonly used in the classroom?
9. Are mediums neutral in their effect on music made with them?
10. Is the computer a single piece of equipment or a toolkit?

Teaching tips

1. Document performances as audio and video recordings to assist reflection and assessment.
2. Use the computer to present music information in a media rich ways that integrate text, image and sound.
3. Encourage students to use multi-media and hyper-linked formats for assignments so they can demonstrate their understanding of the links between information.
4. Use a variety of music representation systems to provide a richer understanding of abstract musical concepts.
5. Remember that making changes in metaphors is required to change thinking, and that changing mediums in not necessarily sufficient.
6. The computer can provide a rich canvas for creative musical activities, particularly in capturing and manipulating performed music.
7. Maximize student learning by using the most appropriate technology for the job, not simply the most available.
8. Always keep in mind that an understanding of the characteristics of the digital medium underpin effective use of the computer.
9. When deciding how best to use the computer, rethink the problem with an acoustic instrument substitute, such that the question become how best to use the . . . piano.
10. As a musical instrument the computer needs to be practiced, like any other instrument. Allow for practice access and time in the teaching program.

Suggested tasks

1. Attempt the same musical arrangement using a variety of music software applications to reveal some of the comparative strengths and weaknesses of each.
2. Audit your musical uses of the computer and see how much you are using it as a tool, medium or instrument.
3. Make a list of the equipment used in your music teaching/learning and describe your use of each as a tool, medium, or instrument.
4. Identify opportunities in your music curriculum where the computer could be used as a tool, medium, or instrument.
5. Experiment with ways that you can include the computer in your musical performances.

Chapter summary

Technologies assist in shaping musical ideas into musical realities. Understanding the nonneutral partnership with technology is important if we are to manage that shaping. The effectiveness of making music with technologies can be advanced if we understand the range of approaches to and the types of relationships with technology. Some distinct approaches include understanding the computer as a tool, medium, or instrument. Understood as a tool, the computer's role is to efficiently assist in achieving our goals and our approach is to direct the computer. Understood as a medium, the computer opens up new spaces of musical possibility and our approach is one of exploring those new spaces. Understood as an instrument, the computer is a sounding board that reflects, shapes, and amplifies our musicality, and our approach is to focus on musical expressiveness in partnership with the computer. Using digital technologies can lead to novel experiences that expose new ways of thinking. We can, in fact, change minds by changing technologies and our relationship with them.

Notes

1   Schafer, R., Murray. *The Soundscape: Our Sonic Environment and the Tuning of the World* (New York: Knopf, 1977).
2   Schaeffer, Pierre, *Traité Des Objects Musicaux*, 2nd ed. (Paris: Éditions du Seuil, 1977).
3   Brown, Andrew R., and Kevin Purcell. "Music Technology: A Transparent Integration." Paper presented at the World View of Music Education: The XVIII ISME International Conference, Canberra, Australia, 1988.
4   McLuhan, Marshall, *Understanding Media: The Extensions of Man* (London: Sphere Books, 1964).
5   Ibid., 67.
6   Kay, Alan. "The Dynabook Revisited," Interview by the Book & the Computer, http://www.honco.net/os/print_kay.html (accessed January, 2003).
7   Ibid.
8   Lansky, Paul. Personal interview, 23 January 1998.
9   Papert, Seymour. *Mindstorms: Children, Computers, and Powerful Ideas* (New York: Basic Books, 1980), 4.

Chapter 2

Philosophical considerations

A range of issues and related tasks inform our use of technologies for music making, and in this chapter we will consider many of them. Exploring these issues will reveal our assumptions and habits when working with a computer and it is useful to expose them and be able to identify their influence. Some of the ideas may be unfamiliar and provide new ways of thinking about and approaching the computer's role in our music making. The issues discussed in this chapter include ways in which computers amplify our decisions, how technologies cannot be invisible in the music-making process, the significance of cultural context on technological design and usage, the importance of metaphor in assisting or directing our activities with technology, what the impact of music technologies are on our notions of musicianship, how the computer can scaffold and support music making, that the motivation or intention of music making does not fundamentally change with the use of the computer, the ways of engaging students with music-making activities through the use a computer, and how the use of computers should not distract us from the importance of musical activities being a meaningful part of a student's life.

Amplification

It is often stated, "that to err is human but to really stuff up you need a computer." The truth behind this statement is that computers have the potential to exaggerate our actions. They provide leverage to achieve more things, of greater scope, in less time, and with less effort than otherwise. The difficulty in managing this then falls back on our ability to make sure that we are doing the appropriate thing in the first place. For example, we can search a lot of information over the Internet but are we asking the correct question? We can easily generate thousands of notes in an algorithmic musical composition, but is the **algorithm** going to produce notes that we will find aesthetically pleasing?

Marshal McLuhan, in the 1960s, championed the notion that technologies extend human capacities.[1] He pointed out that telescopes enhance eyesight, bicycles extend our ability to walk, cranes increase our ability to lift, and so on. The computer is an intellectual amplifier, rather than a mechanical one, so it can extend our ability to solve mathematical formulas, articulate thoughts using word processors, and manage compositional tasks with **sequencers** and music publishing software.

There is some debate about the degree to which computers should be used to enhance human creative abilities, compared with being used to achieve efficiencies of production and perhaps replace some people's jobs in the process. This division corresponds to the usage of the computer as a tool or as a medium discussed in chapter 1. While it can clearly do both, it is true that quite often the computer is relegated to being a tool for drill-and-practice skill development tasks or for the printing of neat musical scores, and its ability to amplify musical creativity through, for example, experimenting with compositional structures, sound design through digital **synthesis**, or interactive performance activities is overlooked.

Maintaining a focus on the important aspects of music making that make it a meaningful experience for musicians and a source of rich culture for communities is important as we embrace new technologies that can quite easily be viewed as only enhancing the superficial aspects of musical practices. According to John Dewey, "The abiding struggle of art is thus to convert materials that are stammering or dumb in ordinary experience into eloquent media."[2] He may as well have been talking today about computing technologies. In exploring the practice of music education with the computer we are drawn into enquiring about the more fundamental relationship between creativity and technology, and in exploring the more philosophical aspects of being technological we are pointed back in the direction of artistic creativity, as Heidegger suggested, "The more questioningly we ponder the essence of technology, the more mysterious the essence of art becomes."[3] To get the most out of our considerations about the use of computers in music education we need to understand that we are, in essence, reevaluating our understandings of music, learning, and technology. Therefore, in a slightly ironic way, through our struggles with the educational role of the computer, it indirectly reveals and amplifies these fundamental understandings.

Invisibility

When we use a musical instrument it mediates our interaction with music. By this we mean that it enables and constrains what music we can make based on its design and material properties. For example, a snare drum has limited pitch variation, a flute plays one note at a time, and a piano cannot control the dynamic of a sound after the note has been struck. These characteristics of the instruments are design features, choices made by the designers that effect our interaction with music when using them. As we interact with music using various technologies as mediators, their design characteristics afford a particular window onto the world of musical possibilities such that some options obvious and others out of view. As a result, the instrument is not musically neutral, or invisible in the music-making process.

The apparent invisibility of technology has concerned sociologists and designers as well. In his writings on technology and culture Neil Postman argues that language is the most serious technology often considered invisible that in fact is full of ideological assumptions and structural directedness.[4] Postman also suggests that in education a curriculum and the institutional organization of instruction are also human constructions, technologies that have significant influence over people but are often considered transparent and uninfluential.

Donald Norman, an expert in technology design, directly addresses this issue in his book, *The Invisible Computer,* where he argues for increased invisibility of the computer and an increased focus on human needs and capacities.[5] Like Postman, he is aware of the strong influence technologies have and as a result, suggested ways to redesign them so that the force of this influence propels users forward rather than stifling them. However, he is also keenly aware that although changes in technologies to suit human needs can be a challenge, the task of shifting human habits and conventions to utilize a new technology, even if well designed, is even more of a challenge. "The problem is," he states, "that whether it be a phonograph or computer, the technology is the easy part to change. The difficult aspects are social, organizational, and cultural."[6]

There should be no misconception that computer music systems are different in this regard from other music technologies including musical instruments; they are not transparent conduits into musical space or into informational space more generally. This is, of course, as ridiculous for computers as it is for any other instrument. This is why the selection of software and hardware is so critical—they impose significant intellectual or physical distortions onto the music-making opportunities, and thus results. The particular characteristics of a computer music system reflect the designer's view of how music is constructed or utilized, and in a way when we choose a piece of music software we are deciding whether of not our needs align with the designers ideas.

This is not to say that all computer music systems are equal in this regard, there is a spectrum of influence. Some systems are quite wide ranging in the choices they provide or quite flexible in how they can be used, others are quite particular about what and how operations are performed. In order to increase ease of use, some systems are based on widely shared understandings and practices, such as when **MIDI** sequencers model audio tape recording practices or when music publishing software model paper-based score engraving practices. These systems will likely seem less constraining because they follow familiar pathways but they may also inherit the limitations of what they model. However, such familiarity should not be confused with invisibility.

Because so much depends on the designer's choices, it is an obvious step that some computer musicians choose take on the role of designer and build their own software that reflects their particular ideas and processes. This does not make the software invisible in a general way, but can mean that it is effectively invisible to that musician because it does not require them to change their working methods. In reality, using software you designed is actually reinforcing habits rather than being transparent so, in a way, self-designed instruments are a mirror rather than a window on musical understandings. There are a number of tool kits for building your own music software, the most common of which is Max/MSP by Cycling 74, but most people will choose to use software designed by others. When doing so it is useful to be aware of what is made visible or invisible as a result of that choice.

Context

It is a truism that no person is an island, that we are products of our physical and social surroundings. This contextual impact is no less critical when using the computer for music making, and can be more critical because the computer is a telecommunications device as well, and can thus become an agent of our social context. But, before pursuing that track, there are important physical contextual issues to consider. As with other musical instruments the computer system is best used in a resource rich learning environment that includes, a quiet room, good **acoustics**, books, CDs, quality audio playback, and so on. This is often overlooked in educational institutions where the computer laboratory, which may be fine for word processing, is unthinkingly adapted for musical tasks. The sight of a clarinet player trying to record a **track** into a sequencer while crammed between rows of tightly packed desks in a computer lab, while others around her chatter and **noise** form the sports field comes through the window is not a pretty one. The computer can be a vital part of a rich music-making environment. Even when it is not at the center of the activity as a sound producing device it can provide communication and information storage retrieval facilities, assist with administrative functions, and more.

The computer's role in creating a social context for musicians is detailed in later chapters however, in brief, it centers around communications over networks that may link people via text chat, voice chat, e-mail, discussion forums, **blogs**, **podcasts**, or **network jamming**. The latter part of the twentieth century saw a struggle for music education to come to grips with popular music. Popular music was not simply a stylistic change that required music educators to adopt new repertoire, it required changes in the process of music making, the skills of musicianship, and cultural value systems. This territory was opened up in Keith Swanwick's publications on music education in the 1970s and 1980s[7] and consolidated elegantly by Lucy Green in her 1997 book *How popular musicians learn.*[8] In particular, the ability to capture and distribute music as audio files, scores, videos, or software provides extensive opportunities for building communities of interest and support to enhance the music learning experience.

Metaphor

The computer is a technological chameleon that can change its color at the double-click of a new software application. A computer performs some tasks that seem like magic, as though there must be some trick, apparently mysterious and unfathomable. While it may be true that some computational processes are complex it is also true that they are made up of simple building blocks. The computer, in essence, only understands numbers—only two numbers 0 and 1, to be precise. However, its complexity is built up from layer upon layer of abstraction and functionality. At each layer new conceptualizations or metaphors are used. The "skin" of the computer software is the Graphical User Interface (**GUI**) and it is here that the most blatant metaphorical masking can be achieved. We can make the computer screen look like a piece of manuscript paper, complete with grain and smudges, or we can make the **reverb** or synthesizer **plugin** look like a physical steel and plastic device. At all times, we should keep in mind that these illusions, while often useful or "friendly" are simply metaphors and can obfuscate as much as they can reveal the operation of the software.

Metaphors can be very useful; they can provide a variety of ways to understand complex phenomena. Musical knowledge can be represented through different metaphors, as for example a timbre's description based on instrument design or its acoustical attributes. A sound may be described as woodwind-like, or brass-like with reference to the instrument design, or as **sound objects**[9] described by their spectral distribution, **amplitude** envelopes, and other acoustic properties, in the manner used in **musique concrète**. These different metaphorical views of timbre, as designed productions or as found objects, can change the way timbre is understood and the possibilities for the use and variation of timbre in musical activities. Metaphor can be useful in maintaining consistency between media. For example, the maintenance of a tape-recorder metaphor for digital recording means that those familiar with tape recording will expect that if the playback is sped up the pitch will increase. If such expectations inherent in the metaphor are maintained then the transference from **analogue** to digital media version should be smoothed. The value of changing technologies without shifting metaphors can be in improved efficiency, financial savings in retraining, and more obvious integration with existing practices; as is the case with substituting manuscript paper for most computer notational packages. But at times maintenance of metaphor may simply result in expensive efficiency gains with little or no change in understanding.

Metaphors can be limiting and misleading. When one has a hammer, the world looks like a nail. If metaphors from previous contexts and media are rigidly adhered too then this can limit the new opportunities that computers can provide. For example, the Desktop metaphor used in many computer systems represents computer data as "files" and places to store them as "folders." One limitation of physical files is that they can only go in one folder. For example, does a student's file get categorized in a folder for her class, for the ensemble she plays in, for the instrument she plays, or under an alphabetical grouping? For quite some time after the introduction of this metaphor in the mid 1980s, the limitation of a single file location was maintained, even though previous computer systems that did not used this metaphor allowed any number of directories to have a symbolic link to a single file thus allowing the student to be located under any category.

Changing metaphors can change minds. The substitution of media, tape to digital recording for example, may not lead to significant changes in thinking if the metaphor of linear tracks is maintained. However, when the difference between media are emphasized, the ability of digital recording systems to randomly access audio segments for example, then new musical possibilities emerge such as granular synthesis. Changes in metaphor can result in significant changes in thinking because new potentialities for understanding the world of music can be exposed. These new perspectives occur with any technological change to varying degrees, but are often little considered. For example, the shift from music performance on recorder to electronic piano has obvious changes from monophonic thinking to the potential for polyphonic and homophonic, and vertical pitch physicality to horizontal, and from discrete octave division to visually smooth transition across the pitch range. However, the change from electric piano to **synthesizer** has similarly important but more subtle implications (at least possibilities) including a shift from a pitch and time focus to a timbre-time focus, from a one-to-one correspondence between gesture and sound-event to a one to many possibility (using complex sounds, arpeggiators, and algorithmic performance options), the ability to determine sonic parameters beyond percussive note onset using **aftertouch** and **modulation** controls, and significant changes in repertoire possibilities particularly to incorporate contemporary music genres.

Being aware of the metaphors that are used in the software allows us to understand it more easily and appreciate why it behaves as it does. Being aware of how the computer operates beneath the metaphor will enable us to appreciate what might be possible or impossible beyond the metaphoric surface.

Musicianship

What are the skills and understandings necessary to operate effectively as a musician? This question has been at the heart of all attempts to establish a musicianship, and the answers to it are as varied as the musical practices and cultures of the world. This variety of answers underscores the provisional and contextual nature of musicianship, and so clearly the increased use of the computer will have an impact on any contemporary definition of musicianship. While this is not the place to answer the definitional question in full, it is reasonable to speculate about the type of computer-related skills and abilities that will be necessary in a contemporary musicianship.

If we look at the ways that experienced computer musicians, electroacoustic and popular, gain their knowledge we see that they share some behaviors including asking questions of their colleagues, reading manuals, searching Internet discussion lists, experimenting with equipment, learning new software languages or terminologies, listening to other musicians music, and various other self-directed activities. The types of knowledge they seek include information about the physics of sound, basic electronics, file types, **sample rates**, **bit** resolution, audio mastering techniques, computer programming patterns, and the location of new information sources on the Internet to further their knowledge and converse with similar artists.

These knowledge areas can be categorized as those concerning the digital nature of music and sound representation, those about the computer system itself, those about music creation more broadly, and those about communicating ideas and music with others. There learning strategies are largely exploratory and research-based, even if in an informal way, accessed on a need-to-know basis, rather than being deliberately mentored or following a set curriculum or being purely experiential. In short, it is arranged around their individual learning needs and success relies on the development of effective research and discovery methods. These practices are clearly reflective of their often noninstitutional settings and may not translate directly to traditional institutional practices. They are more in line with a traditional creative music curriculum than a repertoire based one. Musicianship studies that wish to adequately acknowledge the use of the computer as a part of music making will need to come to terms with these areas of understanding and ways of acquiring skills and knowledge.

Scaffolding

The computer is well placed to provide learning support to students, given that it can mimic the characteristics of many other educational media; it can produce sound, visual, animations, simulations, and provides communication channels between people. We can use these facilities to provide scaffolding or support for the learner as they develop skills and understandings. Notions of scaffolding are premised on the understanding that students build their own knowledge through perceptions of experience. The tenet that knowledge is constructed through experience is strongly argued in the writings of John Dewey and is one of the significant findings from the experimental psychology of Jean Piaget.[10] Constructivist notions are at the heart of many educational philosophies and permeate this book.

One of the more obvious areas where the computer can scaffold student learning experiences is in the provision of accompaniments and backing tracks for performance. The computer can play parts of the composition, which provides motivation by filling out the sound, and stability by keeping the student in time and in tune. The backing can be layered such that aspects of the scaffold are removed as the student gains more confidence and skill. In more sophisticated programs, such as Smart-Music, the computer can also listen to the student performance and adjust to compensate for variations or errors. In some software systems the computer can analyze the performance and provide feedback about how the student might improve.

Network improvisation environments can provide scaffolding by using algorithmic process to generate surface-level detail of performances while students control meta-level arranging and conducting parameters. These environments develop collaborative and ensemble skills through **real-time** networking between computers, either locally or at distributed sites. Programs such as *jam2jam* and *eJay* provide scaffolded performance environments where students control meta-level musical intensities and arrangements.

Networked computing systems can facilitate social and learning support via electronic access to peers or mentors through discussion lists and forums, online chat spaces, and e-mail. Often these technologies are grouped together into structures called learning support systems, which usually add scaffolding for the teacher as well through administrative functions such as assessment and attendance tracking.

Intention

The reason for undertaking an activity is different from the method of achieving the outcome. The use of computers for making music changes little the intention of the musician, which will still revolve around expression, communication, sense making, fun, social relationships, curiosity and enquiry, economic benefit, and so on.

Therefore, like learning other musical instruments, it is important to locate appropriately motivating activities for use of the computer. The computer has some advantages here, in that for many students the computer has some inherent motivational qualities. The most obvious of these is the computers dominant role in contemporary music both as a recording device and, increasingly, as a live performance tool. The increasingly dominant role the computer plays in accessing and distributing music through audio file sharing, downloading and portable music players tie the computer more closely than ever before to musical experience, especially for teenagers. The computer is associated with contemporary musical styles and practices that are likely to appeal to many students, in particular rock, dance and electronic music. Motivation to use the computer may be its association with "fun" activities such as playing video games or chatting over the Internet. Students may also relate to the technical or scientific aspects of the computer and take an interest in how it works (in much the same way that some people are interested in how a piano or automobile operates). Some more musically sophisticated students may be interested in the computer because they can see the potential for musical exploration and development of new techniques and musical forms. As a result of this array of motivational forces, the computer is sometimes used almost exclusively for its role to entice students to music programs. Computing use is becoming so widespread that this ploy will not last for long. Any promise of using the computer for music making needs to become a curricular reality to maintain interest and motivation. This curricular use needs to be based on the constructive and communicative reasons (outlined above) that are inherently motivating rather than relegation of the computer only to less motivating tasks such as drill and practice aural training, surveillance of students in a keyboard laboratory, or administrative efficiencies such as electronic lodgment of student assignments.

Motivation and intention are complex and multilayered. The attractiveness of the computer as a contemporary device is a superficial attractor and therefore music programs would benefit from positioning the use of the computer within some larger frameworks of student intention. Longer term goals might include career ambitions, needs for social acceptance, personal satisfaction through progressive skill enhancement, and so on. Effective learning plans will take account of these overarching motivations that span many projects and often last for years, as well as ones that related to an individual or immediate goal. Some times the very large-scale goals were not immediately apparent, even to the student themselves, and emergent connections between projects become evident only over time.

An important guiding principle when trying to maximize student interest in computer music making is to provide appropriate challenges. Challenging projects are ones that move students into unfamiliar territory or require the learning of new techniques and processes. Challenging computer music tasks include working with unfamiliar software or hardware, developing new tools, or applying existing software to new musical process or outcomes. Musical and technical challenges are important because they motivate the student. Research by Mihalyi Csikszentmihalyi into optimal experience has found that a task is more likely to be engaging if its complexity is sufficient to require the focusing of all a person's energies and skills, but not so complex as to be frustrating. He found that people were happiest when undertaking an appropriately difficult challenge. "The best moments usually occur when a person's body or mind is stretched to its limits in a voluntary effort to accomplish something difficult and worthwhile. Optimal experience is thus something we *make* happen."[11] This suggests that involving students in the setting of targets and milestones in their computer music activities with a deliberate view to them extending their abilities in the process will be an effective strategy in maximizing both their interest and learning.

Engagement

If our music making is most importantly directed by how interested and involved we are with the music-making experience, then it is worth examining more closely the ways in which this involvement can manifest itself as *modes of creative engagement* with music.[12]

The ability of a computer music system to enhance engagement with music is a key measure of its likely impact on learning. There is good reason to think that music making and interaction with a computer are both inherently engaging, given the amount of time people spend at these activities. However, it is also possible for computer software to be boring or frustrating so, as educators, we still need to pay attention to the modes of creative engagement that different systems foster.

In a well-rounded curriculum there are different modes of creative engagement that students should encounter through their musical experiences. The student should find times to be engaged as (Figure 2.1):

- An appreciator—listening carefully to music and analyzing music representations.
- A director—managing music-making activities.
- An explorer—searching through musical possibilities and assessing their value.
- A participant—involved in intuitive music making.
- A selector—making decisions about the value of music or musical elements.

This taxonomy focuses on the phenomenological experience of the student as they undertake musical tasks. At a superficial level, there are similarities with Keith Swanwick's activity focused CLASP taxonomy that suggests student should be involved with Composing, Literature study, Auditioning, Skills, and Performance.[13] The modes of creative engagement share with the CLASP model an intention to provide a way of ensuring that a music program is well-balanced. However, the impact of electronic technologies on music making in the twentieth century has meant that distinctions inherent in the CLASP model between performer, composer and listener have been blurred to an extent that they are no longer clearly identifiable in

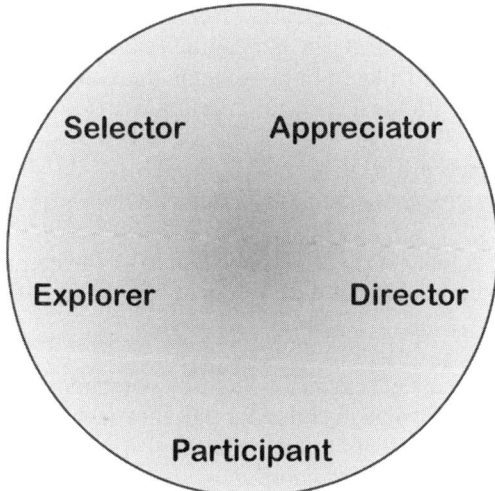

Figure 2.1 The modes of engagement ordered from most objective (top) to most subjective (bottom).

contemporary musical practice. As an alternative view, the modes of creative engagement focus on the roles that students undertake as they produce music and it seeks to focus attention on the musical capabilities the student will develop. For example, within a performance activity the student may be engaged to varying degrees as an appreciator, a director, a participant, or selector of the program. Within a compositional activity the student may use the computer to explorer structural possibilities, to participate with those materials through play and improvisation, to select the final list of materials to be used, to direct the assemblage of those materials within a software environment, and make iterative changes based upon their analysis the emerging result. The interactive nature of the computer allows it to operate as a virtual environment within which each of the modes of creative engagement can be experienced.

A range of computer music software and/or computer-related activities is required to cover all these ways of engaging. When considered as part of the overall music program, computer music activities may fill particular niches that enable the student to be engaged in ways not available in other aspects of the music program.

Meaning

As with any other musical activity, when making music with a computer the experience should be a meaningful one to maximize its educational value, and its personal value to the student. Activities will be meaningful depending upon their relevance to the student and how they connect with the broader value systems of the school and community. Computer-related music-making activities have the potential to be seen as relevant given that so much of the popular and commercial music that students are exposed to is made with computers. If they can use the techniques and processes of the music makers they admire, and achieve identifiable similar results, then they will be very pleased. Meaning can also be enhanced by connecting computer-related activities with students' other musical activities, so that they are normalized as part of an overall music learning strategy rather than seen as separate or special.

A clear description of the types of meaning that music activities can have has been developed by Steven Dillon.[14] In his scheme there are three types of meaning that can be associated with music education activities.

- Personal—the activity is intrinsically enjoyable.
- Social—the activity connects the student with others and these relationships are valued.
- Cultural—the activity is regarded as valuable by the community and, by participating (or succeeding) in it, the student achieves a sense that they too are important.

There can be a range of personal responses to technological change, and it is not uncommon for some people to comment that they feel frustrated by computers. But is also common for students to feel frustrated when learning acoustic instruments, for example, as they try to coordinate several limbs when playing a drum kit. Personal meaning can come of the pleasure of making an interesting sound, composing an intriguing rhythmic texture, or developing a new musical skill. The computer provides a smooth pathway from simple to complex musical tasks. It is a medium rich in opportunities for personal exploration and skill development.

Many inventions and achievements are socially constructed, the result of many people leveraging each other's achievements, interacting or even collaborating. Music, and other performing arts in particular, have a strong social dimension through ensemble activities and public performances. Computer music systems can participate in these traditional forums, and add to the social possibilities through additional interpersonal connections using electronic communications.

The cultural value of music has long been established. Its use at ceremonies and important community and family events is well understood, and seems quite persistent; for example the use of music at the opening of important sporting events. Overlaid upon this is the social significance of computing technologies that seem to permeate many aspects of contemporary Western life and whose importance is reflected in the financial return to those individuals and companies that control the dominant computing technologies. Computer musicians have the opportunity to achieve cultural meaning through their participation in either or both the cultural and technological dimensions of contemporary society.

Making sure that all three types of meaning are accessible to students can assist when selecting music activities using the computer, and also assist in the successful integration of music technologies with existing music education activities. The use of the theory of meaningful engagement as a guide to the integration of computer music technologies into the music is outlined in chapter 23.

Conclusion

In our considerations of music education with computers, it is important to make clear some of the assumptions that we hold and issues we should be aware of. In this chapter through exploration of a number of relevant issues we have seen how the computer can be an important part of a musical education, either as a complementary resource or as a focus for principle study. As we search for a place for new technologies in our music programs, it becomes clear that this reassessment of our priorities is a stimulus for examining many facets music education and musical experience more broadly and the implications and changes the computer makes to music education may be as significant indirectly and they are directly.

Reflection questions

1. Can you think of other issues, not covered in this chapter, that impact upon the use of music technologies?
2. What are examples of a way the computer has been both a positive and negative amplification of your actions?
3. How might the myth of invisibility apply to the piano as a technological conduit for music making?
4. Do you think that physical or social context is more important to successful use of the computer for music?

5. Given that writing on manuscript paper is the metaphor used by music publishing software, what metaphor is used by sequencing software?
6. What computing skills might be considered essential to contemporary musicianship?
7. What are some of the ways a computer might be used to scaffold the learning of music composition?
8. Between which modes of engagement is there likely to be the most overlap?
9. Which types of meaning would likely be present in a public performance of an interactive computer improvisation?
10. In what ways are the most common computer related tasks you set meaningful and engaging?

Teaching tips

1. Use these issues of using music technology as discussion points in lessons to bring students' attention to them.
2. Remind students that they should save their work regularly because a simple mistake on the computer can have disastrous results.
3. Consider the noncomputing resources that you can use or acquire to provide a supportive context for computer music activities.
4. Make students aware of the metaphors employed by the software applications they use and have them analyze where these are maintained or where they are diverge from the metaphor.
5. Include the gaining of computer skill competency in musicianship lessons and tests.
6. Utilize mixed ensembles of electronic and acoustic instruments wherever possible.
7. Ask students to reflect on the musical influence of the technologies they use.
8. Use Schaeffer's categorization of musical objects as an analytical framework for student aural analysis of electroacoustic works.
9. Improve student self-assessing skills by encouraging deliberate reflection on all music activities.
10. Use CD or sequenced backing tracks to scaffold junior student performances.

Suggested tasks

1. Select one piece of software you use and analyze its design and effect with regard to the issues raised in this chapter.
2. Do an engagement and meaning audit of the music program you teach in, and see how evenly the different modes and types are represented.
3. Undertake some follow-up reading of the cited references to pursue areas of interest more thoroughly.
4. List the interface metaphors that are used by the computer software systems you use regularly.

5. It is likely that there are philosophical issues that are important but have not been covered here, explore some of the literature on the philosophy of music education to identify these issues and reflect on how the computer may impact them also.

Chapter summary

There are important issues that drive the development and use of technologies. In educational contexts these become especially pertinent when the lessons learned at an intuitive level can be as influential as the declared curriculum objectives. The issues covered are amplification of abilities, myths about the invisibility of technical designs, the significance of context, the important influence of metaphor in software designs, computing skills as musicianship, how computers provide scaffolding to learners, musical intentions surviving new technological methods, modes of musical engagement, and maintaining meaningful music education.

Notes

1 McLuhan, Marshall, *Understanding Media: The Extensions of Man* (London: Sphere Books, 1964).
2 Dewey, John, *Art as Experience* (New York: Putmans, 1934), 229.
3 Heidegger, Martin, *The Question Concerning Technology and Other Essays*, trans. William Lovitt (New York: Harper & Row, 1977), 34.
4 Postman, Neil, *Technopoly: The Surrender of Culture to Technology* (New York: Vintage Books, 1992).
5 Norman, Donald A., *The Invisible Computer: Why Good Products Can Fail, the Personal Computer Is So Complex, and Information Appliances Are the Solution* (Cambridge, MA: MIT Press, 1998).
6 Ibid., vii.
7 Swanwick, Keith, *Music, Mind and Education* (London: Routledge, 1988).
8 Green, Lucy, *How Popular Musicians Learn: A way ahead for music education* (London: Ashgate, 2002).
9 Schaeffer, Pierre, *Traité Des Objects Musicaux,* 2nd ed. (Paris: Éditions du Seuil, 1977).
10 Piaget, Jean, *Structuralism* (New York: Harper & Row, 1970).
11 Csikszentmihalyi, Mihaly, *Flow: The Psychology of Happiness* (London: Rider Books, 1992), 3.
12 Brown, Andrew R., "Modes of Compositional Engagement." Paper presented at the Interfaces: The Australasian Computer Music Conference, Brisbane, 2000.
13 Swanwick, Keith, *A Basis for Music Education* (London: Routledge, 1979).
14 Dillon, Steve, "The Student as Maker: An Examination of the Meaning of Music to Students in a School and the Ways in Which We Give Access to Meaningful Music Education" (PhD thesis, La Trobe University, 2001).

Chapter 3

A brief history of music technology

Contemporary music technologies are commonly thought to be electronic technologies, particularly the synthesizer, computer, and sound recording devices. These devices are products of the post-industrial or information age in which we now live, an age that focuses on data processing and in which the sonic and structural boundaries of music have been exploded. In such an environment it is all too easy to be overwhelmed by the apparent choice of sounds and ways of dealing with them. While we need no longer take refuge within the boundaries of orchestral instrument timbres, common music notation, or classical forms, it is helpful to take a moment and reflect on the history that produced these technologies and that now continues to lead to new instruments and forms that push beyond them. A historical context also humbles us that our time is not a peak of such development but a unique point along the meandering path of human desire to create meaning and expression that reflect our world and our abilities. This chapter both signposts the histories of music technology and provides some clues about making sense of its directions.

I will begin by providing potted histories from three view points, first, locating some of the major technological landmarks in Western music history, second, an overview of automated music leading to modern recording and algorithmic composition, and third, a brief look at the development of electronic music technology. Having set these scenes, I will discuss what attributes might be seen as persistent and thus may deserve our attention in making sense of the digital technologies that surround us today.

Pre-electronic technologies

Throughout human history there has been a consistent theme of technologies influencing our societal development, with periods of accelerated influence occurring at times such as the Renaissance, the Industrial Revolution, and the information age. This pattern is paralleled by a relatively similar pattern of changes in music technology developments. The earliest harps, horns, and drums are clearly technologies and their usage could be characterized very similarly to the way computers are used for music production in our age. Indeed the ancient Greeks such as Pythagoras could be said to have been more fascinated with the technological nature of music than we are even today.

Other landmarks include the use of written notation from around 500 AD, the development of polyphony in the centuries that followed, and organ building improvements and equal temperament in the Middle Ages. The Renaissance period saw an obsession with music of the spheres resulting from the newly developed field of astronomy, and a peaking of craftsmanship in the violins of Stradivarius and in compositional technique in the Fugues of Bach. The study of alchemy lead to nineteenth-century chemistry and physics providing new metals and efficient methods of manufacture that were used for improved instrument fabrication. This surge in instrument development went hand in hand with increases in orchestra size and industrialization was a common underscoring theme in music such as Wagner's *Der Ring des Nibelungen*. Early twentieth century landmarks include the automation of music via the player piano, the technological abstractions of electronic and recorded sound in the music of Schaeffer and Stochausen, and parallel abstractions in the musical structures and notations of Debussy, Stravinsky, Schoenberg, Xenakis, and Cage.

This history is continuous in its curiosity and creativity, but not deterministic or simply one of increasing complexity. For example, the interests of Pythagoras could be said to closely align with uncovering musical patterns in astrological movements in the renaissance and with Fourier's investigations into sonic spectra, in between these investigations were centuries of developments down other technological paths. The path of technological development is in no way straight or predictable in advance, even if such developments appear.

Automated music

The oldest working automated instrument, according to Thomas Levenson,[1] was a barrel organ of Henry VIII's built in 1502. It was manually driven, but the course of the following century lead to fully autonomous instruments driven by clockwork mechanisms.

In order to increase the repertoire used in automated music machines, a replacement for barrel organs that used replaceable barrels, which were expensive to produce and on which playing time was limited, was sought. A solution to both these problems presented itself in the eighteenth century in the form of the punch card technologies employed by Jacquard weaving looms. Scores were made in the form of holes punched in paper tape or cards, and these punch cards became a new form of musical notation, a notation not efficient for human reading but quite efficient for machine reading. The machine became the interpreter of these machine-specific scores. Such instruments constitute more than an amusement even if their quality of performance was quite low. They enabled musical performances to be captured and transported, to be reproduced on demand, and replayed time and again for closer inspection. Indeed the current popularity of soloist and duo in bars singing to CD and MIDI file backings is not so far removed from the barrel organ-driving busker, examples of which can still be found as a tourist attraction on the streets of many European cities.

Perhaps the most sophisticated, certainly the most popular, automated instrument was the player piano. Although its development historically paralleled the gramophone its sonic quality was far superior for quite a while, and brought music on demand into many homes in the first half of the twentieth century. The availability of automated musical performances in the home changed the role of audience, affecting (not always detrimentally) concert attendance and the social status of musical performance skills. The player piano, more than electronic recording technologies, was the parent of MIDI sequencing in choosing to capture pitch, duration, and force (**velocity**) for each note. The piano rolls were editable and so "near perfect" performances could be created, and composers were not slow to realize that piano rolls could produce music beyond that humanly performable. In this way the composer first became nonperforming producer, involved in all the steps from conception to final sounding.

Another thread that influenced computer music making was the development of Stochastic music where aspects of music were determined by probabilities, and sometimes referred to as chance music. Documentation of the use of chance in music stretches as far back as Mozart's Dice Game[2] and coming into its own in the twentieth century particularly in the works of John Cage and Iannis Xenakis. Xenakis' work constitutes one of the most extensive attempts to produce a music from a standpoint that has a technological aesthetic. Xenakis wrote his early music in the 1950s for acoustic instruments, calculating the probabilities by hand, using math to determine elements of pitch, duration, dynamic and structure. Beginning in the 1960s, he turned to the computer to assist in both element determination and sound synthesis. Xenakis applied his stochastic perspective to music from the micro-structure of sound to the macro-structure of form.

The first public performance of computer music was programmed by Geoff Hill and Trevor Pearcey and generated by CSIRAC (Council for Scientific and Industrial Research Automatic Computer) at the Australian Computer Conference in August 1951.[3] At this time computer music was little more than a computational barrel organ playing popular tunes of the time, however, to do so was not an easy task, especially given the fickleness of the valve components, the timing constraints of the memory using mercury delay lines, and awkward punched paper tapes for describing programs. CSIRAC was the first computer in Australia and a machine intended purely for scientific research, so the achievement is a remarkable example of how quickly people turn any technology to musical purposes.

Computer-based music composition had its start in the mid 1950s when Lejaren Hiller and Leonard Isaacson did their first experiments with computer-generated music on the ILLIAC computer at the University of Illinois. They employed both a rule-based system utilizing strict counterpoint, and also a probabilistic method based on Markov chains (also employed by Xenakis). These procedures were applied variously to pitch and rhythm resulting in The ILLIAC Suite, a series of four pieces for string quartet published in 1957.

The recent history of automated music and computers is densely populated with examples based on various theoretical rules from music theory and mathematics. While The ILLIAC Suite used known examples of these, developments in such theories have added to the repertoire of intellectual technologies applicable to the computer. Amongst these are the Serial music techniques, the application of music grammars (notably *A Generative Theory of Tonal Music* by Fred Lerdahl and Ray Jackendoff),[4] sonification of fractals and chaos equations, and connectionist pattern recognition techniques based on work in neuropsychology and artificial intelligence.

Arguably the most comprehensive of the automated computer music programs is David Cope's Experiments in Music Intelligence (EMI), which performs a feature analysis on a database of coded musical examples presented to it, and can then create a new piece that is a pastiche of those features.[5] EMI works at many levels of detail and convincingly captures not only the note-by-note melodic character, but the textural and structural properties of the works that it analyzes.

Electronic musical technologies

After Thaddeus Cahill's relatively unsuccessful attempt at creating a massive organ-like device using early American telephone technologies called the Telharmonium, one of the first electronic performance instruments was Leon Thérémin's device invented in the 1920s in Moscow. The Theremin, as it was known, was played by positioning each hand at varying distance from two antennae. The location of the hands changed the electromagnetic fields generated by electricity passing through the antennae, one controlling volume the other the pitch of a constant and relatively pure tone. The Theremin made quite an impact with pieces being written for it by Aaron Copeland and Percy Grainger, although the most popularly known example is in the opening of the Beach Boys' hit "Good Vibrations."

The first popular electric keyboard instrument was the Hammond organ, invented in 1935, by Laurens Hammond using electromagnetic components to generate sinusoidal waveforms that could be combined in various combinations using drawbars. The drawbars acted like pipe organ stops, but rather than simply turning on or off oscillators, they controlled their degrees of loudness. The B3 model, first produced in 1936, has become legendary in gospel, jazz and rock music. It provided a relatively affordable and portable keyboard instrument for music performance, and the timbral variety "synthesized" through drawbar settings gave to keyboard players a taste of customizable timbre that would later be expanded by the synthesizer. More details on developments of the synthesizer and other electronic musical instruments can be found later in this book, in chapters 9 and 10.

The solid body electric guitar was developed after some initial production of semi-acoustic electric models in the 1930s. Following early experiments by Adolf Rickenbacker and Les Paul the first production models appeared in the early 1950s from the Gibson and Fender companies. The major technical hurdle being the refinement of the pickups to eliminate noise and to provide a clear signal, which was solved largely by the development of the twin-coil "humbucking" pickup.

Thomas Edison developed mechanical recording technologies around the turn of the twentieth century. However, it was not until electronic amplifiers became available in the form of vacuum tubes that the minute etchings of the recording process could be played back with any fidelity. Even then the making of recorded cylinders was tedious and specialized. Building on this research, the first commercial magnetic tape recorder was introduced in 1948. The ability to record, not only playback, was the shift necessary to motivate musicians to use this technology creatively.

Figure 3.1   The Minimoog synthesizer.

In Paris, in the late 1940s after the Second World War, Pierre Schaeffer developed a compositional use for the previously reproduction-focused, tape recorder. Musique concrète, as it became known, used recorded sounds of both instrumental and environmental origin, and manipulated them through variations in pitch, duration, and amplitude, then collaged sounds into a polyphonic musical form.

Tape-based compositional work was produced by Karlheinz Stockhausen in Cologne from the mid-1950s, which he called Electronische Musik (Electronic Music). As well as treating recorded sounds Stockhausen's focus was on synthesizing new timbres using oscillators, filters, and amplifiers.

The successful commercialization of synthesizers came with the release in 1964 of the Moog synthesizers (Figure 3.1). The technical breakthrough that made these instruments possible was the use of transistors instead of vacuum tubes, which reduced the instrument's size and increased the stability of voltage control. One of the more popular early recordings using the Moog synthesizers was Wendy Carlos' "Switched on Bach," which was a notable achievement at the time, but created a legacy of imitative thinking that still haunts synthesizer usage, as more recently reinforced in the **General MIDI** specification. The most popular of Robert Moog's synthesizers was the Mini Moog, one of the first portable all-in-one synthesizers still highly regarded fifty years after its release.

The use of recording as a compositional and synthesis tool did not change much from the days of musique concrète until the late 1970s when the development in Australia of the Quasar and M8 digital synthesizers by Tony Furse that influenced the commercially successful Fairlight CMI developed by Peter Vogel and Kim Ryrie At the same time, the New England Digital Synclavier was developed in New Hampshire by Sydney Alonso, Jon Appleton, and Cameron Jones. The Fairlight and the Synclavier introduced sampling technologies (short duration digital recording)

Figure 3.2   The Yamaha DX7 synthesizer.

to commercial music making in 1979. Both instruments were also capable of sound synthesis processes and used keyboard controllers for performance, attached to computer systems for storage, display and editing of waveforms.

Digital technologies made their way in to synthesizers first as memory banks for presets, most famously in the Sequential Circuits Prophet V, and later in the sound synthesis engine itself notably with the Yamaha DX7 (Figure 3.2). The release of the DX7 in 1983 coincided with another significant event in electronic music history; the introduction of the Musical Instrument Digital Interface (MIDI) standard.

Developed by Dave Smith of Sequential Circuits, and with input from other major manufactures of the time, notably Roland and Yamaha, the MIDI standard replaced the plethora of interconnecting standards such that equipment from different manufacturers could communicate. MIDI began as a note-based live performance protocol, intellectually indebted to music notation and the player-piano technologies. The MIDI standard has expanded over the years to include file formats, sample transfer protocols, the General MIDI standard sound set, a music XML format, and a range other musical and operational parameters.

The synthesizer, in its keyboard form, has remained quite stable since the 1980s, with some controllers extensions modeled on other instruments including guitar, woodwind, and percussion. There continues to be research into new instrument designs, as there has always been, with STEIM in the Netherlands and the HyperInstrument group at MIT's Media Lab contributing significantly during the 1990s, but developments have expanded quite broadly since then.

The 1980s also saw the increase in personal computer ownership, and with it the expansion of music software. Most significantly, from a commercial aspect, was the rise and rise of the MIDI sequencer. Building on the techniques of earlier electronic sequencers to repeat short series of notes, software sequencers continues to provide more comprehensive musical transformations.

Alongside sequencing, music notation programs were also appearing at this time, although it took the desktop publishing revolution of the early 1990s for all the appropriate technologies to be fall into place, notably postscript and laser printing. Computer music publishing is now the norm rather than the exception. The first program to successfully combine both sequencing and notation was C-Lab's Notator on the Atari computer, which proved the rule that you only need one "must have" program to sell a computing platform.

As personal computer power increased in the late 1990s, synthesis software (long the domain of expensive systems such as the Fairlight, or computer workstations) became accessible. This is evident in the current popularity of hard disk recording systems, such as Pro Tools, as well as real-time signal processing systems that are becoming practical on home computers for reverb and **equalization**, and even real-time synthesis as complex as **frequency modulation**, granular, and physical modeling.

The integration of many of these technical threads in computer-based composing, recording, publishing, and multimedia occurred around the late 1990s and now digital music systems provide rich and expressive tools for the musician. Around the turn of the twenty-first century, the increases in computing power reached a threshold where personal computers were powerful enough to manage most audio and some video processes in real time. This saw the concentration of computer music systems in software or "virtual" versions of what had been previously separate audio components. The laptop computer had become the one-stop digital music workspace.

Layers of persistence

With the virtue of hindsight it becomes clear that there are features of music technologies and their usage that reappear and others that are transient. The degree to which features of technology reoccur I describe as being their level of persistence. The most persistent of all features is a behavioral rather than technical one; the trend to turn scientific (technological) discoveries to creative sonic use. This applies equally to the use of new metallic substances for horns, to applying weaving loom automation to drive automated organs, and to using the earliest computers for music creation. What follows after this experimental stage is a longer-term need to make musical sense of the newly acquired music-making opportunities. The search for virtuosity in expression follows improvements in instrument design.

A less persistent, but still important, aspect of music's technological history is the way that technologies influence musical style. Some technological changes resulted in new musical styles, for example the rise of Hip Hop on the back of affordable sampling systems. However, the effect of digital recording on classical performance is less drastic. This is different from saying technologies are a-stylistic, which they are not. Each technology has a persistent bias toward particular aesthetic outcomes, for example, violin development effected Baroque music, saxophone development effected jazz, and the tape recording created musique concrète. This says nothing about those styles being more or less prone to technological influence, but is simply a matter of historical context. Generally, a stylistic aesthetic is established at a time of some technological development, and the aesthetic is quite persistent, while the effect of continued technological development on an established style is less evident.

Another area where a difference in persistence can be seen is the difference between a change in medium and a change in resolution of a medium. For example, the advances in analogue tape recording quality had less musical impact than the change to digital sampling. The significant changes related to new properties of the digital medium, namely identical duplication of and nonlinear access to data. A more historical example is the shift from slide trumpets to valve trumpets. A valve was not a more fancy slide, it was a revolutionary change not a "resolutionary" change. This is somewhat counter-intuitive because most technological progress is a change in resolution; audio quality recording is improved, the resolution of the television screen becomes finer, the speed of the computer is increased, and so on.

Such changes are changes in resolution; improvements in efficiency. While resolution is adequate, further increases rarely lead to major musical shifts such as the emergence of new styles.

Paying attention to the persistence, or long-term influence, of aspects of technology is important for noticing significant changes, and ignoring insignificant ones. Understanding this will help us to not become overwhelmed by the volume of technological changes, but notice when the persistent characteristics alter, and focus our efforts on making sense and meaning of those changes.

Conclusion

And so as history continues we will continue to seek new ways of seeing or, rather, hearing the world through our technologies. As musicians we will strive to make sonic sense of those new ways of hearing, always mindful of our heritage and what it tells us, yet looking forward to creating a new musical heritage.

As we learn music with computers, it can be enlightening to understand some of the journey that has lead us to this point. We can appreciate why things are as they are, and to question whether that is the way we want them to be to best enable our own music making. It can be reaffirming to know that others before us have struggled to express themselves musically with technologies and to perhaps identify ourselves with a tradition of music-making practices and see ways of appreciating and conserving those traditions while seeking new ways to contribute to them.

Reflection questions

1. What were the dominant technological drivers of the past few centuries?
2. Where do you think current borders of technical innovation are that will effect music making?
3. Given that new materials such as iron and aluminum have shaped the development of acoustic instruments, what changes have driven electronic/computer instrument development?
4. What have been the major developments in automated music described in this chapter?
5. The use of electronics has shaped music making over the past one hundred years, who were some of the musicians to first pioneer the use of electronic devices for music?
6. What has been the impact of audio recording on music making?
7. What was the basis of the compositional technique known as musique concrète?
8. What changes occurring during the 1990s are described in the chapter?
9. Are technological or aesthetic trends more persistent and why?
10. How can a knowledge of history be helpful to music making today?

Teaching tips

1. Have students collate a music discography of works created using a particular electronic instrument.
2. Explore stochastic compositional techniques with students using prepared musical fragments and dice and be inspired by those efforts by the example of Mozart's Dice Game.
3. Have students create a Podcast or radio program about the musical history of a particular technology.
4. Make a musique concrète composition with students that remixes sound material generated by a particular technology.
5. Give a performance using only mechanical music devices such as music boxes, toy drumming dolls, cuckoo clocks, wind-up clappers, and so on.
6. Obtain an old synthesizer and have students explore its sonic potential.
7. Add electronic instrument sounds to any instrument identification tasks students undertake.
8. Analyze the technologies used in a 1980s synth-pop song.
9. Have students reproduce the same musical work using a tape recorder, MIDI sequencer, and digital audio recorder to better understand the difference between these technologies.
10. Help student appreciate the limitations of working with earlier technologies, but setting a composition or performance task that uses limited tracks, memory, notes, functions, or material.

Suggested tasks

1. Obtain an inexpensive Theremin from an electronics store and have students (if in kit form, build it) perform with it.
2. Watch one of the many videos on the history of electronic or rock music instruments.
3. Assemble computer games using consoles from the past decade and listen to the music on each and examine with how computer game has changed over that time as a result of the improvements in console audio features.
4. Obtain samples of recordings done in different eras (cylinders, 78 rpm disks, vinyl records, and CDs) and hear the difference in fidelity and how it does or does not effect your appreciation of the music.
5. Read more about music technology history in one of the cited references.

Chapter summary

When considering contemporary music technologies, we commonly imagine electronic technologies, particularly the synthesizer, computer, and sound recording devices. These devices are products of the post-industrial age in which we now live, an age that focuses on data processing and in which the sonic and structural boundaries of music have been exploded. It is helpful to take a moment to reflect on the history that produced these technologies and how, in each age, music is made with whatever technologies are available. An historical context is also humbling, as we understand that our time is not a peak of such development but a unique point along the meandering path of human desire to create meaning and expression in sound by combining our knowledge, resources, and abilities.

Notes

1   Levenson, Thomas, *Measure for Measure: A Musical History of Science* (New York: Touchstone, 1994).
2   Sohne, B. Schotts, "Mozart Dice Game," in *Machine Models of Music*, eds. Stephan M Schwanauer and David A Levitt. (Cambridge, MA The MIT Press, 1993), 533–38.
3   Doornbusch, Paul, *The Music of Csirac: Australia's First Computer Music* (Melbourne: Common Ground, 2005).
4   Lerdahl, Fred, and Ray Jackendoff, *A Generative Theory of Tonal Music* (Cambridge, MA: MIT Press, 1983).
5   Cope, David, *Experiments in Musical Intelligence*, vol. 12 (Madison, WI: A-R Editions, 1996).

Section II

PRODUCTION

Chapter 4

Audio recording

While much of our current focus on music technology concerns computers, it is really recording technology—in particular the tape recorder—that has had the biggest impact on music making and learning in the twentieth century. The integration of computing and recording in the form of sampling and digital recording makes the distinction between computers and digital recorders, if not quite semantic, at least a matter of degree. The computer has taken over the role of primary recording device and at the start of the twenty-first century its cousin, the Internet, is quickly becoming the primary music distribution channel. Downloaded tracks and original recordings can be transferred to portable music players, such as the Apple iPod, for listening anywhere. In this chapter I will explore ways in which recording technology can be useful in music education, as well as provide a road map of the principles and mediums of recording and production. We begin by looking at how short digital recordings, samples, were the first use of computing technologies for recording, then go on to examine hard disk recording practices that eventually replaced tape recording for the most part.

Sampling

Composers have used recorded sounds since phonographs became available in the 1920s. With the introduction of magnetic tape in the 1930s, the ability to edit and manipulate recorded sounds became possible and lead to new musical techniques, notably musique concrète from the 1950s. Computers have been used for audio processing since at least the 1960s, and the process of digital recording is called sampling. Sample playback became popular in the 1990s when the computer memory required to store the samples became affordable.

There can be some confusion about the term "sample." It can be both a verb and a noun. We can sample a piano, meaning we can take a digital recording of it (a verb). We can play a sample of the piano, meaning that we can listen to the recording we made (a noun). As a noun, the term is used in two ways. In the previous example of the piano recording, the sample is all the data that comprises the recording. However, each single element of the data is also a sample, a single measurement of the signal. So to put all this together we can say that when we sample the guitar we get a sample of samples! As this chapter continues, these separate meanings will hopefully be navigated as clearly as possible.

The process of digital sampling involves the rapid and regular measuring of the audio **signal**. Each measurement of the signal strength is called a sample. This process is analogous to shooting a film, where samples are analogous with frames. In film, each frame is a moment in time, but when played back in quick succession they simulate movement. The rate of audio sampling needs to be much higher than the frame rate of film because the ear is quite sensitive. For CD quality audio, the signal is sampled at a *rate* of 44,100 samples per second. The sampling *resolution* determines the precision of the sample measurement, which affects the accuracy and dynamic range of waveform. As a rule, higher resolutions are better, with CDs using 16 bit resolution. A bit is a single value inside the computer which has a binary value of either 1 or 0. Larger numbers are represented by a series of bits, for example 1101 is the binary representation for the number 13. A **byte** is a series of 8 bits, often called an 8 bit value, and can represent numbers from 0 to 255. Even larger numbers are stored in groups of bytes called words. As a result of this internal organization inside the computer, **sample resolution** values are usually in multiples of 8; typically 16, 24, or 32 bit values.

Digitizing or sampling of audio involves a hardware process called analogue to digital conversion (ADC). The playback of the data requires the reverse process using a DAC. In the ADC process, the size of the original signal, often an electrical current generated by a microphone, is regularly measured. These measurements take samples of the amplitude of the signal. The numbers (digits) generated by these measurements are stored as a list in the computer, and this list is saved as a file. A stereo recording will have two lists, one for the left channel and one for the right, which are often stored together in one file. For replay, the numbers in the file are read back in order and passed at regular intervals to the DAC for conversion to an electrical signal which is amplified and played over speakers. Two variables are important in determining the quality of the digital recording; the time between each sample measurement (sample rate), and the size of the number used to store the measured value (sample resolution). In general, the higher the rate and resolution, the better the quality. CDs use a rate of about 44,100 samples per second per channel, and a 16 bit resolution that allows the amplitude to be represented by over 64,000 discrete values.

Figure 4.1 shows how a continuous analogue signal is described as a series of discrete digital samples. Samples values quantize to the closest grid point, so the higher the rate and resolution the more accurately the sample values represent the waveform.

Due to the expense of memory, the early digital sampling systems in the 1980s captured short segments of sound and used them and variations on them repeatedly. At this time longer recordings of whole songs were still done on tape recorders. A particularly useful method was to sample single notes from an instrument, say a drum kit, which could be used to playback phrases of any length through reuse of the samples.

The range and quality of sampled sounds on a particular synthesizer or software synthesizer vary greatly. In synthesizers supporting the General MIDI specification, the range of samples includes most orchestral and rock music instruments, a selection of classic synthesizer timbres, and some sound effects. Synthesizers

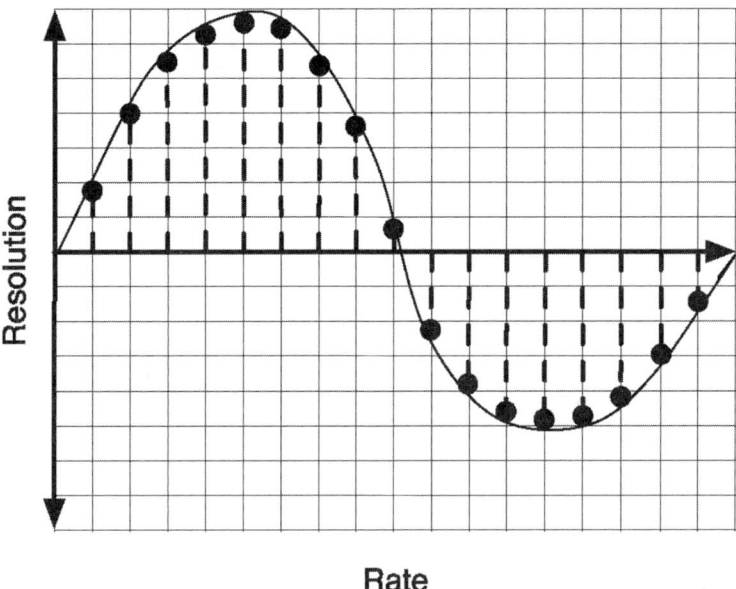

Figure 4.1   Digitizing audio. Dots indicate sample points, dotted line length equates to sample value.

may include a wider range of samples; but the wider the range of samples the more memory is required, which increases the cost. The technical quality of the samples depends on a number of aspects including the sampling rate and resolution, the quality of the electrical components, and the hardware design. The musical quality of the sounds is a subjective judgment and depends on the preferences and skill of those who sampled the sounds and compiled the sound library.

Ideally, for acoustic instrument simulations, there would be a sample of every note of every instrument so that the character of the different registers is reproduced. This is referred to as multi-sampling. In most cases a single sample is used for a small range of pitches, covering the interval of about a three whole steps. If the sample is used over a wider range, the resampling required for higher pitches results in an unwanted change of timbre known as the "chipmunk" effect, and the slower playback of low sounds (while timbrally less problematic) results in a loss of crispness in **attack**. In some synthesizers different samples are used for loud and soft versions of a sound; this is referred to as multi-layered sampling. It is more common for a single sample to be played back at different volumes to achieve dynamics.

Audio file formats

Sampled audio data are kept as wavetables in computer memory and saved to disks as files in one of a number of common audio file formats. Audio files types are distinguished by the way in which the audio is saved to them. Greater detail about audio formats is presented later in the book in chapter 12. For now, it will suffice to indicate that uncompressed audio formats include WAV, AIFF, and AU. Compressed formats that take up less file space, sometimes at the expensive of some reduction in audio quality, include MP3, FLAC, OGG, WMA, and AAC. Most audio editing programs will allow files to be saved in these formats. Files can be converted from one format to another by opening them and resaving (or exporting) to a different format. Most audio recording systems keep files in uncompressed formats to maintain audio quality, while most music players save space by using compressed formats such as MP3. Audio files downloaded from Internet music stores are sometimes in MP3 format, although more commonly in AAC (Apple iTunes) or WMA (Napster and MSN Music).

Manipulating samples

Using samples of individual instrument sounds provides the computer with an efficient way of generating reasonably realistic renderings of sequences. However, sampling's obvious limitation is that the sound selection is fixed unless the user can add their own samples, access additional libraries of samples, or modify the samples there already. With a fixed set of sounds it may not always be possible to get exactly the sound you need. In order to overcome this, most computers and samplers provide a way of importing or recording samples and methods of editing and altering the samples to produce a greater variety of sounds. We will look at some of the more common methods of sample modifications.

Cutting and pasting

A digital recording comprises a list of individual numbers. Sections of this list can be removed or their order rearranged using cut and paste processes. This can be used to edit out unwanted sections or to repeat segments. Segments can be as short as the attack portion of a note, or as long as an entire chorus of a song. These editing techniques can be used compositionally to recreate musique concrète tape splicing techniques, and used to cut up musical material as done in Hip Hop styles. Another obvious ways to change the data is to read the values from last to first, which plays the sound in reverse.

Pitch shifting

Varying a sample's playback rate, not unlike changing the speed on a tape player, will change its pitch. This process is usually achieved using a technique called resampling. Shifting the pitch more than a few whole tones will introduce noticeable timbral variations to the sound. Simple resampling also changes the length of the sample, as it plays faster it is higher but also shorter, and the reverse is true when pitch is shifted down. More sophisticated techniques can separately control pitch and duration of a sample independently. Loop-based sequencing software such as Abelton Live and Sony ACID use pitch-shifting and time-stretching to match tempos and keys between various sampled music clips. Synthesizers often provide the pitch-bend wheel or lever which can control pitch sifting as a smooth glissando, and when set to extreme ranges can produce some very interesting effects.

Filtering and equalization

The timbre of a sound can be altered by changing its harmonic spectra. Filters are used to reduce or accentuate overtones around particular frequencies. Filters, like those on water purifiers, let the signal pass through but extract unwanted elements on the way. Particular filters affect different regions of the harmonic spectra to create the desired effect. While there are many different filter types, usually low pass filters are used to reduce the brightness of a sound, similar to adjusting the treble tone control on a hi-fi system. Equalizers include one or more filters set to specific frequency bands. Mixing desks, both real and virtual, include equalizers (EQ for short) normally labeled Hi, Mid, and Low which correspond the frequency range they effect. More fine-grained EQ control is not uncommon using multi-band or graphic EQs with up to thirty different frequency band controls. Equalization is used to help color the sound as required, in particular to assist in providing clarity to multi-track mixes, accentuate certain sounds, or to de-emphasize unwanted sounds or noise.

Amplitude envelopes

An important cue to identifying a familiar sound is how its volume changes over time. A piano sound, for example, has a quick attack and then decays slowly, while a tuba speaks more slowly and can sustain its volume for some time. By changing this characteristic volume shape, called a volume envelope, sounds can be changed either subtly to better suit the articulation of a phrase, or drastically to create interesting new sounds. Amplitude envelopes are also used in digital recording to cross fade between two sections of overlapping sound, or to provide a short fade in and out of regions to prevent clicks from the abrupt edges where they have been cut. On a larger time scale, amplitude envelopes are used to vary the volume of a track in the mix. Amplitude envelopes are used as mix automation curves in most digital recorders. In digital systems there is a maximum amplitude that can be represented. This limit is the largest (or smallest) value that the bit resolution allows. If the signal is amplified beyond this value, then all values above the maximum are kept at the maximum. This effect is called **clipping**, and results in a distorted effect. When amplifying (or recording) a digital signal, care needs to be taken to avoid clipping. In some styles of music clipping and other **glitches** in digital audio stream are used intentionally as a musical element.

Delays and reverb

Most recordings sound more convincing with the addition of some reverb. The dry sound of the original recording can often be dull and lifeless. Acknowledging this, most systems include reverb and delay processing of samples. A simple echo or delay is an easy process for a computer. To achieve it, the sample **wavetable** can be read once for the original sound, then again for each delay, usually decreasing the volume of each delay. Reverberation is a more complex process of multiple overlapping delays, which simulates the many reflections a sound would undergo in a live space. It is common to say that reverb is like the ketchup of audio processes, you can put it on anything.

Hard disk recording

The process of creating short samples or long recordings is identical on the computer except for the amount of memory required to store the data. Samplers that are used for virtual synthesizers and contain recordings of individual instrument notes usually store their data in the computer's Random Access Memory (**RAM**) where access to it is fast. Longer digital recordings, such as tracks for a complete song, are often too large to be stored in RAM and so are stored on the hard drive, or other more permanent memory. The disadvantage of this is that access to the hard drive memory is slower than access to RAM. To overcome this hard disk recording systems keep the current section of data being heard or edited in RAM and swap memory between the hard drive and RAM as required. As the speed and size of hard drives increases, it is possible for hard disk recording systems to manage more simultaneous tracks of audio at one time. As computer processing power increases, the number and complexity of real-time effects that can be managed at once is increased. Around the turn of the twenty-first century, personal computers reached a stage of development where their digital recording abilities made them the most cost effective means of professional quality record production. It is possible for students in schools to have access to music recording systems with capabilities similar to professional equipment of two decades prior. Technical capabilities are no longer a limitation for recording activities in schools, knowledge of and creative ideas about how to utilize them are now the barrier.

When making recordings, a basic understanding of musical acoustics is useful. Introductions to which can be found in a number of texts. Associated with acoustic understanding is learning to hear how the microphone will pick up sound. Different microphones act in different ways, so experimenting with the microphones you have will build local knowledge, and some study of the basic microphone types and characteristics is helpful.

Signal flow

Except for the most basic recorders, a recording system usually involves several pieces of equipment. It is important to become familiar with what each piece does, how these pieces connect together, and how the sound signal flows through the system. A thorough understanding of signal flow will make problem solving much easier. Methods for understanding signal flow include practice at setting up and un-setting the recording system, working with flow diagrams of various signal flow options, and talking-aloud the signal flow as it is traced through from microphone to recording media back to speakers on playback.

Even though recordings are now stored on hard drives, or other computing media, and many of the outboard effects equipment has been reduced to extra software plugins, the journey of a sound signal through the recording process and back out to the listener is still an important one to be clear about. In fact, as more of the recording processes occur within the computer, the need to understand the signal

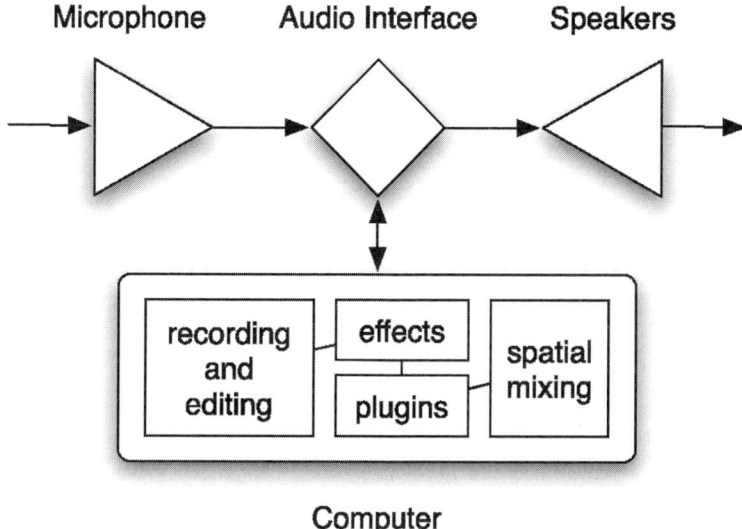

Figure 4.2   Audio signal flow in a simple hard disk recording system.

flow within the system may be greater than ever. It is normally a lack of understanding of this data (signal) flow that causes most frustrations from students trying to work out how a digital recording system operates or to fix problems. Figure 4.2 shows a flow diagram that indicates the main stages of the digital recording process.

Audio is captured by a microphone (or perhaps comes as a signal from a guitar or other electronic instrument) and is converted to digital data by an audio interface. This data is transferred to the computer for storage and editing. In the recording software it may be cut and pasted or stretched and twisted in the editing process. During playback the signal flows out via various plugin modules that add reverberation, compression, and other effects, and each signal (there are normally several tracks of audio) is mixed to the appropriate volume level and positioned in space (panned), usually in a 1D stereo image (two channel) or 2D surround sound plane (six or more channels) that determines which of the audio outputs the signal will emerge from. The data exits the computer and is converted back into an electrical signal by the audio interface so that it can be passed to the amplifier and speakers for all to hear.

There are, of course, a myriad more details in the signal path that vary from system to system, but usually difficulties with recording systems that are not operating as expected comes down to some kink or other in this signal pathway. The most productive way to solve these problems is to trace the signal as it makes its way along the path until the broken link is found. Then, at least, we know where to look in more detail to correct any problem.

Recording mediums

When looking at recording devices, there are three broad categories of recording medium: tape, disk, or memory card. Choosing one over another comes down to deciding which features you require most, and how expensive each is for the amount of storage you require. One significant factor is that tape devices (and some disks) access the data as a linear stream (i.e., to get to a different part of the recording the tape needs to be wound or rewound). Disk and memory card systems are usually nonlinear or random access, which means that different sections of the recording can be accessed at any time, which is usually preferable. A familiar example of this difference is the locating of sections on a video (tape) or DVD (disk). The most commonly available recording mediums and their advantages and disadvantages in educational settings are discussed below.

Tape

Tape devices are the oldest recording medium still in usage. There advantage is their potential low cost. Their disadvantage is there limited availability, linear access to areas on the tape, large physical size, and limited storage capacity.

Cassette

Cassette recording is adequate for most audio sketching and reflection process and even some assessment tasks. Cassette tapes can vary in quality but are usually considered poor to reasonable in quality. They are one of the least expensive recording mediums, both in terms of the cost of recorders and blank media. They seem destined to vanish as a recording medium but are still found in many educational situations.

Reel to reel

There are few advantages to reel to reel recorders in education. Some professional musicians swear by them, but for aesthetic rather than practical reasons. In schools they are cumbersome to setup and operate and the blank media (spare tapes) can be difficult to obtain and expensive. As multi track recorders, reel to reel tape machines will continue to work adequately and do not need updating, but should rarely be purchased new or have expensive repair work carried out

DAT

Digital Audio Tape was once the professional mastering format of choice, but has now been replaced by writable CDs. DAT machines should continue to work well for the next decade, but would not be a wise new purchase for a school. The tapes can be expensive and available only from professional audio outlets. DAT quality is excellent, but memory card, hard disk or writable CDs are more cost effective and usable.

Multi track tape formats such as Alesis ADAT and Tascam DA88 are in the same category as stereo DAT tapes. They work fine if you have them but they are now superseded.

Disk

Disks can be used for directly capturing audio data or for storage of already recorded data. Hard disk recording systems are currently the main method of capturing audio data. They are not a coherent a group, consisting of magnetic and optical media options, but provide the largest storage capacity and good cost-efficiency at this time.

Hard disk

Almost any current model computer can be turned into a hard disk recording system with the addition of appropriate hardware and/or software. The most common hard disk recording system is Pro Tools,[1] but there are many others and most sequencing programs support audio recording. The Audacity program is a free audio recorder and editor that works on most computers.[2] This can make the recording addition quite an affordable extension to existing computer facilities. Almost all hard disk recording systems will be multi track (the number depends on machine speed and hardware add-ons). Quality varies from good to professional depending on the audio interface used to convert the audio signal to and from the computer. The down-side for multiple-user sites, such as schools, is that hard disk space is quickly consumed and backing up or transferring work to another format can be time consuming. Having each student purchase their own hard drive is an option. At least have students backup sessions to a CD as a matter of course to keep the hard drive space free for work in progress.

Mini disc

Mini Discs are situated between the cassette and hard disk recording in quality and convenience, but are being replaced by portable hard drive and memory card recorders. Mini Disc recorder quality is good but not professional. As stereo recorders in schools, the Mini Disc portability is convenient for field recording, but recordable MP3 devices will soon fill this gap.

Compact disc

The main advantages of CDs as a recording medium are that players are so widely available, most computers have CD burners, the audio quality is excellent, and the discs are inexpensive. Also, the mystique of having your own CD is quite motivating to students. The major disadvantage of the writable CDs at present is that most can only be written to once; they are not rerecordable. CDs are an excellent mastering companion to the hard disk recording system.

DVD

Digital Versatile Disks or Digital Video Disks are useful for multimedia or film projects where music and video are used. As a data storage medium, DVDs have a higher capacity than CDs and can be more cost effective. DVD players can decode 5.1 surround recordings, so this will be attractive to students working in surround sound. DVD audio is a six channel high-quality audio format (no video). Burners that support DVD audio are les common than standard DVD but for high-end audio work it is a cost effective solution.

Memory card

Memory cards are being used in portable MP3 players, USB flash drives, in digital cameras, and in some portable recording devices. Memory cards use various forms of solid state memory, with the advantage that there are no moving parts, they can be small and portable, they are reusable, and access to any location is quick. Disadvantages include their relative expense, limited storage capacity, data access speeds can be slow, and there are a bewildering range of formats and physical sizes to navigate. Memory card storage is excellent for educational settings because they provide portable, robust, reusable, and inexpensive storage for students work.

Recording production techniques

Understanding the production techniques, or production values, of the recording process is vital to those making recordings, but also necessary for those, like students, who listen to them. Because most of the music students hear comes to them from recordings, the ability to understand the possibilities of the production process will help them better understand the differences in production style and fashion which are a significant part of defining a musical genre.

The quality of an audio recording is influenced by practices at three stages, capture, editing, and mastering. The choice of microphone, position, and room is critical at the capturing stage, but we will not pay so much attention to it here. Once the audio tracks are captured with a multi track digital recording environment a number of production techniques come into consideration.

Clarity

The recording quality is dictated to a large degree by the equipment and capturing process. However, the use of the techniques below can ensure that each part of the music has its own sonic space. The clarity of the recording can also be improved by editing out extraneous noises such as page turns, coughing, foot tapping, and the like that might be at the beginning and ending of recorded sections.

Tone

Each recorded sound will be colored by the recording process. Once captured, the tone of each part can be adjusted using equalization (EQ). It is good production practice to pay attention to the timbre of each part and add or cut back the amount of treble, bass, or mid frequencies to get the desired sound. EQing can also help clarify the sound by removing booming bass frequencies or emphasizing particular frequency areas in each part to articulate them more clearly.

Balance

The volume mix between parts is very important. Most mixing desks or systems have "solo" and "**mute**" buttons to isolate tracks, which can be used to assist in achieving a balance between specific tracks by contrasting the mix with the individual to make sure its contribution is appropriately audible. Some tracks need to be mixed so that they blend, while others need to be either pronounced or held back. The mix is often not static through the duration of a recording, adjustments at certain points such as bringing up a soloist, may be necessary. After working methodically through the piece section by section noting points of adjustment, the final mix will need to be done "live"—either by hand or using track automation when recording the master version.

Spatialization

A spatial mix of the recording enables tracks to be positioned anywhere around the speaker array using the panning controls. Spreading the sounds across the spatial **spectrum** creates a full sound and can provide each part with its own location in the sonic horizon. At times the initial recording is done in stereo, so those panning positions may need to be maintained. Usually the parts of most importance are panned to the center, such as vocal and bass in a pop song, while accompanying parts are evenly spread to the left, right, front, and rear. Panning can also be used to create an illusion of a stage set up, with instruments being panned to appear around the imaginary "stage." Spatial mixes can be done is stereo (two tracks), surround sound (six tracks for 5.1), or for a custom speaker array set up.

Spatial attributes can be enhanced with various added effects such as reverb, delay, chorusing, compression, and so on. The use of reverb is most common and can make the recording, or parts of it, sound like it is in a hall, small room, a club, or any other space. If the room in which the recording took place has a nice acoustic, then reverb may not be necessary. When it is added it can be applied to the whole mix to provide a general sense of space, or to individual parts to bolster their sound. In complex productions, multiple reverbs may be used.

Effects

Delays are usually applied only to individual tracks to enhance them. Some delay on a lead vocal or instrument is the most common application. Chorusing provides the effect of doubling with a second part slightly detuned. It is usually used to give a greater sense of an ensemble, to string sounds for example. Compression reduces the dynamic range of a track, and is used most often to provide "punch" or emphasis to percussion or vocal recordings which can have a wide dynamic range and are subject to being are subsumed by the rest of the mix in quiet moments. Reducing the dynamic range and increasing the volume ensure that they are always audible.

There are numerous other production techniques, and more detail to the ones mentioned here. Listening closely to commercially produced recordings to hear how they are produced can help students to learn a great deal about record production techniques.

Educational applications of digital recording technologies

The activities to which recording can be put are numerous. In this section we will outline some of the music education activities to which recording technologies can be applied, and provide some examples. From this it should be possible to extrapolate applications suitable for particular circumstances.

Music production

Audio recording is the dominant medium of music creation in our society, perhaps even more prevalent than live performance. Recording is also the dominant music representation format, the medium through which most students will access the musical idea of others. Therefore, the need for music education to help students to be fluent and articulate in this medium is increasingly important. Music production, the creation of music with technologies, includes aspects of composition, performance, and distribution.

To compose directly in the recording medium, multi track recording and sound processing facilities are usually required. Multi track recording on computer is useful for capturing live performances, whether they be in a classical, jazz, or rock style. Digital recording systems are often combined with MIDI sequencing facilities that can be particularly useful for contemporary styles such as pop or electronic dance music where repeated audio sections are combined with sequenced material. Systems with extensive editing capabilities are useful in enabling genres that focus on remixing existing audio materials.

Audio recording can equally support performance activities. These can begin simply as playing along to existing recordings, or creating specific play along tapes. More interactive performances are possible where recording devices are used to delay, loop or otherwise replay parts of the performance which are in turn played against. Such techniques have their history in reel to reel tape loops, but are more commonly found today in dedicated digital sample and delay devices.

Recorded portfolios

One of the original motivations for the invention of audio recording was for the archiving of speech, so using recordings as a record of events and activities has a long history. In music education, record keeping and monitoring of progress is made rich with the use of recordings, these can be as simple as routine classroom recordings of performance progress, to a specially recorded CD of the years' showcase presentations.

Portfolios of recorded material are a useful way to archive and record student activities. Many teachers find it useful to have a storage area for each class or student, on which routine recordings of activities are kept. These can be perused to assist critical analysis, assessment of progress, as a reminder of the work done, or to facilitate communication of standards and progress between teaching teams.

Because recording for portfolios should be a regular activity, some equipment needs to be either permanently installed in the teaching space, or be highly portable so that the teacher or student can carry it with them. Typically, a permanent record-

ing setup with microphones on stands or hanging from the roof is common, or surprisingly good recordings can achieved with portable recordings systems, with an
external stereo microphone assisting to provide the best quality.

Reflection

The most powerful use of recording for learning is its use in providing reflective
feedback on music making. A very efficient use of music technology resources is a
suite of portable sound recorders which can be used by students to record and playback performances, discussions, compositional ideas, and more. Typically, about ten
such recorders could be purchased for the price of one computer system. Such mass
usage enables autonomous learning process across many small groups or individuals at one time. Recorders with removable storage are best so that each student or
class can have it own file storage, greatly simplifying file organization.

Recording for reflection can also make good use of self and peer feedback.
Students seem more willing to take and make criticism of a recording of their work
since the listening back provides a distance and separateness from them personally.
The provision of recording devices for reflection can relieve the need for teachers
to be everywhere in the class at once, since they can defer listening and comments
to a later time when reviewing tapes or they can have students review each others
recordings which is both time efficient and educative.

A number of research studies have shown that reflection is more effective
in discussion situations than through written processes. Taking this into account,
reflective discussions about musical activities can also be recorded for later review.
In this way the student(s) whose work is being discussed can have a recording of the
comments, which might otherwise pass by too quickly to be remembered.

Students can be encouraged to take reflective processes from the class or
instrumental lesson to their practice or home environments. Here the positive critical
feedback process can continue beyond the lesson. Home recording capabilities also
allow the capturing of ideas or performances for later playback to teachers or peers.

Assessment

Audio and video recordings are increasingly being used for assessment purposes.
Their practicality in managing geographic separation, scheduling, selective viewing, and reviewing as evidence is widely accepted. While there is also agreement
that live viewings are preferable, but often the practicalities outweigh these concerns. Also, the use of recording mediums for assessment also enables music produced for that medium—such as computer sequences, electronic music works, and
so on—to be included in the same assessment process.

The increased reliance on recordings for assessment places a greater emphasis on teachers and students to be familiar with recording processes on two counts.
First, they need to be capable of making the best recording possible so that their
work is able to get an appropriate hearing. Second, they need to understand the
medium enough to distinguish the performance/production from the artifacts of
the medium. For example, is the poor tone production due to inadequate microphone
selection and placement or flaws in the performers' technique?

The use of recordings in assessment opens new possibilities that need to be considered. For example, recordings displace time such that performances or compositions from one year or one semester can be compared alongside those of previous times. This might be useful in assessing progress, but may be unfair in assessing students of one era with those of another. Recordings could be submitted for assessment at a number of different times or at a time different from that required. This means that recordings made during the year could be used for formative feedback at the time and then accumulated for final assessment of the year's progress. Such possibilities raise questions not about the technology so much as about assessment practices in general.

Conclusion

Sound recording has become such an influential part of music making in the latter half of this century that competence at making, producing and evaluating recordings is now an essential role for all musicians, and particularly for music professionals such as teachers. Making effective use of recording processes need not involve complex and expensive equipment, and so it not reasonable to limit the music-making opportunities only to styles which rely on multi track recording processes, but to have it available for all students. Digital recordings are used for taking short samples that are used in synthesizers for instrument imitation, and also in creating musical collages and looped based music works. Digital recording on personal computers is also used for larger scale multi track recordings traditionally done on tape in recording studios. These processes mean that the computer provide a versatile range of activities that assist music making and musical development. Uses of digital recording in music education extend from the everyday use in documentation of activities for remembering and reflecting, to creative uses in the roles of composers, producers, and performers.

Reflection questions

1. What technology has reputably had the largest impact on the music industry in the last one hundred years?
2. What is different about the way the computer records sound than how tape records captured sound?
3. What are the three different uses of the term "sample"?
4. Rate and resolution of a digital recording refer to which aspects of the capturing process?
5. Why were samples (digital recordings) originally quite short?
6. What is it that flows as a signal within a computer-based recording system?
7. Which recording medium is likely to be best for portable recording systems, why?
8. How many audio channels are required for the 5.1 surround sound mix?
9. How can recording technologies be used for portfolio assessment?
10. How might the clarity of a recording be improved?

Teaching tips

1. Have students investigate the history of sound recording technologies so they appreciate better the value of the opportunities they have to record music so easily.
2. Students can use recording equipment to make Podcasts (subscription audio programs) about a topic as an assignment submission.
3. Use the creation of a musique concrète composition as a vehicle for teaching audio recording techniques in a creative context.
4. As a way of clarifying their understanding, have students work on definitions for a sound recording glossary.
5. Have students evaluate the recording techniques used in some of their favorite commercial songs.
6. When exploring sample manipulation, use recordings of students saying their own names so the impact of the manipulations is both obvious and fun.
7. Compare the reverberant qualities of different spaces around the school with the different presets on a digital reverb unit.
8. Provide portable recorders for students to do field recordings for use in creating a soundscape composition.
9. Test students understanding of signal flow by having them problem fix a digital recording system that has deliberately set up incorrectly.
10. Use the list of recording production techniques in this chapter as criteria for assessing student recordings

Suggested tasks

1. Compare the characteristics of recordings made over the last one hundred years and assess which technologies made what changes to recording character over that time?
2. Test the capacity of your digital recording system, buy seeing how many tracks and reverb plugins can be accommodated before the computer complains or the audio playback is compromised.
3. Locate, download, and install as many free audio plugins for your computer as you can find, then play with them.
4. Obtain one of the many books on audio recording techniques as a way toward improving your recording skills.
5. Draw a map of the signal flow diagram that corresponds to your digital recording system.

Chapter summary

While much of the focus of music technology is on computers, they were preceded by a series of recording technologies that have collectively had an enormous impact on music making and learning. The integration of computing and recording in the form of sampling and digital recording has the potential to turn any personal computer into a digital recorder. This chapter provides a road map of the principles of digital recording and production. It explores how the technologies of digital recording work, and provides some hints about how to assess and achieve good recording quality. Finally, there is discussion about the ways in which recording technology can be useful in music education.

Notes

1   Pro Tools, http://www.digidesign.com/.
2   Audacity, http://audacity.sourceforge.net/.

Chapter 5

Music publishing

One of the most popular applications of computers in music education is the publication of musical scores. Although musical notation packages are popular with users, their development remains a veritable minefield for software developers as they attempt to accommodate hundreds of years of notational conventions and stylistic interpretations. Conventions of notation that are commonly encountered and understood by musicians can cause significant problems for computers attempting to interpret these incoming musical gestures. Even so, the major music publishing packages do a great job of navigating this minefield and have even become better at making simple things simple. In this chapter we will explore some of the major ways in which computer music notation is being used in schools and outline the potential strengths and weaknesses to be aware of when choosing the right music publishing package.

Notation as a representation

The underlying issue in all music notation is one of representation. Notation is an abstract representation of the ideas and sounds of music. As with all abstractions, musical notation highlights particular elements of music for our attention whilst relying on cultural context and performer/reader interpretation to fill in the remaining elements. It is at these borders of what should be represented and what should be left out that problems arise in musical notation. Computer representations have to deal with these issues in tandem with the more technical problems of digital representation and computer usability.

Despite these challenges for representing music at the margins, most music education applications only have rudimentary notation requirements that the applications handle well, so we will begin by addressing the more relevant question of how computer notational systems are used in education (Figure 5.1).

Figure 5.1 Publishing systems focus on CPN notation but some support TAB or the use of graphic symbols.

Learning with computer-based music notation

It is in the area of music notation that computers in education most obviously imitate an existing media—in this case paper. Music manuscript has widespread uses in music education and will examine some of the more frequent uses of computer music notation systems. These common uses flow naturally from traditional applications of musical scores and because of the strong metaphorical link between computer notation and paper notation, most readers will be able to easily think of additional applications.

Because the computer prints legible and easily readable notation the preparation of arrangements is probably the single most common use of computer notation in schools. The ability to quickly prepare neat scores, easy copying and pasting, automatic extraction of parts, and easy transpositions makes the preparation of scores with computer an efficient task. Given the ease of arranging music with the computer it is particularly useful for teachers who regularly manage ensembles with unusual instrumentation. It can be quite expedient to have a score saved and to quickly create parts for new or substitute instruments as required. Most systems will enable playback of the score for convenient audition of the score status or for audio capture of a completed score as an example of how the score sounds and for the preparation of rehearsal recordings captured at different tempi and with or without some parts omitted. Audio rendering of the scores is particularly useful when a recording of the work is not available.

Educators often need to prepare printed material as handouts, and the incorporation of notation into these is another common application of music publishing systems. Incorporating notation in handouts requires the ability to move the example from the notation software to the word processing software but this process is not always as easy as it should be. Surprisingly, some of the less well-known programs implement this feature best. However, all major software applications do allow some form of capturing score selections to the clipboard for pasting into another application. There can be some tricks to making score segments look correct for handouts, as the layout conventions for a full score may not always be appropriate. Typical

Instrumental Exercises
for Trumpet/Cornet

Introducing Time

$\frac{6}{8}$ time has six eighth note (quaver) beats to a bar, split into two sets of three:

These make up two dotted quarter notes (dotted crotchets):

Other combinations of rhythm can be created which include:

EXERCISE 1

Clap the rhythms above individually and in sequence, to get used to the timing.

EXERCISE 2

Now try playing this exercise, which uses these rhythms and is based on the scale of C major (below). Some fingerings have been added to help you along the way.

C Major scale

EXERCISE 3

Now try playing this melody from a well-known traditional song, but watch out for the accidentals!

Figure 5.2 An example of a music handout prepared in the Sibelius program.

problems often relate to the ability to prepare several self-contained examples in one notation file. Normally a score will have one beginning and one end, so many notation programs assume this in relation to setting and changing key signatures, time signatures, spacing, and so forth. For example, it is likely that clef changes between examples will result in unwanted "courtesy" clefs at the end of lines that cannot be deleted and it can be difficult to turn off automatic features such as sequential bar number counting. Once handouts (Figure 5.2) have been created on a word processor with musical examples pasted in, these can be easily printed or sent to student via e-mail.

As a composition tool, music publishing systems are becoming widespread for reasons of neatness and efficiencies described for arranging tasks. However, because the compositional task not only requires efficiency but also malleability, many composers find their compositional process interrupted or restrained by the limitations and/or implementation of the program's editing capabilities. As score navigation, note entry, and playback features have improved, more composers find programs such as Sibelius[1] and Finale[2] useful compositional environments. Most of the major sequencing programs have support for music notation that is quite reasonable for educational examples and simple scores and the ability to edit in nonnotational views can be an advantage in some cases, but these packages will not be as fully featured for music publishing as dedicated applications. There are a number of simpler music publishing programs including Score Writer[3] that are less featured and often less complex and expensive than Sibelius or Finale, and are quite adequate for the limited demands of score writing and handout preparation in educational environments. There are also a few noncommercial score publishing software environments that usually produce very high quality scores but are somewhat more unconventional in their operation. Notable amongst these applications is LilyPond written by Han-Wen Niehuys and Jan Nieuwenhuizen, which produces excellent output in PDF format, is not too awkward for small examples and can convert from MIDI files as a way of assisting the input of larger scores.[4]

As most computer notation packages have the ability to playback the score, they are very useful for music theory exercises, either as teacher-operated demonstrations or for self-directed student exercises. The addition of aural feedback can greatly improve student response, understanding and appreciation of the rules and techniques being explored. As these activities are often compulsory ones student access is an important consideration. This is usually managed through either access to an adequate number of computer workstations or through careful scheduling of time available on a limited number of computers. For extensive or specialized aural training there are specialized applications that are more appropriate and these are discussed in chapter 18.

Another educational usage of these programs we will explore is the use of notation system for analysis. This area is underutilized, but also not well supported by features in existing packages that focus on publishing. All commercial notation programs can be utilized for analysis through part-muting to isolate elements, comparison of score segments between different tiled windows, and allowing playback of discrete sections at any tempo and with variations of orchestration. Some applications also have features that indicate pitch range boundaries within the score, which can be tweaked for purposes of analysis.

Music publishing systems can be deployed in performance too if required. The most obvious use is to have the program running on a portable computer whose screen can be positioned on a music stand in place of paper manuscript. There are some specialist applications, such as eStand, that are dedicated to this task, but often a music publishing package used to create the score will be sufficient, or even a graphic document reader such as the Acrobat PDF file reader can display score pages saved in an appropriate format.

Finally, because it is often easier to store and manipulate scores in electronic form than on paper, many music publishing systems include software that allows the scanning of printed scores into a digital format. The accuracy of the scanning process varies significantly depending upon the print quality and complexity of the original score. When the scanning works well it can save considerable time in note entry, but when scanning is inaccurate the task of correcting errors in the score can be tedious. Another method of quickly entering note data to a score is to read in a MIDI file of the work. Most applications do a very good job of interpreting the MIDI file into a notated score, even if the MIDI file was created from a human performance of the work. Music publishing systems can usually save scores and MIDI files if required to transfer data to another music application.

Having explored the ways in which a notation systems is to be used, we will now examine how features of different music publishing software applications can be assessed.

What to look for in a music notation system

Music publishing packages are complex software systems designed to accommodate diverse requirements, however, there are some common technical features that everyone needs to be aware of when assessing music notation systems. For educational situations, an appropriate system will also depend on who is using the system, staff or students (and of what age), and the particular needs of the styles of music that will be notated.

Print quality

Rather than starting with input, it can be more important to look first at output when we are concerned with publishing. The way the score looks on screen and when printed depends significantly on the notational font being used. So look for clarity, openness, and readability as you see it. Particular things to notice include note head size and shape, beam thickness and slant angles, and spacing between notes and accidentals (particularly in dense chromatic clusters). The overall notation size(s) may be an issue, particularly is doing music for young audience where larger notes are required or for players who sit well back from their music stands. The ability to view a score on screen in high resolution can help in accurate notation spacing, and reduce the need for excessive draft printouts. Many systems offer a choice of fonts and, for genres such as jazz and early music, there can be specific fonts that give an authentic appearance and access to important symbols.

Input methods

Getting notes into the system can be easy or frustrating depending primarily on choosing an appropriate input method for the music. For example, with rhythmically simple phrases, real-time performance on a MIDI keyboard is quick whereas for rhythmically complex scores, note-by-note input will usually be less frustrating in the long run. Note-by-note methods include mouse-dragging from a pallet or menu, clicking on an on-screen keyboard, use of the QWERTY keyboard, non-real-time MIDI keyboard input and perhaps handwriting recognition. Some note-by-note systems use dedicated hardware such as special-keypads, graphic tablets, MIDI controllers, and so on. It is important to find the range of input methods which suit, first, the complexity of music most commonly written, then match that with the preferences and abilities of the users.

Rhythmic transcription and rendering

While pitches are highly constrained in Western music and hence cause little problem in notation systems, rhythm can be quite problematic. First, some programs simply cannot display certain complex rhythmic groupings (often found in recent contemporary music or non-western music) including arbitrary tuplets, embedded tuplets (one inside another), groupings across staves or bars, or unusual beam groupings within a bar. Second, the ability of a system to appropriately transcribe real-time input can vary greatly. Of particular difficulty are interpreting differences between triplets and dotted note patterns, and the handling of rubato and swing articulation. It is wise to test examples of music containing demanding rhythms with the various applications to see which is best for your needs, keeping in mind that software developers consistently improve such features; be sure to compare current versions of programs.

Staves and articulations

While notes are the central symbols of common music notation, the staves, clefs, slurs, ties, accents, and other articulations form the context and detail around those notes. Most commercial applications will provide a full range of clefs, including alto, tenor, and percussion, and access to percussion staves of less than five lines can be a source of frustration if not available. For guitar music a tablature (TAB) stave is useful. At times the changing of clefs can be problematic particularly if mid-way through a bar. Courtesy clefs are dealt with differently at times also. Staves should be able to be grouped as required. Check some published scores of the style(s) of music likely to be written and make sure all bracketing, beaming, trills, barline extensions, repeat time bars, D.C. and D.S. signs, and so forth are available.

Another variable is the number of articulations that can be associated with a single note and how elegantly they are positioned in relation to one another. Articulations, such as accents, staccato marks, pauses, slurs, and so on are generally well catered for in simple cases. The print quality of slurs, and the ease of positioning and editing articulation locations can vary widely between packages. The styles of music you are working on will determine the set of articulations you require, so make sure the appropriate ones are available. Particular jazz notations, such as pitch fall-offs and symbolic chord notations, can often be overlooked.

Transformation and shifting

Composers often use repetition, sequences, and variation in their scores. Having functions available for moving and transforming can save a lot of input time. Basic copying and pasting functions are to be expected, while the extension of these might include functions to drag-and-drop, creation of multiple-repeats, and the use of aliases (duplicates that reflect any changes made to the original).

Depending on your composition or arrangement needs, the use of note transformations can be either helpful or vital. Transformations include, transposition, duration extension or reduction, and the retrograde or inversion of a phrase, through to more complex functions such as modification by "similarity," automatic harmonization, note range limiting based on instrument ranges, and accidental spelling correction. Programs vary widely in the types of transformations available, and at times the terms used to describe them can also vary.

Text and drawing

Although scores are focused on common music notational symbols, they often include text and simple graphical elements. Text is used for titles, stave names, lyrics, chord symbols, and interpretive indications such as "allegro." The more direct methods of input (clicking anywhere and typing) are quicker and more intuitive for small amounts of text whilst the dedicated text-area approach is more productive for complex scores and large blocks of text (such as lyrics).

Drawing tools are useful for simple lines, boxes, and ovals that can be used to border rehearsal markings, highlight form repeat indicators, and for extended notational conventions; it is surprising how often simple shapes and lines can be useful in a score. An extensive set of tools for drawing is required only for those doing more professional score output, or dealing with graphical conventions often encountered in contemporary works.

Playback and audio rendering

It is often useful to have an audio playback of your score to assist in hearing the progress of the composition or arrangement. It is also useful to be able to make a recording of the score (an audio rendering), or parts of it, to assist in learning and rehearsing the parts or as a demonstration of how the final performance might sound. The ability for music publishing software to perform expressively and with high-quality sounds has increased significantly since the late 1990s. Most packages come with one or more software synthesizers or the option to add one as an additional plugin. These plugin synthesizers allow the user to change the types and quality of sounds used to play back, greatly extending the range of musical styles and uses for which the audio renderings can be put. The expressiveness of the playback can vary between applications on two counts. There can be a general performance interpretation applied to the playback that takes into account emphasis on down beats and subtle variations in note loudness and duration. Second, playback can respond to articulation markings such as dynamics, slurs, accents, diminuendos, rallantandos, and so on.

Priorities for music publishing hardware

The complete music publishing system will comprise a computer, software, a printer, and perhaps a MIDI keyboard, synthesizer/sampler plugin, and audio playback equipment. In this section we will examine the requirements for individual parts of the system, starting with the most important components and therefore the ones where financial resources should be focused.

The most important element, when score publishing is the goal, is the printed output. For student exercises or handouts output quality is less critical. There are two main aspects to printing; quality and size. Printer quality should be as high as is affordable which, at present, means laser printers with a resolution of at least six hundred dots per inch. The common paper size is A4 or U.S. letter, but many score formats are larger including the convention of B5 for orchestral parts, and so access to an A3 printer is a considerable asset if you wish to avoid the need to rephotocopy to the required dimension. An additional consideration with printing is the speed of the printer, often measured in pages per minute. Make an assessment of speed requirements based on the amount of printing you are likely to undertake. Color printing is of little concern in most musical scores, but may be important in making interesting handouts or color coded scores.

After printing, the next priority is the computer screen or monitor. This should be as large and clear as possible. At present nineteen-inch monitors are reasonably affordable, while twenty-three- or even thirty-inch monitors are more luxurious. Note that a standard fifteen-inch display cannot show an A4 page in full resolution. This quickly becomes annoying for publishing purposes. In addition to the screen size, the screen resolution will also determine how much of your score will fit on your screen. The higher the resolution, the smaller the image. Most computer systems allow the screen resolution to be varied, but the screen will have a maximum value. Very high screen resolution is not a substitute for small screen size because the image can become quite small and difficult to read. The most common screens at present are flat LCD screens. These are much easier on the eyes (and desk space) than older CRT models.

The next hardware component to consider is the input interface. Non-real-time input can generally be achieved with the computer keyboard and a mouse, but there are alternatives to the pen such as graphic tablets, trackballs, pens, and so forth. For some users, these mouse alternatives can make a significant difference to efficiency of notational input and editing and at times assist ergonomically. A MIDI keyboard can be used for non- or real-time input and can be useful as an instrument for experimenting with musical ideas before committing them to the score. Audio input (transcription) is possible on some systems, but is less developed and inconsistent.

The playback quality will depend on the synthesizer or sample library being used, and these can vary greatly in quality. Some applications include a plugin playback library of sounds, others allow the user to add a plugin as an additional component. There are a wide range of audio plugins and sample libraries available that support sounds relevant to different musical styles; orchestral, rock, jazz, ethnic, and so on.

Once the output and input hardware has been considered then choice of computer becomes important. Computer speed depends on many factors including, Central Processing Unit (**CPU**) speed and throughput, RAM type and quality, in particular graphics cards, video RAM, and cache memory can make noticeable differences to graphics intensive applications including music publishing systems. The computer's CPU speed is more crucial for large scores involving many calculations for redrawing, and it is useful to take the time to test a one hundred-page score and see what the performance is like under these more demanding circumstances.

Audio playback of the music is an invaluable asset that relies on the quality of attached MIDI synthesizers, on board sound cards, or software synthesizers. For most publishing tasks a software synthesizer supplied with the music publishing software will be adequate. However, if the system is used to produce publishable audio product then more sophisticated software synthesizers or connection to an external MIDI synthesizer should be considered. To hear the output, good headphones of powered speakers will be required. Normally, those available through a computer retail outlet will be inadequate for serious musical use, and speakers or headphones from the hi-fi or professional music store are likely to be of higher quality.

Most notation workstations will be utilized in a room or office beside the printer, keyboard, speakers, and rarely moved from this environment. However, if the notation system needs to be used by many people, in a number of different locations, or for work done at home and at the office, then portability is a consideration. Lap top systems need not be any less powerful than desktop systems, and can be very convenient to use for data input away from the printer/audio area and then output to those devices as required. For even further portability, handheld computers with pen interface make good sense and can even be used in concert halls and other noncomputer-friendly environments, however, serious music publishing packages are not currently available for handheld devices.

Finally, provision for file backup and storage should be considered. Music notation files can be quite large, particularly if saved in some raw graphic formats. In addition, where many students are sharing a system, the hard disk may quickly become full and so offline storage is required. An external **hard drive** is useful for backup and one that doubles as a portable music player seems appropriate. Flash RAM storage devices are also useful for storing a few files and convenient for shifting files between computers. Often a school will have central computer server space on which data can be backed up or stored.

Conclusion

Music notation plays an important part in our music making and learning activities. It is a primary means of storing musical knowledge and a major means of communicating that knowledge. The computer as a symbolic processing machine is well suited to the tasks of handling music notation and the current music publishing applications generally do a good job of this. The computer can assist in publishing neat scores by imitating paper and printing processes, can transform performance gestures into notation and so speed up the writing process, and can provide convenient and powerful notation transformation functions to assist the arranger and composer.

As always, the new opportunities of desktop music publishing bring with them new educational challenges, such as provision of access to the system, a reassessment of how the notational process assists learning, and how the computer's involvement changes the use of notated symbol systems, and more. However, the extensive uptake of the computer for music publishing in education indicates that the many benefits of neatness, efficiency, and audible feedback generally make the journey from pen to computer worthwhile.

Reflection questions

1. What are the ways in which music publishing software maintains or contravenes the manuscript paper metaphor?
2. What are the uses the ability for music publishing packages to render an audio version of the score?
3. How can a music publishing application be integrated with other software for educational purposes?
4. What are some of the potential issues mentioned in the chapter of using a notation package for the preparation of examples for printed handouts, rather than using it for its intended purpose of score layout?
5. Can you e-mail a file from a music publishing software application?
6. Why might some composers still prefer to use paper and pencil over a computer-based scoring system?
7. How might a music publishing system be used for performance?
8. Why might the ability to scan an existing printed score into the computer be useful?
9. Does this chapter suggest that computer power or display quality is more important when choosing hardware for a music publishing system?
10. What graphic functions do you think would be most useful for music publishing systems to have in order to create graphic scores from the twentieth century?

Teaching tips

1. Use computer-based notation tasks as a way to introduce new music theory concepts and new music representation conventions.
2. Have students explore the editing possibilities of the software by creating an entire composition from one bar of original material.
3. Focus student attention on particular areas of score layout by having them finish off those aspects of an otherwise complete score.
4. Use music publishing software for styles of music usually represented as scores and avoid using it for those styles that are not.
5. Have students save copies of their scores as graphic files, such as pdf or jpeg, so that their files are more portable between computing platforms and the scores survive changes in software over time.
6. Provide a range of notation input options so that students can find the method that works best for them.

7. An interesting aural training task is to have students write down a rhythmic transcription, then compare their result to the interpretation of that performed rhythm by a notation package.

8. Remember that guitar tablature is a notation system and often supported by computer music applications, so music publishing packages are relevant for popular music too.

9. Use the table of supported articulations that can be found in the music publishing software's manual as a stimulus for students to investigate what they all stand for.

10. Don't forget to utilize the lyric function of notation software for song writing lead sheets.

Suggested tasks

1. Do a self-check on the difference in efficiency between paper and computer scoring by timing how long it takes to do the same notation task each way.

2. Use a music publishing package to create a music-minus-one audio recording of an arrangement for use in rehearsal.

3. Find out a lot about your music publishing software in a short time by entering in the first eight bars of a complex work such as Stravinsky's *Rite of Spring*.

4. Use a word processor to create a handout that uses musical examples prepared with a music publishing application.

5. Transcribe a score for percussion ensemble in a music publishing package to explore some of the less commonly used stave and symbol conventions.

Chapter summary

One of the most popular applications of computer technology in music, particularly in education, is the typesetting and printing of musical scores. Although musical notation packages are popular with users, their development remains a veritable minefield for software developers as they attempt to accommodate hundreds of years of varied notational conventions and stylistic interpretations. Despite these difficulties, a number of highly advanced software programs are available for writing and arranging music as common practice notation. By using these software programs, the computer can become an efficient tool for the creation of musical scores for performance, for the generation of notational examples for lessons, and for exploring arrangement possibilities by allowing easy variation of musical structures and playback instrumentation.

Notes

1   Sibelius, music publishing software, http://www.sibelius.com/cgi-bin/home/home.pl.
2   Finale, music publishing software, http://www.finalemusic.com/.
3   Score Writer 2, music publishing software by GenieSoft, http://www.geniesoft.biz/.
4   LilyPond, music publishing software, http://lilypond.org/.

Chapter 6

MIDI sequencing

The desire to automate musical playback has a long history stretching at least as far back as the player piano. Audio recording satisfied some of that desire, but its inflexibility as an editable compositional format lead to solutions like the sequencer. The sequencer is a product of the electronic music age which provides a means to automate music without the need to commit it to a static recorded format. The ability to automate provides the musician with extra virtual hands to play many parts at once; it captures ideas for later review assisting our memory and communication of those ideas. The sequencer can do this because it captures and performs the musical gesture rather than the sound itself. In an attempt to acknowledge that sequencing applications handle audio tracks as well as MIDI tracks, these applications are occasionally referred to as Digital Audio Workstations (DAWs). Examples of some of the most popular sequencing software available today are Cubase, Sonar, Logic, Live, and GarageBand. Software packages that have some of the features of sequencers but also operate in different ways include Fruity Loops, ACID, and Reason. For younger children there are also a number of simple step sequencing applications, including free online music tools such as the Beat Machine, Drum Steps, and Composer applications available at the Making Tracks BBC Web site.[1] Another simple sequencer suitable for the primary school is O-Generator.[2] These simple sequencers can be a fun introduction to the concept of sequencing for junior classes, and clearly demonstrate the principles evident in serious sequencing programs. In this chapter we will examine the operation and use of sequencing software such as these and take a look at some of their characteristics, hear about how they have developed, and explore how they can be useful and influential when making music.

Modern sequencing software for music making can be likened to word processing software for writing. Sequencers are the most widely used computer programs for music because of their ability to be used for tasks including composition, arranging, analysis, and recording production. They share with word processors the ability to capture and to flexibly (at times automatically) manipulate music represented as notes or audio files. Sequences of notes, and other actions such as sustain pedal movements, instrument changes, and parameter automation, are commonly referred to as "events" or "objects" in sequencing programs. Modern sequencers receive these events as MIDI messages from performance controllers and send them to synthesizers, virtual or physical, for playback. In this way, the sequencer is a MIDI message recorder and editor, these descriptions of gestures are displayed in a variety of visual score representations including common practice notation, piano-roll matrixes, lists of event data, graphs, and so on. Modern sequencing software also capture and manipulate audio recordings (sometimes called samples or audio clips) and allow for a mixture of event-based and audio-based tracks to coincide within the one song.

Sequencer history

The first sequencers were paper-tape machines used in music boxes and player pianos. Although they started as mechanical devices, paper tapes were also used in some of the earliest vacuum tube synthesizers and computers of the 1950s. Analogue electronic sequencers were used from the early 1970s, well before the MIDI sequencers of today. An analogue sequencer sent regular pulses of voltage which typically controlled the pitch of the sound to analogue synthesizers creating a short melody. Most analogue sequencers consisted of six to twelve monophonic steps which were repeatedly cycled through producing ostinato phrases. Each step had controls for the voltage (corresponding to pitch) and the gate time (corresponding to duration), and the overall speed of the sequence was variable. Multiple sequencer units were required to create polyphonic textures.

These early sequencers obviously did not record performances, they generated them. The technological arrangement of a sequence of notes one-by-one has become known as step-time sequencing. This term is still used today to refer to event-by-event creation of sequences. The characteristic of sequencers to play short repeating phrases meant that sequencers lent themselves to bass ostinati and drum or percussion parts. Sequencers dedicated to drum sounds evolved into drum machines.

The first digital sequencers were modeled on analogue sequencers in that they enabled a series of notes to be specified which were looped to create similar ostinati effects. Early digital sequencers either ran on personal computers, which also produced the sounds, or as dedicated devices which may have had their own sounds or were connected to a particular synthesizer. Early synthesizers often featured a built in sequencer that were often used for playing broken chords and, as a result, became known as arpeggiators. Sequencers developed in several directions, as software programs running on personal computers, as dedicated sequencer units with and without built-in sounds, and as arpeggiation features built into synthesizers. With the advent of MIDI in the mid-1980s, a standard way of communicating between sequencers and synthesizers emerged, and the modern MIDI sequencer evolved as a result. The MIDI sequencer added real-time recording to the list of sequencer functions and acted more like a tape recorder than a loop-based analogue sequencer most of the time.

Modern sequencers

The term "sequencer" is today most often applied to software products running on personal computers, although some dedicated sequencer units are still produced

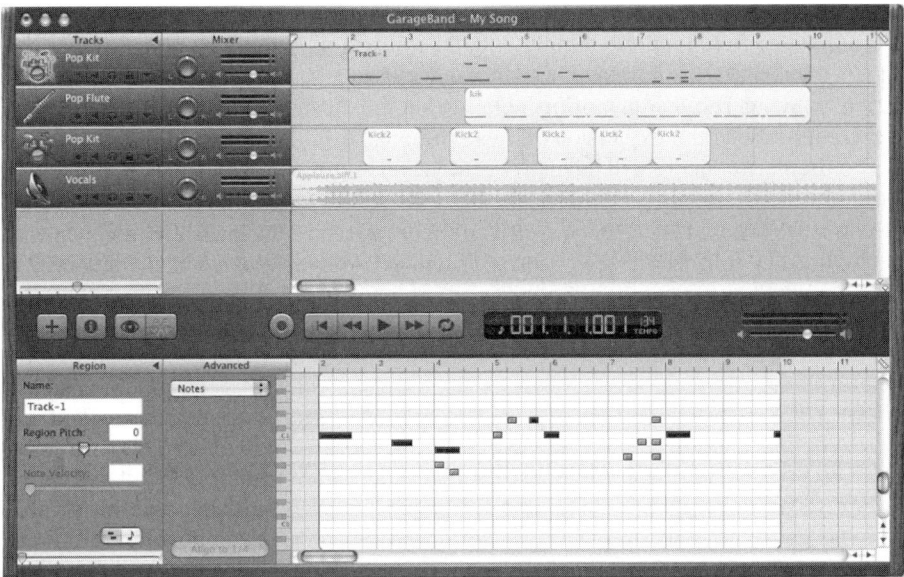

Figure 6.1   The main window of Apple's GarageBand software.

and most "workstation" synthesizers have sophisticated built-in sequencers. Figure 6.1 shows the main window of a typical modern sequencer.

The software sequencer has evolved from its simple beginnings into a sophisticated beast that, along side MIDI sequencing, now routinely incorporates music publishing features, a variety of visual editors, internal and external movie synchronization, algorithmic event transformation, and integrated hard disk audio recording.

Analogue sequencers, like analogue synthesizers, began as single track (monophonic) devices, and many early MIDI sequencers were also limited in the number of tracks (parts) that could be recorded, and the MIDI specification itself only specifies sixteen MIDI channels. This limit, too, can be side stepped by multiple synthesizers which can enable parallel sets of channels to go to each. The number of tracks on modern sequencers is generally limited only by the available computer memory.

Modern sequencers combine and extend both the tape recorder and musical score metaphors. A sequencer records and plays back "tracks" like a tape recorder and utilizes a "transport" control area to house buttons for play, stop, rewind, and so on. Sequencers also displays music like a score with parts vertically layered on a horizontal time line which can be divided into beats and bars, or minutes and seconds, with all tracks following a single tempo map that acts like conductor keeping all the parts together. This track-based organization is often referred to as a linear view of the music. Within this multiple track structure, each track equates broadly to a part in a musical score, and the MIDI sequencer deals with notes as its basic unit of music. A "sequence" is therefore a series of notes. Musically, notes are often grouped into phrases, or gestures, often called patterns, regions or sections which can be arranged on the timeline to form the structure of a piece. Different sequencing software applications provide their own structures for grouping events and managing regions of musical information. Some chunk music into bar groups based on the current time signature, others chunk music into phrases based upon the length of a recording, while others simply list all events in a track ungrouped. Almost all allow arbitrary segmentation of tracks into regions and for the transformation, duplication, copying, removing, muting, soloing, looping, transposing, **panning**, amplifying, compression, and expansion of these regions.

Often sequencers will have different visual editors which display music at different levels of grouping. Higher level groupings such as phrase or patterns can be displayed as boxes on a time line, while individual notes can usually be displayed as notation, a piano-roll matrix, or as a list. Learning when to use each visualization is a key component to becoming a fluent user of sequencers. We will now explore the major data grouping levels found in sequencing applications.

Track view

Each musical part has its own row that follows the time line from start to finish (Figure 6.2).

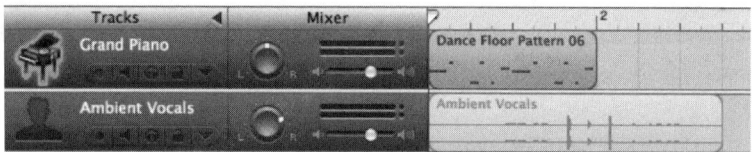

Figure 6.2 Sequencer track view.

Phrase editor

Groups of notes or sections of audio appear as a blocks. A number of blocks can appear on each track and its position indicates is placement in time (Figure 6.3).

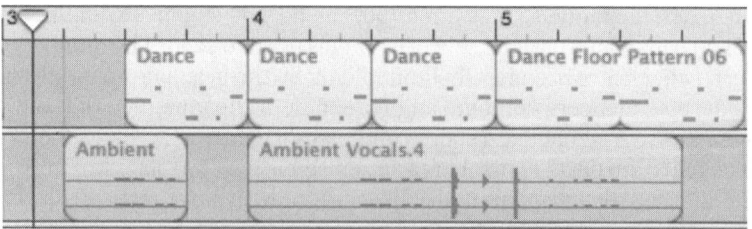

Figure 6.3 Sequencer phrase editor.

Note editors

Each block represents one note, the vertical position of which indicates pitch, while length indicates duration (Figure 6.4).

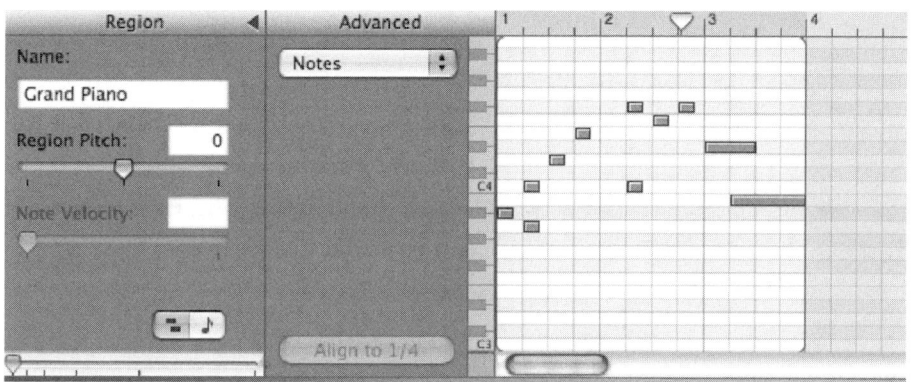

Figure 6.4   Sequencer note editor.

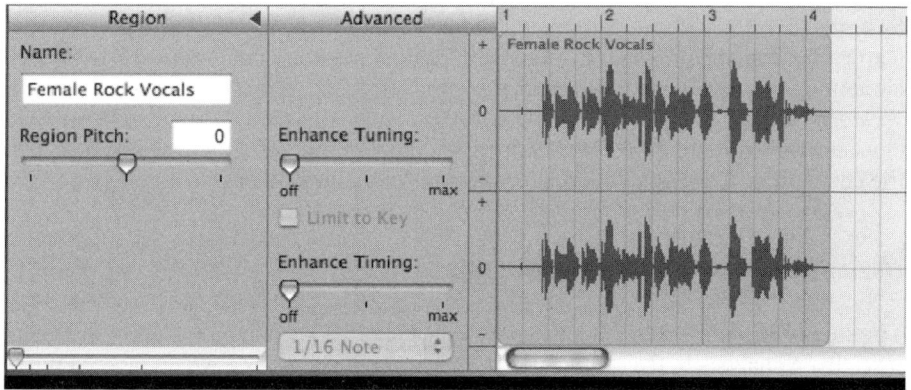

Figure 6.5   Waveform view.

Waveform view

The detailed visualization of an audio segment (Figure 6.5).

Loops

Sequencers allow regions to be repeated several times over (Figure 6.6).

Libraries of musical phrases ready to be used as loops are often provided for sequencing programs to use (Figure 6.7).

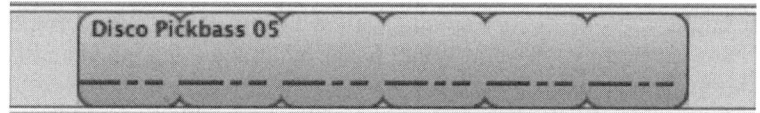

Figure 6.6   Sequencer loop example.

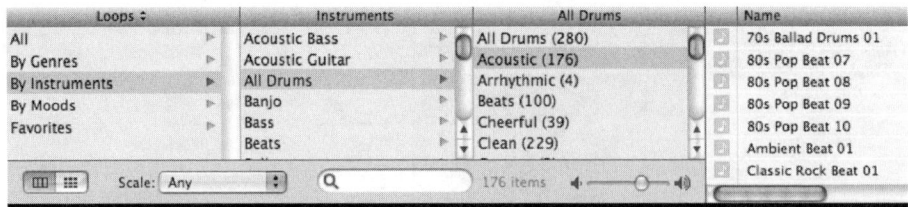

Figure 6.7 Navigating a musical phrase library.

As technologies and their use evolve there is a feedback loop where the technology influences user actions and then the design of the technology is influenced by user demands. In the case of sequencers this evolution is most obvious in two areas. First, the looping feature of early sequencers meant that they were used in ostinati-based styles. Composers of African-American styles were especially attracted to sequencers due to the prominence of repetition and pulse in their music. This feature can even be implicated, along with limited memory sampling, with the development of new styles such as techno. Second, sequencers absorbed conventions of Western musical tradition including common music notation, in their adherence to chromatic pitch resolution, the quantization of rhythms to regular pulse bases, and the convention of a single "conductor" tempo controlling all parts.

Making music with sequencers

The flexibility of the sequencer means that it can be employed for many different tasks from analysis to live performance. In this next section we will explore some of the more common usages of sequencers for music education.

Arranging

Due to its abilities as a MIDI recorder and music notation package, the sequencer is very popular as a tool for arranging music and producing audio and score copies of the arrangement. The more sophisticated sequencing packages provide music publishing facilities that would suit most classroom uses, although they are not as comprehensive as those on dedicated packages explore in the previous chapter. An advantage of sequencers over music publishing packages for arranging is that their audio rendering capabilities are generally more advanced. Therefore, if the quality of a recorded version of the arrangement is important then sequencers will usually have the facilities to edit the performance nuances of the music, then to polish the recorded output with effects such as equalization, **compression** and surround sound mixes. These recordings of arrangements can be utilized for individual practice, ensemble rehearsals and as backing tracks for performances. The ever-malleable nature of the sequence data enables easy production of slightly varied sequences for creating rehearsal tapes with different mixes of instrumentation, or recordings at different tempi, or score parts in different keys and for varied groups of instruments, and so on. The quality of the printed scores in sequencing packages may not be as high as specialist music publishing packages, and a number of sequencing packages may not have any common practice notation representation.

Composing

The sequencer has become the main tool for many composers, particularly those working in contemporary styles or on music for other media such as film scores. At a simplistic level, the sequencer can act as an electronic tape recorder which is easily editable, but this is to seriously underestimate its influence. The transformative and structural functions of the sequencer provide tools for the composer that can shape the composer's ideas and allow relatively easy access to generate-and-test cycles to explore compositional possibilities. Additionally, the ease of editing the music can allow more extensive testing of ideas than would be practical on paper or on tape. This can provide a very supportive environment for the inexperienced composer, where experimentation is encouraged and unsatisfactory attempts easily deleted or muted. The immediacy of hearing back an audio rendering of the work as it develops is particularly helpful to the learner composer. A slight down side of this ability for strong audio feedback can be a reliance on the sequencer's rendering at the expense of developing the composer's aural imagination.

The sequencer's ability to synchronize with recording and video sources has made it a favorite tool for TV and multimedia composers, as it allows the precise control of timing and positioning of events as required. Digital versions of the video material can be imported into most sequencers and will synchronize automatically. For professional-grade work, external hardware can be used to synchronize with tape-based video equipment, but this is increasingly unnecessary as professional video footage is mostly digital.

Looped-based compositional styles, including minimalism, electronic dance music, and most rock and pop styles, are particularly well suited to sequencing applications. Loops can consist of MIDI or audio material and sequencers allow easy arrangement through repetition, variation and duplication of these segments. The track-based nature of sequencers results in layer-based textures where segments drop in and out as the piece proceeds. One of the challenges for composition training with these tools is to help students understand the tendencies of the tools, such as repetition and layering, and be mindful that they are using these features intentionally rather than because they are the easiest options. In short, that aesthetic decisions rather than technical affordances lead the compositional activities.

Production

The definition of a music "producer" has changed meaning across generations. In the twentieth century the term referred to a person responsible for the artistic and technical direction of a recording, in the twenty-first century it refers to a person who makes their own recorded content. This shift in emphasis from the producer as technically knowledgeable to one who is compositionally knowledgeable has been the inverse of the trend of sequencers from primarily compositional tools to being as much audio production tools as creation systems. Modern sequencers are the primary tool for electronic music producers, and the distinction between studio-based hard disk recording systems and sequencers has been blurred almost beyond recognition. The audio functions of sequencer has evolved from simple controls such as volume balance and panning of parts through to control of timbral synthesis variations over time, automation of parameter variation over time. The sequencer has become a host for the growing range of virtual synthesizers and effects processor plugins. Modern sequencers and plugins have conflated the studio to the laptop. The sequencer has grown ever more sophisticated in its ability to help realize the musician's music from inception to completion. This reflects the emergence of the contemporary musician who is part composer, performer, and engineer, and for whom the sequencer is the instrument of choice.

Analysis

The sequencer is underutilized for musical analysis even though it can be a very powerful tool in this area. Many musical works are widely available as digital files either from music shops, mail order companies, or over the internet. For example, the AMEB (graded performance examinations) in Australia has a wide range of music on its lists available in MIDI file format. Music is most widely available as standard MIDI files, but in some cases as multi-track audio tracks, and the ability to record audio tracks into sequencer opens up possibilities for analysis of live acoustic performance. With a work available as a sequence each individual note is accessible for independent scrutiny, unlike a recording where they cannot easily be separated out; except in the mind. Tracks can be isolated to reveal a works structure and the sections can be quickly accessed for comparisons. Works can be slowed in tempo with altering pitch, and performance characteristics such as note duration and dynamic variations can be explored in detail. The effect of arrangement and orchestration choices can be explored through comparative analysis with various alternatives by change the sounds used, register of parts, and variations to the note density and use of ornamentation. Although the statistical features of sequencers are not very sophisticated, most employ a find command which can be used to locate and count pitch classes and to hear the effects of modifications such as changing or deleting notes of a particular class, or within certain durational or temporal boundaries. Some sequencers allow monophonic audio tracks to be transcribed to MIDI data, for rhythmic onsets to be compared against quantized pulse boundaries and, perhaps, for audio data to be viewed as a sonogram to reveal its change in frequency spectra over time. Often direct analysis tasks are viewed as uninteresting by students, however it is possible to engage them in detailed observations when doing remixes or cover versions of songs where an understanding of the original musical material is required as part of the re-creation process.

Performance

In the past, sequencers have been popular with soloists and duets performing in cafes and restaurants as a form of accompaniment, because they are flexible in terms of tempo, key, and orchestration. Sequencers are also utilized for partial accompaniment for some contemporary instrumental works. These days music players, such as iPods, have largely taken over this role. Sequences are sometimes used when a degree of interaction is required. The major forms of interaction include; beat following, where the sequencer "listens" to the tempo of a live performer and keeps in time; sequence triggering, where particular sequences are set off by the performer during the piece allowing a mixture of synchronized and free sections; algorithmic variation, where elements of the sequence are variable according to certain rules, procedures or cues initiated by the performer or environment. There are a growing range of sequencers which employ interactive features that can make for more flexible and interesting performances. Programs such as Ableton Live, and Fruity Loops, enable the improvisational assemblage and variation of prepared musical material during live performance. Laptop computers running these programs are coming to replace turntables in many night clubs and experimental music concerts. The use of external MIDI or control-voltage gesture devices that control interactive sequencers in performance has grown significantly in the 2000s (after having been less popular in the latter decades of the twentieth century). Affordable sensor interfaces and a wide variety of sensors, including accelerometers, flex, light, and pressure sensors, are now available and can help reconnect the physical performance gesture with electronic sound production in the classroom and on stage. Interactive technologies are explored further in chapter 11.

Conclusion

The sequencer has remained a centerpiece of electronic music technologies by constantly reinventing itself to accommodate, as well as influence, the latest technological and musical trends. At the heart of the sequencer is an automation of music represented as a series of **sound events**. Sequencer representations have shifted from electronic to digital and the number and variety of musical and sonic parameters that can be sequenced has continued to expand.

The variety of visual representations most sequencers offer, including track or part, common practice notation view, piano roll, event data, and audio waveform, means that many styles of music and musician can be accommodated by the modern sequencing application. This broad utility is also why it is often the core computer application used for music education. As sequencers evolve still further to combine loop-based and time-line temporal structures in the one package, their use is continuing to expand from its traditional home in compositional activities to embrace performance situations that involve improvisation with prepared materials. There is sure to be a useful application of the sequencer in every musician's life.

Reflection questions

1. What musical parameters were controllable in the early analogue sequencers?
2. The article said that as computer software, sequencers were to music what word processors were to text. What was meant by this analogy?
3. What is meant by the term step-time in relation to sequencers?

4. Is an arpeggiator a sequencer?
5. A linear time line has been at the heart of sequencers for many decades, what clip organizational feature is being added to some recent sequencers that expands their structural organization?
6. What is the difference between a MIDI track and an audio track?
7. What styles of music are suited to the sequencer's ability to easily loop musical sequences?
8. What is meant when we say that composers use a generate-and-test methodology?
9. Given that all tools have tendencies, what are those of the modern sequencer?
10. What is a plugin?

Teaching tips

1. Due to their wide variety of data displays, sequencing applications are useful in musicianship classes when discussing musical symbols and representations.
2. Teach both real-time and step-time data input so that students with and without some keyboard performances kills are accommodated.
3. It is common that, like word processor applications, most people only use a small percentage of the features of a modern sequencer. When selecting a sequencer for use in schools, be careful not to get one that is too advanced (and therefore complicated). Use the ability of sequencers to segment music into notes, phrases, tracks, and so on as a way of underlying the importance of structure in musical organization.
4. Use the looping feature of sequencers to have student quickly create interesting polyrhythmic textures.
5. Have students explore the opportunities (or difficulties) of performative expression in music by adding these changes (tempo, dynamic, note lengths, and so on) to a provided sequence that has limited expression.
6. When ever a teacher considers that audio feedback would assist in student understanding of a musical concept, then consider the sequencer as tool for achieving that.
7. Use the ability of a sequencer to synchronize with a digital video file, as an ideal environment for the student creation of film scores.
8. Loop libraries that come with many sequencer packages, or can be downloaded, are an excellent means of creating compositional scaffolding for beginner composers, who can use these as a basis and add original parts alongside.
9. Arranging tasks can done using a sequencer and an existing MIDI file as a starting point.
10. As audio capture becomes an increasingly dominant part of sequencing, schools should consider providing a quiet space (such as a practice room) set up for student recording.

Suggested tasks

1. Record a MIDI sequence and compare the resolution of the piano-roll and common practice notation displays of the same music; which is a correct view?
2. Compare the feature lists of the major sequencing applications and see, (a) how similar they are, and (b) how extensive their functions have become.
3. Try to circumvent the "conductor" notion of track synchronization in a sequencer by creating a sequence of Steve Reich's *Piano Phase* piece.
4. Use the copy and paste functions of the sequencer to quickly arrange a fugue.
5. Locate and download a number of the free plugins of the type that are supported by your sequencer application.

Chapter summary

Sequencing involves the automation of music playback, which has a long history stretching at least as far back as the player piano. MIDI sequencing software follows the metaphor of a tape recorder with its linear time line, track divisions, and use of transport controls such as play, stop, and fast forward. Sequencers have traditionally captured, manipulated, and replayed musical performance data in the form of MIDI messages, rather than audio, which allows the deferral of static recorded output until the last moment in the creative process. Contemporary sequencers routinely include audio recording and playback, and an increasing number include some algorithmic possibilities. The ability to overlay parts provides the musician with extra virtual hands to play many parts at once. Other uses of sequencers include the capturing of ideas for later review that assists our memory and communication of musical ideas. The sequencer can do this because it captures and performs the musical gesture rather than the sound itself. The output of MIDI sequencers can be saved as standard MIDI files and imported into music publishing programs to created printed scores. The educational applications of MIDI sequencers are vast, including as a composition and arranging tool, a performance partner, and as a window to appreciating the subtle nuances of musical performance.

Notes

1 Making Tracks, simple online sequencing tools from the BBC, http://www.bbc.co.uk/radio3/makingtracks/makeatune.shtml..
2 O-Generator, simple cyclic sequencer, http://www.o-music.tv/product.htm.

Chapter 7

Algorithmic music

One of the more significant advantages of the computer for music making is its ability to be programmed; its ability to automatically execute a series of tasks and to do them quickly. This is, of course, the basis for all software development but can also be the basis for a music making practice. Algorithmic music using a computer takes advantage of this ability to automate a series of instructions (an algorithm) to musical ends. An algorithm is a series of instructions, not unlike a recipe for making a cake, and computers can be very efficient at following such a series of instructions or rules. The challenge for the composer of algorithmic music is to write instructions that lead to interesting and expressive music. Musical algorithms can describe how each of the musical elements are specified and varied as the piece proceeds. This can include control over the pitch, duration, and loudness of notes, the timbre of sounds, the use of structural features such as repetition and variation, as well as tempo, volume balance, and so on.

While some computer musicians use text-based programming languages to design their algorithms, there are other software environments dedicated to making music that use a visual presentation of the algorithms and/or the resulting music. Figure 7.1 and Figure 7.2 show examples of an algorithm that generates a melody based on a pentatonic scale, first using a text-based computer programming language then in a visually-oriented algorithmic music environment.

While all sequencers and notation packages let users automate tasks such as transposition, algorithmic systems allow a number of such manipulations to be combined by the user into a process or algorithm, sometimes called a patch, function, procedure, or macro.

```
(define (melody))
  (play-note (now) piano (random '(60 62 64 67 69)) 100 11025)
  (callback (+ (now) 11025) melody))
```

Figure 7.1   A pentatonic melody algorithm written in the language Scheme for the Impromptu environment.

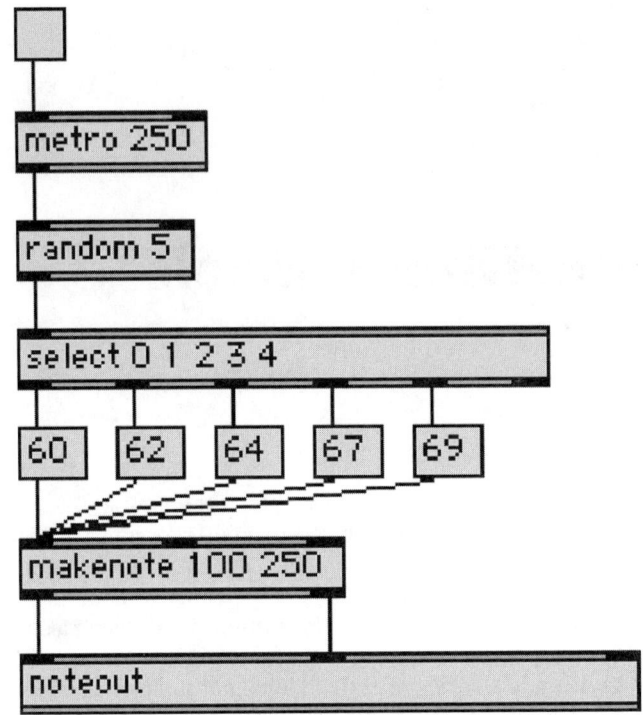

Figure 7.2   A pentatonic melody algorithm written in the Max/MSP visual programming environment.

Introducing algorithmic composition

The ability of algorithmic systems to specify a series of steps for later execution gives rise to the notion that the computer has some autonomy. At its most advanced levels this autonomy is referred to as Artificial Intelligence (AI), most well known through systems such as IBM's Deep Blue for playing chess, and popularized through imagined systems such as Hal in the science fiction film *2001: A Space Odyssey* and androids such as R2D2 in *Star Wars*.

In algorithmic music systems the intention and possibilities are generally far more modest, even though some comprehensive systems, such as EMI by David Cope,[1] can construct complex and complete pieces. Generally, algorithmic composition systems are used for more mundane purposes such as generating a tonal melody of a few bars, creating valid variations in a twelve tone row, suggesting possible chorale harmonization, or sonifying mathematical structures such as fractals or artificial life worlds by converting the numbers generated by formulae into pitches and rhythms.

Many algorithmic systems deal with music at the note level, specifying or manipulating attributes such as pitch, duration, and dynamic. This is historically the most prevalent way of thinking about music and is the basis for common practice notation, so it is not surprising that note-based generative systems are common. Algorithmic processes can be applied in many ways to notes. Small pitch changes at the frequency level can be used for **microtonal** music, or loudness may be controlled by a function introducing a kind of jitter or instability to the note which, if subtle, may add some life to an otherwise static electronic performance. Similarly, subtle changes can be applied to the dynamic levels of a repeated phrase in order to provide variety to mask the machine-like repetition to some degree; we will explore this example further below. Algorithmic systems can be used to generate note-level scores for either acoustic or electronic realization.

Algorithmic processes can be applied to music at a structural level to manipulate bars, phrases, or sections of music, even if the note details of each phrase are unvaried or remain relative to each other within that section. The algorithmic control of musical structure goes back at least as far as the famous story of *Musikalisches Würfelspiel* (Dice Music) attributed to Wolfgang Amadeus Mozart where pieces were composed from sets of short sections designed such that sections could be recombined in many ways. The order of the sections was determined by throwing dice (randomness). More recently, John Cage famously composed pieces as a series of instructions some of which included random or chance events, such as selecting from a deck of cards. In this way Cage encouraged musicians to confront the roles of composer and interpreter through the relationship between score and performer, and to question the need for human-organization for sound structures to be perceived as musical. The possibility of the computer carrying out instructions as musical algorithms challenges us again to reconsider what music is and our role in music making.

Algorithmic composition techniques are also frequently applied to sound generation, the micro structure of music, as well. In a trivial sense it could be said that all synthesis is algorithmic audio, because it follows a set process to produce the resulting sound. However, algorithmic music tends toward processes where the results may be somewhat surprising, even to the writer of the algorithm, because they involve some random or unpredictable choices or because they are so complex that it is difficult to imagine how they might turn out. In this spirit, composers have experimented with algorithmic sound generation using the considerable speed of the computer to make huge numbers of micro manipulations to sounds or sonic parameters to produce a wide array of interesting timbres. Some of the pioneering composers who worked extensively with algorithmic systems to control both micro and macro structures included Iannis Xenakis, with his UPIC and Gendyn software,[2] and Barry Truax's with his POD system.[3] Most modern algorithmic environments, such as Max/MSP, Supercollider, and Impromptu, allow for real-time algorithmic control over macro and micro musical structure.

Uses of algorithmic composition

From this brief introduction it is clear that the application of algorithmic systems can be quite diverse. But why would someone want to use such systems at all? For some it is simple curiosity about the processes of music making, and this is most likely what drove Mozart to compose with dice, and probably played a big factor for Lejaren Hiller and Leonard Isaacson, who were the among the first to do algorithmic composition on computer in the 1950s. Hiller and Isaacson used the rules of counterpoint and statistical analysis of existing works stored in a Markov matrix to generate the Illiac Suite for String Quartet in 1957.[4] The algorithms they used were formalized in MUSICOMP, perhaps the first algorithmic computer system, in the 1960s by Hiller and Robert Baker.

Another application of algorithmic processes is to enable the composer to specify music in a partial way enabling the algorithmic processes to further enhance it. This is used where the composer does not have the desire, skill, or time to specify all elements, and can be seen as an extension of interpretation or improvisation practices, where a score is rendered in detail by an arranger or performer. The algorithmic elaboration processes can also be seen as scaffolding the musician by providing support like an accompanist or assistant. This points to a significant role for algorithmic music in education; programs such as Band In a Box and jam2jam can provide semi-automatic performance support. At a more sophisticated level, PatchWork's interpolation or morphological constraint satisfaction algorithms are used to fill-in details from a partial structure provided by the user. Algorithmic composition programs such as Koan, famously used by Brian Eno, produce generative music from partial or broad-brush descriptions that generate and play back in real time such that each performance is similar but never the same, and versions of this are even available for mobile phones.

Another motivation for the use of algorithmic systems is to provide stimulus and new ideas for the composer or producer by generating alternate possibilities. In this usage, fragments of music are generated that may become part of the composition, or be further modified by the composer, or stimulate further compositional ideas. The algorithms are programmed to provide musical options within a highly constrained space, so that only "reasonable" suggestions are produced.

Algorithms can be designed to create compositional material at the early idea-generation stage, which is often called pre-compositional material. Programs such as OpenMusic[5] are used in this way to play around with musical ideas. The European spectralist school of composers often use such software for analyzing and converting the frequency spectrum of recorded material into pitches in the chromatic scale (or even quarter-tones), which become harmonic material for their instrumental compositions. In addition, algorithmic processes can be applied in the working out stages of compositions to create variations or extensions on existing material. In these cases algorithmic processes are used to generate quantities of music, which are then sifted through to find sections that appeal to the composer. In these cases some or perhaps all of the musical material is generated as a result of applying the algorithms. In this way algorithmic compositional technique is an extension of serialism techniques employed by Arnold Schoenberg, Anton Webern, Oliver Messiaen, and their contemporaries in the mid-twentieth century, where strict rules were used to determine all characteristics of the piece. The Serialist composers worked algorithmically, but generally without the assistance of a computer. These usages of the computer for music making are examples of what is commonly called computer-assisted composition.

As well as providing choices for the composer, the very design of the algorithms can be considered part of the creative process itself. From this perspective algorithmic design not only outputs material for use, but also the design activity itself becomes part of the music thought processes and an expression of musical understanding or intelligence. As a result, algorithmic systems are often conceived as musical instruments and their design as instrument building.

The practice of algorithmic music making with computer can vary from extensive human involvement, as with the interactive performance software Cypher by Robert Rowe,[6] or with David Cope's EMI analysis and composition system,[7] through to simple auto-accompaniment like Band In a Box or jam2jam's style of networked improvisation. Limited programmable environments are available as part of many commercial sequencers and much more extensive features are available as complete algorithmic composition systems in their own right. Some examples of these will be discussed later, but first we will turn to some explanations of the different families of algorithmic processes.

Inside algorithmic processes

While the ways in which algorithmic systems are used is our most pragmatic concern, how they work is interesting because it reflects how people understand music to some extent. Various metaphors of developmental or generative processes can be utilized for music, and we will consider those from the domains of law (rules), mathematics (probability), neurophysiology (connectionism), and biology (evolution). While some algorithmic compositional systems employ only one of these processes, most use elements of several.

Rule-based

The most common of the early algorithmic systems were those that applied rules, of counterpoint for example, to musical choices. These systems rely on the knowledge or expertise of those who design the rules. Rule-based systems create melodies or other musical structures by being seeded with a starting note then selecting successive notes that comply with the rules. A very simple algorithm might, for example, create a melody by these two rules: (1) Always move by scale step, and (2) Select a rhythm to the closest quarter-note step that is either the same as the current one or one step shorter or longer. From these two rules, one for pitch and the other for rhythm, a meandering but somewhat sensible continuous melody will be generated. Rule-based systems can be extremely complex but always rely on the specification of musical heuristics that the designer/composer has as part of their musical knowledge. Musical heuristics and the algorithmic rules based on them can be derived from analysis of existing musical works or metaphorically transferred from other formal structures such as linguistic grammars, and mathematical formulae. In the late 1970s composer Arvo Pärt developed a rule-based system for composition that he calls the "Tintinnabuli" style in which melodic rules are linked to the text to be sung and accompaniment rules are based on triadic tones. This form of compositional process has generated works that have proved to be very expressive and popular.

Probabilistic

In an algorithmic system where choices between various options are weighted, the system is probabilistic or stochastic. If each choice has close to equal weight, then

	C4	D4	E4	F4	G4
C4	0.2	0.1	0.15	0.2	0.5
D4	0.1	0.0	0.2	0.2	0.25
E4	0.15	0.2	0.05	0.1	0.05
F4	0.05	0.3	0.2	0.3	0.1
G4	0.5	0.4	0.4	0.2	0.1

Figure 7.3 A Markov matrix showing the probabilities of pitch sequences.

the choice is commonly referred to as random. For example, the algorithm described in Figure 7.1 and Figure 7.2 makes random selections from a one octave pentatonic pitch set and always uses the same note duration. Randomness is not usually considered all that useful unless applied to small degrees or is highly constrained. A probabilistic system that is biased (weighted) toward certain musical outcomes is more common. To arrive at a set of weightings, a statistical analysis of the note and rhythm occurrences in a sample piece may be done, then the algorithmic system can use the results of that analysis to select notes according to the same weighting as in the analyzed pieces. In such as case, if 10 percent of the notes in the analyzed work are middle C, then about 10 percent of the notes in the generated piece will also be middle C. While this produces a diatonic work with normal tonal distribution, the note order will still be uncontrolled. A more agreeable extension of this is the Markov process, where the statistical analysis also takes into account the local context; for a melody, that means knowing the preceding notes (Figure 7.3). So, for example, if in the analysis 25 percent of middle Cs were followed by D, then in the generated piece whenever a middle C is output there is a 25 percent chance of the next note being D, and so on. The use of Markov chains produces convincing melodies that bear some similarity to those analyzed. However, over time, such melodies can become quite meandering unless higher-level structures such as phrase boundaries and harmonic progression are part of the description.

Connectionist

More recently, algorithmic music systems have used neural networks originally designed for Artificial Intelligence (AI) research. These systems are called connectionist because, like the human brain upon which they are modeled, the system comprises a web of interconnected nodes (neurons). A significant feature of a neural network, or connectionist system, is its ability to learn patterns and then generate the same or, more interestingly, similar patterns. A connectionist system can be trained by being exposed to existing music, at which time it alters the characteristics of the connections between its nodes so they align with the patterns in the input and, after training, the connectionist system can produce an output based on its learned patterns. Because the neural network is based on the neural structure of the human brain, it is, like us, able to tolerate incomplete and unfamiliar information. It also maintains a sense of local context, or history, like a memory that takes into account previous events. For example, it may be trained to remember (identify patterns in) several melodies and afterwards generate new melodies consisting of partial fragments of the training melodies. So, while the results are similar to some probabilistic systems, connectionist systems tolerate unfamiliar or incomplete data and because they can be trained—they don't need a human to do all the statistical analysis for them.

Evolutionist

Evolutionary systems are based on theories of generational genetic mutation and selection. The basic idea is that a melody, or more complex music structure, can "grow" similarly to the evolutionary development of a life form. In one sense, evolutionary systems are similar to rule based systems in that they provide a set of laws that constrain the development of the music. But instead of those rules providing a hierarchical structure distilled from existing musical examples, evolutionist systems provide a small set of laws from which a complex musical structure emerges. The significant difference is that in rule-based systems what is not allowed is forbidden whereas in evolutionary systems what is not forbidden is allowed. This makes evolutionary systems less predictable, which can be either interesting or frustrating depending on your needs. The oldest form of evolutionary computer algorithms is Cellular Automata, which have been applied to music at the note level to create melodies[8] and more complex musical textures, and at the audio level as synthesis and filter generators.[9] Another common class of evolutionary algorithm is biologically inspired Genetic Algorithms, which model the mutation, and recombination of genes. In these systems the "gene" carries data about the music, for example, a gene might be a note and a DNA strand a phrase. Within a gene pool of such musical fragments, new child phrases are created by taking attributes from different parent phrases. Mutations are created by randomly changing the values of some data that, musically, might introduce a chromatic note into a tonal pitch class for example. If the method follows neo-Darwinian evolution, then from the population of phrases generated in this way, the "fittest" or best melody is selected against specified criteria. A person may also act as the selector, by assessing all the variations and choosing the best one, but this can become quite time consuming. On a computer, this cycle of breeding and selecting can be done quite fast, and so the evolution time in computer music systems is much more rapid than in cultural or biological systems. This means that the changes introduced as the music evolves can be heard within the time frame of one piece, or even with in one sound. As with many of these algorithmic music processes, the ability for a student to learn about both musical and biological systems in the one topic has great potential for cross curricular learning initiatives.

Using commercial systems

Getting started with algorithmic composing is made easier by algorithmic extensions to most popular sequencing software such as the Environment window in Apple's Logic program or the Interactive Phrase Synthesizer (IPS) in Steinberg's Cubase, or CAL (Cakewalk Application Language) in Sonar. In these packages algorithmic transformations can be made to sequenced (pre-recorded) or live material. For example, these functions might be used to randomize the dynamic value (MIDI note velocity) of each note in a sequence to provide it with more variety and "life." Also, data from a MIDI controller, such as the pitch-bend wheel, can be remapped to pitch allowing the generation of pitch curves through manipulation of the controller or the drawing of controller automation curves.

Moving beyond MIDI sequencer functions, one of the most popular dedicated algorithmic composition systems is Max/MSP by Cycling 74. This program provides a visual environment where the algorithms appear like a flow chart where boxes of various function are interconnected by lines indicating signal flow, see Figure 7.2. Max/MSP is a MIDI and audio processing program and will work on any computer system capable of running a sequencer. Other algorithmic environments include; Interactor, Kyma, jMusic, Impromptu, KOAN, Algorithmic Composer, Pure Data, and OpenMusic.

Exploring further

While algorithmic composition is often easiest on systems specifically written for meta-control of music, like jam2jam, Band In A Box, and Koan, simple computer-based composition software tools are also available for the younger audience and include Compose World that enable music to be constructed from building blocks of phrases.

For those with some computer programming skills, there are systems with a visual interface, for example, Pure Data, Kyma, Algorithmic Composer, and Max/MSP. For the dedicated musician, there are algorithmic music libraries available to extend for many programming languages. These include Cmix, jMusic, and OpenMusic. In these environments the composer is very free to develop algorithms that particularly suit them and allow for more complex results than dedicated systems. Finally, there are some dedicated music composition languages especially built for real-time operation for improvisational use, whether for composition or performance ends; Impromptu and Supercollider are in this category.

Software for algorithmic composition

Simple applications

Band In A Box   http://www.pgmusic.com/
Bio2MIDI   http://algoart.com/
Compose World http://acorn.cybervillage.co.uk/esp/cw2.htm

Jammer	http://www.soundtrek.com/
Jam2jam	http://explodingart.com.au
Koan	http://www.sseyo.com/products/koanpro/index.html
Music Mouse	http://retiary.org/ls/programs.html

Environments

Max/MSP	http://www.cycling74.com
Impromptu	http://impromptu.moso.com.au
Interactor	http://www.troikaranch.org/interactor.html
Algorithmic Composer	http://www.users.bigpond.com/angelo_f/Algorithmic Composer/
Symbolic Composer	http://www.symboliccomposer.com/
OpenMusic	http://www.ircam.fr/equipes/repmus/OpenMusic/
Pure Data	http://www-crca.ucsd.edu/~msp/software.html

Languages

Cmix	http://silvertone.princeton.edu/winham/PPSK/cmixsource.html
Common Music	http://www-ccrma.stanford.edu/software/cm/doc/cm.html
Csound	http://www.csounds.com/
HMSL	http://www.softsynth.com/hmsl/
jMusic	http://jmusic.ci.qut.edu.au
SuperCollider	http://www.audiosynth.com/

Sequencers with some algorithmic features

Cubase	http://www.steinberg.net/
Logic	http://www.emagic.de/
Sonar	http://www.cakewalk.com/Products/SONAR/

Conclusion

Music composition has always been a balance of art and craft, of inspiration and the application of techniques and technologies. In the twentieth century, particularly, we saw the increased systematization of composition and more computer-based performance. Making algorithmic music requires systematic processes, even if they contain some element of chance, and the computer is greatly expanding the opportunities for exploring the potential of different processes through algorithmic music making. However, getting started with algorithmic music does not even require a computer, only dice or a pencil for calculation, but the efficiencies of the computer make it practical on a large scale. The ocean of opportunities for algorithmic composition is indeed vast, so if it is new to you, be brave, take off your shoes and at least wade through the shallows.

Reflection questions

1. What is an algorithm?
2. What value does a computer bring to algorithmic composition?
3. What musical transformation processes might lend themselves to being used in algorithmic systems?
4. In what ways can algorithmic systems be used as musical assistants?
5. Is the design of an algorithm a creative activity?
6. Who, or what, is the composer of a piece created using algorithmic software?
7. Are algorithmic processes reflections of human thought?
8. What are the defining characteristics of the four types of processes described in the chapter?
9. Is algorithmic music making an art or a craft?

Teaching tips

1. Any step by step musical process is an algorithm of sorts, so teaching algorithmic music is not so hard.
2. Have students create compositions using random values for note parameters by roll dice.
3. Perform works by John Cage that are largely procedural in design.
4. Listen to some algorithmic composition, such as the Illiac Suite?
5. Have students perform with simple algorithmic software such as Band In a Box or jam2jam.
6. Have students create variations of melodies using genetic processes of randomly changing one note and splicing together sections from two melodies.
7. Serialist composers followed algorithms. Listen to and examine the works of Schoenberg, Pärt, Hindermith, and the like.
8. Have students create music from a set of simple rules.
9. Use connectionist music systems as a lead in to discussions about how music is processed in the mind.
10. Discuss what criteria should be used for a "fitness" function to select a best melody or dance beat.

Suggested tasks

1. Algorithmic processes can be done manually. You can start with some paper on which to write rules and results and some dice, to introduce some unpredictability.
2. You can read a more detailed description algorithmic processes and their history in The Computer Music Tutorial by Curtis Roads.

3. For practical exploration, you can start with some of the software from the list provided in this chapter, many of them are free.
4. Examine a score for one of John Cage's aleatoric works and see how descriptions of musical process can be described without a computer.
5. Use the potential of algorithmic music as an excuse to understand more about the computer by learning a new computer programming language that can be used for music making.

Chapter summary

One of the more significant attributes of the computer for music making is its ability to be programmed, to do a series of tasks, and to do them quickly. Algorithmic music on computer takes advantage of this ability to automate a series of instructions (an algorithm) to musical ends. While some computer musicians use general programming languages to design their algorithms, there are many easier options including visual programming environments, or applications that simply require you to move some sliders to change musical parameters. While all sequencers and notation packages let users automate tasks, such as volume and panning, in algorithmic systems the complexity and extent of such manipulations can be combined by the user into a piece that almost has a life of its own.

Notes

1 Cope, David, "Computer Modeling of Musical Intelligence in Emi," *Computer Music Journal* 16, no. 2 (1992) 69–83.
2 Xenakis, Iannis, *Formalized Music: Thought and Mathematics in Composition* (Bloomington: Indiana University Press, 1971).
3 Truax, Barry. "The Computer Composition: Sound Synthesis Programs Pod4, Pod5 and Pod6," *Sonological Reports, No. 2.* (Utrecht, The Netherlands: Utrecht State University, Institute of Sonology, 1973).
4 Hiller, Lejaren, and Leonard Isaacson, "Musical Composition with a High-Speed Digital Computer," in *Machine Models of Music*, 1958.
5 Assayag, Gerard, and Carlos Agon. "Open Music Architecture." Paper presented at the International Computer Music Conference, Hong Kong 1996.
6 Rowe, Robert, *Interactive Music Systems: Machine Listening and Composing* (Cambridge, MA: MIT Press, 1993).
7 Cope, David, *Experiments in Musical Intelligence*, vol. 12, (Madison, WI: A-R Editions, 1996).
8 Towsey, Michael, Andrew R. Brown, Susan Wright, and Joachim Diederic,. "Towards Melodic Extension Using Genetic Algorithms." Paper presented at the Interfaces: The Australasian Computer Music Conference, Brisbane 2000.

9   Miranda, Eduardo Reck. "Evolving Cellular Automata Music: From Sound Synthesis to Composition." Paper presented at the Annual Congress of the Brazilian Computer Science Society (SBC)—SBCM, Universidade Federal do Ceara 2001.

Chapter 8

Sound synthesis

The bottom line in musical activities is the sound. After all the theory and talk, the reward for the musician and audience is the pleasure of hearing a quality sonic result. For this reason musicians on all instruments pay considerable attention to the quality of sound when selecting an instrument and while playing it. The same applies to music making with a computer. No matter how sophisticated the software, or how powerful the hardware, the sound output of a computer system is the front line and final arbiter of sonic quality. Synthesizing a sound is the creation of a sound from basic components or principles.

Understanding how computers (and by implication digital synthesizers) create sounds can inform our understanding of sound, its characteristics and the ways we perceive it. Defining a synthesis process on computer requires a detailed description of the structure of sound and how it behaves; this process of "explaining" music to the computer is educationally useful because it reinforces our own understanding. In addition, the effective use of synthesized sounds in music making requires that we make musical judgments about the sounds, and how they fit the musical context. A thorough understanding of the range of synthesis possibilities will assist in making informed judgments about the sonic possibilities and limitations of music making with computers, just as a good understanding of the orchestral sound pallet is necessary for the instrumental arranger.

We will start of our journey in the world of sound synthesis from a familiar place, the techniques of sound making on acoustic instruments. There are a number of ways to generate sounds on acoustic instruments; by plucking or bowing strings, blowing into mouthpieces or reeds, striking wood or metal, and so on. Similarly, the computer can synthesize sounds using a variety of methods; sampling (recording), adding tones together, filtering a complex tone, modulating or varying an existing tone, modeling acoustic sound sources, and so on. Acoustic instrument sounds are often classified as pitched or un-pitched. From the perspective of acoustics, this correlates with those sounds that have a cyclical waveforms that provide a sense of stable frequency (pitched) and those whose structure changes rapidly over time and whose frequency is unstable as a result (un-pitched) (Figure 8.1 and Figure 8.2).

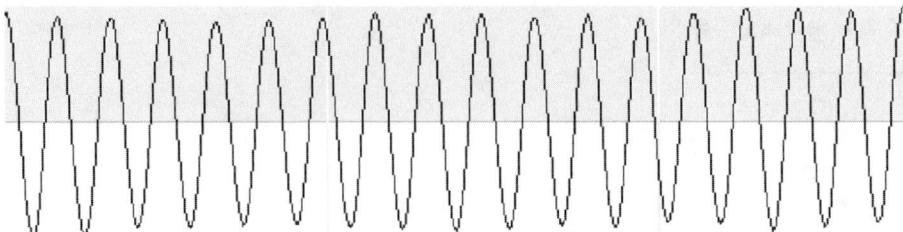

Figure 8.1 A tuned sound (e.g., a flute) has regularity that is heard as a pitch.

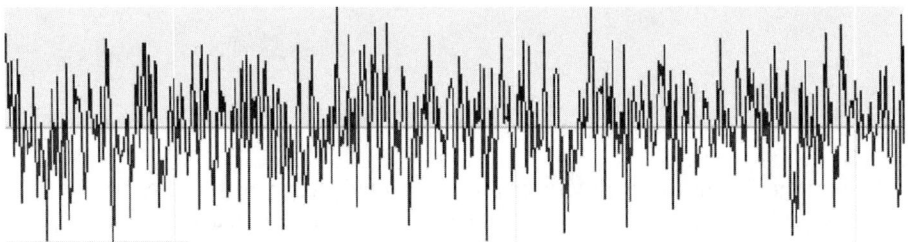

Figure 8.2 A untuned sound (e.g., a cymbal) is irregular and has no sense of pitch.

The articulation and duration of a sound played on an acoustic instrument is controlled by the gesture; wind pressure, bow velocity, piano key speed and pressed time, for example. These are all ways of controlling the volume of the sound over time. In a synthesis processes, this change over time is seen as a curve starting at silence, rising and falling through the duration of the note and ending back with silence. This curve is called the amplitude envelope of the sound (Figure 8.3).

The sound of a guitar is generated by the back and forth vibrations of its sting. This motion is called an oscillation. As too is the motion of a pendulum of a grandfather clock swinging back and forth. For electronic music all motion is provided by the speaker vibrating and so this movement is represented inside the computer as a series of numbers that increase and decrease in a corresponding way. The objective, then of computer sound synthesis, is to have numbers stored in memory or generated by algorithms that represent the appropriate vibrations of the sound that are desired. In this chapter we will explore a few of the characteristics of sound, introduce a number of synthesis techniques, and discuss their musical strengths and weaknesses.

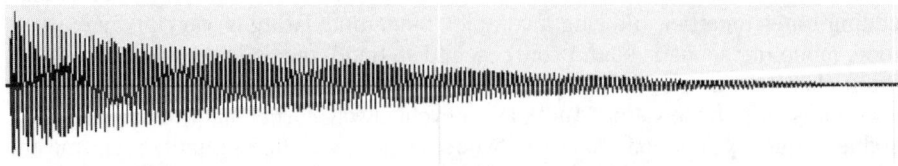

Figure 8.3 The amplitude envelope is visible when its waveform is displayed.

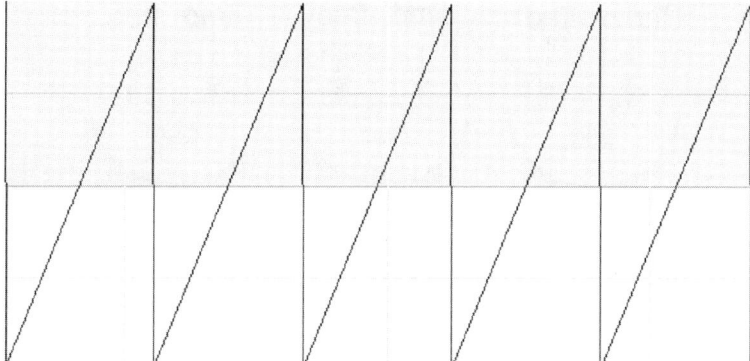

Figure 8.4   A sawtooth waveform has repeating ramp-like oscillations.

Oscillator synthesis

One of the simplest forms of electronic sound is the **oscillator**. This is why we hear it in fire alarms and emergency vehicle sirens. Oscillators are also used extensively in analogue synthesizers, the predecessors of digital systems, and enjoyed a renaissance since the 1990s, particularly for use in electronic dance music. There are more details on synthesizers and their history in chapters 9 and 10. Alarms and sirens often use analogue or electronic oscillators, but a computer uses a digital oscillator created by generating a series of numbers that follow a short but repeating pattern (Figure 8.4).

Oscillators, as a primary source of sound, are used as the basis for a few different synthesis methods. In general, the oscillator-based synthesis methods are not greatly effective at accurately imitating acoustic sounds and better employed to creating interesting new textures. The exception to this rule is additive synthesis that can, in theory, create almost any sound. A simplistic overview of the ways in which oscillators are used for synthesis is that they can be added together, subtracted from, or one can be multiplied by another.

Additive synthesis

In this process oscillators are mixed together to produce a more complex timbre. The frequency (pitch) and amplitude (loudness) of each affects the resulting sound (Figure 8.5).

Additive synthesis has deeply rooted physical and historical connections. It is based on the discovery that a sound can be deconstructed into a set of overtones. Each of those overtones, sometimes called harmonics, is a simple waveform with a frequency related to the sound's fundamental pitch. In additive synthesis, sine wave oscillators can simulate each **overtone**, and many of them can combine to form a complex sound. This process has been used by pipe organs for centuries, and more recently by electric drawbar organs such as the famous Hammond B3. A computer allows precise control over each oscillator, and by independently adjusting the envelopes and pitch variation of each, almost any sound can be recreated. The process is,

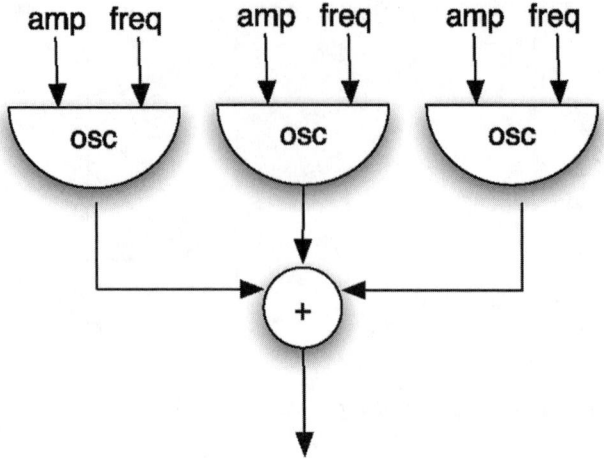

Figure 8.5   The outputs of two or more oscillators can be combined in additive synthesis.

however, quite tedious, and only a few commercial computer music systems support this level of additive synthesis. At a more general level, the combination or layering of any waveforms could be considered "additive," or more correctly, layering or mixing, and this combinatorial process is quite common is commercial systems.

Subtractive synthesis

While additive synthesis builds complex sounds from simple building blocks, subtractive synthesis begins with complex waveforms and filters out components to achieve the desired result (Figure 8.6).

Sometime called analogue synthesis, because it was the most common synthesis method on analogue synthesizers of the 1960s and 1970s, subtractive synthesis can be applied to sample waveforms as well as oscillator waveforms. The classic

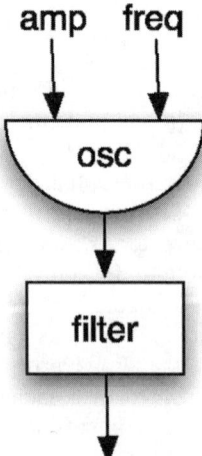

Figure 8.6   In subtractive synthesis oscillator output is passed through a filter.

model beings with a sawtooth, square, triangle, or pulse wave oscillator. Each produces a bright, rich timbre as a starting point. Filters are applied to alter the timbre, usually making the sound less bright or less full. A filter removes particular frequencies from the oscillator, a high-pass filter takes out the lower frequencies and lets the high frequencies pass to create a thinner sound, a low-pass filter does the reverse to create a more dull sound, while a band-pass filter combines both filters to isolate a particular band of frequencies in spectrum resulting in a tight or focused sound. The filters may include a resonance control that increases the overtones in a narrow region around the filter cutoff frequency, creating a more nasal timbre. A distinctive subtractive synthesis sound is the sweeping of a resonant filter creating a timbral effect to the sound not unlike a Jews harp, a desert wind, or the tuning of a short wave radio.

Ring modulation

In a ring modulator the amplitude of one oscillator controls the amplitude of the next. In a computer system this is achieved by multiplying the outputs of the two time domain oscillators together (Figure 8.7).

When the pitch of the two oscillators is in the audible range, the result is the generation of additional partials (overtones) at frequencies equal to the sum and difference of the partials in the oscillators. The frequencies of the original oscillators will not be present in the output. Subtle results can produce sounds that accentuate certain frequencies, less subtle application results in a timbre that is more complex (noisy) than the original and often without a strong sense of pitch.

Frequency modulation

Frequency Modulation synthesis (FM) was discovered by John Chowning based on the use of FM in radio transmission in the 1970s and popularized by the Yamaha DX

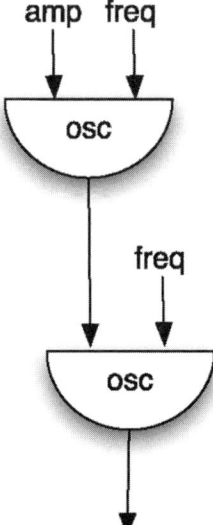

Figure 8.7 The quickly varying output of the first oscillator modulates the amplitude of the second.

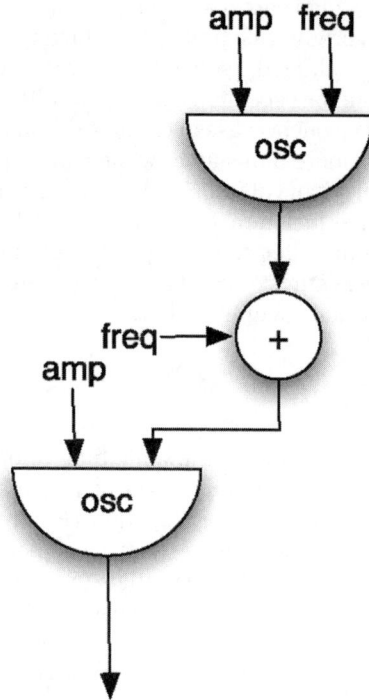

Figure 8.8 In simple frequency modulation, the output from the first oscillator is offset then used as the frequency input to the next oscillator.

range of synthesizers in the 1980s and is also used by some computer sound cards. In FM synthesis the frequency of one oscillator is varied (modulated) by adding the output of a second to it. The modulator output is offset by a constant value that determines the pitch of the carrier (Figure 8.8).

If the frequency of the first oscillator (the modulator) is very low, then the effect is vibrato, but when the modulator frequency is raised into the audible range the effect becomes timbral. Because FM synthesis can produce complex sounds, simple sine wave oscillators are generally all that are required, although theoretically any waveform could be used. The final oscillator is called the carrier, while the input oscillator is called the modulator. The output of the carrier signal only is heard. It is theoretically possible to have any number of modulators and even chains of modulators feeding into each other. The process results in a complex sound where, like ring modulation, side bands are generated above and below the carrier frequency at intervals that are multiples of the sum and difference of their carrier and modulation frequencies. Therefore, if the ratio between the carrier and modulator frequencies is a simple one (1:1, 1:2, 2:3, etc.), then harmonic sounds are created, otherwise the timbre is inharmonic. FM synthesis is an efficient process for the computer generation of complex sounds. It lends itself to percussion sounds, in particular bell-like timbres, and some woodwind timbres, in particular clarinet.

Waveshaping

Like FM, waveshaping synthesis can produce complex timbres from simple oscillator input. It can be applied to sampled sounds but usually results in a highly distorted sound so simple oscillator inputs are often used (Figure 8.9).

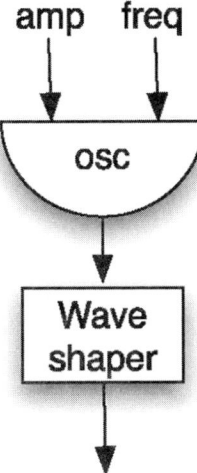

Figure 8.9 Each cycle of the oscillator waveform is distorted by the waveshaping function.

Waveshaping is found on some of the more sophisticated commercial synthesizers as well as in numerous computer-based signal processing applications. In essence, waveshaping changes (reshapes) the waveform input at each **cycle** of the wave according to a transfer function (shape). Waveshaping results in a richer, more complex tone, often containing "noisy," distorted elements. If the transfer function is linear (a straight line), no reshaping takes place; the more irregular the transfer function the greater the **distortion**. Waveshaping can be effectively used to simulate the characteristic of acoustic instruments to distort slightly when played forcefully, and to some degree simulate the effect of overdrive in amplifiers. To do this a transfer function can be set that only reshapes the waveform when the amplitude is high.

Digital synthesis directions

So far we have discussed synthesis methods that are likely to be found in computer audio plugins or commercial synthesizers. As the processing power of computers continues to increase, more powerful synthesis methods become accessible to the personal computer user. In the next section we introduce synthesis methods that are less well known but can create some fascinating sounds. They are generally computationally intensive processes that are quite viable for real-time synthesis.

Granular synthesis

The concept of sound being made up of sonic particles predates computers, and was used for composition by Iannis Xenakis as early as the 1940s with analogue techniques, but is quite a tedious process that is much more viable using a computer. Granular synthesis creates a sonic texture from hundreds or thousands of very short sounds usually less than one-tenth of a second long. Analogies are often made between granular synthesis textures and dust particles or clouds (Figure 8.10).

Each **grain** usually has an amplitude envelope applied so that it does not have a sharp start or end that would cause unwanted clicks in the sound. The sound grains may be

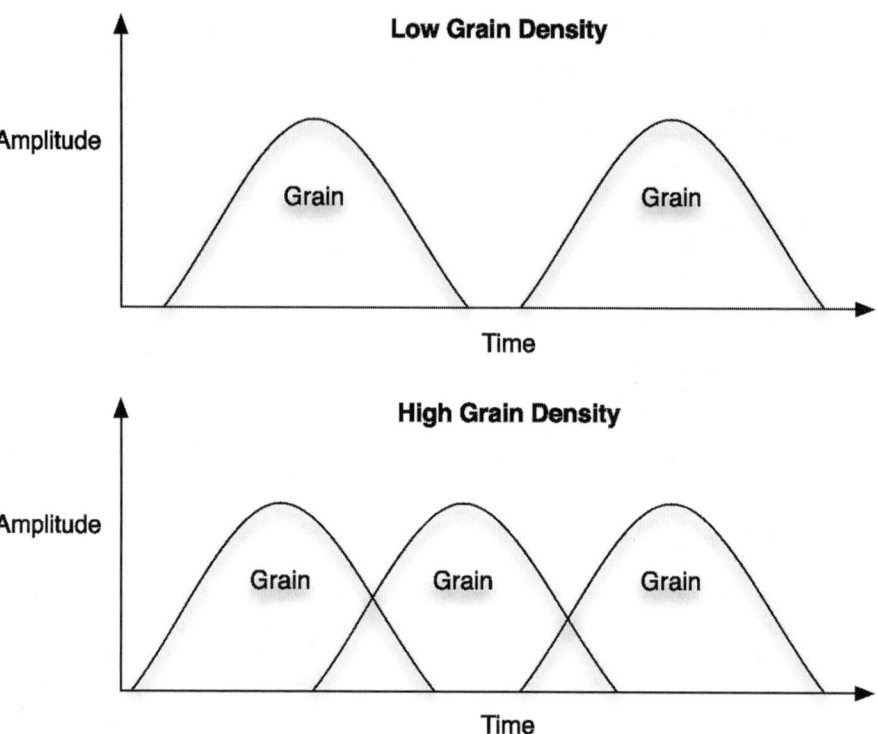

Figure 8.10   Grains are very small bits of audio that can be assembled for playback at different densities.

organized for playback infrequently such that the click of each grain in heard (low density) or so frequently that they overlap to produce a continuous sound (high density). Grains may be created from any sound or synthesis source. One interesting application is to start with a sample (e.g., a person talking) then to chop the sample into grains and replay the sound with various changes to, and reorganization of, the sound grains. Alternatively, grains from different sources can be combined to generate a mixed timbre. The resulting sound of granular synthesis can be affected by changing the length, pitch, or amplitude of each grain.

Physical modeling

All of the synthesis methods presented so far have introduced new ways of thinking about sound, and new terms to describe them such as oscillator, filter, envelope, waveform, **partial**, grain, and so on. These new ways of thinking help us to reshape our concepts about sound and music, but may seem abstract from the physical world of acoustic instruments. Physical modeling approaches the generation of sound by trying to emulate the properties of the physical object that creates sound—in particular, acoustic musical instruments. For example, a guitar model includes an exciter (the plucking and vibrating of the string), and a resonator (the body of the guitar).

There are a number of different varieties of physical modeling. Each attempts to mathematically model the physical characteristics of acoustic instruments within the computer. This mathematical simulation is then "played" or excited and the changes in the model that result are mapped as vibrations causing sound. For research purposes, the closer the sound is to the real instrument being modeled the more accurate the model is deemed to be. However, the truly exciting prospect raised by physical modeling is the ability to adjust the simulation to create instruments that have not, or even could not, exist, and then to hear what sounds they make. For example, imagine combining a clarinet mouthpiece with a ten-meter long steel string and put the result through the bell of a trumpet with a Harmon mute inserted.

The various types of physical modeling simulate the physical attributes of instruments in different ways. Most methods create models for different parts of the instrument. The approaches to physical modeling differ in how they describe the parts.

The mass-spring approach treats the string like a series of objects with some density connected by springs that have certain elasticity, and models the movement and energy transfer of the string. The model simulates the movement of instrument parts (e.g., a guitar string) as a row (or matrix) of small masses connected by springs. "Hitting" the row will cause the masses to move about. Monitoring the movement of one or more of these masses can provide a vibration pattern that can be synthesized.

The waveguide approach models the movements, such as the string, as delay lines that correspond to the time taken for the sound wave to travel through the instrument; along the length of the string. This approach was first used commercially in the Yamaha VL series of synthesizers but is now much more common in synthesizers from Korg and in many virtual synthesizer plugins.

The sounds produced by physical modeling synthesis can be very life-like, and at times require significant skill to control in performance, thereby opening up new opportunities for expressive live electronic music. The process is quite demanding in its use of computer power, and each family of instruments that is to be modeled requires the design of new techniques which slows down the rate at which these systems come into commercial use. Working with physical modeling synthesis systems is not only fun but can be a good stimulus for better understanding how acoustic sound sources work.

Experimenting with sound synthesis

Computers systems today are more than capable of real-time generation of sounds using almost any synthesis process. A growing number of software synthesizers are being introduced. Some of these imitate existing synthesizers, analogue modeling, or "virtual" synthesizers, while others create sounds using new digital processes. Also available are synthesis toolkits that enable users can build their own synthesizers on-screen. A number of audio editors are available that allow simple generation and manipulation of sounds. In sum, there are plenty of ways to access these synthesis processes on your computer.

Plugins and hosts

Computer music systems are increasingly modular. This allows the user to get the features and components they need. The technology that is driving this customization most markedly is plugins. These are specialized tools that perform a single job well, typically as synthesizer, or audio effect such as reverb or compression. There are also plugins for MIDI processing as well but these are less common. Plugins are not limited to music applications, but are available for a wide variety of purposes including the graphic arts.

Music plugins can accept audio and/or MIDI input, can manipulate or use that input or generate new material, and they send out audio and/or MIDI data. Plugins are able to be linked together in chains to create compound effects. There are a number of formats for music plugins including VST, DirectX, AudioUnits, RTAS, and MAS. For most purposes they are functionally equivalent. As you might expect, they are not interoperable so a plugin for one format does not work across the others. Fortunately, many music systems support a number of different plugin formats and many plugin developers compile versions of their plugin for a number of different formats. To use a plugin, it must be installed on your computer. There is usually a plugins folder in which they are put and many plugins come with an installer that will put them in the correct location. Plugins (and host applications) are available for download over the Internet. Some are free, others shareware, and others are fully commercial applications. Many music software applications will also come with a range of plugins included.

Software programs that are plugin hosts will look for available plugins when they launch. There will usually be a drop-down menu in the host application that allows selection of the plugins. A host application is one that supports a particular plugin format. Some hosts do very little apart from managing a chain of plugins, while other hosts use plugins to augment an already feature rich application. All major sequencing and hard disk recording applications are plugin hosts.

Synthesis toolkits

One of the most flexible ways to experiment with sound synthesis is to use a software synthesis toolkit. These programs will consist of synthesis components, such as oscillators, filters, envelope generators, and so on, and will allow the user to construct their own synthesis algorithms by combining those components. Most of these systems will use a visual display of the components/modules/objects such that the final construction looks not unlike the flow diagrams used earlier in this chapter.

One of the most prominent synthesis toolkits is Max/MSP from Cycling '74. Other similar packages are AudioMulch, Pure Data, Reaktor, Alsa Modular Synth, and Kyma. Some synthesis toolkits have a text programming interface that some people find more flexile than the visual display, but it is usually less intuitive to use for the beginner; examples include: Common Lisp Music, Supercollider, Csound, Cmix, Impromptu, and the MusicKit.

Signal generators

A number of sound editing packages, such as Amadeus II or WavePad provide some simple tone generation functions. These can be useful for creating test tones, or complex tones for later processing in the editor. A few of these packages include simple FM synthesis generators as well. These can be a simple starting point for students to hear and visualize the differences between various waveforms, and the editors often include filters and other effects that can be applied to the sounds.

Useful links

Information about many of the applications mentioned in this chapter can be found at the Web addresses below. These are good starting point for exploration into sound synthesis.

Dedicated plugin hosts

These programs are lightweight host applications into which audio plugins can be loaded. They provide only a skeleton infrastructure for audio and MIDI input and output and all the major functionality is provided by the plugins. There are many other programs, such as sequencers and hard disk recording software, that also support plugins other than those listed here. They are heavyweight hosts that have a lot of their own functionality and for them plugins are added extras.

Rax	http://plasq.com/rax/
VSTI Hos	http://www.defectiverecords.com/vstihost/index2.html
Niall's Pedal Board	http://www.niallmoody.com/niallspedalboard.htm
V-Stack	http://www.steinberg.de/ProductPage_sbdff5.html

Synthesis toolkits (graphical)

AudioMulch	http://www.audiomulch.com/
Pure Data	http://www-crca.ucsd.edu/~msp/software.html
Reaktor	http://www.native-instruments.com/
Kyma	http://www.symbolicsound.com/kyma.html
Alsa Modular Synth	http://alsamodular.sourceforge.net/

Synthesis toolkits (textual)

Common Lisp Music	http://ccrma.stanford.edu/software/clm/
Supercollider	http://www.audiosynth.com/
Csound	http://www.csounds.com/
Cmix	http://www.music.princeton.edu/winham/cmix.html
Impromptu	http://impromptu.moso.com.au
MusicKit	http://musickit.sourceforge.net/

Sound editors with tone generators

Amadeus II	http://www.hairersoft.com/Amadeus.html
WavePad	http://www.nch.com.au/wavepad/index.html

Conclusion

Making sounds is the bottom line for musical activities. While there are some musical activities involving computers that don't rely on quality audio, such as music publishing, most do. Being aware of the synthesis possibilities is an important step in using the computer for music making, and this chapter has introduced the most common methods. The next step is to explore some sound editing with the synthesizers and software you currently have or can easily obtain, adjusting sounds to best suit your music. Exploring sound synthesis is also a useful method of learning about the physics of sound, the acoustics of musical instruments, and to develop a better appreciation for audio quality and a more discriminating perception of timbre. Exciting new synthesis possibilities exist and advances in computer power are making them more and more accessible. The exploration of digital sound synthesis can be a rewarding exercise in itself and is fundamental to interesting sonic output from music making activities using a computer.

Reflection questions

1. What is an oscillator?
2. Why is it that sine wave oscillators of different frequencies can be added to create any sound?
3. What are the differences between ring modulation and frequency modulation synthesis, given that both produce more complex sound spectra?
4. What types of filters are typically used in subtractive synthesis, and what do they each do to the sound?
5. Do audio plugins work in all plugin formats?
6. Typically, how small are grains used in granular synthesis?
7. Why do synthesizers need to control the amplitude envelope of a sound?
8. What is the difference between frequency and pitch?
9. What types of elementary components would you expect to find in a synthesis toolkit software application?
10. Generating signals using audio editing applications is probably the cheapest and simplest place to start when introducing students to computer-based sound synthesis.

Teaching tips

1. Use one of the many electronic dance music tracks that use subtractive synthesis methods extensively to get students interested in understanding timbre and acoustics.
2. Tuning forks are simple tone generators. Use them as a physical example of what is occurring in an oscillator.

3. Popular music often featured sound synthesis methods popular at the time so find examples of subtractive synthesis from the 1960s, FM from the 1980s and discuss these timbres in an aesthetic context.

4. When you use a plugin, virtual synthesizers based on real ones find photos, reviews, and example audio tracks of the original to enrich students understanding of the history of synthesizers and synthesis.

5. Set students a task to imitate sounds using virtual (or real) synthesizers. Use both electronic and acoustic sounds as references to imitate.

6. Have students explore the synthesis functions and plugins they have on their home computers.

7. Have you school install one of the synthesis music toolkit software applications and get some keen students to explore it then demonstrate it to other students.

8. Synthesis has strong connections to physics and electronics, so look for co-curricular opportunities relating to acoustics or signal processing.

9. Use everyday oscillators such as sirens, beeps, and warnings, as examples of the relevance of electronic sound synthesis to our society (wouldn't it be nice if they were more aesthetically pleasing?)

10. Some of the early electronic works of Karlheinz Stockhausen and Edgard Varese are good examples of the first musical uses of electronic tones and oscillators.

Suggested tasks

1. Obtain a synthesizer with lots of knobs and sliders and work out which controls relate to the synthesis methods outlined in this chapter.

2. Do a Web search for audio plugins and try to locate at least one that uses each of the synthesis methods mentioned in this chapter.

3. Create, or locate, examples of tones made with additive, subtractive and FM synthesis and describe the general difference in quality between sounds produced by each technique.

4. Read more detail about sound synthesis and software systems in Eduardo Miranda's book *Computer Sound Synthesis for the Electronic Musician*.

5. Check out what plugin formats your music software supports.

Chapter summary

No matter how sophisticated the software, or how powerful the hardware, the sound output of a computer system is the front line and final arbiter of sonic quality. Understanding how computers (and by implication digital synthesizers) create sounds can inform our understanding of sound, its characteristics and the ways we perceive it. There are two primary ways for computers to produce sounds, either by the playback of recorded sound (sampling) or by generating sounds from mathematical formulae (synthesis). This chapter explored sound synthesis and chapter 4 explored sound recording. Understanding synthesis involves a detailed awareness of the structure of sound and how it behaves; and the process of designing a sound using the computer reinforces that awareness. In addition, the effective use of synthesized sounds in music making requires that we make aesthetic judgments about the sounds and how they fit a musical context. A thorough understanding of the range of synthesis possibilities assists in making informed judgments about the sonic possibilities and limitations of music making with computers.

SECTION III

PRESENTATION

Chapter 9

Synthesizer performance

The synthesizer is one of the more recent instruments of Western music, and one that was specifically designed for music performance, unlike other recent instruments such as the turntable and laptop computer that were designed for other purposes and commandeered for use as musical instruments. While it has come a long way from the early valve instruments of the 1950s, the modern digital synthesizer is, along with other electronic instruments, still finding its place in our music education system. The synthesizer is often found in the music classroom as a sound effects device, a substitute for a piano, or as a MIDI input device for sequencing. The synthesizer's performance role has been largely left unexplored except in some school keyboard laboratories where artistic expectations can are quite modest. This slow acceptance by educationalists of new electronic instruments, including the synthesizer, was lamented by Pierre Boulez at least twenty years ago when he commented that;

> It is hardly necessary to add that this state of affairs [the completely blocked evolution of musical instruments] is faithfully reflected in education, where the models selected for teaching are drawn from an extremely circumscribed period in the history of music, and consequently limit — from the outset — the techniques and sound materials at the musician's disposal; even more disastrously, they given him a restricted outlook whereby his education becomes a definitive absolute possession.[1]

Since these harsh words were spoken, synthesizers have found their way into many music education programs, and this chapter explores some of the ways to expand their use. As a useful metaphor, imagine the synthesizer as the twenty-first century xylophone. In the same way that Carl Orff expanded the horizons of music experience through the application of xylophones and other percussion instruments, the synthesizer has the capacity to influence music education in its exploration of even richer gestural and timbral possibilities.

In what ways is the synthesizer like a xylophone for music education? First, the synthesizer often has a keyboard interface more restricted than a piano. This enables visualization of pitch relationships, equality of performance effort at all pitches, and is easy to make a sound on but capable of virtuosic mastery. Second, it comes in a variety of sizes and qualities to suit all situations and budgets. Third, it can be played monophonically, polyphonically, or automatically sequenced enabling it to function in a variety of musical roles. Fourth, it provides a versatility of sound timbres in excess of and unlike previous instruments.

What is a synthesizer?

As a general description, a synthesizer is an electronic musical instrument for the creation of sounds that can be controlled in real-time by the actions of a player. A synthesizer is the sound generating part, and there is often an array of dials, sliders, and other controls to adjust the synthesis parameters. Synthesizers can often a keyboard interface for performance, but some have no performance controller, and a few have controllers based on other acoustic instruments; in particular wind controllers with Boehm fingering, guitar controllers and percussion controllers are commercially available. Any of these performance controllers are usually accompanied by one or more levels, dials, sliders, or foot pedals to control other performance features such as vibrato, pitch bending, volume, and so on.

As a sonic-chameleon, there are many different sounds that the synthesizer can play. It therefore has no one distinctive sound of its own. And following the use of the synthesizers as a tool to imitate acoustic instrument in performance and sequences, many modern synthesizers follow the General MIDI (GM) specification: having a set of sounds arranged in banks, such as pianos, organs, brass, pipe, ensemble strings, guitars, drums, and other imitative sounds. In addition, the GM sound list contains classic synthesized tones such as "Warm **Pad**" and "Sawtooth Lead". By adhering to the GM specification synthesizers can be used to replay music

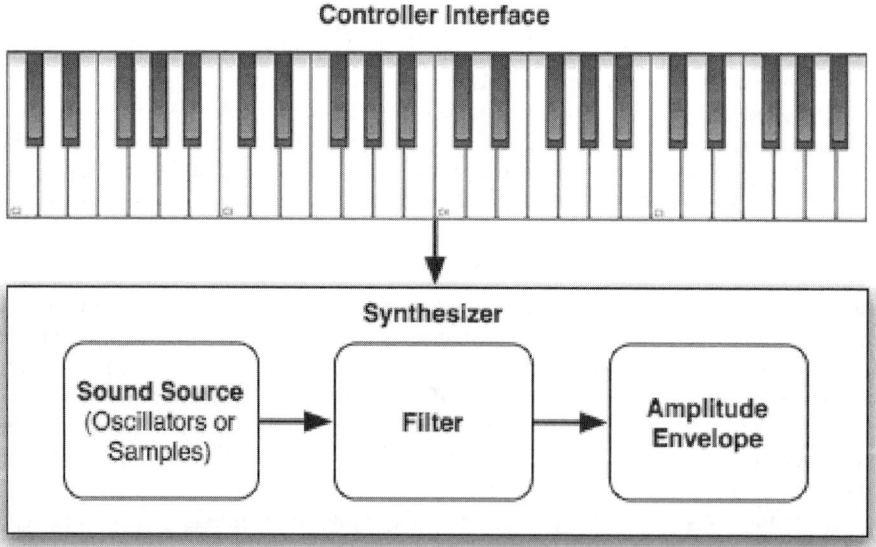

Figure 9.1 The architecture of a typical synthesizer.

or sequences written for the specification with little adjustment, also the user can be sure that a particular set of sounds will be available. However, another effect of GM is that it can provide limitations on timbral diversity that Pierre Boulez warned against in the quote above.

Software synthesizers provide many of the features mentioned above with regard to sound design, and rely on external controllers, at least the computer's mouse but usually a MIDI keyboard, to turn a computer into a synthesizer. Software synthesizers are available as stand-alone applications or as plugins to be used within sequencers and other music applications. Many of these virtual synthesizers mimic established hardware synthesizes from the later twentieth century, but many others provide some innovative flexibility as would be expected given the malleability of the computer as a sonic medium.

The range of sounds produced by a synthesizer depends largely on the type of synthesis used. Most commonly at present is the use of sample or Wavetable playback, usually with the addition of some analogue-style filtering, modulation and effects. This simply means that the sounds of the synthesizer are recordings replayed with the possible addition of a brightness control, vibrato, and added reverb. Any new sounds are variations or combinations of one or more of the samples. These variations can be quite dramatic and unrecognizable from the original sources given sufficient editing flexibility. Other synthesis systems available include subtractive synthesis, frequency modulation, additive synthesis and physical modeling. These were discussed in greater detail in chapter 7.

The sounds need to be heard, so a synthesizer always needs a playback system. Often this is via built-in speakers, or external amplifier. While built-in speakers are the most convenient class-room option, synthesizers and the speaker systems themselves are often not of the best quality in these models. As with all electronic instruments headphones can be used for private listening.

Choosing a synthesizer for educational use

The range of synthesizer instruments is vast and educational circumstances diverse, so any attempt at prescription will be in vain. However, in this section some guidelines for stand-alone (not virtual) synthesizers that will be useful in a variety of creative circumstances in schools are provided.

Sound quality and quantity

Is there a wide variety of sounds? Does it support, and is it limited to the General MIDI sound set? Is the sound quality going to provide a rich sonic experience for the students, or is it thin and lifeless? Are there effects available such as reverb, delay, and chorus?

Ability to edit and create sounds

Does the synthesizer allow users to modify the sounds and to create new sounds and save them? Are there controls for timbre change, amplitude envelope control, and real-time manipulation of sounds during performance?

Types of performance controllers

What is the main controller type, keyboard, wind, percussion, guitar or other? Does it support velocity sensitivity and aftertouch? Are there other controls for pitch bend lever, modulation, sustain, and volume? Are there built-in speakers or does it require an amplifier and speakers?

Connections

Dose it run on batteries or have a power supply? Are there MIDI or USB connections to a computer music system? Is there a headphone connection? How many audio outputs are there, and what types of connections are supported? Is there an audio input?

Educational applications of synthesizers

A rich instrumental environment is stimulating for music students, and the availability of synthesizers as a resource in schools adds to this richness. While many synthesizers have a keyboard interface, there are many other controllers available, some based on acoustic instruments such as the saxophone, drum kit, guitar or trumpet and other new interfaces such as breath controllers, light beams, pressure pads, ribbon sliders, and so on. This enables students with a diverse range of techniques to access the advantages of synthesizers.

Individual work

Individuals can use synthesizers whenever they need an instrument to explore or perform with. The use of headphones can make individual synthesizer use both productive and unobtrusive. Students can be working on arrangements, transcriptions, theory exercises, composition, or performance practice in a focused environment.

Class ensembles

The synthesizer and xylophone metaphor brings to mind their use for class ensemble performances. Having a range of pitched and non-pitched sounds means that they can be used for the performance of class arrangements or soundscapes. The ability of synthesizers to play across various pitch ranges enables them to be bass instruments, chordal, melodic, percussive, or to provide sound effects. By using synthesizers with different controllers—some keyboard, some wind, some percussion—a variety of articulations are possible and any live presentation of work always looks and sounds more interesting and fun with a mixed ensemble.

For best ensemble participation, synthesizers need to be portable so that ensembles can be formed in various arrangements in the classroom as required. This may mean keeping power extension cords handy and purchasing small powered speakers (rather than large guitar amps) if the synthesizer does not have any built in speakers. In any case, greater flexibility is available if synthesizers are not built into fixed furniture.

Composition

Synthesizers come to their fore in the exploration of sounds, or in creating music where a range of sound textures is useful. Following the lead of the experiential learning methods encouraged by Schafer,[2] Paynter,[3] and others, sound exploration pieces are ideal for film music, art instillation soundscapes, and music for dance. Simple adjustments to sound parameters such as envelope and filter changes can take minutes to teach and lead to hours of musical exploration. It is important to make sure that such editing of sounds is possible, as it is with synthesizers by definition, but not on many electronic keyboards that only have **preset** sounds.

The synthesizer for solo performance

As an instrumental study in its own right, the synthesizer has a large history of informal practices. These have mainly supported its use as a popular music instrument. Keyboard players in pop bands are the traditional users of synthesizers in performance, and it is expected that such performers have facility of a range of keyboard instruments including piano, organ, clavinet and synthesizer. With the ability of synthesizers to sample each of these other keyboard instruments, and being more portable than the others, it is generally the dominant performance instrument in contemporary popular music. Synthesizers are used for electronic dance music productions, as these become increasingly interactive during live performance synthesizers, often in their virtual form, are once again at the forefront of live popular music.

A number of educational authorities allow performance on synthesizer as an instrumental study, but not all do this yet. There is some notated repertoire available, mainly from the pop music literature of the 1980s and 1990s. Performers in the early part of the twenty-first century seem more interested in semi-improvised performances than in performing repertoire works, and there is a wide range of combinations of prepared and improvised musical material used in these performances.

One of the most serious impediments to school-based synthesizer performance tuition is the scarcity of repertoire. Although the synthesizer has decades of composers writing for it, the styles in which it was commonly used, electroacoustic music and popular music, have different cultures than Western art music, which undergirds Western music education. In particular, the music for synthesizer from the electronic music community is often specific to now-obsolete instruments or unpublished and difficult to obtain, while popular music has an aural tradition (i.e., the body of notated works is limited).

Performance skills

The aptitude for synthesizer performance is generally similar to other instruments, however, a heightened interest in sound timbre and some creative drive seems to characterize the synthesizer player. Jeff Pressing lists the following specific skills for a synthesizer performer: sight reading with a wide notational understanding similar to a conductors, improvisational ability, synthesis programming, knowledge of a wide diversity of styles, technique on the controller, familiarity with MIDI, audio devices, and computer software.[4]

Performance techniques for synthesizer extend beyond note, dynamic, and rhythm selection. They include the addition of pitch bends, modulation control for variations over a note's duration, and the ability to change sounds and associated articulation demands during performance. These techniques, and the need to program sounds, demand of the synthesizer player a quite detailed knowledge of the workings of the instrument, of acoustics and synthesis techniques. There is often considerable programming effort as part of preparations for synthesizer performance in order to make the performance itself sonically rich and responsive to gestures.

Synthesizer ensemble performance

The synthesizer ensemble comes in a variety of forms. In a school setting, synthesizer ensembles can be a rich source of musical output for students who might not otherwise experience ensemble music situations (e.g., pianists and electronic music composers).

Synthesizer-only ensembles

Synthesizer ensembles have been successfully run in many schools since the 1980s. These groups often begin with a small group as a keyboard ensemble then add alternative controllers to this group to provide visual interest in performance and wider participation. Experiments with sound systems can also add interest, multi-speaker performances can easily be arranged with individuals or small groups of players dispersed around the space each with their own amplifier, or a **mixer** can do a sound diffusion over a speaker array as part of the performance.

Mixed electroacoustic ensembles

Ensembles of synthesizer and acoustic instruments can range from rock and jazz band line-ups with rhythm sections, to art ensembles using any available grouping or traditional and experimental instruments. The synthesizer's versatility in such ensembles usually means a workable balance can be achieved. Percussion and synthesizer combinations are an effective ensemble mix, both timbrally and visually.

Issues to be considered in mixed ensembles include; tuning, balance, and sound spatialization. Synthesizers are always out of tune (or always in tune depending on your view), they are usually set to mathematically perfect equal temperament, and not even the piano sticks to those rules. It is necessary to retune synthesizers so that they are stretch tuned; sharper in the higher registers and flatter in the lower registers, so that they stay in tune with the acoustic instruments. Some synthesizers may not allow for this, but all reasonable quality ones do.

Being amplified, synthesizers should be able to balance within any ensemble mix. However considerable attention is often required to control volume levels. These can vary between sounds, and between works and sections of works. Although velocity sensitivity will go a long way to enable this, the use of volume control by hand slider, foot pedal, or breath controller is to be encouraged.

Another result of being amplified, is that mixed ensembles can sound spatially incohesive without careful attention to sound quality and speaker position. Reverb is common on modern synthesizers, this needs to be used with taste in a mixed ensemble; in most cases live performance is best with little or no reverb so that acoustic and electronic instruments sound "in the same space." Another alternative is to bring the acoustic instruments into the amplified space by amplifying them to some degree. Speaker location needs to be considered for two reasons, firstly so that the sounds can be located with the instrument that is producing them and, secondly so that the acoustic and synthesizer sounds appear to be transmitted from the same location. Often it is useful for each synthesizer player to have their own small amp next to them in the ensemble.

Interactive performance

The use of synthesizers in an interactive performance with computers is another exciting ensemble possibility. Interactivity in this sense is more than playing-along with a taped or sequenced backing, although this can itself lead to rewarding performance outcomes, it requires that the actions of the performer effect the accompaniment as well as their own part. Repertoire for interactive synthesizer performance is usually equipment specific, and so is often generated by the performers themselves or by composers writing for them. A number of popular sequencing packages, such as Apple's Logic, allow for such interaction, and algorithmic compositional languages such as Max/MSP, Pure Data, AudioMulch, or Impromptu are frequently used for this kind of piece. There will be more extensive discussion of interactive performance in chapter 11.

Instrumental teaching of synthesizer performance

A synthesizer teaching course may aim to increase the skills for a whole class, an ensemble, or a synthesizer soloist. In any case, areas of study should include: sound design, technical and reading skills, aural perception, creative organization, repertoire, contexts and literature, and performance practice. When teaching synthesizer performance research shows that lessons should be practically focused, emphasize listening and reflection, should make significant use of media other than print including audio recording, video, sequencing, and multimedia, and provide a positive social context.[5] In the classroom situation, synthesizer teaching activities can include playing prepared ensemble pieces, creating soundscapes, exploring sound editing, studying acoustics, and composing, or arranging small mixed ensemble pieces. In instrumental lessons, activities can additionally include learning repertoire on a theme, preparing for a particular performance, studying a new synthesis method, and programming new sounds.

Piano students who learn the synthesizer as an instrument often say that they enjoy the instrument because it enables them to participate in ensembles, that it gives them access to relevant sounds and musical styles, and that it makes a connection between art and technology that brings together significant aspects of their culture. Good teachers can make use of these inherent motivations to make synthesizer playing a vital part of their curriculum.

Conclusion

The synthesizer is commonly seen as an input controller or sound device for computer-based sequencers. It is important to not simply to see it only as a tool, because it has much more musical potential than that when treated as an instrument. Just as educators don't stop at using xylophones to teach musical note names, but use them for creative exploration of sound, and for some as a vehicle for virtuosic musical expression, so the synthesizer has the potential to open up a world of music to students in our schools, if only we learn to play it, not just use it.

Reflection questions

1. What was Pierre Boulez's concern about music education?
2. In what ways is the synthesizer like a xylophone for music education?
3. Is the synthesizer a keyboard instrument?
4. Why is the synthesizer described as a sonic-chameleon?
5. What does the General MIDI specification specify?
6. What criteria are important to consider when choosing a synthesizer for educational use?
7. Which synthesizer ensemble formats are suggested in the chapter?
8. What performance skills did Jeff Pressing suggest synthesizer player should focus on?
9. How might synthesizers be amplified for a mixed-ensemble performance?
10. What aspects of the synthesizer are likely to help motivate students about music studies?

Teaching tips

1. A variety of different synthesizers will be more interesting than a set of identical ones.
2. Revisit the pedagogical practices that surround Orff instruments and similar ones for music education with synthesizers?
3. Imitating acoustic instrument sounds with a synthesizer can be a good opportunity to investigate the acoustics of musical instruments further.
4. Try to have a variety of different synthesizer controllers so that students with all manner of instrumental skills can work easily with them.
5. Software synthesizers can be inexpensive, even free, so consider using computer-based systems to explore the timbral potential of synthesizers.

6. Students often work well in pairs when exploring synthesizers.
7. Consider using synthesizers in ensembles where there is an instrumental gap to fill.
8. Consider adding an acoustic instrument to an electronic ensemble to add variety to the sonic possibilities.
9. Exploring sound programming on a synthesizer using headphones can be a useful extension activity when a student has completed other work ahead of time.
10. Don't forget the constructivist approach that a student will learn more about synthesizers by building one (even a virtual one) than using one already built one.

Suggested tasks

1. Locate a synthesizer with a non-keyboard controller and have a play to experience the different a controller makes to the type of sonic gestures than can be produced.
2. To get an idea about the synthesis techniques currently in use, tabulate a list based on promotional material from a music shop or music technology Web site.
3. Explore some of the leading research in new electronic music interfaces by reading over the proceedings from the international conference on "New Interfaces for Musical Expression."
4. Try playing a simple musical phrase using different synthesizer sounds and feel how the different amplitude envelope and dynamic response across sounds changes the playing style required.
5. Locate a CD of a classic synthesizer performer (e.g., Steve Winwood, Keith Emmerson, Chick Corea, Steve Pocaro, or Joe Zawinal) and create sounds that imitate one of the sounds they use.

Chapter summary

The synthesizer is one of the more recent instruments of Western music. While it has come a long way from the early analogue instruments of the 1950s, the modern digital synthesizer is still finding its place in our music education system. Despite its widespread use as a source for new sounds and textures in contemporary popular music, the synthesizer is generally used in the music classrooms as a tool, replacing a piano, or as a MIDI input device for sequencing. The synthesizer's performance possibilities in ensembles and soundscape settings has been largely unexplored. This chapter explores some of the potential of the synthesizer for creative music making in the classroom and as a performance instrument for the stage.

Notes

1 Boulez, Pierre "Technology and the Computer," in *The Language of Electro-acoustic Music*, ed.Simon Emmerson(London: Macmillan Press, 1986), 6–7.
2 Schafer, R. Murray, *The Soundscape: Our Sonic Environment and the Tuning of the World* (New York: Knopf, 1977).
3 Paynter, John, *Sound & Structure* (New York: Cambridge University Press, 1992).
4 Pressing, Jeff, *Synthesizer Performance and Real-Time Techniques* (Oxford: Oxford University Press, 1992), 391.
5 Brown, Andrew R., "Teaching Synthesizer Performance: Issues for an Instrumental Music Program for Synthesizer," The University of Melbourne, 1994.

Chapter 10

Live electronic music

Live electronic music performance on various devices with all manner of interfaces has a strong, if not well-known, history and is increasingly popular among younger people, especially in dance and experimental music settings. This chapter will discuss the operation and performance potential of electronic music devices including laptops, turntables, beat boxes, signal processors, and various electronic devices including stomp-boxes, and toys. The field of live electronic music provides rich opportunities for music education. It is a practice at the crossroads of many important considerations; its connection with popular culture motivates students, its emphasis on performance gives it a connection to the embodied nature of musical experience, and its focus on experimentation provides opportunities for creative expression and the fostering of an enquiring attitude.

Introduction

Live electronic music is, in the early twenty-first century, mostly aligned with musical styles broadly described as electronica, which is strongly associated with dance music but also includes more experimental tendencies. Electronic music refers to music produced using electronic components, such as synthesizers, samplers, computers, and drum machines. It may also incorporate guitar effects pedals, modified electrical devices (circuit bending), and amplified acoustic sound sources.

According to Wikipedia, "In the United States and other countries like Australia, electronica (and the other attendant dance music genres) remains popular, although largely underground, while in Europe, and in particular the UK, it has arguably become the dominant form of popular music."[1]

Electronic music often consists of mechanically precise and, at times, complex rhythmic material. The popular versions of this music focus on how danceable this rhythmic material is. The sounds come primarily from electronic sources often featuring altered samples from vocal, instrumental, or found-sound sources, and can be mixed with vocal or instrumental live performances. Rhythm, timbre, and texture are dominant elements in the music with harmony taking a less prominent role. Live performance of this music involves a combination of direct gestural control and meta-level arrangement and mixing of elements and can include well-established interfaces such as music and computer keyboards and turntables, or more idiosyncratic controllers.

Live electronic music has a history of mainstream and experimental activity stretching back to the beginnings of the twentieth century from which contemporary practices are built (knowingly or not), and so an overview of this history is presented in this chapter. The chapter will also explore the equipment and practices of contemporary live electronic music and discuss some ways in which educational opportunities are inherent in improvisation with technologies that define the live electronic scene.

History

This historical overview will focus mainly on performers and also some composers. Instrument developers and designers of synthesis techniques have also made a significant contribution to this field, this is well covered elsewhere.[2]

Edgard Varèse set the tone for the electronic music community in the early twentieth century with his constant striving for new technologies with which to expand the sound world and the possibilities of musical structures. These desires found expression first in unusual instrumental combinations and extreme rhythmic changes such as in the composition *Ionisation* for multiple percussion instruments, and more relevantly in the musique concète work *Poème électronique* written for eleven-channel tape projected over 425 speakers in the Phillips pavilion at the 1958 World Fair in Brussels. Varèse was an advocate of new electronic instruments and wrote *Ecuatorial* in the 1930s that included parts for two Theremin, later rearranged for Ondes Martenot in the 1960s when Theremins were no longer readily available.

Early instruments

The opportunities for electronic music making that Varèse insightfully anticipated were exposed by the emergence of electronic technologies toward the end of the nineteenth century. Along with inventions such as the light bulb and telephone, a few inventors worked on electronic devices for making music.

Canadian Thaddeus Cahill is credited with building the first electronic instrument, the massive Telharmonium in 1897. The Mark II version cost an amazing US$200,000 in 1906. Using state of the art technologies of the time, electromagnetic generators made signals, which were sent to telephone receivers with acoustic horns like those in phonographs for amplification. This was before the days of vacuum tubes and electric amplification. The Telharmonium was controlled by keyboards, numerous pipe organ-like stops, and foot pedals.

Leon Theremin and Maurice Martenot created more modest electronic instruments that are still in use today. The Russian physicist Leon Theremin had created the instrument that now bears his name by the 1920s, and the release of a commercial version meant that it was well known by the 1930s. The Theremin produces a sound using heterodyning oscillators controlled by the proximity of each of the performer's hands to two antennae; one controlling pitch the other volume. The Ondes Martenot used similar technologies to produce a sound but used a keyboard and slider for step and glide pitch control. These instruments also saw the rise of the first virtuoso live electronic musicians, including Carla Rockmore, who toured performing the Theremin in the 1920s, and Maurice Martenot and his sister, Gillette, who were frequent performers and teachers of the Ondes Martenot. A number of musicians continue to specialize as performers of this latter instrument, and affordable reproductions of the earlier have seen it become popular again in the early years of the twenty-first century.

The famous Australian-born pianist, composer, and instrument inventor Percy Grainger was constantly experimenting with new musical devices, both new instrumental techniques and machines. He, like Varèse, was inspired to musical experimentation by Ferruccio Busoni, and he wrote music for the Theremin, experimented with manipulations of recorded phonograph discs and Pianolas, and used chance processes in his *Random Round* composition in the 1920s. He went further, however, to invent a number of musical instruments based around his Free Music principles, notably the Free Music Machine built with Burnett Cross that used eight oscillators and paper rolls with cut contours that, when scrolled, guided sets of mechanical arms along the paths adjusting oscillator parameters for pitch and amplitude. Both instruments produce a continuous pure tone capable of vocal-like expressivity.

New directions

In the late 1940s and early 1950s, following the Second World War, a number of electronic technologies had matured and became increasingly affordable, in particular valve electronic components such as oscillators and amplifiers, and the tape recorder. A new group of musicians took advantage of these developments to develop innovative forms of music making.

Pierre Schaeffer developed a style of composition using the tape recorder called musique concrète where recordings of everyday sounds were collaged into a musical structure. This was not easy work at the time because tape recorders were in their early development and editing the recording meant literally cutting and resplicing (sticking together) sections of tape, and use of multiple parts required several machines that could not be synchronized accurately. In using the technology in this creative way, Schaeffer was the first to successfully approach the tape recorder as a musical instrument. In these activities in studios at Radio France in Paris, Schaeffer was accompanied by Pierre Henry, who became a well-respected composer in the style. Musique concrète techniques were the forerunner to sampling and remixing practices used in electronic dance music. Live performances of this music also developed a unique approach of sound projection, where the recorded composition was dispersed over an "orchestra" of loud speakers. The live performance involved distributing the music around the auditorium by operating a mixing desk to change the volume levels of various speakers placed around the space. Music projected in this way later became known as acousmatic music.

Not far across Europe, in Cologne, Germany, Karlheinz Stockhausen was doing parallel innovations in music making using electronic devices originally designed for radio to synthesize sound. Stockhausen made some of the earliest purely electronic music with his serial compositions *Studie I* (1953) and *Studie II* (1954) that layered multiple tracks of enveloped sine tones. Most of Stockhausen's compositions, however, combined electronic and acoustic instrumentation, and many works with tape used recording and manipulation techniques not unlike those employed in musique concrète. Performances of many of his works feature spatialization through multiple loudspeaker projection. His continued experimentation with and enthusiasm for new methods of music making has made Stockhausen a respected and influential figure in Western music generally and in electronic music especially.

The influence of the American composer John Cage in redefining the boundaries of music in the twentieth century is legendary. And, although some of his works used musique concrète techniques in the 1950s, it is his influence on the use of electronics in live music that is most significant here. Especially given that it was within a context that was very much focused on tape-playback of electronic works. For example, in his composition *Cartridge Music* (1960) he instructs the performers to replace the phonograph needles with alternate materials, such as toothpicks, and to use these modified players to play cartridges (records) along with "small" sounds made with furniture that are amplified by use of contact microphones on the objects. These types of techniques are still regularly employed in experimental electronica. These, and other, sonic techniques were combined with Cage's strong reliance on performer improvisation and the use of random events and juxtapositions to determine musical structure at the time of performance, rather than being worked out at the time of composition (as with serialism) and specified in the score. This spirit of improvisation and acceptance of contextual serendipity is still strongly present in live electronic music.

Experimentalists

The 1960s and 1970s were times of significant experimentation in music, and with affordable electronic synthesizers coming onto the market and hobbyist electronics enabling a wider range of people to build their own electronic devices, the range, and quantity of live electronic music expanded significantly.

Commercial synthesizers such as the Mini Moog enabled composers like Wendy Carlos and Isao Tomita to create electronic versions of pieces in the Western repertoire, Carlos' *Switch on Bach* (1968) being the most famous. Electronic music was becoming more wide spread in alternate popular culture, Carlos' score for the film *A Clockwork Orange* (1971) being a clear example.

A number of musicians, including Tristram Cary, Gordon Mumma, Tony Furse, and David Tudor, worked at designing and making electronic instruments as well as making music. Others, including Alivin Lucier, Philip Glass, and Pauline Oliveros, were interested in designing and building their own systems from various electronic devices that were available, including tape machines, echo devices, distortion circuits, record players, and such. Performance presentation was a significant concern to these musicians and they often collaborated with dancers or artists using different media. Dedicated digital instruments developed around this time with early examples including the Fairlight CMI, New England Digital's Synclavier, E-MU's Emulator, and Ensoniq's Mirage sampling keyboard instruments.[3]

Connecting with rock music

Rock music is a product of music technology, and with its dominant use of the electric guitar, it could be argued that it *is* electronic music. However, from the 1970s to the 1990s the influence of electronic music and the ideas of those who had pioneered its development were strongly intermeshed with rock music. This effect can be hinted at earlier with, for example, the image of Stockhausen appearing on the cover of the Beatles famous *Sgt. Peppers Lonely Hearts Club Band* (1967) album, but as electronic instruments, in particular the synthesizer, became more common this effect was more pronounced.

A host of musicians working in rock genres understood that the electronic technology was not simply a means to an end but it was a revolution in the ways music could be understood and made. Among these were Klaus Schultz, Brian Eno, Todd Rundgren, and David Sylvian. These musicians experimented with new electronic instruments, and understood that the recording studio was an essential part of the musical experience, not simply a tool for capturing sound. This is the same insight that drove Pierre Schaeffer some decades earlier. Live performance had always been a part of rock music tradition, and even as these musicians innovated in the studio, the challenge to reproduce this music in a live setting continued to drive innovations in the use of electronic instruments and effects on stage.

Other performers were even more overtly engaged with electronic instruments in their music and live performances and some had some success in the popular market also. Artists such as Devo, Kraftwerk, and Laurie Anderson were almost techno before there was techno.

A less aggressive electronic pop music style was pursued by artist including Vangelis, Jean-Michel Jarre, Yello, Tomita, and Enya. They used the electronic sounds, but maintained conventional harmonic and melodic conventions. These artists also were popular as film composers, Vangelis' score for *Blade Runner* being a notable example. They also took electronic ensemble performance to new heights with large outdoor concerts featuring theatrical staging and lighting, foreshadowing many of the later festival-like electronic music events.

Rock music produced its share of electronic music superstar performers, including Keith Emmerson, Steve Pocaro, Patrick Moraz, and Rick Wakeman, members of major bands who rose above that to be notable musicians in their own right. Keyboard virtuosity was at the core of their performance practices, and in this era too many synthesizers were never enough. It was common that these performers could hardly be seen on stage for the stacks of equipment that surrounded them as they played.

There were a number of bands in the 1980s that challenged the dominant rock sound of electric guitar and drum kit by featuring synthesizers and electronic drum sounds in their music. This resulted in a slightly less aggressive music that suited pop artists such as Pet Shop Boys, Duran Duran, Eurithmics, Howard Jones, The Human League, and Yazoo. Many of these artists were pushing the limits of the sequencers and synthesizers of the time. The electronic basis for their sound allowed these groups to reproduce the slick studio aesthetic in live performance and this attention to presentation was matched by a polished visual appearance that was appropriate given the growing importance of the video clip to a band's success.[4]

Dance music

Electronic music as a genre found a new voice as dance music for playing in nightclubs beginning in the 1980s and establishing itself in the 1990s. Electronic dance music emerged as techno and house in the United States and later as acid house in the U.K. and trance in Germany. European musicians seemed to dominate the production of electronic dance music in the early twenty-first century. The technology used by these bands was similar to that used by electronic pop bands—synthesizers, samplers, drum machines, and effects units—but the musical focus was more on groove and evolving instrumental timbre than on melody and vocals. Also, the pace of textural change in electronic dance music was slower and the overall form and duration more extended than in rock or pop music. Some of the notable artists that were prominent in this development, and are now considered landmark artists, include Underworld, The Orb, 808 State, Coldcut, The Chemical Brothers, Massive Attack, Aphex Twin, The Prodigy, Autechre, and Fatboy Slim. These acts were popular in the dance music scene, and some were successful in the mainstream music charts as well.

Equipment

The music technologies used in live electronic music congregate around the equipment that was accessible at the time of its stylistic development in the 1980s. This review will focus predominantly on equipment used in electronic dance music, while the range of electronic and digital devices used in more experimental electronic music goes well beyond this gear to include any electric device that does, or can be made to, make a sound.

Hardware synthesizers

Synthesizers have been, and continue to be, at the core of much electronic music. Electronic (analogue) instruments have largely been replaced by digital synthesizers based on computer technology but the older ones are much prized and newer releases of older models an also be found. Some of the classic analogue synthesizers include those made between the 1960s and 1980s from companies such as Arp, Korg, Moog, Oberheim, Roland, Sequential Circuits, and Yamaha. Newer synthesizers often focus on replicating the instability in the classic equipment that gave the sound a particular warmth through a process called analogue modeling. Keyboard synthesizers that feature this include the Access Virus, Alesis Andromeda, Hartman Neuron, Korg Z1, the Nord Lead, the Yamaha AN-1x, and the Roland V Synth.

Samplers

The second stream of influence in electronic music, along with synthesis, is sound recording, and this influence is represented in the form of recordable media (records, CDs, and audio files) and digital samplers. Samplers allow the recording, editing, arrangement and performance of sound. They are typically used for shorter sound clips that are can be looped, triggered, and arranged into larger structures. Early samplers, such as the Fairlight CMI, featured keyboard controllers. But the use of samples moved to a focus on rhythmic interest rather than on pitch control. By the 1990s, most samplers featured trigger pads rather than keyboards. Keyboard samplers have been produced by Alesis, Casio, Emu Systems, Ensoniq, Fairlight, Kurzweil, New England Digital, Roland, and Yamaha. Percussion-based samplers include the Akai MPC2000, Korg ES1, Roland MV8000, and Yamaha RS7000. For performance purposes, samplers allow real-time control over pitch, duration and timbre of samples, and the triggering of sound using on-board or external controllers.

Drum machines

Rhythm is at the heart of electronic dance music, and therefore the drum machine has played a prominent role in defining the sound and style of this musical genre. Drum machines were sequencers for percussive sounds created by, at first, synthesizing then later sampling drum and percussion sounds. Like synthesizers, drum machines from the 1970s and 1980s have become classics; originals are highly valued and later technologies frequently emulated them. The classic drum machines include the Roland TR-808 and 909, Alesis HR16, and the Linn M1. Around the 1990s, drum machine features were incorporated into percussion oriented samplers, although a few dedicated drum machines are still produced. Software drum machines are widely used in computer-based systems. In live performance, drum machines allow rhythm patterns to be edited on a note-by-note basis, preset rhythms can be selected on the fly, and the timbre of the sounds produced can be manipulated.

Turntables and mixers

Despite the replacement of vinyl records as a mainstream music distribution format by the CD in the later part of the twentieth century, their use in electronic dance music has kept alive their production. The mixing and scratching of vinyl as a method of musical expression emerged from the Jamaican Dub music culture that evolved from the practice of live playing of records over sound systems for street parties and was further popularized and transformed by being blended with other electronic music technologies in the United States. Turntable systems consist of two tables and a mixer used to cross fade between them and make some minimal timbral variations. The Technics SL-1200 phonograph is the turntable used by most DJs, and for turntablism using CDs, the Numark, Denon, and Pioneer DJ CD players are widely employed; chunky two channel mixing desks from Numark, and Behringer are used to direct and manipulate the audio signals.

Software

Computer-based systems for live electronic dance music became popular in early twenty-first century as the cost effectiveness and flexibility of software-based real-time audio processing turned laptop computers into powerful musical instruments. Software emulations of synthesizers, samplers, drum machines, turntables, and mixers became increasingly common. There are too many of these to mention here, but the economics of production ensure that, increasingly, new technologies are released as software applications rather than physical devices. Virtual versions are often created as plugins for use in software environments.

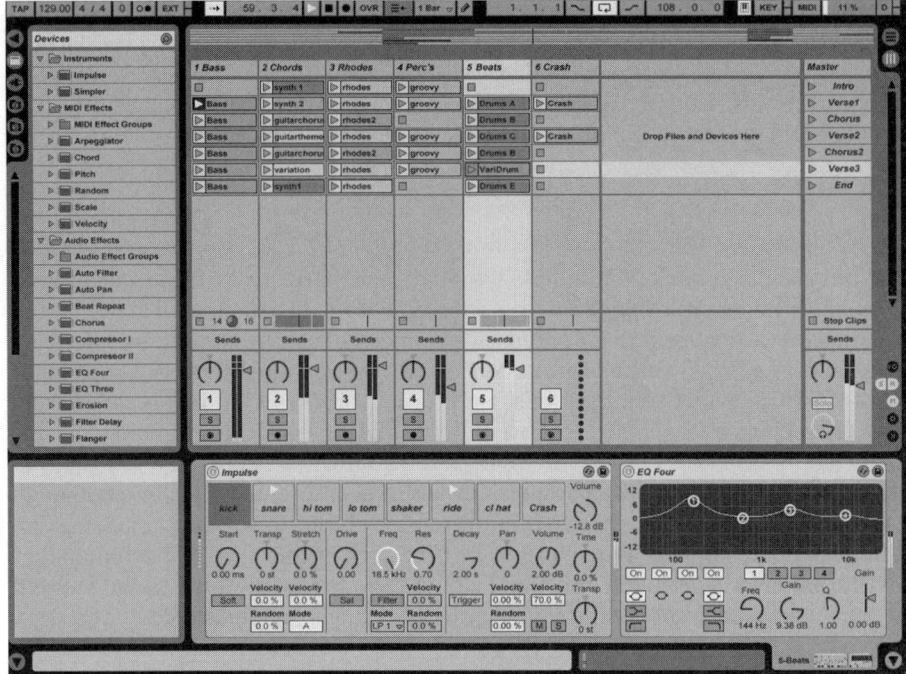

Figure 10.1   Ableton Live features a matrix of musical loops that can be varied in real-time.

Since the earliest electronic music, the notion of arranging components of either equipment, processes or audio material has been a strong element in this style. This modularity provides a flexibility that matches the unpredictable nature of creative ideas and allows for re-patching during live performance. Software sequencing environments, developed for music production rather than performance, utilize a strict linear time line that is not conducive to live performance. As a result, software systems with a modular and nonlinear structure became popular for live electronic music, these systems include Ableton Live, Reason, FruityLoops, ACID, Max/MSP, and Reaktor (Figure 10.1).

Controllers

To maintain the physicality and performativity which has been a feature of live electronic music, a number of devices can be used to control the software environment during performance. The Stanton FinalScratch system, for example, uses a record with an audio timecode to enable synchronization between a turntable and computer. It allows traditional scratching techniques to be performed with the computer as sound source. Another example is the Hercules DJ Console which emulates an entire two turntable and mixer set up in one unit that connects to the computer and controls audio files stored on the hard drive. The Korg Kaoss Pad is another popular controller with an x-y pad that also does audio and video signal processing itself rather than simply controlling processing on the computer. Various MIDI controllers with an assortment of buttons, dials, sliders, and switches can be connected to the computer to adjust parameters during performance.

Headphones

Headphones have become an integral part of a DJ's equipment list because they are used to cue tracks and other musical material prior to it being mixed into the signal being heard by the audience. Headphones for this purpose usually have enclosed speaker capsules that cover the ears to isolate the listener from other sounds in the room.

Performance practices

There are a number of factors that influence electronic music performance practices including the level of musical activity, how a musician's actions relate to changes in the sound, the size and frequency of gestures, the performance context, the size of the ensemble, the performers interaction with the audience, and so on. It is generally true that required electronic music performance gestures are minimal, in the same way playing notes on the piano only requires a small finger movement. Gestures like record scratching are more akin to bowing actions on a stringed instrument. In addition, each artist has their own approach to the degree of intervention into the live musical process they want to have, from a DJ who selects a new song every few minutes, to a performer activity playing lines of a keyboard or adding percussive parts from a drum pad. The duration of a musical element used has a significant impact on the required level of activity. User of a prepared recording requires little input, a series of looped samples or algorithmic processes requires some arranging and mixing to maintain interest over time, and the use of short sounds treated as notes requires a constant interaction more akin to acoustic instrument performance. These activities can be done in a calm manner sitting behind a laptop or they can become a manic running around stage from device to device adjusting, playing and triggering frenetically. The size of the ensemble also changes the performance dynamics; where there are more performers each may not need to be so busy to provide visual interest, and the interaction between them will also add to the performance experience. In an age of automated machine music, it is not necessary for electronic music performance to involve large ensembles so typical group size is from one to four performers. In addition to operating instruments, vocal performances, dancing, and visual display or manipulation are other performance activities regularly used for live electronic music.

The venues for live electronic music are many and varied, but they rarely include the concert hall, even though the earliest electronic music events often used these venues. More common are nightclubs or bars where there is a social and informal atmosphere. Large public events are also common including rave parties, and music festivals at which many artists perform over many hours and often on many stages. While many of the musicians involved in improvised electronic music are also involved in the rave or dance music scenes, the experimental music presentations are more designed for listening than for dancing and use small spaces such as cafes, art galleries, or small theaters.

Learning to make live electronic music

As a vehicle for music education, the range of activities in live electronic music presents many opportunities. Given that activities such as creating playlists is easy to do, it can be a good way to introduce critical listening and musical aesthetics. It can relate to the simplest form of DJing. Judgments about program selection and order present challenges relating to the matching or contrasting of musical elements and purposes.

The presentation of these playlists can then involve live manipulation in the form of mixing, starting with cross-fading between tracks, EQing, and controlling audio diffusion in an acoustmatic sense.

Electronic and computer based instrument can be used for improvised live performances from sound collages and film scores to dance parties. This can include using a range of MIDI controllers and triggering devices, Theremins, cheap domestic electronic keyboards, and so on. The preparation and control of synthesized, sampled and sequenced or recorded materials is fun, skillful, and requires aesthetic judgment. Improvised activities are more immediate and accessible than formal compositional processes tend to be, particularly for inexperienced musicians. For the student interested in electronics, there are many kit-based synthesizers and gestural controllers that can be assembled.

Computer-based environments, such as sequencers and modular audio patching systems, enable students to construct quite sophisticated sonic material and structures. Students can build their own patches for use in live performance, or the experienced can be challenged with live coding in which they build and play during the performance without prepared material.

Conclusion

The building and playing of music with electronic instruments has a heritage going back one hundred years. As the technology has become more powerful and portable, the ways in which it can be incorporated into live performance have multiplied. Musicians in the electroacoustic, rock and pop and dance music cultures have each embraced live electronic music in their own ways. The impact of the Internet, music file sharing, wireless communications, continued miniaturization, and increasing computation power seem to ensure that live electronic music has even more surprises in its future than in its past.

Reflection questions

1. What is the definition of electronic music given in this chapter?
2. Which musical elements are the focus of electronic musicians?
3. When did electronic music begin?
4. Who were some of the early pioneers of electronic music?
5. *Poeme Électronic* was produced by which composer?

6. Why might the word concrète in musique concrète have been chosen for this process?
7. What tones were used by Stockhausen in the piece *Studie II*?
8. Which different electronic dance music styles are mentioned in this chapter?
9. Name one classic synthesizer and one classic drum machine now revered by electronic dance music artists.
10. What is turntablism?

Teaching tips

1. Have students pick one of the musicians mentioned in this chapter and find out more about them and listen to some of their music.
2. Have students build from a Theremin from a kit and then perform with it.
3. Students could create an improvised work, using a *sampler*, from sound recordings they collect.
4. Small group improvised performances to a section of an old silent film can be fun with electronic sounds.
5. As an aural training experience have students compare the audio quality of the same music recorded on different media (cassette, CD, MP3 file) and comment on the differences.
6. In the spirit of Wendy Carlos and Tomita, have students perform electronic versions of classical repertoire.
7. As a lesson in music representation, have students translate rhythmic patterns between a 16th note drum machine grid and common practice notation.
8. Hold a turntable festival for students.
9. Discuss with students the merits behind the use of minimal and overly theatrical performance gestures through comparison between laptop and art rock synthesizer performances.
10. Set up an acousmatic audio diffusion system at school using mixing desks and as many speakers as can be gathered, then have student perform projections of their own stereo works over the system.

Suggested Tasks

1. Grab a turntable and mixer and experience how difficult accurate rhythmic scratching and beat matching can be.
2. Listen to recordings from each era of electronic music history mentioned here.
3. Locate some toys that make electronic sounds and use these to create a composition.
4. Watch one of the films with an electronic music soundtrack and pay particular attention to the score.
5. Go to a local music store and explore some of the latest electronic performance equipment.

Chapter summary

Live electronic music performance on various devices has a rich history of innovation in Western music throughout the twentieth century and seems to be increasingly popular, especially in dance and experimental music settings. A variety of musical practices have emerged over that time including musique concrète, acousmatic music, electronic music, electroacoustic music, and electronic dance music. A range of electrically powered technologies have been used for live performance including tape recorders, oscillators and amplifiers, computers, turntables, drum machines, signal processors, and even electronic toys. The presentation of live electronic music has included formal and informal settings, large and small venues, minimal and expansive active human input, and collaborations with a range of other art forms and media. The educational potential of live electronic music stems from its caché within youth culture, its accessibility through meta-controls and improvisation, and the ability to bridge popular and high art musical ideas and conventions. Live electronic music provides an additional pathway to creative musical expression, and thus to greater musical understanding.

Notes

1   Wikipedia entry of Electronica, http://en.wikipedia.org/wiki/Electronica (accessed October 2005).
2   Evidence found is several locations including, Barroso, Koldo, and Naomi Niles. 2003. Electronic Music Timeline, http://www.intuitivemusic.com/techno-guide-time-line.html (accessed October, 2005).
3   Burns, Kristine H. 2005, History of Electronic and Computer Music Including Automatic Instruments and Composition Machines, http://eamusic.dartmouth.edu/~wowem/electronmedia/music/eamhistory.html (accessed October, 2005).
4   Hass, Jeffrey, 1999. Electronic Music Historical Overview, http://www.indiana.edu/~emusic/elechist.htm, (accessed November, 2005).
5   Chadabe, Joel, *Electric Sound: The Past and Promise of Electronic Music* (Upper Saddle River, NJ: Prentice-Hall, 1997).
6   Prendergast, Mark, *The Ambient Century: From Mahler to Moby — the Evolution of Sound in the Electronic Age* (London: Bloomsbury, 2003).

Chapter 11

Interactive computer music

Imagine the scene. On stage in a solitary spotlight is the clarinetist Gerard Errante. His clarinet is surrounded by a number of small microphones on flexible stems attached to the instrument. Beside him is a table supporting a laptop computer and a stack of electronic modules. To begin the piece, Errante reaches over and presses the spacebar. As he begins to perform on the clarinet, the room fills with synthesized accompaniment from the PA system. As he continues to play, the accompaniment ebbs and flows with him, becoming more dense and frantic or sparse and light in response to the lines played on the clarinet. It is clear that phrases and rhythms from the clarinet part are echoed back as part of the accompaniment, not always in their original form but still containing the nuances of phrasing that connect them with the original. As the last clarinet note trails off, the synthesized accompaniment emits one last quiet phrase and the piece ends.

The term "interactive music" may seem like a statement of the obvious; of course, music is interactive. What is meant by interactive music with computer technologies? There are two aspects to this question. First, due to the primitive state of early electronic and computer technologies the music made with them was historically non-real time. That is, a composition was created by splicing pieces of tape together, or by a computer processing a short audio segment for a few seconds, minutes, or even hours. Interactive music relies on the computer reacting like an instrument, in real time. Second, unlike performance on most physical instruments, interactive performance with a computer usually implies a one-to-many relationship between external event and computer response. This is unlike a piano, which, when pressed, a key plays a single note, as does a flute when blown, even the sustained sound from a violin requires continued bowing. In interactive music the computer can act in a semi-autonomous entity carrying out a series of operations from a single trigger or adapting what it plays automatically based on a performer's actions. Interactive performance occupies the space between a one-to-one direct physical relationship typical of acoustic performance, and the playing along with pre-set accompaniment, Karaoke style. In short, in interactive performances the computer plays more or less autonomously responding to real-time feedback from a person or environment. This form of interactive algorithmic improvisation is considered by Roger Dean to be one of the most fascinating possibilities of computer-interactive improvisation, permitting what can be considered "hyperimprovisation".[1]

One form of interactive performance is the algorithmic computer accompaniment, just like that described in the opening section, as used by Gerard Errante and documented by Roger Dean. A number of such systems have been designed, usually for use in a particular composition, by researchers in the computer music community such as Laurie Spiegel, Joel Chadabe, Max Mathews, Roger Dannenberg, Barry Vercoe, Robert Rowe, Todd Winkler, Richard Teitelbaum, Jean-Claude Risset, Todd Machover, David Wessel, and Cort Lippe, among others. Other forms of interactive performance can use multiple technology systems involving audio, video, and lighting as used by Laurie Anderson, or it might be as simple as the use of a digital delay device and sample triggering in the performances of Linsey Pollak. It can be highly technological and invested with serious social comment as with performances by Stelarc, or it can be more entrainment focused and use commercial samplers and turntables as in the work of DJ Spooky. The music of interactive performance with computers can be complex and challenging or simple and accessible. Whatever the case, many musicians are attracted to its combination of performance excitement, compositional control, and technological intrigue.

Software-based virtual instruments are an accessible place to start student off when exploring interactive computer music. Virtual instruments are often based on a traditional acoustic instrument such as a piano or drum kit, but need not be. A variety of more experimental interactions are increasingly common with products such as Spongefork and Musolomo that allow you to synthesize or manipulate sounds using the computer keyboard and mouse as controllers. The manipulation of a graphic object with a mouse to create variations in sounds, musical and otherwise, is not uncommon in interactive computer music environments. Interactive instruments at their most fundamental simply trigger sound samples on user actions, but can extend to include dynamic timbral variation through synthesis functions and performance of prepared musical phrases or longer audio segments.

The interactive experience

As a learning experience, interactive performance can be useful beyond any intrinsic value. Even more than recorded or sequenced accompaniment, interactive performance can scaffold a learners' performance. These are systems based on machine listening and performance designed for this specific purpose, such as SmartMusic from Coda software and InTheChair that allow prepared accompaniments to follow the student soloist, and Home Concert that follows MIDI performances using any MIDI file as input. The preparation of interactive performance pieces requires investigating the nature of musical interaction. Such analytic and reflective activity can improve the learner's understanding of ensemble playing and help him appreciate the complexity of musical communication.

A number of interactive performance systems put the user in a controlling situation not unlike a conductor or director, where balance, tempo, and other parameters are adjustable as the piece plays. These can provide opportunities for the less skilled musician to experience controlling some of the expressive characteristics of highly complex music. The sense of autonomy, self confidence, and musical understanding gained through such experiences can be very rewarding. For the less experienced performer, interactive systems can provide a responsive accompaniment or duet that adds value to their necessarily limited output. The more experienced performer can use interactive performance systems to supplement and extend ensemble experiences, and to explore new musical challenges.

In addition to being a vehicle for supportive performance, interactive performance systems can open up opportunities for composition. In fact, it is quite common for live electronic music performances to be improvisational and for the framework for these improvisations to be composed by the same musician. The algorithmic nature of interactive systems require skills of composition and sound design in their construction prior to the performance, and then the understanding and manipulation of these elements during performance.

Computer listening and response

A computer music system used for interactive performance needs to both listen and perform. In order to listen, the computer receives data from human performer(s), usually in the form of MIDI or audio signals. One of the important decisions in machine listening is to decide what aspects of the performance to monitor. MIDI signals send gestural information about notes pressed, including their pitches, loudness, and timing, as well as the movement of **continuous controllers** such as sliders and dials, and of switches such as foot pedals, triggers or drum pads. The computer can be set to respond directly to these MIDI messages and therefore is monitoring performance gestures directly. Audio signals provide the listening machine with direct access to the amplitude change of the sound, but all other information including pitch, timing, and timbre needs to be derived from analyzing the audio signal. This is possible but not trivial. The process of analyzing the audio signal has similarities to the human processes of "perception" or "understanding." In the audio case, the computer is monitoring the results of the performance and may need to infer performance parameters from that. In other cases, knowledge of how the audio was produced are not critical and the machine will respond to features of the signal, such as its volume or frequency spectrum, directly.

The computer might listen for events that trigger a response, such as the playing of a particular pitch, or it might look for patterns in the data such as a specific phrase or an increase in the average loudness of a performance. In response, the computer might play an answering theme or harmonization, or follow with a similar change in its own volume level or an increase in textural density.

Robert Rowe defines three methods by which a computer responds to data from a performer; with music that is sequenced, transformative, and generative.[2] A sequenced musical response is one that is preset or prerecorded and does not change from one performance to the next. These are useful in music where performances are similar each time or where a more predictable response is necessary. Sequenced responses can be either quite short (a single note), or long (several bars/minutes), and of any simplicity or complexity.

A transformative response is one that utilizes the signal input (or an analysis of it) to form the response. A simple example would be the playing back of a performed phrase that has been transposed or elongated. Transformative responses are quite common and musically satisfying, since imitation and repetition are the basis of much compositional and improvisation music in any case. An interactive music system that employs this technique extensively is The Continuator by François Pachet, and its use for stimulating musical creativity in young people is well documented in Pachet's research.[3] Such responses also give the listener the impression of a dialogue between the musician and computer. Even if this dialogue is quite superficial, comparable to the *Eliza* computer conversation programs, it can be musically quite interesting. A simple way of implementing this is to have a sampler that catches moments of a performance that are then fed back into the performance, these samples may also be varied, extended, segmented, or otherwise altered.

Creating computer transformations of data relies upon compositional devices used in many musical genres, such as reversal, repetition, and counterpoint, and more recent schemes that have only become practical with the use of the computer, such as the use of Markov processes and genetic algorithms. Methods of transforming the data can be classified into several categories: constraining, which includes processes such as filtering, limiting, thinning, quantizing, and compressing; transforming, which includes delaying, transposing, scaling, reversing, and gating; and extending, which includes repeating, elaborating, harmonizing, or evolving. Interactive performance can offer a situation where these musical ideas can be explored in an active way.

A generative response is one composed by the computer. The response is often unpredictable to some degree but usually constrained to provide a similar but not identical outcome each time. The computer might, for example, generate a pulsed percussive performance based on a random selection of rhythms and sounds. Methods for generating new material with a computer include the use of mathematical formulae such as probability theory, serial techniques, and evolutionary variation. Music can also be generated by structuring fragments (cells or motives) that might be stored prior to performance, taken from the performance data, or generated from basic principles. These fragments might also be transformed in many ways, including those mentioned above. A generated response may take into account the performance data, as does for example the GenJam system created by Al Biles,[4] or it may simply provide generated material within some constraints that is stimulus for the live performer to work with.

Most practical interactive performance systems will utilize a combination of sequenced, transformative, and generative responses to suit the predictability and aesthetic preferences of the composer.

Human input

Performing interactively with a computer requires the use of some type of interface between the performer and computer. This might be a MIDI controller such as a keyboard, or a control surface with various buttons, knobs and sliders, or a trigger device such as a foot pedal, or percussion pad. Or it might be a microphone that captures the sound of the performance. MIDI controllers based on acoustic instruments include synthesizer keyboards, wind controllers from Yamaha and AKAI, Gary Lee Nelson's MIDI Horn, Dexter Morrill's MIDI Trumpet, the Chelletto by Chris Chafe, MIDI and Electric Violins from Zeta, Percussion controllers ranging from the MIDI

Xylophones to various MIDI drum pads, and numerous drum machines featuring drum pads.

Less conventional controllers include various Glove devices such as the P5 Data Glove. Baton-like devices include the Airdrums and the Digital Baton. Some performers prefer wireless controllers, which may include video-based systems such as the Very Nervous System by David Rockehy and 3DIS by Simon Veitch. Infrared, ultrasound, and radio signals were used in systems where the performer was not wired to the computer. This feature is found in the Lightning by Donald Buchla, and the D-Beam used on some Roland products. Not all these interfaces are commercial products, some are experimental prototypes.

The interface might take an audio signal from a microphone or pickup. The human performance may directly result in a computer response, or it may be recorded by the computer for later use. For simple interactive performances, the audio signal can be passed directly to digital effects processors that provide delays' reverb, and other effects. Effects units provide an inexpensive but immediately exciting way of entering the world of interactive performance. Electric guitarists have used a simple delay pedal to enhance their performances for many years. Building up a complex musical layer with one or more delay units is a nice way to extend performance practices with digital technology. It is not technically interactive; rather it is an imitative response but interesting none the less.

A pitch to MIDI converter can be used to convert the audio signal to MIDI message, which can then be processed by an MIDI-based music package, however pitch to MIDI converters can be unreliable at times and work better with some instruments than others. An alternative is to use one of a wide variety of dedicated MIDI controllers based on acoustic instruments that have been designed to specifically interface with computer systems.

Yet another alternative is for the performance gestures to be tracked by video, infrared sensor, or other non-tactile method. This is particularly useful when the performer (e.g., a dancer) does not want to be tethered to a controller device. Video senor data can be processed to derive motion tracking information such as location within a region (for example, a dancer moving to a certain part of a room), or behavior information about movements (such as quickly changing direction at the bottom of a conducting gesture). An example is the Cyclops system developed by Eric Singer and distributed by Cycling 74 does video tracking and outputs MIDI data (Figure 11.1).

Synthesizer hardware that includes many controls, like the Roland Groovebox, or loop-based software systems such as Ableton Live, can be used to adjust sequences in real time by mixing parts in and out, switching between present patterns, controlling tempo, and so on. These are popular with live techno musicians but with some imagination can be used for music of different styles as well. Dedicated computer software systems such as M by Cycling 74 (Figure 11.1) provide easy to use visual interfaces that can be used to create interactive environments. The M software allows the user to construct loop-based sequences that play via MIDI synthesizer, and enables parameters or sections to be changed in real time. A "conductor" area can be used to easily control two variables at once as the mouse is dragged across the conductor grid. More sophisticated environments that you to graphically build interactive performance systems include AudioMulch, Algorithmic Composer, SoftStep, and Max/MSP. There are a few real-time computer music languages, such as Supercollider and Impromptu, that provide the power of general-

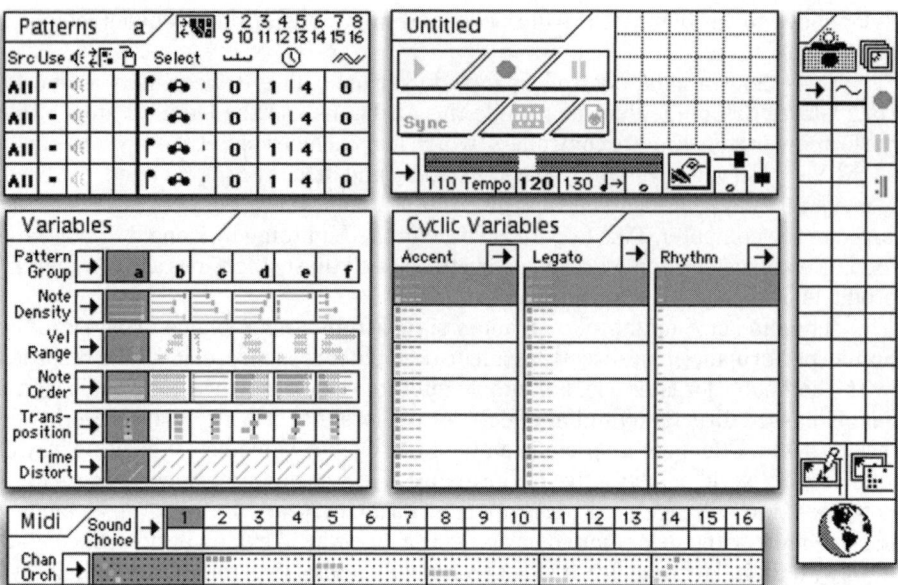

Figure 11.1 The interface for M, an interactive MIDI-based software application.

purpose languages with a library of music-related functions with which to program sophisticated interactive music systems.

Performance partnerships

When working with a computer for interactive performance, the computer becomes the instrument, often with a controller extension. Like any musical instrument, the performer often needs to take time to learn to work with it to control the musical outcome. Through this interaction a partnership develops that might range from one characterized as performer and accompanist to one more like an improvisational duet. Through these musical partnerships the interactive performer is enabled to explore a range of control over the algorithmic nature of the computer, from order to chaos, or from prerecorded playback to random samples. The musical challenge then is to find a space between order and chaos where there is predictability but challenge, and organization but interest. The boundaries of which will change from person to person, between styles, and over time.

Interactive performance can also be seen as a balancing of responsibility and control. The decision for the composer is about which aspects of the music will be controlled by the performer(s) and which by the computer. It is a matter of setting up constraints within which the interactive performance takes place. All technologies have built-in constraints such as the set pitch limitations of the piano and the polyphony limitations of the flute. The computer has limitations of speed and processing power manifest in limitations on polyphony, timbral complexity, and speed of interactive response. The computer is programmable and therefore provides great variety in the way it can respond to performance and over the level of autonomy it can be asked to exercise. While the responsibilities of the saxophone player and saxophone are relatively fixed, those between the interactive performer and computer may change from work to work. Exploring the musical boundaries of the performance partnership can be very rewarding even, and for some people especially when, the musical partnership includes an interactive computer music system.

Remote control

Interactive performance over the Internet is a growing area of interest, as the speed and reliability of Internet connections increase, and as many performers are seeing this as just another venue within which to perform or collaborate. Despite earlier technical challenges, there were a number of pioneering efforts in networked music making. In the mid- to late 1970s, the group called The League of Automated Music Composers formed in California and performed works where computers communicated over a network to influence each another's musical output. Some members of this group formed The Hub in the early 1990s who continued this work with more reliable MIDI-based networks. Carla Scaletti's *Public Organ: An Interactive, Networked Sound Installation* (1994) was one of the more ambitious of the early projects in interactive performance over the Internet. While pieces such as Scaletti's are actually human interactions mediated by computers, rather than interaction with the computer as partner, they point the way toward new music making opportunities in interactive performance where the computer's role can vary from medium to instrument to performer. Scaletti's experiences in this area contributed to the Kyma computer music system used by many musicians for interactive sound works.[5] Another Internet-based interactive music project is William Duckworth's *Cathedral* (1997), which has a variety of activities from Webcasts to music games.

Networked improvisation is an interactive music activity where people jam over a network connection. The connection may be local, simple between two computers in the one room, or global, via an Internet connection to another geographic location. Software such as jam2jam simplifies network improvisation by using generative musical processes to assist in making the music. Adjusting parameters on the software can control these music processes, and the meta-level control changes are sent over the network to keep the various jamming nodes coordinated. More sophisticated systems enable interactive performance over the Internet by streaming MIDI or audio data between locations. These systems can be awkward to coordinate and synchronize because of the variable speed of data transfer over the Internet.

Useful links

Information about many of the applications mentioned in this chapter can be found at the Web addresses below. These are good starting points for exploration into interactive music.

Dedicated applications

eJay   http://www.ejay.com/
Jam2jam (network jamming software)   http://explodingart.com
M (intelligent composing and performing system)
    http://cycling74.com/products/m.html
Musolomo (software instrument)
    http://plasq.com/musolomo/
Spongfork (software instrument)
    http://www.spongefork.com/
The Continuator (details and video of the imitative software in action)
    http://www.csl.sony.fr/~pachet/continuator.html

Software environments

Algorithmic Composer (a MIDI-based graphical music environment)
    http://www.smartcontroller.com.au/AlgorithmicComposer/algorithmicCom-
    poser.html
AudioMulch (interactive music and sound environment)
    http://www.audiomulch.com
jMusic (Java-based algorithmic music library)
    http://jmusic.ci.qut.edu.au
Kyma (algorithmic music and sound system)
    http://www.symbolicsound.com/
Reason (modular virtual synthesizer and sequencing software)
    http://www.propellerheads.se/
Max/MSP (graphical environment for music production)
    http://www.cycling74.com/products/maxmsp.html
Pd (graphical music programming language)
    http://www-crca.ucsd.edu/~msp/Pd_documentation/
SoftStep (an algorithmic sequencer)
    http://algoart.com/softstep.htm

Multimedia tools

Cyclops (video analysis and tracking for Max/MSP)
    http://www.cycling74.com/products/cyclops.html

Auto-accompaniment software

Home Concert (auto accompaniment software)
    http://www.musiconmypc.co.uk/art_music_making_software.php
InTheChair (accompaniment and performance monitoring software)
    http://www.inthechair.com/
SmartMusic (auto accompaniment software)
    http://www.smartmusic.com/

Conclusion

Interactive performance with computer is still a growing and expanding area. It has a history as old as the computer itself and seems to have yet to be fully explored as an opportunity for music making with the computer. At present, most commercial interactive performance systems are focused on adaptive accompaniment for instrumentalists following known repertoire, while systems that aim toward a stronger sense of partnership and improvisational interaction between performer and computer are still experimental. Some of the accessible systems for school applications include *M*, which enables layers of loop-based phases to be controlled by mouse and MIDI gestures. The eJay software is a simplified virtual DJ console where prerecorded audio files can be mixed during improvised performances. The jam2jam software enables meta-level interactivity as the user control parameters of a generative music system in real time. The jam2jam software also enables collaborative interaction because several jam2jam systems can be networked together. Hence, the performer is interacting with both their computer and with others in the network improvisation session. Interactive computer music is an exciting area in which the challenge is to create software systems that achieve musically meaningful and aesthetically rewarding outcomes that stimulate both artists and audiences.

Reflection questions

1. How does interactive music differ from a play-along audio or MIDI track?
2. In what ways can interactive performance systems scaffold learner's actions?
3. What does the SmartMusic software do?
4. What are the similarities between a conductor and a musician using an interactive music system?
5. In what ways can a computer be said to "listen"?
6. Describe the differences between sequenced, transformative or generative music.
7. What sort of wireless performance controllers are available?
8. A pitch to MIDI converter does what?
9. What is the difference between the jam2jam and M software applications?
10. What is meant by the term "network improvisation"?

Teaching tips

1. Have students begin interactive activities with systems they control with a mouse, such as M, jam2jam, and for the slightly more advanced try Propellerhead's Reason.
2. Students can research and report on the interactive music activities of one of the musicians mentioned in the chapter.
3. Students can better understand the nature of musical interaction by comparing the experience of playing and improvisation with another student and with an interactive music system.

4. Use an algorithmic computer music application to provide a backing track for student performances, and have one student vary the algorithmic parameters during performance.
5. Use an auto accompaniment system for instrumental students to rehearse repertoire.
6. Comparative experimentation with a range of performance controllers can provide insight into expressive control requirements.
7. Use a guided listening to the musical responses of an interactive music system to stimulate understanding about the bounds and conventions of musical styles.
8. Challenge senior students to explore an environment used by professional interactive musicians, such as AudioMulch or Max/MSP.
9. Interactive music systems need not be for soloists, a small group of student can play along with an interactive music system.
10. Make links with another institution and engage in a network improvisation over the Internet.

Suggested tasks

1. Prepare a live performance using an interactive music system.
2. Ask for a demo of an interactive accompaniment system, you might be surprised how well the systems follow a live performance.
3. Look up, and listen to, the interactive works of those people from the computer music community named in the chapter.
4. Think carefully about the difference between a word processor application "responding" to a save file command, and a computer music system "interacting" with a performer.
5. Download and watch the videos of The Continuator application being used by young children to see the excitement interactive music can bring.

Chapter summary

Interactive computer music involves a computer system that has some semi-autonomous behavior such that it generates music that responds to input from a human performer or the environment in real time. In traditional performance the interaction is with other performers and the audience, in interactive performance the interaction is with a responsive computer music system as well. Interactive music can be as simple as a person controlling and algorithmic music process, or it can be as complex as a system analyzing a human performance and generating appropriate music in response. Often interactive systems involve a degree of improvisation, although some auto accompaniment systems rely on the fact the performers are playing a known score in order to keep track. Interaction with computer music systems can be via a microphone that picks up the acoustic sounds, sending data from a MIDI controller, using a mouse to control a graphical interface, or by using any other method of sensing a performer's activity. The performance activity is mapped or analyzed by the computer to produce some musical output that becomes part of the performance. While these systems can be very complex, a number of easy to use options are available including eJay, M, and jam2jam that you can get going with quickly. Interaction is a key ingredient in music making and so interacting with a responsive computer music system is a rich area of musical experience to be investigated.

Notes

1   Dean, Roger, *Hyperimprovisation: Computer-Interactive Sound Improvisation*, (Middleton: A-R Editions, 2003), xxiii.
2   Rowe, Robert, *Interactive Music Systems: Machine Listening and Composing* (Cambridge, MA: MIT Press, 1993).
3   Pachet, François, "The Continuator: Musical Interaction with Style." Paper presented at the International Computer Music Conference, Göteborg, Sweden, September 2002.
4   Biles, John A, "Genjam: A Genetic Algorithm for Generating Jazz Solos." Paper presented at the International Computer Music Conference, San Francisco 1994.
5   Scaletti, Carla, "The Kyma/Platypus Computer Music Workstation," *Computer Music Journal* 13, no. 2 (1989): 23–38.

Chapter 12

Digitizing and visualizing music

The representation of information effects its interpretation and meaning; therefore the careful presentation of information is a mainstay of education. Modes of educational presentation have included the telling of stories, the drawing of pictures and diagrams, the writing of texts, and the production of videos and software. The presence and potency of the performer, or presenter, in this communication cannot be underestimated, however, in this chapter we will pay particular attention to the role of digital media representations in communicating musical knowledge.

The history of presentational mediums includes cave walls, blackboards, overhead projectors, computer data projection, and Internet Web sites. Presentation of musical information varies in dimension also, from generalized information about a century of music making to the specific timbral spectrum of a work of musique concrète, from encyclopedic volumes to single page summaries, and from the vast resources of the Internet to brief notes stored in a mobile phone. This chapter explores various representations of music and sound with a particular focus on their ability to facilitate editing, analysis, and presentation.

Introduction

Computer-based presentation of material can include computer projection of slides using a program such as Microsoft's PowerPoint, the posting of support materials on the Internet as HTML documents, the distribution of files to students on disk or over a network, or by creating CDs, DVDs, or other digital recordings as pedagogical materials.

The medium of presentation is an important pedagogical choice because it advantages content that is easily presented by it and that, in turn, may lead to a distortion of perceptual priorities in the student, or other observer. The medium of paper privileges static information, text seems most readable on paper, and diagrams and musical scores are additional static representations of music that have evolved with paper-based presentation. Paper is editable, but electronic and digital media are even more malleable. Digital information, stored as discrete numbers, can be copied and changed any number of times without degradation, unlike analogue mediums (i.e., paper or audio tape). The ability to work with digital presentations, such as building Web pages, enables the user to explore many alternatives without the risk of damaging the material. This flexibility of a medium has an impact on the exploratory tendencies of thinking done with that medium. Another advantage of digital data is that it can be used to represent a variety of traditional media, text, image, animation, photography, film and sound. The benefits of being able to work directly with sound on the computer, rather than with representations of sound as notation on paper, include the ability to deal directly with the medium of music, sound, rather than through an intermediary interpretation.

Building on the work of Jean Piaget, Seymour Papert reminds us that children are concrete thinkers, and that the relationship between knowledge and its medium of presentation is critical to understanding. "The traditional epistemology," he argues, "is based on the proposition, so closely linked to the medium of text— written and especially printed. *Bricolage* and concrete thinking always existed but were marginalized in scholarly contexts by the privileged position of text."[1] Writings about music are, in Papert's terms, a "proposition" about music; an abstraction. With computer-based presentation of musical information there need not be such a high-reliance on the abstractness of text or graphical representations, but rather, we can encounter sound itself and complement that with other temporal media such as animations and video.

The use of time-based media, such as audio recordings and video, for music presentation is clearly beneficial not just for educational purposes but simply as a rich experience of music, clearly evident in the popularity of music videos as a way of consuming music. Temporality is inherent in time-based media, but can also be present in the reading of static media. For example, a written score is rarely taken In in one look, rather it is scanned and read in a way that results in a temporal experience of the score. It might even be argued that the ability to randomly access a score or book presents some advantages over the linear playback of an audio recording. The computer can fortunately combine both the random access and the direct encountering in music software systems where a visual overview is combined with audio rendering or recording of the music.

There is a strong tendency to align teaching practices with information availability. Most curriculum documents are text-based, and thus have an (often unintended) bias toward textual and score-based representation of music that share a similar symbolic abstraction, and are often treated to a related semiotic interpretation. Digital presentation of information can often amplify this abstract quality as a result of its innate segmentational nature, but can also go some way to overcoming static abstraction through the ability to represent motion, both as video and sound. An increasing number of curriculum "documents" are now being produced with multimedia materials that exemplify or elaborate on the curriculum. In the following sections, various methods and formats of digital capturing and presenting of musical information will be examined in some detail, with the hope that a better understanding of them will assist in better communication and expression of ideas about music.

Audio formats

Digitizing audio is a primary concern for musical presentations. Its use is quite pervasive in our society in the form of CDs, which store sound as a stream of digital data representing the music. Digitizing of audio is also called sampling. "Sampling" is also the term used widely in the popular music world to describe the capturing of musical phrases for later recombination in beat mix, techno, and related styles; see chapter 8 for more detail on digital audio recording. The use of digitized music is also becoming prevalent for distribution of music on the Internet. On the Internet sound files can be sent as a whole file, usually in a compressed form such as MP3 or AAC, or as streamed audio where a series of small audio chunks are played then discarded. Common streaming formats are Real Audio, Flash, Windows Media, and QuickTime.

The way in which the sample data is stored is defined by its file format. It can be confusing that there are several file formats for audio (not to mention those for video, text, and so on) but the most common ones are widely supported. It is always important to check which formats your presentation medium accepts so that you can save the audio (or other material) appropriately for later inclusion. In addition to the information below, more information on these and many other file formats can be found at FileInfo.com.

PCM audio

When a sound is recorded it is captured as raw audio by a process technically known as Pulse Code Modulation (PCM). Many audio file formats store this data directly, including WAV and AIFF formats. This is also the format used for audio on CDs. The PCM audio data can vary in quality depending upon the sample rate, bit resolution used. CDs use a sample rate of 44,100 samples per second and a sample resolution of sixteen bits; therefore these audio specifications have become the most common. Lower values are often found when recording spoken voice (e.g., in Dictaphones) and higher values are often used for professional studio recordings. The audio files can contain a number of audio tracks. Mono (single track) and stereo (two tracks) are the most common, but in theory the files can contain any number of tracks.

The process of getting the audio data from a CD or DVD and into a file on the computer is called ripping. The technical process is relatively straight-forward given that the data is already in a digital format and just needs to be copied.

MP3 files

MP3 is an abbreviation of MPEG 1 Audio Layer 3 and utilizes a form of compression that exploits the limitations of human hearing. The MP3 encoding process starts with a PCM audio signal and attempts to eliminate frequencies in the signal that the human ear cannot hear distinctly, while keeping the other frequencies. As a result, MP3 compression is said to be "lossy." The advantage of MP3s is that their size is significantly less than an equivalent raw audio file, such as a WAV or AIFF file, typically about one tenth of the size. This makes them ideal for transmission across the

Internet or for storage on a portable music player. The smaller the file size, the less download time and the less memory space the music takes up.

If you want to take a CD or wave file and turn it into an MP3 file, you need a software encoder. Many audio applications, such as Microsoft's Windows Media Player and Apple's iTunes, include an encoder to allow the saving of audio recordings or PCM audio files in MP3 format. The MP3 encoding can be done a different rates and with a variety of different settings to produce smaller or larger amounts of compression. The compression amount is measures in kilobits per second, with a bit rate value of 64 to 96 being low, 128 to 192 is average, and 256 high. Lower bit rates result in smaller files of poorer quality, and vice versa. Determining an appropriate encoding rate required depends on how large a file size or level of sound quality is wanted.

To playback an MP3 file a decoder is required, but this process is less computationally intensive than encoding, and is easily achieved in real time. MP3 players are common, not only in software but in mobile music players and mobile phones.

AAC

The Advanced Audio Coding (AAC) format is another audio compression codec that operates similarly to MP3, and therefore the previous discussion encodes, decoders and bit rates apply to this format too. ACC encoding also results in smaller files and arguable has a better sound quality for the file size than MP3. The AAC format is part of the MPEG 4 video compression standard and is also used by Apple Computer in their popular iPod music player and iTunes music store.

Ogg vorbis

Another compressed audio format is the unusually named Ogg Vorbis. It's files have the .ogg file extension. It uses similar psychoacoustic data reduction processes as MP3 and AAC codec's and achieves results comparable to AAC. Ogg Vorbis differs in that it is a free format, whereas developers of MP3 and AAC encodes pay a small license fee. Because it does not have the backing of large companies its use is not as widespread and locating software to encode and play Ogg files is more difficult. The Audacity audio editing software is a free program that can save and load Ogg files.

FLAC

Given that musicians are concerned with audio quality, the lossy nature of MP3, AAC and Ogg Vorbis files may present some concern. Audio can always be saved as PCM data in Wav or AIFF formats, for example, but their file sizes are quite large. One alternative that provides a compromise solution is the Free Lossless Audio Codec (FLAC). The FLAC encoding achieves compression amounts of about 30–50 percent of the original, about half that of MP3. FLAC encoding is widely used for audio archiving and for audio file transfers and streaming where audio quality cannot be compromised. In this regard its value for music education seems quite high.

Audio visualizations

When presenting and working with audio on a computer a visual representation is useful and common. Sound is usually depicted on a graph that has instantaneous time, like an oscilloscope, or with time as a horizontal axis. With time lapse displays the vertical axis can either indicate loudness, as in a waveform display, or frequency, as with a spectrogram. These graphs can be either two or three-dimensional. Most audio editing software packages, including the freely available Audacity software, can display audio in a variety of ways.

Oscilloscope

An oscilloscope is a device for visualizing differences in electrical potential. Electronic musicians have long used oscilloscopes to display the waveform generated by their equipment. An oscilloscope displays the signal over a small time frame, redrawing the wave across the screen at a fast rate. Digital versions of oscilloscopes work in real-time displaying the audio signal being captured by the microphone at the time, they do this through an iterative process of **buffering** and displaying a short sample of the wave (Figure 12.1).

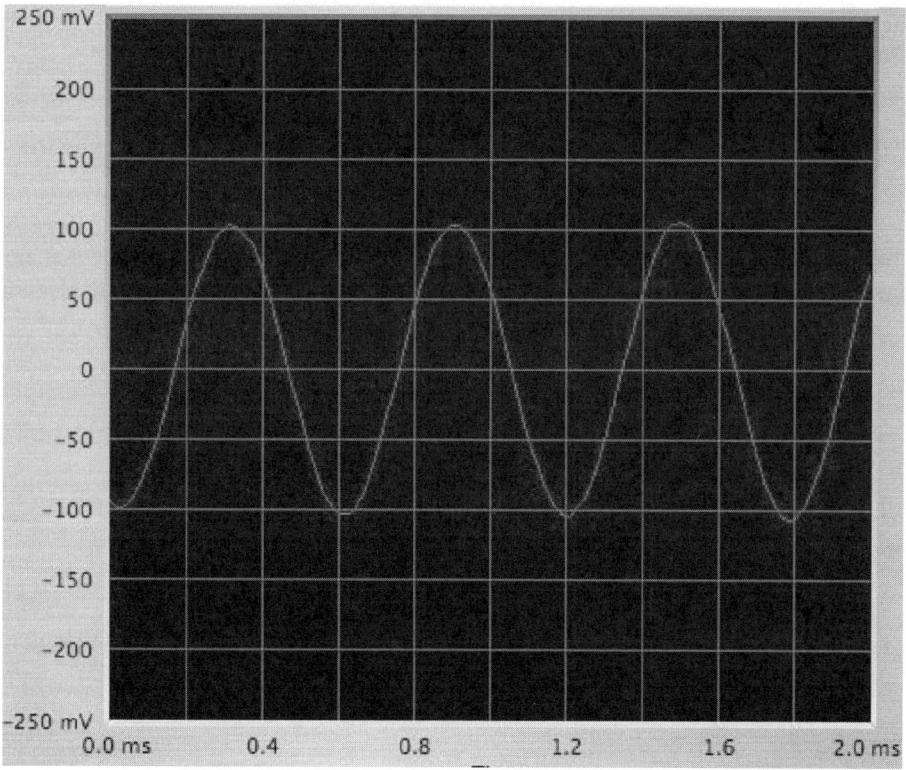

Figure 12.1   A simple waveform displayed in a software oscilloscope.

Oscilloscopes and other real-time displays are excellent tools for helping students understand the relationship between sound elements and their visual appearance. They can see that more noisy timbres have a more jagged shape, louder sounds are larger on the vertical axis and that higher pitched sounds have more tightly packed (shorter) cycle lengths. Because these features are immediately visible students can experiment with different sounds in front of an oscilloscope and quickly get a feel for the relationship between heard and seen representations of sound, and a clearer insight into sonic elements.

Waveform display

A waveform display shows the sound signal similarly to the oscilloscope, as an amplitude-time graph. However, the waveform display shows a recorded sound file over any duration, rather than a fleeting glimpse of the sound in the moment that the oscilloscope gives. Because the waveform display is a static, nondynamic, display it can be understood like a "score" for audio. It has the same advantages as a score of being a great vehicle for reflection, analysis, editing and arranging of sound data. As a result, the waveform display is the most common visualization of music in computer music software. The digital waveform display is a graph that looks like a continuous line but is, in fact, a line that joins-the-dots between the individual samples. This can often only be seen when the display is zoomed in to see the waveform at its most detailed level, because the time between samples (dots) is very small (Figure 12.2).

Spectrum analyzer

The spectrum analyzer shows the instantaneous frequency distribution of a sound. Unlike the oscilloscope and waveform display that work in the time domain, graphing amplitude over time, the spectrum analyzer operates in the frequency domain, graphing amplitude over frequency. The piano keyboard also covers the frequency

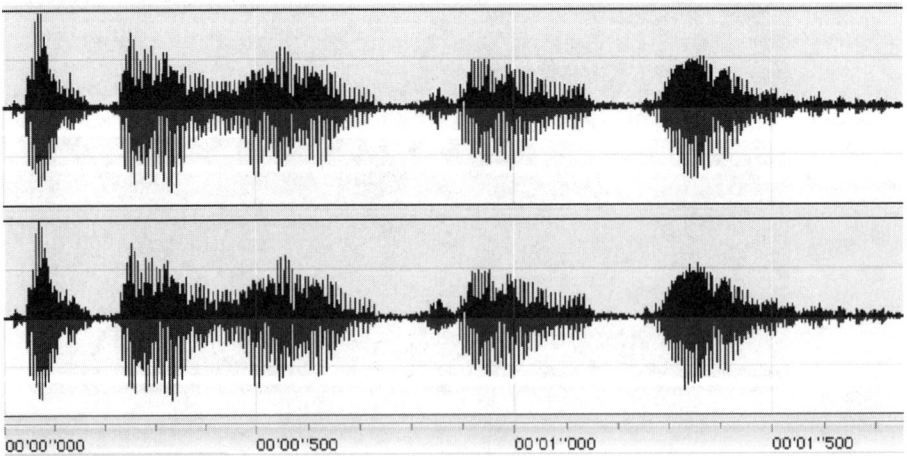

00'00''000   00'00''500   00'01''000   00'01''500

Figure 12.2 A stereo waveform, left and right channels have their own tracks.

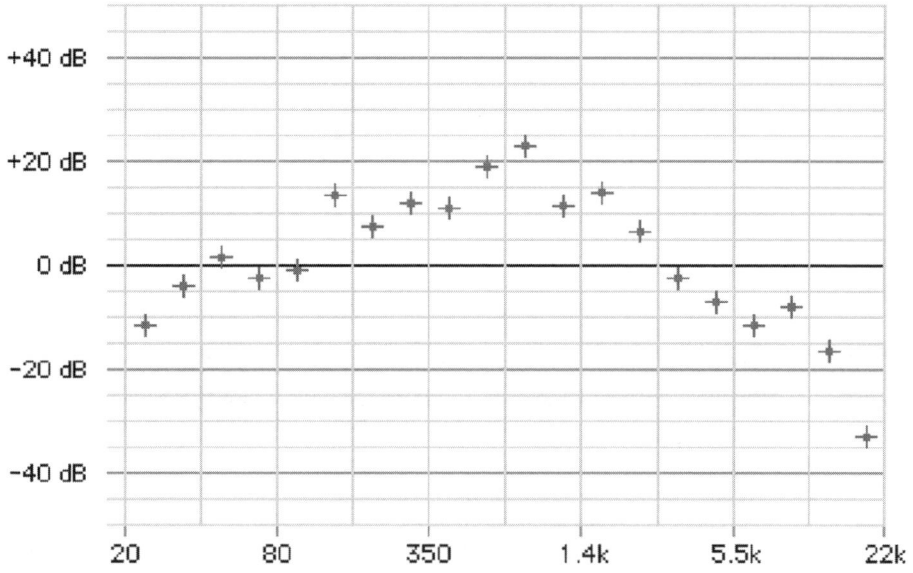

Figure 12.3 A twenty-band spectrum analyzer, each cross represents one frequency band.

spectrum, from low notes up to high notes. In the same way the spectrum analyzer plots the frequency from low to high on the horizontal axis. In a similar way that the piano divides the pitch range into eighty-eight keys, a spectrum analyzer divides the frequency spectrum into a number of bands, typically between about ten and thirty. On the vertical axis, it indicates the loudness or intensity of each frequency band. Because audio recordings capture sound in the time domain, the signal must be processed to obtain data about the frequency spectra. This process is usually done using a Fast Fourier Transform (FFT), which breaks down the sound into its component harmonics. The spectrum analyzer operates by repeatedly capturing a small segment of recorded sound (called a window), doing an FFT on that data, and displaying the results. This can occur so quickly is appears instantaneous, which is why we refer to it as a real-time process (Figure 12.3).

Spectrum analyzers operate in real-time and the height of each frequency band dances around as the sound signal varies. Like oscilloscopes, spectrum analyzers are useful for immediate feedback of timbral features, and have the similar education value in developing aural perception of timbre through experimentation. They are useful for checking the frequency (instrumental) balance within a recording or live ensemble and are often used in live performance as a way of determining the frequency of microphone feedback.

Spectrogram

A spectrogram, often called a sonogram, shows the frequency spectrum over the duration of a sound. The spectrogram is to spectrum analyzer what the waveform is to the oscilloscope; it does the same process but shows the accumulated results over time and operates on a file rather then real-time input. The spectrogram reveals

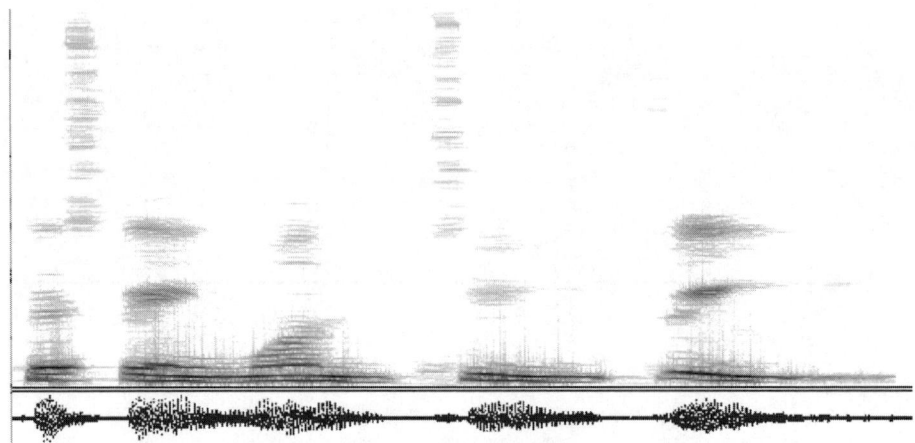

Figure 12.4 A spectrogram with the corresponding waveform view below.

the frequency distribution of the sound over time, and the changing frequency spectrum within a sound (e.g., in a crash cymbal that started with a wide frequency range and narrows over time) can be clearly seen (Figure 12.4).

Each "line" in the spectrogram display corresponds to a frequency band and the intensity of a line indicates its amplitude. The frequency range is on the vertical axis with low frequencies at the bottom. Because the frequency range is so wide and the frequency scale is logarithmic, it is not uncommon for linear spectrograms to have a lot of activity in the lower regions. Spectral analysis of recorded music is often used as an analytical technique in the same way a textural analysis of a notated instrumental arrangement is, to reveal the timbral variety and structure within a musical work.

MIDI representation

Apart from digitizing audio another common way of representing music is via the Musical Instrument Digital Interface (MIDI) standard, and the more restricted General MIDI subset. One of the main advantages of MIDI representation is that the files are very small. This is because MIDI files store information about the start and end of a note, while audio files represent the state of the note at every moment. The small file size makes them easily transportable and allows extended musical passages to be efficiently stored. Also, the note-level editability of the MIDI format means that examples can be easily changed in tempo and transposed as required. MIDI files, however, rely on a built-in or external synthesizer to replay the music so the audio results are dependent on the quality and capabilities of the synthesizer. For example, this means that nonstandard timbres and vocals are usually not able to be represented.

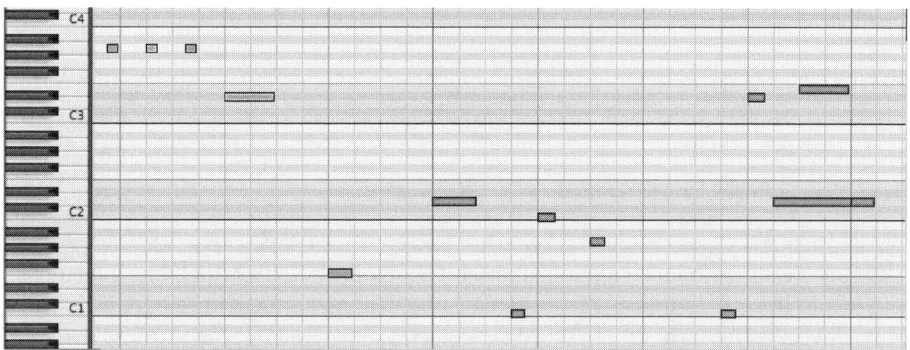

Figure 12.5   MIDI data viewed on a piano roll display.

MIDI visualization

The common way of representing MIDI data is as a piano roll display, where each note is represented as a rectangle on a pitch and time graph, the length of a rectangle corresponds to a note's duration and often some other indicator such as color represents the dynamic (loudness) of each note. Piano rolls were originally made of paper with elongated holes cut to let air through which triggered the piano hammers. Players used pedals to drive bellows that both scrolled the paper roll and drove pistons that pressed the piano keys. The digital displays are based on this model, but are usually turned on their side so that the pitches are on the vertical axis and time scrolls across the screen (Figure 12.5).

The piano roll display is similar to staff notation in many ways expect for the scales of the axes and the note icons. The piano roll has a chromatic vertical scale, rather than diatonic, the horizontal time axis is linear rather than variable, and the note icons are uniform. As a result, students often find this display more intuitive than common practice notation.

Textual representation

Music can be represented as text, not only poetically as a literary description, but also as a notation. There were many early computer music systems that represented a musical phrase as "c d g a e d c" often with the addition of octave and durational numeric symbols as well. One quite advanced version of this scheme is the abc music notation language invented by Chris Walshaw.[2] A small example of music in this format is shown in Figure 12.6. The value of a text-based system is that computers can easily manipulate text data, the files can be easily compassed or sent via e-mail, and there are many other text-based languages with which it can be incorporated, include Postscript, HTML, and XML.

A number of specialized computing tools are available for creating, editing and translating music in the abc format. There is a range of other text-based music

```
T:Paddy O'Rafferty
C:Trad.
M:6/8
K:D
dff cee|def gfe|dff cee|dfe dBA|dff cee|def gfe|faf gfe|1 dfe dBA:|2 dfe dcB||
~A3 B3|gfe fdB|AFA B2c|dfe dcB|~A3 ~B3|efe efg|faf gfe|1 dfe dcB:|2 dfe dBA||
fAA eAA|def gfe|fAA eAA|dfe dBA|fAA eAA|def gfe|faf gfe|dfe dBA:|
```

Figure 12.6 A melodic fragment in the abc music notation language.

languages each with its own particular focus, including Koan, which encodes music and sound information into a text string to be sent as an SMS message, NIFF and MusicXML, using form music score description, and DARMS, which was used for musical analysis.[3]

Structural representations can also be as visually interesting as they are informational, and the field of data visualization has a number of examples of music being a stimulus for artistic visualizations. One particular example that is both structurally informative and quite beautiful is Martin Wattenberg's The Shape of Song process.[4] The potential for cross curriculum projects between music, visual arts, and computer science around music visualizations is rich indeed.

Music fonts

While it might not be common for music educators to use text representations to describe entire music scores, it is more common that text documents may need to include elements of music notation. Including graphic files of music notation is quite feasible and is elaborated on in chapter 4, but adding the odd symbol or two in a sentence means that "two quarter notes equal a half note" can become a mixture of musical and normal characters, as shown in Figure 12.7. In fonts, each letter has an associated number and the display renders each letter based upon a font description. Music notation fonts can be used to embed notational symbols in text documents. This can be very useful for making text explanations more musically readable, or for setting up simple music theory tests in a word processing document. For example, the Sonata font displays a crotchet (quarter note) in place of the character "q," a quaver (eighth note) is "e," a treble clef is "&," and so on. Each letter in the font is mapped to a musical symbol.

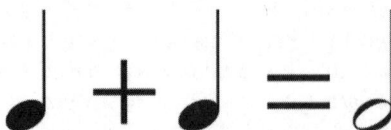

Figure 12.7 Mixing music and standard fonts in a document.

Graphical representations

Music has long been represented graphically, and such representation can be within a structured system like common practice notation or it can be a more abstract visual representation such as a collection of curves and arcs that describe pitch trajectory, as used by Iannis Xenakis with his UPIC computer music system.[5]

Computer-based visual notations can be saved as graphic files. Most music publishing software systems enable saving of scores in this way, some even allow saving of selected sections of a score. In cases where the program does not output a graphic file for inclusion in presentations then a picture of the screen can usually be taken and edited as required. There are any number of software painting and drawing tools that can be used to create graphic scores or to import and standard score and add additional graphic enhancements.

Graphic formats

In order to achieve an appropriate output for graphic presentations, it is wise to understand a little about the types of graphic file formats and their strengths and weaknesses. As with audio formats, graphic formats vary in their priority with regard to file size, image quality, the ability to be resized, and color accuracy. Graphic formats fall into two broad categories, those that are *bitmaps* which have a dot-by-dot representation of the screen display stored in the file, or those that are *vector*-based. Digital photos are bitmapped images and, of course, photos of instruments, ensembles, techniques, people, and so on are useful in musical presentations. Printed or film-based photos can be digitized as bit maps by a scanning device and saved for inclusion in an appropriate file format. The quality and size of bit mapped files vary proportionally with the resolution of the image, and large bit mapped images can occupy a lot of space, although generally they are compressed with a lossless codec such as GIF or PNG or a lossy codec such as JPEG. Vector-based graphic formats, such as SGV, Postscript, PDF, and Flash, describe the graphic image as a series of scalable atomic elements including lines, curves, and shapes. This allows for the maximizing of display quality even when the size of the image is altered, or the output resolution is changed vector-based images can also be stored efficiently. This can be important for presentations where images are to be projected or printed at varying qualities.

Animations can be constructed from a series of images, and can be useful for showing how a process, technique or procedure unfolds over time. Some image formats, notable GIF 89a, support step frame animation, which is particularly useful for displaying a series of still photos. The Flash format allows for animated vector graphics and is an efficient method for creating drawn animations in a small file footprint, and has a rich tool set for creating animations.

Video formats

It is not big step from animations to movies because video footage is digitized as a series of individual still images. Video material is ideal for demonstrating music performance activities and practices and is an very effective self-assessment tool often used to improve sports skills but under-utilized for musical skills training. Movie files are very large compared to audio and image files and so compression codecs are of even greater importance in this field, and there are a wide variety of them. Digital video is both a medium and the name of a video format. DV video is a common format for hand held movie cameras and used by many computer-based movie editing software applications. The Motion Picture Expert Group (MPEG) standards are also widely used for storage and playback. MPEG 2 is the format used by DVD, and MPEG 4 is common in digital devices and computers. H.264 provides excellent quality and compression and in increasingly being utilized.

Video, as with text, audio, and still images, can be embedded in many word processing documents and certainly in presentation software and Web sites. The combination of these can provide rich teaching resources that engage many of the senses and account for different ways of knowing. Students will benefit by describing their understanding in media-rich ways as well and the computer, as the centerpiece of digital convergence, can assist in the preparation, and presentation of these educational materials.

Presenting

In order to present musical information that contains text, music, and image some integrating format in required. This can be a word processor, multimedia authoring environment, presentation package, Web page, or dedicated computer software. Media players, such as QuickTime and Windows Media Player have become core technologies on computers and are relied upon by many applications to provide support for media-rich content in documents, and for the Web these and other players such as RealPlayer and Flash Player help make online content as rich if not richer. When preparing media-rich documents there are many choices of document type. The most appropriate will depend upon which media type is the primary one for the presentation, for example elaborated reports best suit a text-centric application such as a word processor. Another consideration is the format and audience of a presentation, for example a presentation to a school assembly may suit a slide show. The information organization is another key differentiator, for example a documentary would suit a DVD and a self-help tutorial would be effective as a Web site.

Word processor

The humble (or not so humble) word processor in most cases displays a lot more than text. They can be used to include sections of scores, scanned images and diagrams, and audio or video annotations to produce interesting and informative handouts. Word processing documents with temporal media, such as an audio file, can be distributed electronically to students and even computer projected for class presentation. The facilities for screen-based presenting directly from the word processor may not always provide the most sophisticated presentations but they are certainly functional and widely available.

Digital slide show

Dedicated software applications such as Microsoft's PowerPoint and Apple's Keynote are built for integrating different media into a slide show presentation. They function similarly to word processors as just outlined, but are focused more toward on-screen presentation than printed output. Information is organized as a series of pages, or slides, each of which can contain any digitized media. When projecting presentations, it is useful to consider that text and image sizes should be large enough to be seen clearly from the back of the room, that appropriate stereo application is available to playback audio samples or MIDI files, and that presentations contain supportive material rather than a repetition of what is said or in a printed handout.

HTML

Web pages are constructed using the HyperText Markup Language (HTML). At its most basic, HTML refers to the appearance of text, but Web browsers interpret HTML and also handle specific graphic formats, usually GIF and JPEG files. HTML files are text files and can be viewed in a word processor that may show all the HTML commands embedded in <angled brackets>. These commands are interpreted by the browser rather than displayed and relate to the text immediately following or preceding them. HTML code can be written in any text editor or by one of numerous **WYSIWYG** editors, such as the free Nvu, which generate the HTML code automatically as you manipulate content and layout. Because HTML files are text only, they are quite small and can easily be distributed on disks or via e-mail as well as over the Internet. Media other than text (images, audio, and movies) are stored separately from the HTML file and referenced by HTML commands called tags. A growing number of word processors, including Microsoft Word, include the ability to save a document as a HTML file, which makes the creation of a basic Web page very quick and easy.

Web browsers use helper applications, often called plugins, to play media types such as audio, MIDI files, and movies. Creating pages using the plug-ins that come standard with the major browsers is the safest policy when creating a Web presentation. Common audio formats on the Web include WAV, AU, AIFF, and MP3 files. Common streaming audio formats include Real Audio, WMA, and QuickTime.

An overview of all the features available in HTML is well beyond the scope of this chapter, but two features deserve some attention. Most importantly, HTML documents can have hypertext links. Text or images can be a hot spot that, when clicked, load another HTML page. Pages can be divided into regions called frames. Each frame is a HTML document in its own right, which allows sections of the display to remain constant while others are updated as links are followed. More commonly, the screen can be divided in regions using a table layout that divides an area in to a number of rows or columns. Another HTML feature is the ability to have forms that allow for user feedback by providing check boxes, text fields, popup menus, buttons, and so on. Completed forms can be emailed with a single click. Forms can be very useful for questionnaires, or student/teacher feedback and communication.

PDF

One file format that has become widespread in the early years of the twenty-first century is Adobe's PDF format. This format is a vector-based graphical description compressed into a small file. PDF documents can be read with a freely available viewer program, they can be rescaled for printing or presentation and are thus very useful for distributing musical scores. With some advanced editors, PDF documents may contain media elements and hypertext links.

Podcasts

Audio, and optionally video, material can be stored as files for downloading to a portable player, such as Apple's iPod, a process that has been dubbed Podcasting. Podcasts can involve subscription services and automatic downloads and so on, but even manual downloading of material is not uncommon. Many radio programs are providing shows as Podcasts on their Web sites, and some people offer alternative audio guides to museums and other public sites as Podcasts, which can be downloaded prior to a visit. This can form a viable option for audio tutorials or archives of classes or lectures for students to review. Students can download the files and listen as they travel to and from school or some other convenient time.

CDs

The making of audio examples on CD is a high quality and relatively inexpensive tool in educational situations. Once music is digitized it can be burned to CD from computer with a CD writer and the blank CDs are inexpensive. In effect, distributing CD musical listening examples, aural training exercises, or even audio lectures is quite practical.

DVDs

DVD authoring became quite mainstream in the early years of the twenty-first century and has many of the advantages mentioned for CDs but with the obvious addition of video material. Editing and burning video material is inherently more time and computer intensive than audio alone, but provides robust storage and convenient portability for material that can be viewed either at school or at home. Music performance documentation and assignments as documentaries lend themselves to the DVD format.

Using digital presentations for teaching and learning

Given the array of presentation options available, some important questions arise about their appropriate usage for music education. Is a medium best for teachers or students? Are presentation mediums most useful for exposing, discovering, or generating information? To what extent is a presentation about content, presentation, or delivery? What musical knowledge can be contained in or stimulated by a media-rich presentation?

Earlier in this chapter it was suggested that the sonic and performative nature of music making lent itself to media-rich presentation of musical ideas, so it seems clear that teachers should be encouraged to utilize these means wherever practical. However, it is commonly understood that the best way to learn something is to teach it, and so students should be encouraged to use these as a way of organizing and communicating their understanding too. In fact, student use of digital media capabilities and equipment may well be more educationally efficient that their use by teachers. In summary, the digital convergence onto the computer platform of previously separate mediums provides the opportunity for explicit connections to be made between different knowledge representations that can assist both the development and expression of musical interpretation and understanding.

Reflection questions

1. Why does the medium of presentation matter educationally?
2. What differences between paper and digital mediums are mentioned?
3. In the quote by Seymour Papert, what is meant by the term *"bricolage"*?
4. How is it suggested that a static medium like a printed score can be understood as being temporal?
5. In relation to audio, what does the acronym PCM stand for?
6. What are the differences between WAV and MP3 audio formats?
7. What are the differences between Ogg Vorbis and FLAC audio formats?
8. Oscilloscope and waveform displays are similar in what ways?
9. How can music fonts be useful, outside of their application in music publishing software?
10. Contrast the features of bit mapped and vector graphics formats.

Teaching tips

1. Enrich printed handouts with images representing the music and sound that is being investigated.
2. Provide access to a digital camera and digital video camera for students to document their music activities.
3. Encourage students to create a media-rich Web site as part of portfolio assessment.

4. Students could keep their work as a portfolio on a data CD or DVD if all activities were digitized.
5. Use hyperlinks in a Web-based assignment task to enhance understanding about the links that exist between people, music, places, and ideas.
6. With in-class presentations require students to include audio and image elements to ensure that they engage with the sound of the music they are studying, not just textual descriptions of it.
7. Explore the differences between audio file formats with students so they understand why the choice of file type is both aesthetically and technically important.
8. Have students bring all manner of noisy object from home for a session with real-time visualization tools including an oscilloscope and spectrum analyzer.
9. As a way of experimenting with music representations have student invent a new notation system based on iconography or color.
10. Work with the ITC teacher to explore how best to enable media-rich documents to be created on the schools computers.

Suggested tasks

1. Gain insight into a familiar piece of music by listening to it while watching its effect on a spectrum analyzer.
2. Explore the possibilities of inserting audio, image, and video into the document applications that you use most often.
3. Search the Web for Podcast aggregators to get a feel for the variety of content being produced for that type of delivery.
4. Revise some of your frequently used presentations to see how you might make them more media rich.
5. Think about where you can do less talking and more playing of music or videos in your teaching.

Chapter summary

The convergence of previously separate media forms onto the computer as digitized text, sounds, image and structure, presents opportunities for the creation of media-rich presentations for use in music education. Musical knowledge can be represented in many of these media forms, and probably least effectively of all as text, which has been the traditional medium for knowledge representation in education. Understanding how these media operate in the digital space and some of the terms and conventions used in the software tools will help better exploit the opportunities for media-rich presentations. Therefore, this chapter discussed some of the main features of digital media formats, codecs, and files, and the main categories of presentational formats including word processing, Web sites, CD/DVD and slide shows. The tools and techniques for presenting material in media-rich ways can be used by educators to create resources and for assessment and by students for reflection and for expression.

Notes

1   Papert, Seymour, *The Children's Machine: Rethinking School in the Age of the Computer* (New York: Basic Books, 1993) 156.
2   Walshaw, C., abc, a music notation language, http://staffweb.cms.gre.ac.uk/~c.walshaw/abc/.
3   Selfridge-Field, Eleanor, *Beyond MIDI: The Handbook of Musical Codes* (Cambridge, MA: MIT Press, 1997).
4   Wattenberg, Martin, 2005. The Shape of Song, http://www.turbulence.org/Works/song/, (accessed October, 2005).
5   Lohner, Henning, "The Upic System: A User's Report," *Computer Music Journal* 10, no. 4 (1986): 42–49.

Chapter 13

Music for visual narrative

Creating music for film, TV, visual art exhibitions, or dance productions are some of the more popular school music activities, as well as being exciting projects for professional musicians. There is a strong tradition in many of these collaborative fields, including the opera, ballet, musical theater, film scoring, TV program themes, music video, and so on. There are many reasons why musical collaborations with other creative arts disciples can be fruitful and inspiring. It has become common place for composers to do entire music sound tracks on computer, and the ability of computers to handle digital image and video has made the integral creation of cross disciplinary work viable. Rather than explore all of this rich territory here, we will focus on some of the issues, techniques, and processes for utilizing the computer to create, synchronize, and deliver music for events and productions that are driven by a visual narrative in particular.

Sound and image

The connecting thread between all the activities discussed in this chapter is that they have a linear narrative and can usually be characterized as story telling, even if this is at times obscure. (Chapter 14 will explore computer music in nonlinear or interactive situations in more detail). In a film, a dance, and even an art exhibition there is a plan to take people on a journey through the work. The role of music is to enhance that story, often at an emotional level. During presentation of the work, music can also add to the physicality of the experience, filling the venue with sound to envelope the audience in the work.

Unlike music for the concert hall, music for visual narrative is often a supportive and suggestive emotional adjunct. Taking into account the collaborative role that music plays when accompanied by a visual narrative, the responsibility of the music to carry that narrative or convey a mood is changed. This changed role can result in reduced density and complexity of the music so as not to overwhelm the images. As Earle Hagen writes in his book *Scoring for Film*, "The natural tendency for a composer starting out in film is to overwrite. Too much music, and not enough time to say it."[1] This is good advice for the student film composer and also hints at why music for visual narrative can be educational effective; it does not require complexity and the skills required to manage that. This is not the same as saying it is easy, however, effective results can come from minimal but appropriate compositions within the capacity of school students.

When working with other media, there will be constraints imposed by the artistic vision of the overall project and, often, the musician may not be in control of that vision. This can be turned into an educational positive. One of the most difficult tasks is to be "creative" without any constraints. It is usually much easier to have some defined boundaries within which to work. Collaborative projects provide such limitations where the general, or specific, themes, styles, or moods are specified and the musician needs to produce the most effective result that archives the specification. Writing to a brief can be pedagogically useful in focusing a student's compositional attention on elements of the task that are required by the curriculum.

Creating music for film, dance, theater, or any other collaborative project usually provides another constraint, time. Deadlines and the lack of time influence the rhythm of production, and it is common that the creative process under these circumstances will be set by the beat of another drum.

The utilitarian nature of producing music for a visual narrative can provide a stimulus for creation, but often the result when combined is different from how the musician imagined it working. Because these activities tend to come together only at the last minute it is important for the musician to develop the skills of imagining the music they are working on in context. This development of musical imagination is a musicianship that extends beyond the aural to the performative. Students should be encouraged, when undertaking such tasks, to work with the context in mind. Having visual materials in front of them when working can assist students to contextualize their compositions. Materials useful to support this contextualization can include draft edits of films or scripts, rehearsal videos, storyboards, and so on. The digitization of these media can allow the integration of such materials into the computer music workspace.

There has been an assumption thus far that students are creating the music for these visual narratives, but this need not always be so. Many situations require the selection of appropriate music rather than, or in addition to the production of new music. The task of music selection is a valid musical activity and can be an excellent starting point for the student when trying to understand the role of music in the visual contexts. There are notable examples, such as the film *2001: A Space Odyssey,* where source music originally used as a placeholder became the film soundtrack.

Given that people have previously produced excellent sound tracks for film, dance and so on without computers, what is the role or value of the computer in this process? There are three major advantages:

- interoperability of media,
- flexibility of editing, and
- conflation of the writing and recording process into one production process.

The ability for video in particular but other visual media also, to be incorporated into music production software greatly enhances the ability to connect the sound and image. Videos can be synchronized to the music track, chorographic software can synced to music software, stage plans, scripts, and set designs can be readily available and cue points marked in them. All this can happen within the one virtual working environment, be saved into one directory on a hard disk, and taken with the musician wherever he (and his laptop) goes.

Creative processes are fluid at the best of times, and collaborative ones can be volatile in the ways aspects of the project change. As a result the flexibility of the production process and tools is vital. Because the commitments made to elements of the score or audio components in a digital system can be changed easily by cutting, pasting, dragging, and so on, then these systems are very useful. For example, it is can be powerful to have a production meeting around the computer where the implications of changes to the structure of a work can be explored as part of the decision-making process.

Media productions in the twentieth century were typically assembly line processes where elements of a production passed from task to task. For example, film scoring started with a script and cue sheet, then a composer wrote a sketch score, an arranger orchestrated the core, a conductor and orchestra played the score, foley artists created sound effects, actors provided dialogue, a recording engineer mixed the score, effects and dialogue and post-production houses integrated the score into the film. In the twenty-first century, all these processes can be achieved on the computer, and most of them done in one or two software applications. While large studios may still have specialists, smaller filmmakers handle the whole process with one or two people. This conflation of processes into music production systems has blurred boundaries between composer, arranger, performer, and sound engineer, and these tools, at least simple versions of them like Apple's GarageBand and iMovie, are quite accessible for use by students in schools. The integration of these skills means that students can be transdisciplinary in their abilities and understandings and so the educational processes need to reflect this blurring of tasks and disciplines as well.

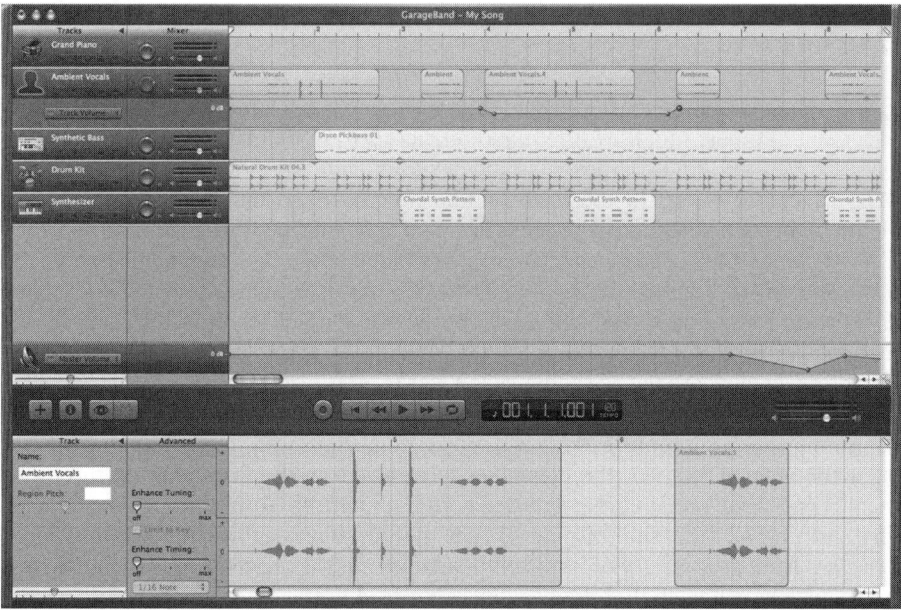

Figure 13.1 Sequencers such as Apple's GarageBand can be used to create music for videos.

In the following section we will explore in more detail some of the considerations for music making with the different visual contexts of video, theater, dance, and exhibition.

Video

There is a century-long tradition of music for motion picture, beginning with live performances to silent films in the early 1900s. These became more elaborate with score written for live orchestral performances to silent films. Stylistically the tradition of musical scores running most of the way through a film lives on music for animations and cartoons. Sound pictures saw replaced of live performance with pre-recorded sound tracks; not without some agitation from musicians at the time. Also, the addition of spoken word as a sound source changed the role of the score quite significantly. In this period the film composer became quite a prominent figure in the artistic direction of a film. Significant film composers in the mid- to late twentieth century include Eric Korngold, Bernard Herman, John Williams, James Horner, and Jerry Goldsmith. At the same time, other sound elements, particularly spoken voice and sound effects, became important sonic elements in film. The advent of the television in the mid-1900s expanded the opportunities for musicians with music being used during show titles, as underscore in dramas, and for TV advertising. Streaming video on the Internet became widely available in the 1990s and, as the twenty-first century proceeds, networked video delivery is becoming increasingly common.

Despite the changes in technology, there are some basic processes and principles that are important for film composing and with which the computer can assist.

Structure

Apart from the opening and closing credit music, the constraints on the duration and placement of music in a film (the macro structure) are determined by the way the scenes are edited. The composer, sound designer, and director will usually collaborate on deciding where the music and sound effects will go and what the role of each should be in each scene. This process is called spotting the film. From the spotting process comes a list of cues, special events or moments in the film and places where music should start and stop. As a result, the composer will have a cue list and a plan of where and why music needs to be produced. Most music sequencing and recording applications allow for markers or cue points to be added to the timeline. These provide a visual reference as the musician works on the score. Usually there will be editing functions to enable the moving or stretching of material to match cue points. Before the use of computers for music production, there were many tedious manual calculations necessary for the composer to ensure that the duration and timing of musical passages would correctly align with the pictures. Applications usually support zooming of the visual display so that the musician can quickly see a musical structure from at a variety of levels of detail, and allow larger structures in the film to become evident such that they can be reinforced in the music.

Another structural element in visual narratives, particularly in film or video, is the use of character themes. Once written, these themes can provide good starting points for musical sections within the work. Music under particular scenes can be based upon the themes or motifs of the characters in the scene as the starting point for that section. The connection between the musical ideas and characters also helps reinforce the narrative and can be used to refer to characters that are alluded to in the script but are not present in the scene. Because there can be reuse or variation of material in this way, the ability for computer software to easily copy and paste and edit can be of great assistance.

Synchronization

A key technology in video or film production is synchronizing elements, such as different video streams and camera shots and audio tracks including voice-overs, sound effects and musical score. Traditionally this involved complicated interconnection of different machines, using click tracks, time code and all manner of connecting standards. Fortunately, the digital process has made synchronization of video elements much easier and this is an almost transparent process in computer-based editing software. Normally opening a video file in a music application will create a window for the file and synchronize it to the current project with a default assumption that they should both start together. Setting the start locations of different tracks (audio and video) should be all that's required and they will stay in time after that. It may be necessary to synchronize computer files from different applications, for example sound effects recordings from an audio editing package with the video and music in a sequencer. At these times, the ability to accurately position a sound file on the time will be critical and an understanding of video frame rates and time code conventions may be helpful. There can be conflict between musical beat timeline subdivisions and video time and frames subdivisions that may not align. These are usually only a matter of setting timeline preferences to an appropriate convention or overriding quantization with some option to allow microscopic dragging or moving of material on the timeline.

Given that the timing of cues in films and videos needs to be very accurate, there can often be musical decisions required about how to shorten or lengthen a phrase to fit the allotted time. Most composers advise as a first rule of thumb, not changing the phrase structure, but rewriting to add or remove notes, before changing the tempo. If the musical style allows, then modulating the phrase with some rubato can slightly change its performed length. In addition, there can be speed changes, done with MIDI data as a change of tempo or with audio through time stretching or reduction processes. Working through these issues can help students to better understand the subtle musical effect that tempo, melodic shape, and rubato have the aesthetic qualities of music.

Theater

There are many occasions in schools where music for plays and theatrical productions is required. This is a good chance for composition, performance, and sound design activities in the music program to connect with a visually dominant presentation medium. In this section we will focus on how these can be enhanced by assistance from computing technologies. We will avoid direct discussions of musical theater although that activity will be informed by these discussions.

Sound design

For many theater productions the sonic requirements are more heavily focused on what we might call sound design rather than composition or performance. This could involve the creation of foley effects including gun shots or automobile engine sounds, the assemblage of atmospheric soundscapes such as thunder storms or party chatter, and the selection of appropriate musical clips for use as transitions between scenes. In these situations, the focus is on the tasteful application of music and sound and probably the live performance of those sounds during the show. The preparation of these materials can be done using sound recording and editing software, and techniques discussed in chapter 8. The performance of the sound design could utilize a loop-based sequencer such as Ableton Live, which allows sounds to be triggered in real time, or even a time-based sequencer with each sound spaced out on a time line (although this would make overlapping cues awkward to play).

Audio spatialization

An important consideration in live theater is the placement and movement of sounds in space, the spatialization. Good spatialization can greatly enhance a theater production. It requires that a multi-speaker array be installed in the theater and that appropriate multi-channel mixing equipment is available. The uses are many and varied, including the position of foley effects to match their physical (or off stage) location, the positioning shifting of ambient sounds (i.e., weather or traffic noise) so that the audiences feel they are inside near the production, and the playback of music or DVD tracks in 5.1 or other surround formats. The heart of a digital multi-track playback capability is a computer with a multi-channel sound card or interface. Each output can be sent to a different speaker located around the theater, and most major audio applications will allow multi-channel mixing of each track to position the track as required. The preparation and delivery of spatialized audio requires careful listening to the real-world environment that is trying to be imitated and the creative imagination to create virtual spaces as required by the theater production. These tasks can greatly enhance the audio awareness of students, and affordable multi-channel audio systems make this achievable in school environments.

Music

Selecting or writing music for a theater production provides many of the challenges that were discussed for film music, including contextual appropriateness given the topic of the play. Some works are period pieces that require research into the musical styles and conventions of that period or culture. Shakespeare's plays, for example, are often put into contemporary settings and so the focus would be on identifying the emotional or narrative intent of the original and how that can translate into a contemporary context. This approach allows students to use music of their time and to re-evaluate its meaning and how such meanings can transcend time and place.

At times the music requirements are to provide underscore ambiance, as is often done for film, and digital sequencing and recording software packages can be applied here as for any other compositional task. It can be quite successful to have students perform these ambient musical tracks live during the theater production. An electronic music ensemble is appropriate here because of the sounds they can produce and because the control over volume can be important. The requirements to be subtle and to allow for actors vocal delivery to be heard can be useful constraints from which students can learn to appreciate the subtle power of music in reinforcing narrative.

Dance

Choreographed dance productions almost always have a strong musical element. This affords the musician the prospect to create music for a cross-arts collaboration where the music has quite a high profile, and where artistic license can be quite liberal. The history of music and dance goes back further than we know, with examples in indigenous cultures traced back tens of thousands of years. Even in Western fine arts history, the ballet tradition is well established. In the second half of the twentieth century, choreographers were quick to collaborate with the emerging electronic and experimental music scenes (e.g., the notable partnership between the composer John Cage and choreographer and dancer Merce Cunningham). Connections between rock music and dance are inherited from Afro-American traditions and have produced genres such as jive, disco, punk, soul, and techno, each with their own distinctive dance style. Based on this popular music tradition, many schools hold rock music dance contests, usually playing well-known songs. While such activities are essentially theater studies, there are opportunities for musical involvement through the production of remixes or cover versions of the songs that retain the character of the song but customize its structure and arrangement to be even more appropriate for dancing, or at least the choreography of the production.

Collaboration

The music producer and choreographer can have strong collaborations because both art forms have a degree of abstractness that provides flexibility. Contemporary dance projects can often enable the composer to escape tight cue points and even strict tempo or rhythmic constraints. However, as noted earlier, freedom from constraints can also make the production of appropriate music somewhat nebulous, and a number of attempts at draft ideas may be required before a composer and choreographer agree on a suitable direction. Often, example music selected by either party can serve as a way to explore possible directions quickly. Avoiding the attachment to the draft example, sometimes called demo love, can be tricky and it can often be best to give in and allow the use of the existing track rather than write another in its shadow.

Once a general direction of the work is established, a computer music system can be a useful tool for discussion of macro structure and pacing, because of the ease with which sections can be arranged and tempo maps can be drawn and redrawn. Working with a flexible tool can speed up the collaborative process enormously compared with having to wait for redrafts and re-recordings when using less dynamic media.

Gesture

Another connection between dance and music, and possibly the reason they are so strongly related historically, is that they are both about gesture. A key element to understanding what music may be appropriate for a dance is to work at the level of gestural correspondence, not necessarily in a simplistic imitative way, but rather as a similarity of intensity. Are the dance gestures slow and fluid or sharp and fast? How does the fluidity of the gestures change in different sections of the choreography? Are there polyphony or unison textures in the dance that could be structurally parallel in the music? When writing with a focus on gesture it can be worth exploring ways that gestures and drawn curves can use utilized to make these connections. Curves are routinely used in music software for parameter control, for example, volume, dynamic range, pitch bend, amount of reverb or delay, spatial positioning, and so on. Simply using the mouse to draw curves with an appropriate gestural style and then mapping these to elements in the music is a way the computer can be used to connect gesture and sound quite directly.

Experimentation

It is not uncommon in contemporary dance performances to have dance gestures directly controlling musical events using MIDI dance suits, pressure pads, light sensors, video tracking and other interactive technologies, as discussed in detail in chapter 11. These can work quite effectively in an abstract or simple triggering situation, but not so well where tight synchronization is required given that there is some margin or error in many of the tracking systems. Gesture capture can be used to trigger single sounds, to start or end musical processes, to control parameters of compositional processes or sound synthesis, and act as cues to the music system.

Much choreographed music is tightly scripted and is usually best accompanied by a recording of the music given that there will be little variation between performances, however, in more loosely choreographed works where there are elements of improvisations then it makes sense that the music can also be performed live in a semi-improvised sense. In this way the piece can take its own direction at each performance. A mixture of prepared recorded material, improvised electronics, and acoustic sounds can provide a rich pallet of timbres and structures and, in schools, small ensembles can be formed from interested students to work on such projects. The combination of prepared material and semi-structured improvisation provides enough continuity for the choreography but still allows for a responsive performance that takes into account the physical context, mood of the audience, and the variations in delivery that inevitably occur.

Exhibition

Music for visual art exhibitions can likely be more imaginative than having a yet another string quartet play Mozart's *Eine_Kleine_Nachtmusik* at the opening. While traditionally visual art exhibitions have been silent affairs, the increase in electronic and digital works, sometime called New Media or Media Arts works, has been accompanied by an increase in audio as part of the exhibitions. Digital media art works often have visual and sound created by the one artist, reflecting the convergence of forms into the digital space, but it is not uncommon to have collaborations between visual artists and musicians.

A number of school-based projects have been inspired by Modest Mussorgsky's *Pictures at an Exhibition* to have combined audio visual exhibitions where students compose music inspired by art works, often done by other students. The presentation of these can follow several conventions. Each artwork can be hung in a different gallery space with its own sound system, or a linear presentation can have each work on video with accompanying music played live or pre-recorded, or the pictures can be hung in a standard gallery space with the musical works saved as audio files for playback on mobile music players. In the last scenario, each visitor has their own player and headphones and can visit the works in any order they choose then select the appropriate track.

Sonification of digital images

Sonic rendering, sonification, of visual artworks are also possible with computing technologies. The data is a digital image can be mapped to sound with pixel location representing pitch and time as in the work of the vOICe image sonification applet. The process of steganography uses pictures as a spectrograph image, which

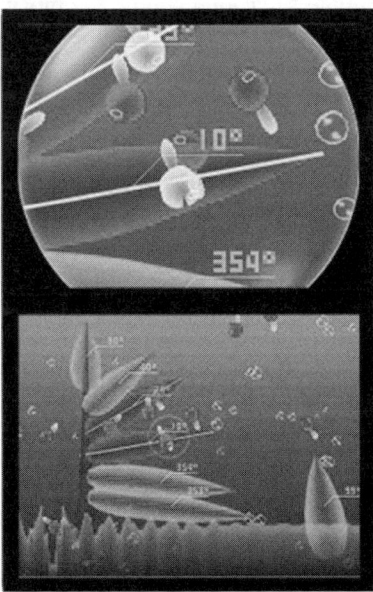

Figure 13.2 A still image from one of Toshio Iwai's Electroplankton games.

is transferred to a sound using an inverse Fourier transform. This technique was used by the techno musician Aphex Twin (Richard James) in a section of his track *Windowlicker*.[2] Some software based on a similar approach used by software such as MetaSynth allow users to "paint" music by having a pallet of colors that represent particular timbres and that can be applied to a canvas with a timeline. Other music painting programs turn the visual gestures into musical parameters, as with the Kyma system controlled with a pen tablet. The Gendèr program by Peter McIlwain allows the user to draw harmonics in an additive synthesis system. The harmonics fade over time creating a constantly varying timbre.[3] Some systems allow you to draw musical phrases that can be played once or looped, as with a number of the musical games on Toshio Iwai's Electroplankton.[4] Interactive works like these are also discussed in chapter 14.

Mood

Producing music for an existing visual art work, perhaps a painting, sculpture, animation or installation, the artwork can provide a starting point for the composition, a stimulus, and an invitation to understand another artist's work in more detail. Musicians will often try to reflect the mood or ambience of the work and the challenge can be to understand the structure and range of interpretations that the work presents. This range can become a stimulus for sections of the music or for layers within the musical texture.

Temporality

Unlike any of the previous art forms we have discussed, visual art works are often fixed in time, not temporal like music. This presents a challenge when writing music to accompany an image or a sculpture, for example. How long should the music be? Should it loop or be triggered by the exhibition visitor? At what tempo should the music be played?

In one sense, the reading of a fixed visual art work is always temporal, so hints about how to approach timing in the musical work can come from the musicians own experience of viewing the work. There can also be parallels drawn between levels of activity and intensity in the colors and shapes in the work that can translate to musical activity and pace. In another sense, the lack of an obvious temporal frame can be liberating for the musician who can please themselves about what music will complement the visual work.

Presentation

The way in which visual works are exhibited and viewed is quite different from the performing arts concert situation and this means that consideration about the presentation of music in exhibitions requires some thought.

Vision is directional and sound is not. It is fine to have several art works in a single room because a visitor can face each work in turn, ignoring the others behind and beside them. Sound fills the space, using conventional speakers, and so multiple sound works in the one space are problematic. A simple solution is to present just one sound work. This can be fine if the exhibition is coherent enough that the music suits all works. This approach also allows multi-speaker sound diffusions to be used, so long as the sound design does not have an obvious directionality that is important to the work because people will face in all directions in the gallery and there will not necessarily be a "front" location. Another approach is to have several sound sources but to keep the volume low. This is a poor solution from the musical perspective as the low volume rarely does justice to the music, and audio spill is problematic. Using headphones at each artwork solves the previous two problems of isolation and presentation volume. Wireless headphones can be used to enable the visitor to view the artwork from any location while still listening to the music. One drawback of headphones is that they can only be used by one person. A variation of the headphones-at-each-work option is to allow visitors to have their own mobile music player with headphones. This works quite well, but can detract from the social aspect of gallery attendance, as people feel more isolated and less likely to communicate with others for fear of interrupting when listening to music on headphones.

Working through the aesthetic and practical considerations about presenting music in galleries can be a useful comparative exercise for music students who would rarely otherwise be challenged to question the concert-stage mode of music presentation.

Conclusion

Writing music for film or video is the typical example of writing music for visual narrative. As we have seen, there are a number of other cross arts activities where music supports a visual experience for the audience, including theater, dance, and visual art projects. Computer-based music processes including composing, scoring, recording, performing, and sound design can be applied to these media-rich activities and are explored in detail in the production section of this book.

Making music that fits with other art forms requires a reflection on what it is that is unique about music and what it can contribute to these collaborations. This, in turn, strengthens our music practices away from such collaborations as we better understand the expressive power of music and how it can add emotional value to activities generally, well beyond staged artistic events. These lessons may be subtle and not highlighted on any curriculum document, but afford significant learning opportunities nonetheless. As we ask students to create music for projects where narrative is clearly articulated, as it is in film and theater in particular, they come to understand that music can tell a narrative too. The fact that students find these activities very engaging makes them doubly valuable.

There is also an important technical understanding to be gleaned by working with sound and image within the computer and that is to appreciate the abstractness of the digital representations. Given that the computer can represent not only music and sound but text, image, and moving picture, we start to glimpse the structural similarities between these modes of expression and to imagine the possibilities for future expression in what might be called a digital narrative.

Reflection questions

1. What activities, apart from film scoring, were suggested as providing a narrative visual experience for which music could be produced?
2. What is the difference between creative works with a linear and nonlinear narrative structure?
3. How does the role of music in creative art collaborations differ from its role in concert hall presentations?
4. What was Earl Hagen's advice to student film composers quoted in this chapter?
5. How can the constraints imposed by collaboration be constructive for the creative process?
6. Why is the flexibility of computer-based production tools useful for collaborative projects?
7. In film scoring, what is the process of spotting?
8. Merce Cunningham was famous in which creative arts discipline?
9. What is sonification?
10. What are some of the challenges of presenting music in visual arts exhibitions?

Teaching tips

1. Use movie trailers as short film scoring exercises for students.
2. Students can use a piano roll MIDI editor to draw a picture in notes, or write their name, then play it back to hear how it sounds.
3. Borrow student works from the Art Department as inspiration for compositional activities.
4. Examine the school timetable to find what other creative arts classes are running at the same time as your music classes and approach those teachers about doing collaborative projects.
5. Encourage small ensembles to rehearse pieces for performance with silent films as a backdrop.
6. Make use of sound editing software for students to create sound effects for the school's theater production.
7. Locate some videos of contemporary dance productions and have students do a simple analysis of how the music and dance integrate.
8. Student can log on to the vOICe sonification Web site to explore the possibilities of hearing images.
9. Create a "Pictures at an exhibition" DVD with contributions form each student who shoots a short video of a public art work and produces a musical score for it.
10. Conduct class debriefing discussion sessions following each creative project to help tease out the important lesson learned by the experience.

Suggested tasks

1. Watch the film *Blade Runner* by Ridley Scott to hear how Vangelis demonstrates that an electronic music score can be very effective.
2. Try syncing a movie to music. Download a movie trailer and import it into music sequencing package and record a simple sequence.
3. Explore composing to a strict time limit by writing a short melody and then modifying it to create versions that are exactly two seconds shorter and longer than the original.
4. Produce a sound collage as if for a theater production that sounds like an open-plan office.
5. Check out the Image Filter room in the *MetaSynth* program for a close integration of visual images and sound.

Chapter summary

Producing music need not only be for music-focused outcomes for the concert hall or for recorded media, but it can play a supportive or partnering role for visual experiences such as film and video, theater, dance, or visual art exhibitions. Combined with a visual stimulus, the narrative and emotive nature of music is emphasized and the complexity of the music need not be as great given that there are visual stimuli also contributing to the narrative. These attributes make music for visual narratives a good educational experience, they need not be complex and they draw attention to the emotional power of music and sound. There are a number of considerations when producing music for visual narratives, some of which are unique to this situation others that apply more broadly. These include working within the constraints imposed by the collaboration, coordinating and synchronizing music with other events, understanding that music intelligence is required for tasks such as music selection and sound design, meeting the challenges of presentation in different performance environments, and appreciating the similarity of structures across art forms and media and how these come together in digital space. Musical collaborations with other art forms can be supported by computational tools that can integrate multiple media in the one space and can provide a flexible production environment for creation and presentation.

Notes

1   Hagen, Earle, *Scoring for Films: A Complete Text* (Miami, FL: E D J Music, 1971), 74.
2   Aphex Twin (Richard James), *Windowlicker*. Sire records, 1999.
3   McIlwain, Peter, "A Survey of Software Designs from the Sonic Art Group," in *Proceedings of The Australasian Computer Music Conference*, edited by Paul Doornbusch, 81–90. Melbourne, 2002.
4   Iwai, Toshio, "Electroplankton." Musical Media Art work for the Nintendo DS game console. Nintendo, 2005.

Chapter 14

Rich media environments

There are two threads emerging in digital arts that are combining to create a new genre of creative practice. First is the digital convergence of a variety of media including still image, moving pictures, sound, and text. In the digital space, these forms become interoperable and practices previously considered hybrid or multi are now integrated. Second is the increasing capacity of real-time computation that allows more and more processes to be controlled by gestures. Emerging from these threads is the possibility of incorporating many media types into the one document or virtual environment. Creating rich media environments draws together and builds upon practices in creative use of sound, image, text, and video to create both live and document-based interactive experiences.

The most pervasive rich media environment is the Internet. World Wide Web content is increasing making use of a wide range of media elements, including music and sound. The World Wide Web is a network of documents that use rich media and interactivity to convey their message. There is also an interactive media culture around creative practice, either as live performance with technologies or interactive installations and software applications. In the 2000s, the sophistication and tight integration of media types in real-time computing systems has seen an accelerated activity in rich media environments, as evident in popular culture with the increasingly rich media Web sites, the use of 3D gaming technologies for educational purposes, and the increasing number of books and blogs about digital media culture (Figure 14.1). In this chapter we will pay particular attention to the use of digital audio in these contexts and how they can be applied to assist music education.

The skills and abilities that music students need to acquire to flourish in rich media environments include a strong understanding of sound design, an awareness of the structural connections between sound, image and textual expressions, and an intuition about the importance the performative nature interaction design. These skills brings together the traditional skills of the composer, performer, conductor, sound engineer, and producer, and overlay skills of the computer scientist, visual artist, graphic designer, filmmaker, and communications theorist. This skill list is not meant to seem overwhelming, but rather to provide a license for the music educator to draw on a wide range of knowledge, skills and activities to excite students about

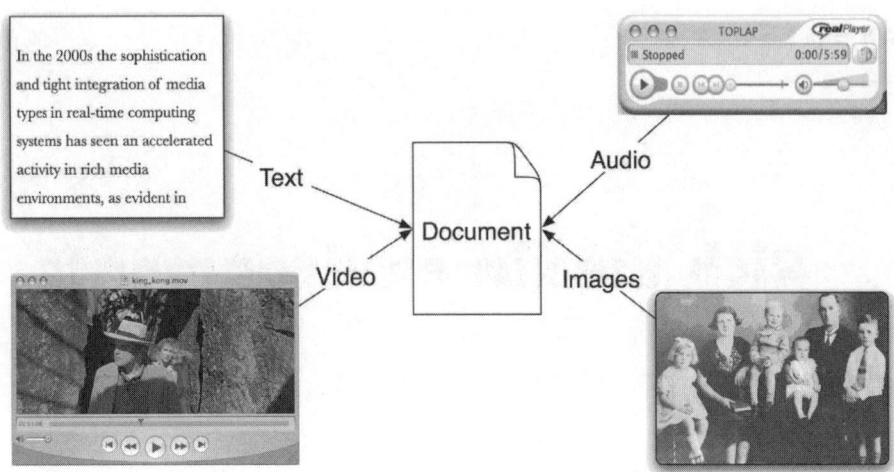

Figure 14.1 Rich media documents incorporate multiple types of media on one page.

the importance of music and sound in contributing to the growing domain of rich media environments. Therefore, we will examine music students as sound designers, look at the basics of digital audio technologies that make interactive media possible, and addresses the changes to curriculum that these imply.

Another area of education impact is assessment, where the use of interactive media for capturing and presenting student activities has resulted in changes to the delivery and evaluation of student work. Students are now able, not only to learn from viewing multimedia presentations, explore databases and communicate with others over the Internet, they can also demonstrate their understanding through rich media assessment items and interactive performances. These advances have resulted in changing the minds of teachers and curriculum developers about best learning and assessment practices. Moderating videoed performances done at local sites rather than holding central examinations is a case in point. The ability for students to present assignments as Web pages rather than as printed pages creates opportunities for integrated sound and video examples, while audio documentaries enable verbally orientated students and musical performers to express themselves fully. A student may produce an assignment based around one of her arrangements that included a score, a MIDI sequenced demo, a video of a live performance, and a written report describing the objectives, arrangement techniques and a critique of the outcome. In a multimedia environment these formats could be integrated digitally and links between them established.

The interactive layer that can connect rich media documents, as done in a Web site, allows the links and connections between ideas and activities to be concretely articulated. Students can demonstrate their understanding of the network of connections surrounding a topic or activity by creating multiple pages and hyperlinking between them and relevant external sites. This kind of activity is a rich media extension of footnoting or referencing in text publications, and reinforces similar educative values.

Digital media

Media arts productions on computer have been made possible by the melding of disparate media types into the one digital format, where all things are represented as numbers through the medium of the computer. Digital audio is commonly used in hard disk recording, sampling, compact discs (CDs), and Digital Versatile Disks or Digital Video Disks (DVDs). The advantages of digital audio include cost-effective storage, wide dynamic range, random access to any point in time, and the absence of degradation with repetition or copying. More details about digital audio are covered in chapter 8. The process of digitizing images is similar expect that the images have two dimensions, width and height, which increases the amount of data per frame significantly over audio. For example, a stereo audio recording has only two values for a frame, the left and right channel, while a small digital video, with a resolution of 320×240 pixels, results in 76,800 values for a frame. Fortunately for video the frame rates are low, typically around 30 per second, whereas for audio frame rate (sample rate) is typically 44,100 per second. Still, at these rates, one second of sound generates 88,200 digital values while the same duration of video generates 2,304,000 digital values. These numbers should make it clear why processing digital audio and, especially, digital video requires substantial computational power.

Music and visuals have been used in art forms for a long time. Opera, musicals, and film, are notable examples. Audio in interactive media functions in many ways similar to these established forms, but also in some unique ways. These functions apply to many interactive media outcomes and formats.

Audio functions for interactive media include:

- Communication of moods and emotions
- Narrative, particularly through dialogue
- Smoothing of abrupt visual/spatial transitions
- Spatialization and motion enhancement
- Reinforcing structural linkages
- User action feedback

Forms of interactive media

Interactive media come in a variety of forms each of which has its own uses and properties. In this section we will examine two of them, virtual reality simulations and rich media documents.

Virtual reality simulations

Much interactive digital work falls into the category of virtual reality, where imitative or imaginary spaces and objects are created. Many games, simulations, and even interface metaphors fall into this category. There are simple tools such as Kahootz that enable students to create their own 3D worlds, and others that more powerful but not so simple including Squeak-based project *Croquet* for creating networked

3D worlds. The Kahootz product has a strong teacher and student user community where environments and lesson ideas are exchanged. For senior student who want to get into high-quality virtual environments and games affordable game engines such as Torque are appropriate.

Audio provides significant experiential enhancement to such environments by adding sound effects and atmospheric music that adds realism to spaces, objects, actions and interactions. Elements of dimension and spatialization can be introduced through appropriate use of reverb, delay, and filtering. Such processes give rooms a size and objects a distance and density. The presence and movement of objects can be reinforced through sound localization and displacement. Elementary but effective techniques for localization can be achieved by panning sounds within a stereo image. Forward and backward movement in the stereo sound field can be achieved through changes in loudness and reverberation. Vertical displacement is more difficult and requires significant dynamic equalization. Moving sounds in three dimensions usually requires either a greater number of loudspeakers and control over each separately, as implemented with surround sound in cinemas. Independent movement of many sounds originally required significant signal processing power as achieved by the Convolvatron and Maxitron by Chrystal River Engineering or the Huron by Lake Technology to enable three-dimensional movement of multiple sound sources respectively. More recently, these capabilities have found their way into high-end music sequencing and hard disk recording systems.

Rich media documents

Interactive media documents, most commonly Web pages, often create their own interfaces with audio elements; buttons "click" when activated, voice-overs announce or direct proceedings, and spot effects of various sorts alert users to visual or nonvisual activities. Audible feedback enhances visual cues and can often be more effective than visual cues, so the quantity and selection of such sounds can significantly alter the usability of multimedia interfaces. Because the interpretation of a sound's meaning can vary between users, it is best to keep them subtle, brief, scarce (but not absent), consistent, and to always test them with the target audience. Educational resource materials have been one of the major areas in which interactive documents have been used, and tools for their creation are becoming increasingly common. Most Web site design products including Dreamweaver, Nvu, and GoLive can be used to create a rich media document as an educational resource.

Rich media document toolkits (e.g., TK3) enable the creation of rich media documents. There is also Adobe's Acrobat Professional for creating PDF documents that can contain media elements. The Sibelius music publishing program can be used to create rich media worksheets that include musical staves on which notes and music can be played back (Figure 14.2). The Macromedia Flash software is frequently used to create animated elements or whole documents. A good example of a rich media documents is the *Cesca Chair* online book that describes the processes of chair design. It is an award winning creation by Rick Pawla and Kevin Henry that contains text, animations, video and hyperlinks.[1] Audio data can be incorporated into Flash presentations in a range of formats. Flash supports the playing of audio loaded with the presentation, often used for navigational effects or for background

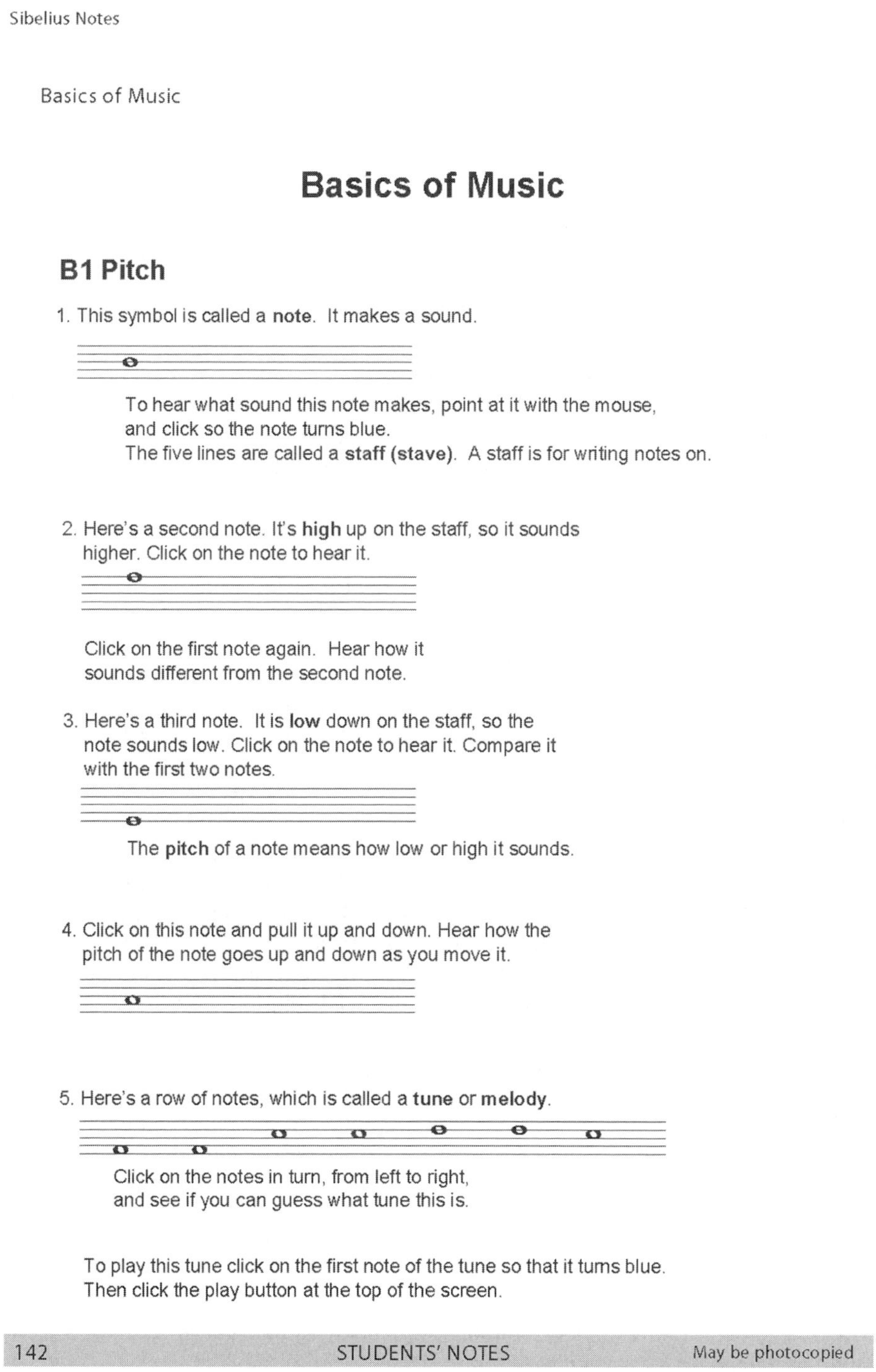

Sibelius Notes

Basics of Music

Basics of Music

B1 Pitch

1. This symbol is called a **note**. It makes a sound.

To hear what sound this note makes, point at it with the mouse, and click so the note turns blue.
The five lines are called a **staff (stave)**. A staff is for writing notes on.

2. Here's a second note. It's **high** up on the staff, so it sounds higher. Click on the note to hear it.

Click on the first note again. Hear how it sounds different from the second note.

3. Here's a third note. It is **low** down on the staff, so the note sounds low. Click on the note to hear it. Compare it with the first two notes.

The **pitch** of a note means how low or high it sounds.

4. Click on this note and pull it up and down. Hear how the pitch of the note goes up and down as you move it.

5. Here's a row of notes, which is called a **tune** or **melody**.

Click on the notes in turn, from left to right, and see if you can guess what tune this is.

To play this tune click on the first note of the tune so that it turns blue.
Then click the play button at the top of the screen.

142 STUDENTS' NOTES May be photocopied

Figure 14.2 Sibelius Notes uses the ability to embed scores that can be played to bring worksheets to life.

music where looped playback is common. It also supports the streaming of longer audio files. Some interesting use of Flash for games and music toys can be found at the Australian Broadcasting Corporation's Rollercoaster site.[2]

Sources of audio content

Sound designers will normally build up a library of sounds and music that they can call on for projects. For those not so motivated, the sounds built into synthesizers or sound effects CDs can be purchased. In any case, one of the first steps to developing audio content, after deciding what it will be, is the collector or creation of appropriate sound elements.

Sampled sounds and musical excerpts can be quite large if used on the Web. Media products can use MIDI files for music where performance information is stored in a relatively small file and played back using sounds from a sound card or software synthesizer. The major advantages of this method are that the Standard MIDI File format is widely supported and that only a small file size is required for a reasonable audio quality from a synthesizer or sound card. The disadvantage of MIDI files is that only a set, and limited, range of sounds can be used. Most lower-cost MIDI equipment conforms to the General MIDI sound specification that includes a list of instruments and sounds focused on replicating orchestral and rock instruments.

Algorithmic composition packages of varying sophistication provide great potential for use in multimedia packages. An algorithmic composing program uses a formula or procedure to create music. Such procedures can vary from tightly defined pop music styles, as used in programs such as the popular Band-In-A-Box, to open-ended compositional environments, such as Max/MSP, AudioMulch, Algorithmic Composer, jMusic, Impromptu, Chuck, or Pure Data. The benefit of algorithmic systems over MIDI sequences is that variety can be introduced each time the music is played because it is being re-created each time. Also, the algorithm description of music can be even smaller than a MIDI file because it describes the musical structure rather than the note-by-note surface level. The down side is that much more knowledge is required to implement and algorithmic music solution, so most students will probably stick with audio or MIDI solutions.

Since most rich media documents are viewed, or read, on personal computers, the major enabling technology for digital audio has been the increased out-of-the-box audio capability on those computers. This includes the standard inclusion of CD/DVD drive and good stereo sound and perhaps 5.1 surround sound capability. More sophisticated audio hardware is always available, at a price, in the form of external audio hardware.

Digital audio editing software is commonly available, allowing recording, and manipulation of various kinds. The number, speed, and quality of the manipulations generally determine software pricing. Manipulations such as cutting, pasting, merging, volume adjustment, and panning are standard. The ability to adding echoes and reverb, playing backwards, normalizing, equalization, and gating are not uncommon. See chapter 8 for a more in depth overview of this area.

Audio file formats differ between platforms and software packages. The necessity to transfer between these is widely recognized and most audio software allows importing and exporting of the major formats. At present the MP3, AIFF, and WAV formats are quite widely utilized on the Internet for audio files played in browsers, and streaming formats such as RealAudio (RAM), Windows Media Audio (WMA), and QuickTime are common for longer files or Internet radio transmissions. For music downloads to portable media players MP3, WMA, or AAC (M4A) formats are most common, and are also used for download or mms messaging to mobile phones along with the smaller and lower quality AMR or MIDI file formats. See chapter 12 for a more detailed overview of audio file formats or visit the audio pages of FileInfo. net.[3]

The musical challenge of interactivity

Interactive systems move control away from the system toward the user. In music this is similar to moving control of the orchestra away from the conductor and to the audience. In principle it should be fine, in practice it can be treacherous. The dominance of vision in human perception means that users pay more heed to graphical cues than sound cues. Another feature of this perceptual difference between vision and sound is that visual systems cope with cutting from one scene to another in, literally, the blink of an eye, while the auditory system maintains temporal and linear continuity even when vision is refocused. Audio refocusing is more of a perceptual than physical action. This has implications for virtual rich media environments in which digital structure need not be linear, therefore music's (and dialogue's) linear nature needs to be allowed for in the structure of interactive multimedia productions. The most common problem is the awkward interruption of musical phases by a user's navigational choices. This situation can be controlled by disallowing navigation at times, or by programming the elegant handling of sound with amplitude fades, or maintaining music playback during visual changes.

Another aesthetic challenge of nonlinearity is that the structure of a work may not be predictable, that is, users may access pages within the document in any order or navigate the virtual world in any direction. This requires that the composer/sound designer create a musical pallet of sounds that can follow each other in a variety of combinations. Musically this has implications for key, modality, tempi, timbre, and mood of the musical sections or sound library. The nonlinearity can provide opportunities as well. Sections of a multimedia document may be visited in an unpredictable order, and some pages can be repeatedly revisited. The aleatoric selection of musical segments can provide interest and stimulation to the sound design.

Current multimedia authoring packages allow little "elegant" control of sound. As algorithmic music compositional techniques become more integrated into multimedia environments they will allow the sound designer to more easily handle the unpredictable structural possibilities and to add variety to an otherwise static or deterministic environment. From a more technical point of view, multimedia development systems would better handle multiple media demands, such as sound continuing while vision changes interactively, if they supported parallel processing of these media. As such features become more common in software systems the sound designer's job will require much less compromise.

Skills of the sound designer

Sound designing for rich media products can involve several tasks; dialogue recording and editing, sound effects, music composing, atmosphere sounds, audio mixing, multimedia authoring, and computer programming. In most cases, one person has to do most of these tasks, in other cases a programmer takes care of technical tasks and the sound designer acts mainly as artists, providing both music and sound effects as audio or MIDI files.

Many multimedia projects are created by teams, and so interpersonal teaming skills are required beyond those normally associated with a solitary composer, but these ensemble skills are quite well developed in musicians through group music activities. It is increasingly evident that media artists will be required to work across graphics, video, sound, and programming tasks, particularly in smaller projects, but for larger productions a specialized sound designer will always be necessary. On the other hand, as media production standards continue to rise, specialization will increase as it has done in the computer game industry as games become big-budget productions heading toward those used for Hollywood movies, so there is likely to be an increasing need for musicians highly skilled in rich media sound design and production.

Rich media curriculum documents

Rich media document formats require changes in the curriculum in terms of skill development for authorship, criteria for critical evaluation of new media forms, and adequate infrastructure for creation, storage, assessment, and feedback. Questions for educators implementing such curriculums include: Do the students and teachers working in media formats have flexible and sufficient computer resources to create and assess such work? Are timelines varied to reflect changes in development and production from text or performance equivalents? Are the curriculum objectives able to be met by, or redefined to account for, such changes in media? How best are the artificial barriers between instrumental and classroom music education dissolved to enable a focusing on integrated music education that embraces music production outcomes?

Importantly, to enable significant curriculum development, the music curriculum as a text document needs to develop into a rich media document form. One writer who recognizes this effect is Steve Dillon who, in discussing music education and multiple logics, notes that "Print and its linear processes no longer dominate thought and communication and we now combine the word with images and sound in multi media communication which represents actual or imaginary experiences."[4] We have seen how changing technologies directly influences the understandings of students, but we need to recognize the same is true for educators. We know as musicians that different media and their associated properties, conventions and metaphors determine what can be expressed with them, so we need to accept that the curriculum "document" needs to expand its communicative power by becoming a rich media document. Communicating our artistic curriculum intent only through text involves unnecessary abstraction and disembodiment, as William Barrett noted in the mid-1980s;

Statements may be the instruments of enlightenment, but not the only ones. As soon as we are freed from the notion of the single proposition as the ultimate locus of truth, which [sic] each proposition carrying its truth on its back like a rider on a saddle, we are also freed toward understanding other modes through which truth may be realized. In particular, we might begin at last to ask seriously in what way truth may be embodied in works of art.[5]

Introduction of rich media curriculum expressions is evident where CD-ROMs of exemplar materials are being prepared as support material for music syllabuses. The changes that rich media curriculum development will produce are impossible to predict, but we can be confident that the possibilities are more likely to be sympathetic with musical understanding if curriculum documents includes sound.

Useful links

Information about many of the applications mentioned in this chapter can be found at the Web addresses below. These are good starting points for the developing rich media environments.

Document creation tools

Acrobat Professional (PDF document creator/editor)
      http://www.adobe.com/
Dreamweaver (Web site design tool)
      http://www.macromedia.com/
GoLive (Web site design tool)
      http://www.adobe.com/products/golive/main.html
Nvu (a complete Web authoring toolkit)
      http://www.nvu.com/
TK3 (toolkit for rich media documents)
      http://www.nightkitchen.com/

Interactive systems

Croquet (networkable 3D world building toolkit)
      http://www.opencroquet.org/
Kahootz (a simple 3D world builder)
      http://www.kahootz.com.au/
Squeak (a digital media toolkit for creating environments)
      http://www.squeakland.org/

Media creation tools

Algorithmic Composer (a MIDI-based graphical music environment)
      http://www.smartcontroller.com.au/AlgorithmicComposer/algorithmicComposer.html

AudioMulch (interactive music and sound environment)
     http://www.audiomulch.com
jMusic (Java-based algorithmic music library)
     http://jmusic.ci.qut.edu.au
Pd (graphical music programming language)
     http://www-crca.ucsd.edu/~msp/Pd_documentation/

Examples

Cesca Chair (interactive industrial design education)
     http://interactive.colum.edu/students/rpawela/productDesign/cescaChair/
     CescaChair.html

Conclusion

As the nature of nonlinear digital media presentations makes new demands on the linear nature of music and sound, sensitive implementation of rich media environments for students to work with and work in will create new opportunities and lead to richer understanding in a shorter time. Sound design, the core skill for preparing audio elements of rich media environments, is a complex mix of musical, technical and creative abilities, and often requires a willingness to work as part of a design and production team.

Both students and teachers can benefit from working with rich media documents. Teachers can express ideas effectively to students through rich media environments, but more importantly, reshape their curriculum the encourage the use of rich media documents. Students can use rich media environments to express themselves using sound, diagrams, video, text and animations in a way that suits their abilities and can help to develop their communication skills. At the very least, any document that can include sound has a prima facie case for success in music education.

Reflection questions

1. What are the two trends suggested as leading toward the expanded availability of rich media environments?
2. What is meant by the term "rich media"?
3. Name some of the rich media environments that are discussed in the chapter.
4. Why might rich media documents be useful for music education?
5. What changes to curriculums are suggested to take advantage of rich media environments?
6. How might rich media documents be useful for assessment?
7. What are some of the activities undertaken by a sound designer for rich media environments?
8. Why is the nonlinear capacity of digital an issue for music and sound?

9. What are the circumstances that mean both skill generality and specialization needs exist for musicians working in the production of rich media environments?
10. Why are collaborative skills likely to be required by a sound designer?

Teaching tips

1. Rich media documents can be made in most word processors that allow imbedded audio and image files; start by adding audio annotation to text documents.
2. Creating Web documents is much easier with an editor such as Nvu or Dreamweaver; make sure there is one on the computer in the music department.
3. Use a whiteboard to map out the connections between all media that has been collected on a project before making a rich media environment from it.
4. Have students create a rich media profile of their own music making, complete with examples of their music and photos of them producing music.
5. There can be technical hurdles in using digital media software. Make sure that students have a few practice tasks before they are to do one for assessment.
6. Using frames in a Web site can help keep music persistent while text and image data changes. Put the audio file for playback in a persistent frame that does not update.
7. Have music students collaborate with media students on a rich media environment to allow the music students to spend most time of sound design, rather than page layout details.
8. Set a project where students create a document about an imaginary topic that challenges them to invent a sound world rather than simply record it.
9. Teaching is a good way of learning. Have students design a Web site that is a tutorial for younger students on a topic you want them to learn about.
10. To encourage student to look for connections between information set a requirement that a rich media documentation project should have a minimum of five links per page.

Suggested tasks

1. Visit the Web sites of some musical artists to see how they present themselves in a rich media way.
2. Download a demo of Kahootz and learn to build a simple 3D world.
3. Look over a music curriculum document and identify how it could be enhanced by the addition of musical examples and images.

> 4. Advertisers are profession communicators, so look closely at how they use multiple media in TV ads and pick up some tricks for your own teaching materials.
> 5. Look at some of the projects at the Squeak Web site for some inspiration about how to use digital media in education.

Chapter summary

The bringing together of a variety of media including sounds, still images, moving pictures, and text into a rich media environment or document presents sound design challenges and opportunities for musicians and educators. The opportunity is the ability to be able to express ideas about sound as sound within the legitimate space of a "document" rather than as an appendix or add-on extra. The challenge is to acquire the skills with which to create and edit rich media documents, from Web pages through DVDs to 3D virtual worlds. Music and sound design for multimedia brings together the traditional skills of the composer, performer, conductor, sound engineer and producer. The basics required for acquiring these sound design skills include understanding the digital audio technologies that make rich media documents possible and understanding the nonlinear nature of digital environments and how this impacts on the linear nature of music and sound.

Notes

1   Pawela, Rick, and Kevin Henry. 2005. *Cesa Chair*, http://interactive.colum. edu/students/rpawela/productDesign/cescaChair/CescaChair.html (accessed November 2005).
2   ABC Rollercoaster — Interactive games and music toys, http://www.abc. net.au/rollercoaster/games/.
3   FileInfo is a site describing computer file formats, http://www.fileinfo. net/filetypes/audio.
4   Dillon, Steve. "The Student as Maker: An Examination of Making in Music Education and the Implications for Contemporary Curriculum Development" (Master of Education thesis, La Trobe University, 1995), 21.
5   Barrett, William, *The Illusion of Technique: A Search for Meaning in a Technological Civilization* (New York: Anchor Press, 1978), 143.

Chapter 15

Music distribution in the age of the Internet

The impact of the Internet on music distribution is more significant than any technological change in the music industry since the advent of music recording in the late nineteenth century. The Internet was designed to allow people to communicate data to one another and this is precisely what occurs with file transfer systems. The Internet has been open to commercial interest sine the mid-1990s but the widespread availability of broadband Internet connections and the efficient compression of audio files by MP3 and similar codecs has made the downloading of files as large as audio files, a viable activity for a large number of people. The distribution of musical scores in electronic form is also significant but, because of the much smaller market, is less often in the public consciousness. If we follow this trajectory, then video downloads or streaming services such as YouTube, which involve even larger file sizes may, in the future, challenge broadcast TV in the same way that streamed music is an alternative to terrestrial radio and music downloads have challenged retail CD sales. Another factor in music distribution has been the ability for people to listen to music more conveniently when they are mobile. The popularity of mobile music was first demonstrated by portable radios and the popularity of radios and music players in cars. It was reinforced again by the success of Sony's Walkman portable cassette players and the portable CD players that replaced them, and has been evident in the early part of the twenty-first century in the popularity of digital music players such as Apple's iPod.

While broadcasting is a fast and efficient method of getting music to people at any time, and the sales of physical media like CDs enables people to choose the music they want to listen to and when they listen to it. The Internet, as a music distribution medium, combines both these attributes. The challenge for our societies is to find a way that this can be harnessed to create fair and sustainable ways of communicating musically with each other.

The distribution of recorded music is relevant to music education for a number of reasons. First, in the course of music education access to recorded musical examples and score repertoire is critical. Music educators and students are significant consumers of recorded music. Second, many music students will go on to be professional producers of music and having a solid understanding of the operations of and issues concerning the distribution of music will be a prerequisite to a successful career. Third, it is useful for the outputs of music education activities to be shared with parents and others in the education community and the Internet provides an effective vehicle for archiving and showcasing the music, performances, and other work of students.

Playing music on the Internet

In order to listen to music from the Internet, one needs: an active Internet connection and computer; an Internet browser such as Internet Explorer, FireFox, or Safari; music playback software such as Flash, Windows Media Player, QuickTime, or RealPlayer; and some amplified speakers attached or built in to the computer (or headphones). To hear some music go to a free music download site, such as Elektrobar, which links to electronic music artists who are interested in promoting their music, and follow the links to download or stream the music. With the music players installed correctly, music should playback inside the browser (or in a popup window that appears) or there may be an option to download the entire music file to the hard drive then opening it in a music player for playback locally.

There are a few technical differences between modes of playing music from the Internet. The first distinction is between downloading and streaming. When downloading a music track, the whole file is copied to your computer. It may be possible to start playback before the whole track arrives, or it may be necessary to wait for the track to completely download. Streaming music is different in that only a small section of the music is downloaded at the time. As one section is playing the next section downloads. When a section is finished playing it is discarded. The second distinction is whether the music data is in RAM (memory) or on your hard disk drive. When listening to music played from a browser the data is generally loaded into the computers memory for playback. The implication is that when you close the browser window or turn off your computer memory is cleared and the music data is lost. Downloading music files transfers the data to a file on your hard disk and they will remain there until you deliberately erase them, even after the computer is turned off.

Stakeholders and issues

Having discussed the basics of playing music, we can take some time to examine the people involved in the production and distribution of music on the Internet. There are a number of perspectives about music distribution on the Internet and it is important to understand the preferences and motivation of each stakeholder..

Artists are interested in creating great music, the promotion and distribution of their work to an audience, and being able to generate a fair living for their efforts. Publishers and record companies are concerned with promoting the works they represent and to monitor the usage of the music they publish such that it is being used legally. Internet providers, and telecommunications providers generally, are concerned with increasing the amount of data traffic on their network and therefore encourage increased music distribution over their networks. Retailers wish to be able to aggregate and distribute music as widely as possible, for a profit, and to provide the easiest access to their music content for the audience. Broadcasters and DJs wish to be able to select and use music for their shows with as few financial, legal, and technical hurdles as possible. Audiences would like to locate music they like, or are likely to appreciate, and to listen to it at their convenience in as high a quality as possible at the lowest cost.

The reoccurring themes across these different perspectives include the selecting and collecting (aggregating) collections of music, enabling and controlling access to these collections, and the costs of distribution or access. These themes are not unique to Internet distribution of music, they have been debated with regard to live music performances, radio and television broadcasting, and CD sales. Even the solutions are not new in kind, they tend to come down to legal rights of control over the music (copyright and so on), and technical gate keeping control over access (media formats, distribution channels, and so on).

Ownership

The ownership of musical material has a number of layers primarily arising from copyright laws, which are covered by International treaty but also vary slightly between jurisdictions. Copyright can cover any material version of a work, such as a score or sound recording. There rights over a work reside in those that produce the work. In music this generally means that composers hold the rights over the song or other composition, so long as it is written down or notated, and these are often referred to as the publishing rights. This publishing ownership applies regardless of who performs or records the composition. Those who produce a recorded work hold rights over that version of the composition. The people who own the recording (usually those who paid for its production, e.g., a record company) and the musicians performing on the recording have rights in the produced work referred to as mechanical (tape, audio, file, CD, etc.) and performance rights. There can also be rights relating to the use of music with other media, such as film, which are referred to as synchronization rights.

Approval from rights holders needs to be obtained for legal public use of musical material. For example, the use of existing music as a soundtrack for a film requires authorization of the holder of the synchronization rights. When an artist records a song for commercial release, the authorization of the composer is required. When sections of a recording are sampled and used in a subsequent work, authorization from the mechanical rights holder of the sampled recording is required.

There can be exceptions to the use of copyright material for fair use in educational activities, but these are limited and may not extend to public presentation, so it is important to take care when displaying student work on public Internet sites, for example, that copyright is not being breached. The simplest way to avoid copyright entanglements is to have students do productions of their own compositions.

Seeking permission from the owners of copyrighted music to use it in music educational activities can be an awkward and time consuming process. One alternative is to look for music that is covered by one of the creative commons licenses where authorisation for sharing or noncommerical use is provided. Creative Commons licences are used by many artists, and the creative commons Web site (or Google advanced search) allows Internet searching to locate and download music,

Figure 15.1   ccMixter, a site with music available for remixing under creative commons licenses.

or other creative content, that is availible under the Creative Commons licenses (Figure 15.1). Use of music distributed under creative commons licenses requires attribution that is acknowledgement of the orginal author.

The Creative Commons licenses allow the author of a work to permit no commerical use of his material or for his work to be used in derivitive works, that is, remixed or used in a collage with other material. Because these permissions are explicit in the Ceative Commons licenses, it is not necessary to contact the author to check how you can use their work. It is also possible for students to distribute their work on the Internet under such a license; this will allow them to decide how they want their work used by others who might download it.

Access

While there are legal protections covering the use of music material, many artists and record companies attempt to use technical measures to restrict illegal use of their music. This has become a particularly hot topic in the digital age where exact copies of a digital audio file can be made quite easily. With previous media, such as vinyl records and cassette tapes, copies of the material were imperfect and repeated copying of copies resulted in a significant degradation of sound quality. This meant that original recordings were more highly valued than copies, but in the digital age this distinction is less true. One way of mimicking this effect of quality differential on value is for artists to allow lossy compressed versions of their music, such as low bit-rate MP3 files, for download to stimulate interest in the full fidelity original versions, such as CDs.

Another frequently used method of using limited access to create interest, is to have short segments, or teasers, of works available for download. Most of the online music stores use this strategy. Streaming of music can provide some protection from copying from the average computer user. When music is streamed, only a small section of the music is maintained by the local computer at a time and so, like radio, once played the music data has disappeared and is not available to be copied. Like radio, however, it is possible to record the streamed audio output as it plays. To protect complete files that are downloaded, many online music distributors alter the files to restrict some activities. This process is called digital rights management (DRM). These alterations to the files should not affect the audio quality of the music but will impose other restrictions, such as setting a limit on the number of times a file can be copied or set an expiry date after which the file will not play. Less invasive DRM processes include the addition of a "watermark," an inaudible change to the file that can be read by appropriate software. If a watermarked file is copied, the mark is copied with it, therefore it can be possible to trace copied files back to their origin if a register of watermarks is maintained. Most online music distributors include DMR technologies in their files and most record companies require that their material be protected by DMR technologies. As with any digital encryption process, the "arms race" between the developers of DRM techniques and computer hackers who break the encryption is ongoing. In most countries it is illegal to circumvent such encryption, but for the purposes of fair use there have been some exceptions to this situation.

For the most part DRM technologies need not effect the educational use of music distributed online. It certainly need not be a concern for the posting of student work online, and for music purchased online the only implication may be that a song with DMR may not be copied onto many computers, such as a school computer lab, but doing so may be illegal use in any case in some countries.

Distributing music over the Internet

Any of the methods used for commercial distribution of music using the Internet can be used by educators to distribute student work. In this section we will canvas a number of approaches to distributing music over the Internet.

Physical distribution

While most of the attention on Internet music distribution focuses on file downloads, there is a substantial use of the Internet to support the physical delivery of CDs and DVDs. Online ordering of physical goods from books to groceries has been an expanding market since the 1990s with e-commerce sites such as CDnow, Amazon, and eBay growing into very large businesses over that time. These stores usually allow you to listen to excerpts of the music, purchase by typing in credit card details, and the CD or DVD is delivered to your door a few days later. The convenience of being able to audition CDs and see images of the cover art online makes online sales a convenient method of purchase for many. However, many other people would still rather have the physical copy of the music, even if they intend to make a copy for their MP3 player for the majority of listening.

There are a number of business models for the online sales of CDs. There are music retailers who have both a physical store and a parallel online catalogue. This provides choice for their local customers and extends their customer base beyond the local geographic community. Others are online only stores who have the advantage of reduced costs of a retail store, but still need to warehouse inventory. Some distributors are using the global reach of Internet distribution to provide niche markets that may not be viable in a single geographic location. The specialty of the store may focus on a musical genre, media type, or distribution model. For example, Classic CD Exchange deals with second-hand classical music CDs, the Electronic Music Foundation (EMF) specialize in experimental electronic and computer music, EMusic focus on independent record labels, and CD Baby provide distribution for independent artists that provides a larger return for the musicians without major record company mediation.

The physical distribution of music on CD is thriving in the age of the Internet, in the early years of the twenty-first century physical distribution accounts for the vast majority of music sales, however, distribution through file download has been accelerating quickly.

File distribution

The digital delivery of music is the revolutionary element of Internet music distribution. The viability of this was demonstrated through the success of music file sharing networks, notably Napster, where users shared music files they had converted from CD (ripped). A number of technologies combined to make file sharing popular. First, there was increased access to the Internet starting with students using university networks and then expanding to broadband Internet connections in the home. Second, the use of the MP3 file compression format reduced the file size by a ratio of about ten to one. Third, music files contained one song rather than a whole album. These three things combined to make the digital transfer of music files easy. Fourth, the use of peer-to-peer technologies enabled the aggregation of large databases of music that could be accessed by a broad range of people to locate the music they wanted in one location. The down side of Napster and other early file sharing systems was that such sharing of files was illegal, and in fear of reduced revenue artists and record companies rallied to close down illegal services.

Peer to peer systems are an elegant and efficient method of file sharing over the Internet. The sharing itself is not illegal if the material being shared is in the public domain or licensed to allow such sharing. Even after the closure of Naspter and some other high profile music file sharing systems, peer to peer software continues to be popular using software such as Gnutella and Limewire. Unfortunately for educationalists such systems do not discriminate in relation to content and illegal and pornographic material is difficult to avoid on these services.

Rather than throw the baby out with the bath water in closing down illegal file sharing, some companies tried to turn the popular but illegal activity of file sharing into a popular and legal one. There were two trends in this direction. The first was to have sites where the music available for download was supplied and authorized by artists themselves. Sites such as MP3.com started in this way where much of the

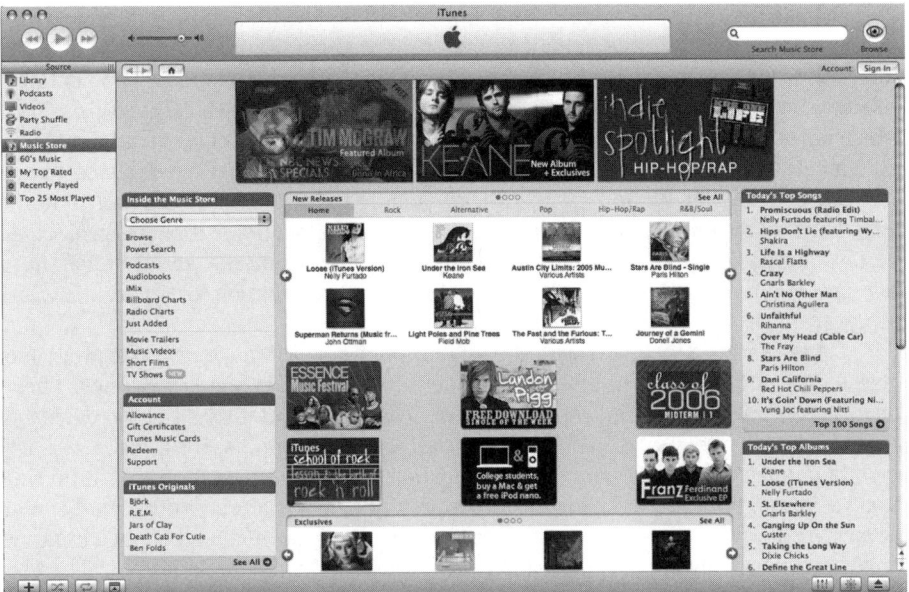

Figure 15.2   The iTunes music store.

music was available for free, some available by donation, and some popular tunes by payment. This worked fine but did not include the music people wanted the most, the popular and famous artists whose material was controlled by the major record companies. Apple Computer brokered a solution to this with their iTunes store making music from the major record companies (and others) legally available as a pay-by-song download. Apple used a DRM technology, FairPlay, to limit the use of encoded files on unauthorized computers. They also developed a simple integration of their iTunes download store with their portable music player, the iPod (Figure 15.2). The combination of an attractive and convenient mobile music player and affordable and easy access to popular musical material proved to be a successful combination than many other organizations emulated.

The use of audio file downloads for playing on the iPod and other portable music players was not restricted to music. A growing trend to distribute audio recordings of talk shows, interviews, museum guides, radio dramas, and more, emerged to take advantage of this music downloading infrastructure. It is called Podcasting; the name derives from a combination of iPod and broadcasting. Podcasts are often produced as a series that can be subscribed to, but also include one-off productions (i.e., independent audio guides to a museum or art gallery). Many traditional broadcast companies began to include Podcasts of their content for download as a way of time shifting access to their material. Podcasts became so popular that Apple included a directory of them in its iTunes music store. As music players began to take on video playback capabilities, originally to show music video clips, animations, and TV shows, video Podcasts became popular too. The generation of a Podcast requires the same sound editing skills as the making of a radio play or a radiophonic soundscape.

Music file transfer process need not only to be used for completed music productions. As a collaborative compositional tool, the sending and receiving of audio files opens up new opportunities for music making. Several composers can collaborate on a work by sending drafts of the work or elements of it to each other via e-mail. Musicians can trade sounds and musical ideas as audio, MIDI or application files. In an educational setting this allows students who are not normally collocated to collaborate on projects. It allows students or teachers to work on projects both at home and at school by simply transferring the files between locations. It allows projects to be distributed amongst a class for work on sections of elements, and then for these to come together as the pieces are lodged in a central location for structuring and mixing.

Another area in which digital distribution of music was been a run away success in the early years of the twenty-first century is mobile phone ring tones. These have a reputation for being aesthetically unpleasant and offensive, but the design of appropriate ring tones can also be imaginative and ingenious. Ring tones in early mobile phones followed a particular file format and were monophonic with no timbral variation, but most phones now are able to play polyphonic synthesized tracks or any MP3 or Wav file as a ring tone. Interestingly, prices of a ten-second ring tone have been routinely twice that of a four-minute song download on iTunes! The creation of a ring tone audio file is an interesting and manageable creative musical task for students, and they can use it in their phone when complete.

Internet radio

A Webcast is similar to a radio or TV broadcast but for distribution over the Internet. An Internet radio is an audio-only Webcast. A Webcast is initiated by a server application on a computer that can send out multiple streams of the content; usually an audio file or video file. A client application on another computer can connect to the server and "listen" to one of the streams. Webcasts can stream content at a specified time, like a normal radio station, or they can start a stream on demand when a user connects. According to Wikipedia, the amount of Internet traffic devoted to Webcasts has double each year since 1995.[1] Many of the online music stores that require a subscription include access to up to one hundred Internet radio stations as part of the subscription service. Most commercial terrestrial radio stations also have a parallel Internet broadcast or allow streaming of radio programs on demand.

Setting up a student Internet radio station can be even more successful than the many terrestrial stations, because the content need not be real time and so a repertoire of Internet radio shows can be accumulated over time and thus produced at a more relaxed pace that fits more easily within the curriculum. Internet radio stations do not need a license, as do terrestrial stations, but you do need to make sure that you have cleared the rights to broadcast all the material that will be on the radio. Using only student content is the simplest method of staying legal. Setting up an Internet radio server is not too difficult but will require the assistance of a network provider or institution IT support staff. Programs and music prepared for an Internet radio show can also be made available for downloading as Podcasts.

Music commentary on the Internet

It is not only the music itself that has been influenced by the Internet but also talk about music. Internet sites devoted to music are everywhere, and include a wide range of interests and intended audiences. Some are music news sites about new music releases or gossip about artists, some are fan sites devoted to particular musicians, others focus on music equipment from iPods to violins, some are designed to be informative and focus on a particular topic such as Classical operas or DJ technique and some, like the Coverpop site, are for music shoppers.

Traditionally, Web sites have been static pages that were designed once and remained the same for some time. This does not suite the dynamic nature of information in the Internet age and is best used for sites that need very little updating over time, for example, information sites about historical events or topics. The most popular form of dynamic Internet commentary is the Web log (blog). A blog contains a list of posts, or entries, with the newest post at the top of the list. In many ways a blog is simply a public online journal or diary in which thoughts can be written as often or as infrequently as desired. In a blog, a certain number of posts are displayed on the Web page and earlier ones are archived. A blog is usually searchable and posts are often arranged by topic so that particular categories of information can be selected. Adding a post to a blog involves logging into a Web-based editor where the text for the entry is typed and associated images or other media are added. Blogs are quite easy to use and sites, such as Blogger, allow anyone to set up a blog. Alternately, many blogging software systems are available for installation on a server that can be customized to look and operate as you would like. Blogs can be useful for music education as part of a portfolio or journal that the student keeps about their work. Blogs set up on a school server need not be public and can be password protected to restrict access.

A wiki is another form of dynamic Web site creation. A wiki is like an online shared document that one or more people can read or edit. A blog is useful for information sources like news stories where more recent stories are most important, or for personal diaries where information is stored chronologically. Wikis are useful for information that needs to be updated or elaborated upon over time. Many open source software user manuals are wikis, thereby allowing anyone in the software community to add, fix, or elaborate on aspects of the manual. With many people working on it adding their own contributions the whole document grows quickly and robustly. The most well-known wiki site is Wikipedia, an online encyclopedia that can be viewed and edited by anyone. Despite looking like a recipe for chaos, the information in Wikipedia is quite robust given that any incorrect information can be easily corrected, so time since an entry has been edited is some indication of its correctness (or obscurity).

Examples of music-related wikis include the wiki of the Choral Public Domain Library, which contains information and scores for thousands of vocal works. The Sequenza is a wiki encyclopedia of new music that focuses on composers, genres and repertoire from the twentieth and twenty-first centuries. The Young Composers wiki is a site where students can set up a Web page for themselves or discuss issues with other young composers in online forums.

Because many dynamic Web sites, including blogs and wikis, are regularly updated, it is useful to know when there are new entries to look at and to see a summary of them to decide whether of not to visit the site. A service that does this is RSS, Really Simple Syndication. An RSS application can subscribe to a Web site that provides an RSS feed. The RSS application will check the site to see if there is new content and show the title and summary of that new content. This saves the user manually surfing to each site to check for articles they have not read. The RSS feeds send information in a text format called XML (eXtensible Markup Language) and so sometimes the XML symbol is used instead of RSS to indicate a subscribable Web site. RSS readers such as NetNewsWire or SharpReader are widely available, and some Web browsers incorporate RSS aggregation features. Subscribing to RSS feeds from Web sites can save considerable time unnecessarily revisiting these sites if there is no new information to read. Adding an RSS service to a Web site can be particularly useful when it is updated infrequently, such as a music band Web site, and you want to allow readers to be notified of new updates and information, such as new concert dates and so on.

Promoting music on the Internet

The Internet offers good opportunities for the promotion of music, whether it be as part of promoting the school or college music program or for individual students and their music. We will discuss a number of issues related to preparing to promote music on the Internet in this section including the preparation of materials for promotion and sales, establishing a Web presence, and communicating with the press and public.

Getting ready to promote music on the Internet starts with getting all the materials together and ready to go. First, of course, is writing and producing the music tracks. For downloading the files there will need to be MP3 version of the music available. These should be of reasonable quality, at least 160 kbps data rate. It is wise to have short demos of each song available as lower quality MP3 files, these may even be mono and the segments should be between 30 to 60 seconds in length. When preparing the MP3 files make sure the ID tags are filled in with the name of Artist, song title, e-mail contact and possibly Web site address so that the artist can be contacted by interested people. It is useful to have some text materials that describe the music and the artist. These should include the style or genre of the music, its highlight features, and a story about the songs and the artists' background. This text can be used for general public information and for press releases. Photographs of the artist and album cover artwork will be required, and it may be useful to have a combines the text and images into a PDF promotional document.

A major step for Internet promotions is having a Web presence, so it will be necessary to establish a Web site for the artist. There are a number of Web hosting sites such as Überlabel, AudioStreet, ArtistLaunch, or DMusic that will set up a site and handle sales of music for a percentage of sales and varying types of fees. At MySpace music an artist or band can have a free site that includes a music player that allows people to listen to examples of their music. It may also be an option to set up an independent Web site. This will require getting some Web space with an Internet Service provider (ISP) and designing a Web site. It is important to make the site look appropriate for the style of music being promoted (Figure 15.3). The site will appear more professional if a domain name that relates to the artist name

Figure 15.3   The front page of ArtistLaunch.com, a music promotion service.

is obtained, and this domain can be delegated to point to the Web site. To sell music at the Web site an e-commerce facility will need to be established. Web hosting services may provide this, otherwise there are options provided by e-commerce providers such as Esellerate, PayPal; many banks will also take care of processing credit card transactions.

Having made music available and provided information about it, another consideration is communicating with people about your music. Make sure that contact details including an e-mail address is available for contacts from the press, record companies, live performance bookings, CD customers and so on. Make sure that a list of current and future performance and other appearances and events are regularly updated. Provide the opportunity for people to give feedback about the music and the site, and to sign up to an e-mail list for notifications about new releases and new concerts.

Once a Web presence has been established, it is time to make sure people know that it exists. If a professional music hosting service has been used, then, hopefully, they will do some advertising. References to the music and site can be e-mailed to the music press for reviews. The Web address can be included on concert posters and tickets, and paid advertisements can placed at popular music blog sites.

Useful Links

Information about many of the applications mentioned in this chapter can be found at the Web addresses below. These are good starting points for locating information about music distribution.

Music sales and promotion

Amazon	http://amazon.com
CD Baby	http://www.cdbaby.com
CDnow	http://cdnow.com
Classical CD Exchange	http://classicalcdexchange.co.uk
EMusic	http://www.emusic.com
iTunes	http://www.apple.com/itunes/

Music promotion

ArtistLaunch (Web music hosting and sales)	http://www.artistlaunch.com/
AudioStreet (Web music hosting)	http://www.audiostreet.net/
DMusic (Web music hosting)	http://www.dmusic.com
Überlabel.com (Web music hosting)	http://www.uberlabel.com/

Music information

Choral Wiki
        http://www.cpdl.org/wiki/index.php/Main_Page
Coverpop (searchable collages of items)   http://www.coverpop.com
Internet Archive (educational resources page)
        http://www.archive.org/details/education

Sequencza 21 (new music wiki)	http://netnewmusic.net/wiki/
Wikipedia (online encyclopedia)	http://en.wikipedia.org/
Young Composers wiki	http://www.youngcomposers.com

Rights and commerce

Creative Commons (licenses for creative works)	http://creativecommons.org
Electronic Music Foundation	http://www.emf.org
Esellerate (e-commerce service provider)	http://www.esellerate.net
PayPal (e-commerce service providers)	http://www.paypal.com

RSS tools

NetNewsWire Lite (Mac OS RSS reader)	http://ranchero.com/netnewswire/
SharpReader (Windows RSS reader)	http://www.sharpreader.net/

Conclusion

The digital music revolution emerged with the CD but has blossomed in the Internet age. The ability to send music as a stream of data across the world in an instant with no loss of quality in the process has revolutionized the way music is distributed and consumed. The impact has been felt by all stakeholders from artists, to record companies to retailers and consumers. There is now much more recorded music available to people than at any previous time in history and the implications of that access to music are social and technical, as reflected in the evolution of licensing, rights management and business models surrounding digital music distribution. The implications for music education include changes in the way teachers and students access music and information about music, also the opportunities available for making and communicating music. Even as the trends of Internet distribution seems to be established in online CD sales, song downloads and Internet radio streams, the potential of wireless networks, and increasingly portable data storage on music players and mobile phones threatens to continue disrupting patterns of music sharing for some time to come.

Reflection questions

1. What are the technical factors that combined to produce the acceleration of Internet music sharing in the 1990s?
2. What computer-based music player applications are available to support Web-based music distribution?
3. What is the difference between downloading and streaming music?
4. Who are the stakeholders in the digital music industry listed in the chapter?
5. What is the difference between publishing and mechanical rights for musical works?
6. What are some of the ways a creative commons license differ from a standard copyright license?
7. What is DRM and why might mechanical rights holders want it?
8. Apart from file distribution, how can the Internet be used to enhance music distribution?
9. What is a Podcast?
10. Why is the content of MP3 ID tags important for promoting music on the Internet?

Teaching tips

1. Listen to and evaluate MP3 audio quality and file sizes at different data rates to provide students with a good understanding of the relationship between compression and audio quality.
2. Provide students with free and legal download sites for the music that is being studied to encourage student to listen to more music more often as part of their music education.

3. Have students set up a blog for their music studies to encourage reflective practice and to increase communications between student and teacher.
4. Ensure that the blog includes audio, and perhaps video, elements as well as
text entries.
5. Actively document music performances and other events with audio, photos,
and video so that these can be posted to the Web as promotion of these activities to the community.
6. Students can put music criticism skills into practice by contributing reviews of
CDs to music sales sites such as Amazon.
7. Podcasts can be used to distribute annotated descriptions of students music
work to parents as a supplement to written reports.
8. Use audio downloaded from the Internet that is released under the creative
commons sampling license for creating musical soundscapes.
9. Set up a compositional collaboration between students at distant schools and
use music file transfers as a means of communicating drafts of work between
them.
10. Have students create a Podcast review of a school music concert that includes
interviews with performers.

Suggested tasks

1. Take some time to visit iTunes or other online music store to get a sense of the
scale and sophistication of music distribution services.
2. Research information about creative commons licenses and why they are
useful.
3. Visit the official Web site of a technology-savvy music artist (e.g., Björk, Prince,
or Brian Eno) to see how an artist can promote their work using the Web.
4. Tune in to an Internet radio station that plays music you like.
5. Explore some new online CD stores as a way of expanding your music
sources.

Chapter summary

The extent to which music is experienced in live or formal presentation contexts is
quite minimal compared with the amount of private listening to pre-recorded music.
The computer has not only increased the production of recoded music but has also
revolutionized its dissemination—in particular through digital recording, first onto
physical media such as CD and DVD and then via file distribution over the Internet as files and Internet radio streams. The key technologies involved with digital
music distribution include file formats, digital rights management techniques, and
file transfer systems. Key social issues include authenticity when copies are perfect,

licensing arrangements and control of legal rights, and economic models that work for all stakeholders. As a result of these challenges, the music industry is changing, and with it music education. There are new opportunities for the creation and distribution of student's music, new opportunities for sourcing music repertoire and information about music, and an increased challenge to help students understand how digital music distribution will effect their musical life now and in the future, either as a consumer or producer of digital music.

Note

1   Wikipedia,http://en.wikipedia.org/wiki/Webcasting (accessed October 2005).

Section IV

REFLECTION

Computers and music research

As music educators strive for a relevant focus, they pursue music-making activities in all their forms. Research and reflection upon our musical activities is a vital part of a complete music education. Music research includes musicology, which has a history of being very document-centric, and also embraces practice-based reflective activities. There are many research sources including books, journals, people, and places that can be used as well an Internet sources, but this chapter focuses on the sources made available via the Internet.

Music education discussions often focus on musical praxis, experience, expression, and aesthetic awareness. However, contextual understanding remains important. While educators in the 1970s focused on experiencing music, in the 1980s on balancing composing, performing, and listening, in the 1990s on media integration, reflection, and competence, and in the early 2000s on meaning and engagement, research activities endure in the form of history, musicology, sociology, and other contextual studies. If there was any hesitation in admitting the importance of musicology research in our school and college music programs, the Internet is here to revitalize it as we embrace the new century.

The place of research in the music curriculum

The image of research involving long hours pouring over dusty old books or music manuscripts in order to find some obscure fact is now replaced by a vision of searching online databases full of colorful graphics, sound bites, and video segments. In fact, surfing the Internet is closer to watching TV with a remote control in hand than anything else. Research using the Internet can also include investigation through email dialogue, involve the game-like intrigue of seeking out a vital source and fact, and it can bring together a student's intellect, performance skills, sense of narrative structure, and their visualization abilities, in the creation of a media rich assignment.

The media used in the final output is in partial acknowledgment of the saying that "Writing about music is like dancing about architecture."

Having argued for investigation to be proudly added to production and criticism as a cornerstone of music education, the rest of this chapter will explore the opportunities and pitfalls of music research on the Internet, provide a path through some technological and methodological forests, dare to consider censorship and copyright, and encourage student creation of multimedia documents as research reports.

Opportunities on the Internet

Apart from a sexy image, is there any substance to the Internet as a research tool? While the debate is inconclusive, it is clear that the quantity of content on the Internet is increasing rapidly. But then so are the number of cable TV channels! It is clear that the opportunities of the Internet need to be more than quick (or not-so-quick) access to what is already in books.

The number of online databases with music information is steadily increasing and some materials are now only available online. While the book volumes dominantly sit on library shelves, and *Encyclopedia Britannica Online* and *Grove Music* online require a subscription, there are plenty of reputable online music sources. These include educational institutions providing lesson materials for their own students, companies providing information of their wares, various professional and amateur associations, academic journals, community resources such as *Wikipedia*, and enthusiastic users (Figure 16.1).

Searching

As well as known sites, such as encyclopedias, the major tool for Internet research, are the search engines, including Google, MSN Search, Yahoo, and Ask Jeeves.

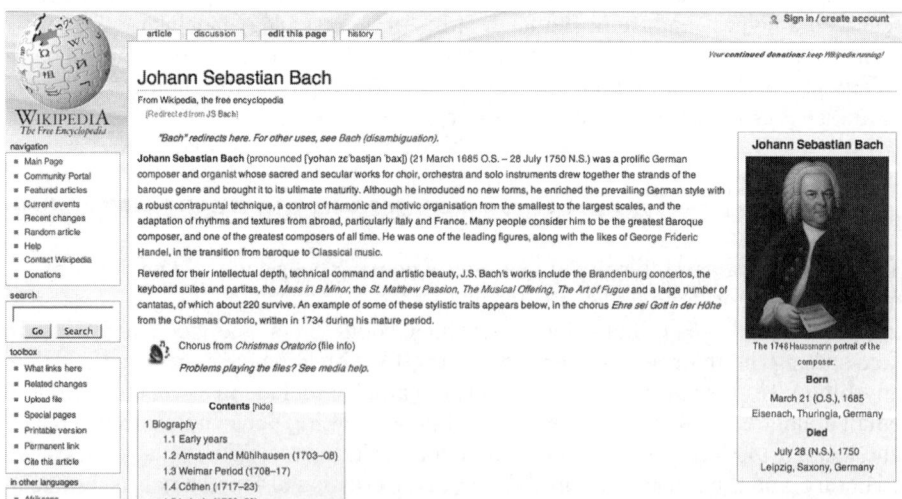

Figure 16.1   A portion of Wikipedia's entry on J. S. Bach.

Using these in an effective manner requires selecting appropriate keywords that identify the topic without being too board. These search engines have all introduced features that try to identify searches for musicians, composers, bands and record titles so that they can additionally link to music download sites and other music-related sites. Database querying techniques such as the use of AND, OR, site: and "quoting phrases" can greatly improve the accuracy of search results. Specialized searches, such as Google Scholar can limit the types of documents to those more relevant to music research, and the useful books on a topic can be found and searched using Google Print or Archive.org. There are some specialist music search engines such as Allmusic.com that provide searchable information on an extensive range of popular and classical music topics.

Most academic journals have online catalogues that show the name and abstract of the article and many have full document downloads available. There may be a local institutional library that has a subscription to the online journal allowing downloading of the article, or at least the appropriate articles can be located then read in the library from the hard copy journal.

The Creative Commons search engine will provide access to legally useable materials such as audio, images, video, and text. Easy access to legal media can be particularly useful for students obtaining examples to augment written assignments or as the basis for sound design projects.

Convergence of media

As more and more information is digitized, including scores, performances, and writings, the access to this will increasingly be via digital conduits, via the Internet. This convergence of media brought to popular attention in the late 1960s by Marshal McLuhan in his book *Understanding Media*, is a powerful trend.[1] A significant aspect of online databases is that they can be media-rich documents. They can include sound and moving vision as well as text and graphics as discussed in chapter 14. This richness of data should not be underestimated for music research. There is much to be gained from accessing a digital video clip on Chinese flute playing compared to reading a book about it.

Forms: online data collection

Research is not only about reading the ideas of others, it is also about gathering data and generating one's own conclusions. Fortunately, the Internet is not a one-way highway. An increasing number of researchers are using the Internet to gather field data using email communications and Web page forms. Forms are widely employed in Internet commerce to allow users to enter personal details or to provide feedback to a company, but they can successfully be used for research. One example is an adaptive music project at the Queensland University of Technology where a student has designed an automated music program and put it on the Web. Visitors to the site, announced through online discussion groups, listen to the music program and provide comments via a form that is e-mailed back to the researcher. Thus a worldwide response is possible. Setting up dedicated Web survey's is not too difficult but and even simpler method for getting feedback from site visitors is to use Web log software that enables visitors to comment on blog entries. A simple questionnaire could

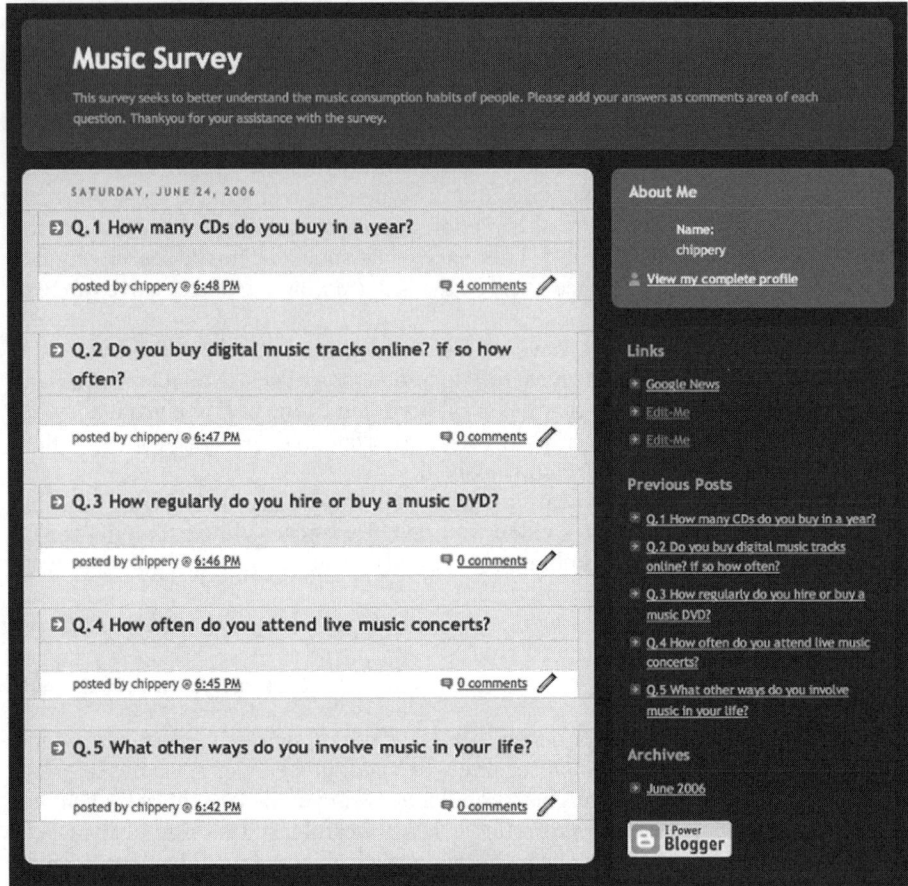

Figure 16.2 An example of an online music survey created as a blog.

be set up with each question being a separate blog posting so that visitors could leave responses to the questions as comments on the blog. This is easy for students to set up with free blog tools such as Blogger.com as shown in Figure 16.2.

Cooperative projects

The dialoguing possibilities of the Internet have given rise to other modes of musical research. The MICNet project at Northwestern University School of Music and other sites like it allow students to exchange compositional ideas by swapping music files, and network jamming software such as jam2jam enables group improvisational sessions over the Internet. Similarly for music research, cooperative projects can be conducted between many sites through exchange of draft and final research documents, data and materials. This can be a linear process where drafts of one document are moved back and forth or a distributed process where each student works on different aspects of the project and so contribute to a final report. A more interactive approach can utilize shared documents using, for example, a wiki or even real-time collaborative document editing with programs such as SubEthaEdit or Google Docs. Cooperative projects also require students to articulate their ideas and to communicate using musical terminology that can enhance student's understanding of the field. In addition, the use of keyword searches enables subtle changes in vocabulary to make significant differences in search effectiveness. Internet music research requires students to focus the research and sift through irrelevancies to find what they needed to know.

Access

For the student, usually familiar with surfing the Internet, the opportunity to do research this way builds on their existing experience. The information on the Internet is relatively unencumbered by geographical location, and the volume significantly overwhelms that of any single educational institution's own resource centre. There is still some inequity on availability and financial grounds, but schools usually make inroads into this by providing Internet access in libraries and classrooms. Most governments are at various stages of linking all their schools to the Internet.

The degree of access also relates to the motivation inherent in the media. Research might just become fun, while being somewhat TV-like, and somewhat game-like, the task of music research using the Internet may be seen as less hard work.

Internet surfing tips

As with most technologies, the Internet's strength is its major flaw: too much information. Sifting through the vast array of classifieds for second hand Bach (the brand) trumpets in search of some facts about J.S. Bach's writing for trumpet, can be frustrating. As many schools choose inexpensive Internet services, the World Wide Web has quickly become known as the world wide wait, because of significant delays in waiting for requested information to be sent.

Tip 1: Do some background research in traditional media to identify the precise informational needs prior to searching.
Tip 2: Be explicit about search keywords, not general.
Tip 3: Use a variety of search engines simultaneously and compile results.
Tip 4: Save interesting sites to the hard drive for later examination, so that online time can be spent searching rather than reading.
Tip 5: Keep records of useful sites and follow secondary links and references from these useful sites.
Tip 6: Use news groups and discussion lists to ask for help and recommendations of information sources. This makes use of other's experience, and saves time.

Discerning "good" information

While there might be an enormous volume and range of information available via the Internet, there is also a wide range of quality. With more traditional forms of publication, such as books, CDs, and videos, there is a financial filter (i.e., the publishers provide some level of quality control). Publishing a Web page on the Internet is very inexpensive by comparison, and so it is important to know whether the information about, for example, the musical attributes of the Chemical Brothers music is from a twelve-year-old fan of the band or from a professor in contemporary music at a university. As with book publication, the Internet publisher can be used as some measure of quality control, in relation to the accuracy of information. For example, the Smithsonian Institution's science history information should be trustworthy, as should Stanford University's tutorials on sound synthesis.

Where the authorship or publication details are not known, methods of quality control can include triangulation of sources, checks against ones own empirical evidence, or the seeking of negative cases, or conflicting information. To avoid over-reliance on Internet, sources use it to quickly assess the range of issues surrounding a topic and then obtain detailed information on the identified issues with more traditional (or trustworthy and available) sources.

Another educational issue relating to information quality is the detail of the information. The variety of sophistication and language level of Internet sources can be problematic for music research activities in schools. One solution to this can be the accumulation of a library of "suitable" links. As part of each research project, have students and staff add to a page of useful sites that can be revisited for subsequent projects.

Censorship

Censorship issues always surround new media such as the Internet. One of the duties of educators is to ensure that information is appropriate. While supervision of Internet sessions and direction to identify "suitable" links will generally be helpful, complete protection will always be impossible (as with all activities).

Reasonable steps to protect students that don't require constant teacher supervision involve a combination of regulation and restriction. In the United States, a law aimed at restricting pornographic content on the Internet was introduced in 1996, the Communication Decency Act (CDA).[2] Due to constitutional concerns by 2006 it had yet to come into full effect. In 1998 the Child Online Protection Act was introduced but was also blocked by potential constitutional limitations. In 2000 a more focused bill, the Children's Online Privacy Protection Act (COPPA), was passed in the United States. The bill applies to the online collection of information about children under the age of thirteen.[3] In Australia, the Australian Broadcasting Authority (ABA) is responsible for content regulation of mass media, including TV, computer games, and the Internet. It has a coregulatory scheme established under Schedule 5 of the Broadcasting Services Act 1992, which includes a code of practice and the authority to investigate complaints.[4] European countries have similar solutions that involve individual banns on particular material regardless of medium and encouragement of responsible and diligent action by ISP and users.

In response to concerns that regulation does not, or cannot in the case of the Internet, always protect children from undesirable content, many Internet service providers (ISPs) and software companies provide customers with options to establish lists of either "undesirable" or black-listed sites that cannot be accessed or, alternatively, a white-list of allowable sites.

One method of regulation being considered is content rating, which would inform users or service providers of the content via labeling, as used for films and video games. This leaves the decision about access to material of a specified rating to the user (or guardian). An extension to this is that sites would have ratings embedded in them and browsers would be set to only download sites with appropriate rating labels. One of the leading systems being considered in this area is the Platform for Internet Content Selection (PICS) rating system.[5] Given the quantity, diversity of producers, and the global jurisdictional issues, it is unlikely that a rating system will be practical in the near future.

Educational providers can limit access through black or white listings of sites for their Internet connections, however, students need to be taught to manage the Internet against possible harmful effects as well. A combination of reasonable protective measures along with teacher/parent and student self-regulation should enable Internet research to be a positive learning experience and no more harmful than other media.

Copyright

The technologies that create the ease of access to materials over the Internet for music research, enable a corresponding ease of copying. The digital copies are, moreover, identical to the originals. Such ease of access and copying means that some increased awareness of copyright responsibilities may be required to avoid illegal (if well meaning) activity. The digitization of all media means that picture, text, sound, or movie data on the Internet is treated equally in relation to copyright.

Copyright relates to the making of copies, so it is worth considering what constitutes a copy. Viewing an Internet site on a computer involves making a copy of the data in the memory of your computer (RAM). In most countries the law does not consider the holding of data in RAM as a breach of copyright. However, if the information is saved to disk, printed out, or recorded onto another medium, then that is considered copying.

If there are no restrictions to accessing the information over the Internet, such as password protection, then there is assumed to be an implicit agreement for use (but not copying) of that information. If there are any notices restricting use or claiming copyright, then normal off-line copyright provisions apply. E-mail documents and information posted from Internet forms, either personally or to a discussion list, are also covered by copyright law; the copyright remains with the author. So when using or quoting from e-mail, the permission of the author is required. It is good practice to seek a blanket agreement of the participants at the outset of the project for use of the data.

An increasing amount of material on the Internet, from text in blogs to audio files and animations, is being made available using Creative Commons licenses. A major advantage of these licenses, as opposed to traditional copyright, is that explicit agreement for limited usage can be assigned by the author at the outset. This means that you do not need to contact the author to know if you can use the material, the license makes its clear under what conditions you can (and can't) use their work. The options within the range of Creative Commons licenses concern the commercial or noncommercial use of the material and what sort of modifications to the work are allowed. It is therefore possible to locate images, music, and text that can legally be collated into a research presentation, particularly for noncommercial purposes like education.

Referencing

It is important that the source of information and ideas are attributed to those who originated them, therefore references are used to give people credit for their work. First, we will consider the citation of electronic documents in a research report. The practice for citation of electronic documents is quite similar to nonelectronic documents. Remember that a citation exists to acknowledge the source of information and ideas, and to enable a reader to check the sources if they wish. Therefore, the citation should include the author and document details, date and place (electronic) of availability. If no date of publication is available, which is quite common, then the date of access can be acknowledged.

The American Psychological Association (APA) publication manual provides the following format for referencing online sources:[6]

Johnson, D. (1997). The History of the Flute
Available: http://www.abcd.org.au/music/flute.html

Second, the methods of referencing within an electronic research report can vary. Standard printed document processes can be applied, and a slight variation on these is to make each reference in the text, for example (Jones, 1987) or [12], a hypertext link to the full citation at the end of the report. Having the full citation itself hyperlinked to the original source document, assuming it was an online document, can further extend this process.

Sound on the Internet

When dealing with music research, one of the exciting features of the Internet is its ability to contain sound recordings or videos of performances. The use of sound and video on the Internet is not standardized to the same extent as text, there are a number of issues relating to quality and accessibility that need to be considered. In this section I will refer to sound, but all comments apply equally to video.

Sound over the Internet can come in a variety of formats. The various methods of getting music files can be grouped into two categories: files that can be downloaded to the user's machine before playback, and those stored to the user's machine in chunks, a process known as "streaming." An overview of audio file formats is provided in chapter 12 and a more detailed introduction of playing back music from the Internet is provided in chapter 15.

An alternative to downloading music as audio, is to have music represented as a MIDI file. Because MIDI files contain gestural information rather than sound information, they can be quite small. MIDI files replay on the sound hardware of the computer, so the audio quality of them varies accordingly. MIDI file players are standard in Internet browsers but their use is decreasing as compressed audio formats, such as MP3 become more widespread. Combinations of MIDI and audio data format, such as Mod files or Beatnik, are a way to find a middle path between audio-only or MIDI-only formats. An example of effective use of such a format would be the transfer of a musical backing via MIDI with accompanying vocal track as an audio signal.

The increasingly dominant way of accessing musical examples is with audio streaming that allows sounds of any length and of reasonable quality to be heard over the Internet. Presently, sound in such formats require extensions to browsers, called plugins, to play back but these are often included with the browser. These plugins are usually free but do need to be installed. The most common streaming formats are Flash, Real Audio, Microsoft Media Player, and QuickTime. For music research, streamed audio allows access to substantial musical examples. However, it does not allow the saving of these files for latter reference.

The Internet is an entertainment medium as well as informational one. As a result, trends in audio for cinema and computer games are finding their way onto the Internet. In particular, surround sound reproduction is beginning to be prominent. For a system to utilize surround sound a decoding amplifier, as required for surround videos or TV, is required, but also may be built into the computer's audio hardware. The music researcher may see little immediate benefit in this development, but in areas of critical performance recreation a three dimensional sound space may contain important cues, although only for research of an advanced nature.

Reporting research as multimedia documents

While accessing the Internet for information can be exciting and useful, the creation of research reports as media rich documents, such as Web pages using the Hyper Text Markup Language (HTML), is equally important. As with all representation systems it is important that students cannot only read them but write them too. The most obvious advantage is that the research report can contain examples of performances as video or sound recording combined with color photographs and text. The use of media rich documents is outlined in detail in chapter 14 but some applications to music research are outlined here.

Narrative versus hypertext

A major difference between paper-based reports, even those employing color photos and graphics, and Web documents is that the data within a HTML document can have associated links, called hyperlinks. A hyperlink enables a click within one document to take the user to a linked document, or section within a document. From an educational standpoint, the addition of hypertext links to a research report document encourages the student to see connections between information and issues (Figure 16.3). This ability for the Web documents to reveal the organizational structure within the students mind can provide opportunities for student reflection and for teachers to gain an insight into the thinking and understanding of the student.

Narrative flow of information, although interruptible by hypertext, is still an essential element of Web documents. The basic structure of each Web page is a linear narrative from top to bottom. So the overall assemblage of information can be displayed in this way while embedded hyperlinks point to additional or supportive information.

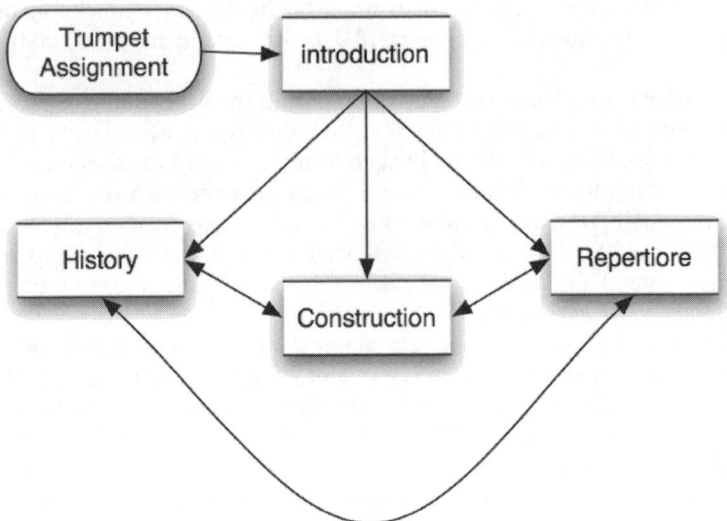

Figure 16.3 A mind-map or flow-chart can be directly converted to a hypertext document, maintaining the richness of interconnections between information.

Music production skills

In order to fully exploit Web documents for music research reporting, students will have to acquire music production skills to produce and embed sounds. The recorded presentation of a student's musical skills, either compositional or performance based, is becoming a fundamental skill for music students. This can simply involve an audio recording and digitization into a suitable file format, or can extend to digital manipulation of the recording to enhance or totally reinterpret the recording. More details on audio recording practices are covered in chapter 8. With electronic presentation of music productions overtaking (in terms of quantity) in-person presentations, music students should clearly be developing skills in media rich online presentation methods.

Empowerment over knowledge

As students create in a medium they gain understanding of the medium as well as the content. This statement should be a mantra for music educators sympathetic to constructivist learning philosophies, and is no less true for music research presentations. When students prepare research reports as Web documents, they become increasingly critical of the Internet sites they explore for information. As they become aware of the strengths, limitations and tricks of creating Web documents, they can "read" other's documents more succinctly and quickly. They become aware of issues such as audio format differences, the design and informational balance between text, graphics and sound, choices between file size and loading times, the importance of site structure and information presentation models, and the develop discrimination between good content and good presentation.

Conclusion

Research activities in educational music programs can be given a new lease of life with the Internet as a source of data and a vehicle for presentation. The use of the Internet can make investigation an equally appealing partner to production and criticism in the music education curriculum; the Internet also provides a means of global communication for both research into and presentation of music making. It enables music research to involve sound and gesture, not only text and score. Educators should value Internet capable computers in their classrooms, and view the Internet as a two-way avenue for integration of the school and the world; use of the Internet for music research and publication can be both a window on the world and a global stage.

Reflection questions

1. How has the Internet changed the practice of music research?
2. What are the benefits to students of using rich media (HTML) documents for research reports?
3. What are the opportunities for music learning opened up by peer-to-peer collaboration over the Internet?
4. What might be barriers to students accessing the Internet in schools? How can these be overcome?
5. What range of research resources is typically available in schools?
6. What level of source referencing detail is appropriate at differing levels of schooling?
7. What is the difference between streaming and downloading audio over the Internet?
8. How important is computer audio playback quality when students are searching the Internet?
9. Why is it important that students be able to write, as well as read, HTML documents?
10. How does the Internet make music research more appealing?

Teaching tips

1. Take students through a tutorial on advanced Internet searching techniques.
2. Have students learn how to create forms and create online surveys.
3. Encourage students to join an Internet discussion group on a music topic that interests them.
4. Make posters outlining the six Internet surfing tips and post them near computer terminals in the music room.
5. To ensure research validity, require students' research assignments to include triangulation of sources, checks against empirical evidence, and deliberate seeking of negative evidence.

6. Facilitate student discussions about identifying information quality from the Internet and other sources.
7. Have a guest speaker come to talk about Creative Commons licenses and how they affect musicians.
8. Require students to submit research reports as hypertext documents with links to external reference sources.
9. Develop skills in recording and digitizing audio for embedding in HTML pages.
10. Have the school IT section set up an audio streaming server and "broadcast" recordings of student's music over a school Internet radio.

Suggested tasks

1. Find out which online journal databases your library subscribes to and see how many music journals are included in those databases.
2. Check out the advanced search pages and associated tutorials at some of the major search engine sites to improve your ability to do Internet searches.
3. Design a collaborative music research project that can connect several schools and devise some ways that the Internet can be used to help gather and communicate data as part of that project.
4. Practice preparing media-rich Web-based presentations by doing one on a music topic that you know quite well.
5. Do some research on the pros and cons for artists of Creative Commons licenses.

Chapter summary

Research and reflection upon our musical activities is a vital part of a complete music education. Current music education discussions revolve around musical praxis, experience, expression, and aesthetic awareness, however, contextual understanding remains important and computers, and the Internet that connects them, have revitalized music research. Research activities have traditionally included analysis, history, musicology, sociology, and other contextual studies but can also include the exploration of music-making techniques in areas such as acoustics, instrument building, arranging, marketing, copyright, and so on. If there was any cringe in admitting the importance of music research in our school music programs, the computer as an analysis tool and the Internet as an information conduit are here to revitalize it as we embrace the new century.

Notes

1   McLuhan, Marshall, *Understanding Media: The Extensions of Man* (London: Sphere Books, 1964.
2   Access to copies of the CDA act at these sites:, http://www.fcc.gov/telecom. html, http://www.house.gov/feeney/downloads/feeneyamd/protectactfinal. pdf.
3   Access a copy of the COPPA act at http://www.ots.treas.gov/docs/r.cfm?48721. pdf.
4   Access information of ABA Internet codes and standards of conduct at http:// www.aba.gov.au/internet/codes.shtml.
5   Access information about the PICS specification at http://www. w3.org/PICS/.
6   American Psychological Association, *Publication Manual of the American Psychological Association*, 4th ed. (Washington, DC: APA, 1994), 218. APA style manual information online, http://www.apastyle.org/.

Chapter 17

Music and sound analysis

The computer is widely used as an analytical tool, most obviously in business where spreadsheets are routinely used to track and forecast financial and inventory details. Similarly, musical statistics and patterns can be revealed using a computer. There are some dedicated musicologists working with specialized computing tools for musical analysis and some of these tools will be mentioned below, but music analysis on computer can also be done with more widely available software. It is possible to turn familiar music applications, such as sequencing, recording, and publishing tools, to the task of musical analysis by using the computer to capture music as MIDI data and use the visualization abilities of these applications to examine music using familiar displays such as common practice notation and piano-roll views. As well as using music applications for analysis, the comprehensive resources of spreadsheets can be used to do statistical analysis of music after converting notes or audio data to numbers. These familiar tools are more likely to be available in music education settings; however, it is worth examining the more specialized tools to understand what is possible and to support more advanced levels of study. This chapter covers the issues and processes of musical analysis with computers and explores the potentials and the pitfalls.

Strategies for music analysis

Analyzing music generally involves a search for features arising from such questions as what key is the piece in? How many times does the theme reappear? How and when does the tempo change? What is the frequency distribution within a recorded work? There are a number of general strategies for music analysis including data reduction or "zooming out" to reveal larger-scale structure, pattern matching where repetition and reuse are identified, statistical analysis where the frequency of occurrence reveals tendencies in the work and, metaphoric description where music is discussed in ways that provide some insight into a particular interpretation of the music.

Data reduction

A common technique for analysis is data reduction; limiting notes to a pitch class set, for example, or consolidating phrases into larger forms such as sections or movements, or selecting key surface features that are used to identify higher order structures—as in Schenkerian analysis[1] or *A Generative Theory of Tonal Music*.[2]

Music analysis generally focuses on some aspect(s) of music and ignores others. The isolating of an element can make particular features come to light that might otherwise be difficult to observe in the full context. This process is similar to creating a map. Maps can show different features depending upon their function, which might be geographic, political, or climatic. Geographic maps might indicate population centers, transportation routes, or topology. In the same way, a musical analysis can be a map of the music that outlines particular features while it obscures others. A musical analysis might focus on harmonic progression, metrical structure, timbral evolution, texture, melodic contour, dynamic contrasts, musical expression or interpretation, sound spatialization, lyric context, or any other feature which the investigator considers important.

Pattern matching

It is widely recognized that coherence in music is largely determined by the reuse or similarity of material. Searching for reoccurring patterns in the music can help identify significant elements or features, including those that may not always be obvious to the casual observer or listener. Choosing the elements to pattern match is easier if we know what is sought. If looking for structural boundaries, then cadences or rhythmic aspects would probably be appropriate, if looking for thematic development, then matching proportional intervallic and rhythmic relationships can be helpful. Often the analysis question is more vague, such as seeking to uncover the composer's processes, or perhaps even the composer's intention. Perhaps the aim is to uncover what features define a style or a performance practice. In these cases, a systematic exploration of several aspects of the music is necessary. One of the most difficult, but perhaps most profound, tasks might be an analysis which searches to reveal aspects of a piece which make it meaningful. In this realm, the significance of elements is not at all obvious, and nonsonic elements such as listener history and social context may become quite influential.

Statistical analysis

Statistics are commonly used for helping with insights into sporting contests. The number of hits, catches, goals, or runs is often used as a measure of sporting performance, either for an individual or a team, in one game or across their career. Similarly, how often events occur in music can provide clues to the elements of a genre or the preferences or habits of a composer. The frequency of pitches can indicate the key of a piece, the distribution of rhythmic values can help predict the difficulty of performing a work, and the average and standard deviation of pitch range of a musical part can help determine suitable instrumentation for an arrangement.

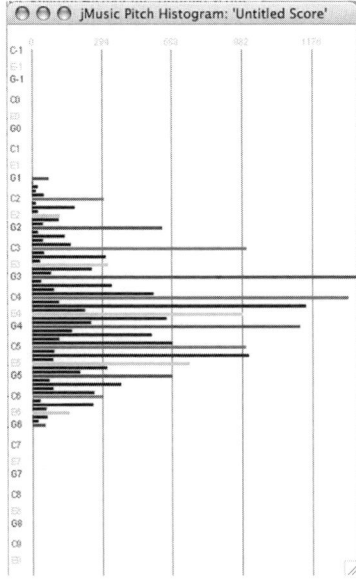

Figure 17.1 A pitch histogram of the first movement from Beethoven's First Symphony in C major, Op. 21.

Statistical features of music can be usefully visualized using graphs. Graphs are useful in showing trends, such as indicating potential harmonic tendencies by displaying the occurrence of pitch classes. A common statistical visualization is a histogram, as shown in Figure 17.1.

The image in Figure 17.1 was generated by the Music Histogram program written by the author that produces these graphs from a standard MIDI file.[3] The graph shows how many notes of each chromatic pitch are present in one movement from Beethoven's Symphony in C Major. The dominance of particular notes in the key can be seen in the histogram, where C and G notes (red and blue lines) are clearly most frequent with note D and E being the next most common. Chromatic notes outside the scale are least frequent. Also interesting to observe is the bell-like distribution of notes around middle C. The generation and analysis of graphs like this can help students to see that theories about scales and keys is more than simply an idea, that the evidence for note priorities occurring in real pieces backs up the theoretical abstractions.

Metaphoric description

Another, less qualitative, method of analysis is the description of music through analogy, or metaphor. Music can be considered to "flow like a river," "spiral downwards like a staircase," and so on. Music can be described as "mechanical," "organic," "spacious," or "dense." While it is possible that these terms might describe individual elements of the music, they are more likely to relate to the way several elements work together, or how the music is interpreted at an emotive, rather than functional level. As a result, they can be useful in pointing students' attention to features of the music, without having to wade through masses of analytic data. It can also be useful to correlate intuitive impressions of the music with statistical measures so that each can help inform the other as a way of more deeply understanding musical works.

Linguistic descriptions can be emphasized in a review or critique of a music production, as part of a peer review processes or as an initial or conclusion stage in a more formal analysis. A poetic or cultural perspective on a work is often expressed through metaphors and the ability to articulate musical features identified statistically in a written report or verbal discussion requires appropriate naming and describing.

Computer assisted analysis

When people analyze music they look, listen, think, discuss, and describe. These are not attributes we normally ascribe to computers, but one way or another, if the computer is to help in analysis it needs have musical input, to process that data, and to communicate the results. The computer's equivalent of hearing is receiving input from audio or MIDI sources. When digital recordings are examined as amplitude or frequency over time, they can reveal a great deal about the sounds that were recorded. Much of the analysis of music is done at a symbolic, or iconic, level where we are concerned about notes, phrases, parts, and voices, rather than samples or sounds. For symbolic analysis, we often rely on the Musical Instrument Digital Interface (MIDI) description of music as notes that start and stop.

If audio and MIDI recording is the computer's equivalent of hearing, then its equivalent of music reading is to have the music coded into a notational scheme. Considerations for such a scheme include readability, coherence with perceptual categorization, and integration with historical analytic techniques. Another important consideration is that with any coding scheme we loose detail. As Robert Rowe points out,

> The transformations of musical information made by listening systems are not lossless. In other words, the abstractions made do not produce a representation that can be transformed back into the original signal, as, for example, a Fourier analysis can be changed back into sound pressure wave. The abstraction of MIDI already throws away a good deal of timbral information about the music it represents.[4]

An encoding scheme such as MIDI only approximates the performance nuance that generated it, ignoring dynamic changes within a note's duration for example, and common practice notation as dots on a stave is even more abstract. When we analyze music as notation or MIDI data, we need to be aware of the fact that we are assessing a musical abstraction, from which we can get some very useful information but not all aspects of music.

Common practice notation is an iconic system. Notational marks indicate both audible (notes, accents) and nonsounding (barlines, key signatures) aspects of music. A great deal of music analysis deals with the score, so, for the computer, the score needs to be encoded. Once encoded, the score can be processed by the computer. Apart from MIDI other common coding schemes for music analysis are Kern and DARMS.[5]

The limitation of musical encoding for computer analysis is not the only obstacle of computer assisted analysis. Music is more than the sum of its parts, so even if all its features could be captured, the analysis of emotive aspects such as tension, excitement, embarrassment, and so on still present problems and challenges to the music researcher.

Score analysis

While musical scores have traditionally been represented on paper as notes on a stave, and may also be on a computer screen, inside the computer most commercial music applications represent symbolic music as MIDI data or some variant of it. It is also most common that for analysis purposes musical scores will be most easily accessible for computer analysis as a MIDI file. Therefore, it is useful to examine the characteristics of MIDI data for use in score analysis on computer.

The MIDI data representation was designed for performance and deals with music as a series of events. In MIDI, notes have a beginning (note-on) message which indicates the channel (1–16), pitch number in semitones (1–127; 60 is middle C), and dynamic (1–127). The note-off message is similar except the dynamic (called velocity) is zero, indicating that the note should stop. A stream of MIDI messages, each a group of numbers, represents the notes in a piece. There is no time information inherent in the MIDI messages, so the computer program must time-stamp the arrival of each message to determine the duration and spacing of notes. Other events, such as pitch bend or volume change, have their own messages.

MIDI sequencers have many ways of visualizing music, and many of these were discussed in detail in chapter 5. These views, in particular the piano roll and common practice notation displays, are also useful for analysis. The ability of the sequencer to zoom in and out of a display can greatly assist in seeing different perspectives of the music, from the small details to the overall structure. Figure 17.2 shows an overall view of *The Rite of Spring* by Igor Stravinsky.

From this visualization of the well-known Stravinsky piece it is clear that dramatic changes in texture and pitch range are present. Also, the sections of frequent time signature change, especially in the "Prelude," can be seen in the different density of vertical bar lines. It will be much easier for students follow a large scale graph like the one in Figure 17.2 when listening to the piece for the first time than the note-buy-note detail of a CPN score.

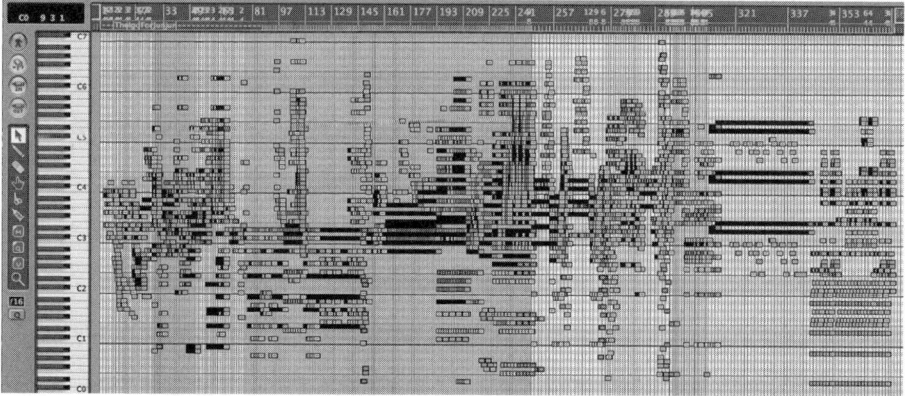

Figure 17.2 An overview of Stravinsky's *The Rite of Spring* in a sequencer piano-roll display.

Sequencer applications can also be useful for locating details within a work. Many of them contain filtering or selection functions that can isolate frequently occurring pitches, sections or phrases. The can also be of use in hearing sections in more detail through the muting and soloing of individual parts as the sequence plays, and by changing tempo without effecting pitch the sequencer can help students unpack complicated phrases by slowing down playback or listen to the larger scale effects by playing quickly through the piece.

Most music publishing software programs can be used for simple score analysis through comparison of parts and sections in multiple screens, muting and soloing playback, and zooming out for score display. However, the searching and finding capabilities are usually quite limited, and generally there will be little advantage over a printed score. The Sibelius program does allow the scripting of music analysis functions in its ManuScript language.

Many forms of analysis attempt to reveal the larger scale form in music, the ways in which musical sections are organized, repeated, ordered and so on. While the software for doing this structural analysis is either quite complex or not widely available, it is nevertheless worthwhile seeing what is possible with computer analysis and what is likely to become more accessible as the twenty-first century progresses.

A very elegant visualization of musical structure is Martin Wattenberg's Arc Diagrams where a semicircular arch is drawn to connect sections of music that repeat. Figure 17.3 shows three arcs.[6] With this view, it is possible to analyze the multiple layers of repetition, and thus structure inherent in a work. Work generated with Arc Diagrams is as beautiful as it is practical; examples of it have been exhibited as art. The InForm music analysis software uses similar arc images to show musical structure. Students can create their own diagrams by printing computer rendered scores and coloring in arcs by hand as an introductory analysis task.

David Cope's EMI (Experiments in Musical Intelligence) program is famous for analyzing and reconstructing music in the style of various composers. In the process, EMI does a comprehensive pattern matching and grammar extraction analysis based around identifying characteristic musical patterns called "earmarks" and "signatures." Cope has made available a cut-down version of EMI called SARA—available on the CD **ROM** of his book *Experiments in Musical Intelligence*. SARA requires the score to be coded into a particular format. Each note entry contains a list including start-time, pitch (MIDI number), duration, channel number (part), and dynamic.

Figure 17.3 Arc diagram view shows the links between repeated sections.

SARA performs pattern matching processes on the data that does layer analysis and is not dissimilar to Schenkerian structural reductions. A Schenkerian analysis is based on the work of Heinrich Schenker who viewed music as having layers of structure; the foreground in which all notes and ornaments are considered, the middle ground containing just the harmonically pivotal notes, and the background where any "well composed" tonal piece was reducible to one of three patterns based on the tonic scale and triad. SARA identifies features which characterize the musical style of a particular composer which Cope calls "signatures." With the SARA software a user can specify the pattern matching latitude of various parameters that change how similar two segments need to be in order to be considered a match.

A more sophisticated technique for revealing hierarchical structure in a musical work is available in *A Generative Theory of Tonal Music* (GTTM). It is, according to its developers, designed "to specify a structural description for any tonal piece; that is, the structure that the experienced listener infers in his hearing of the piece."[7] The theory is designed to infer the kinds of structures that we hear as listeners, rather than purely statistical features. There are four sets of rules, metrical and grouping rules to analyze rhythmic features, and time-span and prolongational rules to examine interaction between pitch and rhythm. The result is a multileveled reduction of score detail through the rejection of all notes except those at structurally significant points in the score. Computer-based analysis based on *GTTM* has been explored by researchers including Masatoshi Hamanaka and Keiji Hirata, but software for doing *GTTM* analysis is not readily available.[8] Rules from *GTTM* can be a useful starting points for computer-based musical analysis tools, such as Humdrum.

David Huron's Humdrum Toolkit is one of the most widely used computing tools by musicologists for score analysis.[9] Humdrum is divided into two parts,: (1) the Humdrum syntax, which defines how musical data is to be organized and, (2) the Humdrum toolkit of software functions for analyzing the data. The Humdrum Toolkit is very flexible and open, however, the process of encoding the score can be time consuming if is not one of about 10,000 already coded works available in the associated Kern music format. Conversion between MIDI files and Kern are possible. Humdrum Toolkit functions include pattern matching, user-defined similarity checking, and statistical measurement of any coded attribute. The application is command-line driven and while powerful is not for the faint hearted, musically naïve, or younger student.

While applications such as SARA and Humdrum are flexible and powerful they can be somewhat finicky to use. A simpler solution for doing statistical analysis on a musical score is to convert a MIDI file of the music into numbers that can be analyzed in a spreadsheet. The Midi2Text program, written by the author, does just this.[10] It reads in a MIDI file and creates a tab-delimited text file that contains a table of each note's start time (in beats), pitch (MIDI note numbers), duration (in beats), and dynamic value (MIDI velocity numbers). The text file can be read into a spreadsheet and will be displayed similar to the data shown in Figure 17.4. The sorting, calculating, and graphing functions of the spreadsheet can be used to analyze and display the musical data.

Each of these score-based analysis methods rely on the encoding of music in a symbolic way where notes are objects with properties and a series and/or hierarchy of them constitute the musical work. In the next section we will consider music analysis of music represented as sound.

◇	A	B	C	D
1	Start Time	Pitch	Duration	Dynamic
2	0	76	0.5	64
3	1	76	0.75	64
4	1.75	77	0.25	64
5	4	77	0.5	64
6	5	77	0.75	64
7	5.75	79	0.25	64
8	8	76	0.5	64
9	9	76	0.75	64
10	9.75	77	0.25	64
11	12	77	0.5	64
12	13	77	0.75	64
13	13.75	79	0.25	64
14	0	72	0.5	64

Figure 17.4 Music data in a spreadsheet.

Audio analysis

The analysis of digitally recorded audio is becoming common for analysis of electro-acoustic music and electronica, and is often used in ethnomusicology where there are no "scores," in the Western sense, that utilize a written symbolic system. Audio waveforms provide amplitude and time information directly and timbre information through conversion. The visual displaying of the recorded data as waveforms and sonograms is discussed in more detail in chapter 12. The direct components of these visualizations, amplitude in the case of waveforms and overtones in the case of sonograms, can be analyzed directly or used to find second order features such note start positions, rhythmic timing, and change of instrumentation through calculations based on onset peaks and variations in frequency spectra. Many computer music programs display audio waveforms and these can be used in simple cases to look at the music at different levels of scale by zooming in and out, like that described above for the use of MIDI sequencers in displaying score views.

Graphical symbols can be used to represent sound samples in soundscape works that do not lend themselves to conventional notation. A significant example of this usage is the mapping of sound-objects in musique concrète and electronic music. In such representations, each visual symbol corresponds to a sound, and visual manipulations of the symbol, such as stretching or splicing, indicate similar changes to the sound object. This method was used by Pierre Schaeffer to articulate his theories of *sonemes* (sound objects).[11] As a method of analysis, a graphical representation can be constructed from listening to a recorded work, timing section durations, and observing changes visible in waveform of sonogram views of the audio data. The process of constructing the graphic score is an analysis task that focuses listening and the development of a symbolic key requires classification of sound types and observation of their structural organization.

More detailed timbral analysis of an audio signal is possible using the process of Fourier Transform which identifies the frequency of each harmonic and their

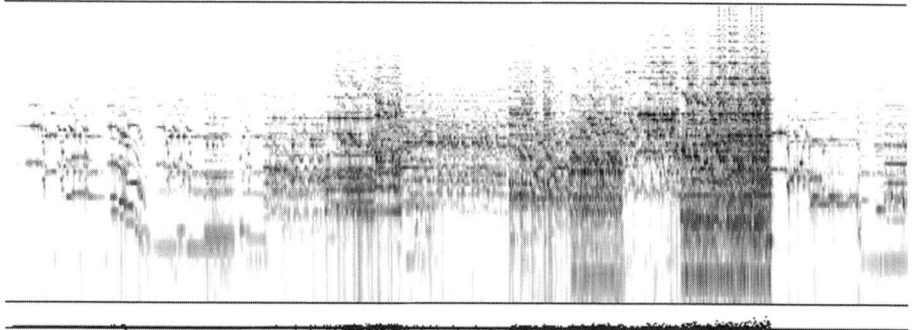

Figure 17.5 Pitch contours are evident in a sonogram with a logarithmic frequency scale.

amplitude over time. These are often displayed as 2D or 3D graphs or sonograms that can allow detailed comparison of instrument, ensemble, or architectural characteristics. A sonogram of the prelude from Stravinsky's *The Rite of Spring* is shown in Figure 17.5. The similarity with the first one-fifth, or so, of the MIDI display of the whole work in Figure 17.1 is clearly seen. The sonogram can be assessed by a number of criteria—whether the spectrum is diffuse or compact, the amplitude is high or low, and the sound durations are short or long.

A number of inexpensive audio editors can display sonograms, including Audacity, which has support for spectrum display and pitch detection, AudioSculpt, which has a very clear sonogram display, and Amadeus, which has a wide variety of visual display options. Spectral composers make use of Fourier analysis to generate pitch (frequency) sets for their compositions. This enables them to use a sound as a pitch source as well as a timbral component. Analysis of works by spectral composers, as well as producers of electroacoustic music and electronica often involves investigation via sonogram.

Conclusion

Even from this introduction to computer assisted music analysis it is clear that the computer can contribute in many ways to musical research. With tools ranging from the flexible audition of scores in sequencers and music publishing applications, to detailed statistical analysis in Humdrum, computers can help investigate a score at any level of sophistication. Audio analysis tools can reveal section structure through waveform and frequency display of digital recordings.

Music analysis can seek to isolate the elements within music or focus on the music's overall structure and organization. Analysis can be seen as a purely theoretical music practice or as the careful study of music that creates understanding and leads to meaning. In any case, computers have an increasingly important place in that reflective analysis, but their use does not change the fact that through our investigations we know more, but the more we see is still unknown. As we grasp the music with our analytical tools, like snow, it disintegrates and melts through our fingers. But, nevertheless, computers do help increase our grasp.

Reflection questions

1. What is the analysis value of being able to zoom in and out of a piece of music on computer?
2. What is meant by describing music metaphorically?
3. How is analysis like creating a map?
4. What are some of the features a musical analysis might focus on?
5. What are some possible aims of pattern matching in music analysis?
6. A histogram can show what information?
7. In what way can a computer "hear" or "read" music in order to analyze it?
8. How is a piano roll display used for analysis in Figure 17.2?
9. What does the Midi2Text application do and where do you download it?
10. What criteria are suggested for analyzing music viewed as a sonogram?

Teaching tips

1. Make sure analytical questions are clearly stated before beginning so that students understand what they are trying to find.
2. Contrast zoomed-in and zoomed-out views of the same music on screen to help student understand what information is hidden or revealed in each case.
3. Have student practice "reading" audio waveforms and sonograms of sounds they record before analyzing whole music works as recordings in this format?
4. Use the mapping metaphor, have students drawn "maps" of a larger musical work as a first step toward more detailed analysis.
5. Compare pitch histograms of tonal and atonal music to see the difference in pitch usage.
6. Students can draw arc diagrams above a computer printed melody showing where note groups are repeated.
7. Have students write a review of a work in text first, then attempt to use other analysis techniques to confirm their first impressions.
8. Discuss which music elements are emphasized or hidden in each type of music representation they use, CPN, MIDI, audio, graphical score, and so on.
9. Senior students should explore the possibilities of analysis afforded by the Humdrum Toolkit.
10. Use sonograms to show the connection between notated score and frequency spectra in the resulting performance.

Suggested tasks

1. Locate the opportunities for analysis in the curriculum and match them with appropriate computer-based methods and tools.
2. Download one or more of the programs mentioned in the chapter and try them out.
3. Locate MIDI files for the major works in the curriculum so they are available for analysis.
4. Compare sonograms of works from different genres to become familiar with the differences in spectral patterns between them.
5. Use the Midi2Text application to put MIDI data of a favorite piece into a spreadsheet.

Chapter summary

The computer is widely used as an analytical tool for music as it is for other tasks, such as understanding physics or financial markets. Musical analysis can be assisted using widely available tools such as sequencer, hard disk recorders, and music publishing applications. However, for more detailed analysis specialized programs exist to perform functions directly related to musicological theories that reveal musical and sonic patterns and structure. There are four types of musical analysis commonly examined; data reduction, pattern matching, statistical analysis, and metaphoric description. Music analysis of any of these types can be undertaken on symbolic representations of music, such as notated scores or MIDI data files or on audio recordings of musical productions or performances. Symbolic representations make it easy to examine structure and note organization within the work. Audio analysis can clearly reveal timbral and dynamic trends in the music. Various visual displays can be used to show the results of the analysis from numeric table, graphs and graphic scores to waveforms and sonograms. The computer can be a useful aid in music analysis due to its speed of processing data and ability to translate digital audio to digital graphics. However, despite the great advances of computer-supported analysis, there are still many aspects of music that we know are powerful but that we cannot explain.

Notes

1   Forte, Allen, and Steven E Golbert, *Introduction to Shenkerian Analysis* (New York: W. W. Norton & Co.), 1982.
2   Lerdahl, Fred, and Ray Jackendoff, *A Generative Theory of Tonal Music* (Cambridge, MA: MIT Press, 1983).
3   Download a copy of the Music Histogram program at http://jmusic.ci.qut. edu.au/applications.html#histogram.

4   Rowe, Robert, *Machine Musicianship* (Cambridge, MA: MIT Press), 2001, 120.

5   Tools for working with music in DARMS format are described in Pool, Otto Ede, "The Apollo Project: Software for Musical Analysis Using DARMS," in *Computing in Musicology: An International Directory of Applications*, Volume 10., eds. Walter B Hewlett and Eleanor Selfridge-Field (Stanford, CA: CCARH, 1996), 123–30.

6   Wattenberg, Martin. 2005. The Shape of Song, http://www.turbulence.org/Works/song/ (accessed October, 2005).

7   Lerdahl and Jackendoff, *A Generative Theory of Tonal Music*, 112.

8   Hamanaka, Masatoshi, Keiji Hirata, and Tojo Satoshi. "Automatic Generation of Grouping Structure Based on GTTM." Paper presented at the International Computer Music Conference, Miami, 2004.

9   Huron, David. 1999. Humdrum Toolkit, http://www.humdrum.org/Humdrum/ (accessed November, 2005).

10   Download a copy of the Midi2Text application from: http://jmusic.ci.qut.edu.au/applications.html#Midi2text.

11   Schaeffer, Pierre,*Traité Des Objects Musicaux*, 2nd ed. (Paris: Éditions du Seuil, 1977).

Chapter 18

Aural and musicianship training

Acquiring basic skills in musicianship and aural perception continue to be a core aspect of music education. For the purposes of this chapter's discussion, the term "aural training" is defined as the development of an ability to perceive sonic features in music. These features are normally the raw elements of music or combinations of them as outlined, for instance, in George Pratt's book *Aural Awareness*.[1] While the recognition of timbres, melodies, harmonies, rhythms, and other musical elements underpin aural perception, the basis of musicianship is music notation literacy, audio acoustics, social context, and historical positioning. A contemporary musicianship would also include some familiarity with activities including music sequencing, audio recording, mixing, digital music representations and computer operation. However, as the twenty-first century gets going, not all musicianship programs include these elements of contemporary musicianship. The aim of aural and musicianship studies is to develop skills and intuitions in students to move them from novice to expert musicians, to assist them to move from deliberate or conscious thinking-in-action to a habitual and automated intuitive response. A significant part of this journey involves understanding the elements of music in a sonic or physical sense, and this is what much of the aural and musicianship software focus on, however, other vital elements that lead to a deep musical understanding include the informal, contextual, situational, and other cultural elements of music, these latter elements are less obviously assisted by the computer. This chapter explores the issues involved in choosing and using a computer for developing aural and musicianship skills and, along the way, highlights some software applications that support the development of these skills.

There are several approaches to the development of musical skills or understandings and the appropriateness of these approaches depends upon the background of the students, the curriculum intentions and the amount of time available for work in this area. Many programs, particularly for aural training, follow an approach of repetition and graded skill acquisition. Typically, with this approach, students are presented with a series of short tasks or questions and their success at answering these leads to further tasks at the next level. Examples of software using this approach are the Auralia and Musition applications from Rising Software, which put a strong emphasis on progression, monitoring and assessment. The use of short-term tasks that accumulate to level changes is also the approach that many video games utilize and a number of music applications attempt to emphasize this game association, however, other developers view this as a trivialization or distraction and are therefore more austere in their presentation. These task-based applications are most useful when specific skills needs have been identified or when close measurement of student progress or ability is required.

Other programs, particularly those focused on contextual understanding, follow an approach that emphasizes information breadth and connections. They often approach musical understanding from the perspective of a case study, for example a particular musician, genre or composition, and provide multiple perspectives on a musical topic including relevant techniques, skills, social circumstances, and historical context. These case-based applications are most useful when the meaning of musical knowledge is important and the order of musical knowledge acquisition is not critical. A range of computer applications support a mixture of task-based and case-based approaches with varying degrees of emphasis, but the underlying enabler for all of them is the computer's ability to combine media rich resources in a programmable, thus adaptable and interactive, framework.

Media-rich computer programs in music education, ranging from informational tours of musical works to drill and practice sessions on the recognition of key signatures, usually gain their advantage over printed resources through the integration of sound, vision, and text and interaction with the user. These programs can be Web-based, server-based, or run from the local hard drive. The audio component is

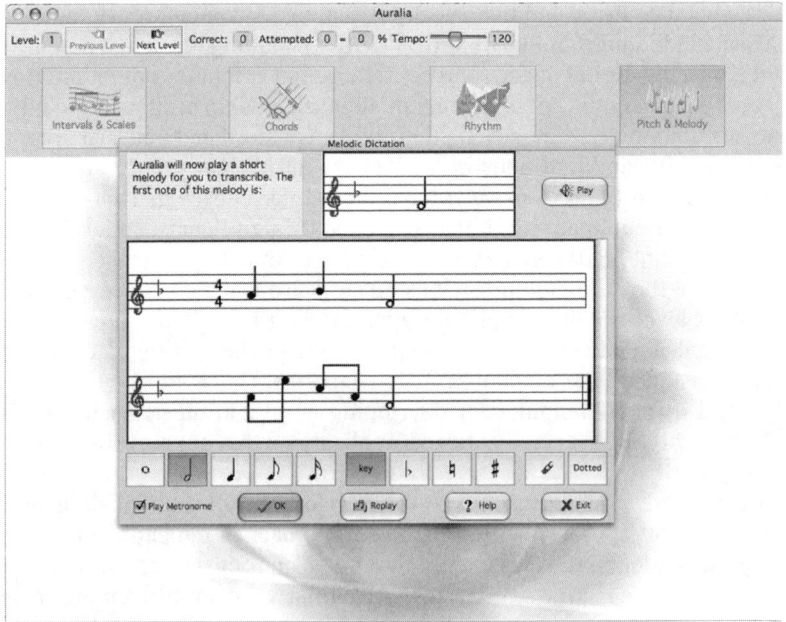

Figure 18.1   A melodic dictation window in Auralia.

typically generated through audio recordings (samples) or MIDI playback using a software synthesizer. A particular advantage of MIDI-based examples for this type of application is the capacity for music to be easily generated or varied in tempo, key and timbre, resulting is a more flexible and adaptable question database. Examples of this genre of software include the Interactive Musician series from Alfred's publishing that focus on pitch training, rhythm, and sight singing and a colorful, notation-focused software environment.

As well as having the advantage of integrated sound and vision, computer-based musicianship recourses can incorporate game-like elements that make them fun to use. This enhances student motivation in these otherwise repetitive and tedious curricular areas, and this is a powerful reason for their use in music education. Despite these motivating elements, long sessions on repetitive tasks can still be tedious and so the judicious use of aural training software as a music education strategy is important. It is not useful if a student achieves good music test results at the expense of "learning" that music is no fun at all.

Another potential disadvantage of computer-based training for aural skills and musicianship is a student's lack of access to computing resources. Typically, computer software in this area is designed for individual use, or perhaps for work in pairs, requiring high student to computer ratios. To cope with this, teaching strategies need to include student rotation, use of computer-based training as a remedial or extension activity, and its use as an individual homework activity. Access to computing resources may potentially limit regularity of practice too. Musicians have long known that musical skills, be they physical or mental, benefit from regular practice. Therefore, as computers become widely available in homes or as portable devices, the opportunity for students to spend some practice time on musicianship software increases. One barrier to student homework on computer is software licensing restrictions, and therefore Web-based systems, free software, or licenses that allow home installation by students can be useful in these circumstances. Sites such as Good-Ear and musictheory.net that provide free online aural training or musicianship exercises (respectively) are a good place to start for resources that are easily accessibility at both school and home.

Software features

The teaching of musicianship can follow a continuum from imitation to application, and a good computer program, like a good curriculum, will include activities along this continuum. Musicianship activities usually focus around musical representations other than sound, and so the multimedia nature of computer programs should provide the link between sound and symbol. The matching of aural and theoretical concepts can create useful associations in the mind of the student, and computer programs where these links are evident are most likely to be useful. Below are some of the musicianship activities found in computer programs:

- Identifying/naming—in this approach, flash card or similar activities help reinforce identification and labeling. Contextual examples can be used here, where a number of features of a musical excerpt are expected to be named, including meter, instrumentation, style, tempo, and so on.

- Matching—in this approach, associations between representations are rein-forced (e.g.,the locating of notes on a stave and keyboard and guitar fret board).
- Structuring—students demonstrate their understanding through appropriate use of musical materials. This can include sorting notes into meter groupings, writing melodies to lyrics, harmonizing melodies, and so on.
- Demonstration—this is the reverse of naming. Students are asked to relate, describe, or to demonstrate, their understanding of musical terms and sym-bols. This can include performing a diminuendo, or singing an intervallic step.

When selecting software for aural or musicianship training, there are a number of features that will differentiate applications from each other and may make some more suitable than others for particular circumstances. These features include the degree of interactivity, ease of set up and access, the types of music representations employed, and the styles and genres supported.

Interactivity

A variable in the quality of aural and musicianship software is the appropriateness and regularity of feedback to users on their progress. Some programs provide sim-ple true or false responses to student answers, with allowance of a limited number of attempts before providing the correct solution. Some applications provide hints after incorrect answers and only a few include complete instructional courses provided as required when students are not able to provide the correct answer.

The basis of all training programs is repetition, but the sophistication of such repetition can vary widely, from game-like routines, where students hop from one activity to another within a virtual arcade, to programs that control incremental progress based on student performance. Programs aimed at musicianship often use a repetitive quiz model with some allowing content to be added by the teacher. Some applications also allow the student to freely explore material of any type or difficulty. Some of the best examples employ a combination of exploration and achievement-based incentives and progression. Of course, the role of the teacher in choosing appropriate software, setting appropriate tasks, and providing learning activities when misunderstandings are identified is critical in the successful use of such musi-cal software.

A number of music training systems include the ability for students to answer tasks by singing or clapping. The computer "listens" to their performance by record-ing and analyzing their responses. Programs that support this include most singing tutors and aural training packages such as Practica Musica, which provides tasks for sight reading as well as aural recognition.

A number of user interactions are possible, and aural and musicianship train-ing programs usually focus on one or two of these, although more comprehensive packages may utilize more than this. User interaction approaches can include:

- Recognition/identification—intervals, scales, rhythms, or tones are played and usually a multiple choice response is required of the student.

- Repetition/dictation—students are required to imitate by singing, writing, playing, or drawing. These activities are often more contextual and open ended, and usually preferable to simple identification activities.
- Prediction—students are required to suggest possible extensions of an example. This might include the closing of a cadence, or the rhythmic completion of an incomplete measure. These activities need not be true or false, but can provide clear indication of a student's problem solving ability within a tightly constrained task.
- Description—is similar to recognition, but goes further to require a justification of why an answer was given. This higher-order cognitive requirement can be useful in clarifying alternatives in open-ended tasks, and for responses to contextual examples where several musical elements interact.
- Analysis—extends description to include critical judgments regarding a musical example. Students should be encouraged to reach this level where they can comment on music in an articulate fashion, but few software programs extend to this level.

Access

The time required to start-up and access information about music from a computer needs to be worth the effort for both teacher and student. Thus, it is important to determine that the computer-based musicianship tutorial or database presents information in an effective fashion that utilizes the integration of sound, vision, and text and does not required complicated physical set up of equipment to get gong. In some instances, where the software is poorly designed, it might be easier to open a book or listen to a CD instead.

Another issue of access is how easily students can get to a computer to use the programs. Teaching styles vary, but schools are usually designed around group work and supervision, which can be at odds with an individual development focus prominent in aural and musicianship skill acquisition. A simple (simplistic) solution to this quandary is the use of computer labs where each student works at their own computer. While appropriate for rudimentary skill acquisition, labs are usually not appropriate for the majority of music education activities and entire labs of computers are a significant expense, it is also important that the skill acquisition tail does not wave the music education dog in this regard. As well, many labs are isolated from the rest of the music resources, such as instruments, books, CDs, and may unduly

Figure 18.2 Music learning games such as Mozart can be played by students on a PDA or phone.

segment aural and musicianship skills from music making in the minds of the students. Alternate solutions include students rotating through activities within the music spaces one of which is the use of aural or musicianship software programs, students can work on aural skills development in their own time either at school and at home, using a PDA or phone while traveling to and from school, or students can accesses skill development software in "down time" from other activities where long-term achievement goals are set and students work when they can toward these and as often as they need in order to achieve set competency standards (Figure 18.2).

Music representations

While aural programs deal with music as sound they often support examples with common practice notation (CPN) using a stave and note position on instruments such as keyboard or guitar. For example, the Listen software from Imaga includes a keyboard, guitar fret board, and stave views in its interface. Musicianship programs mostly deal with CPN but there are some programs, written usually for younger children, which employ pitch as keyboard note positions or, less conventionally, as graphic representations—typically, lines for melodic contour, pitch-color relationships, or cartoon-like height and length metaphors such as staircases. Many students learn guitar and may be more familiar with guitar tablature than CPN and in these cases it can be important that programs can represent music as tablature as an alternative view.

While CPN is pervasive in education systems often teachers also use coding systems including solfa, solfege, French time signs, and so on. The programs available to support these representations are less common, as are programs using English, rather than American, duration terms (crotchet, quaver, and so on). It is wise to remember that in choosing a computer program its language and symbols should integrate with those you wish to support and that students understand.

Genre and styles

The areas of aural training and musicianship are significantly grounded in culture. Most programs tend to revolve around diatonic Western music lending themselves to eighteenth- and nineteenth-century art music and contemporary rock and folk music. This is usually appropriate but also limiting, so when choosing aural training software make sure it covers the curriculum areas required; including, for example, jazz chord terminology, atonal melodic material, poly-meter rhythmic examples, or electronic and acoustic sampled timbres. It maybe necessary or useful to get a program that focuses on some special aspect of your program; for example, Absolute Pitch is a program that focuses on atonal pitch recognition.

When choosing packages that integrate with the curriculum, it is important to choose those which cover the full range of elements required. While pitch, harmony, and rhythm are well covered in most aural and theory programs, few deal with timbre and texture and, if they do, they often limit themselves to orchestral norms in these areas. It is rare to find programs dealing with tuning systems other than Western equal temperament, while some explore modal tonalities, non-Western tonalities are not well supported. To provide appropriate focus on stylistically appropriate musical elements some musicianship packages specialize in particular genres, for example the MiBac musicianship tutorials include the Music Lessons software for "classical" Western music and the MiBac Jazz software specifically for jazz education.

One of the most subjective areas in assessing aural and musicianship programs is judging their "musicality" even while it is arguably one of the most important considerations. Musicality of the program generally refers to the aesthetic quality of the examples both compositionally and in sound quality and expressiveness of playback. In assessing the musicality of such programs, it is worth considering the attention paid to phrasing, placing examples in a musical context, and the audio quality of the sounds and instruments used. Programs such as MacGAMUT pay particular attention to the musicality of their generated examples, and a few systems such as Calma allow musical examples to be specified by the teacher for ultimate control (but also additional effort).

As many of the tasks in aural training revolve around melodies, the phrasing of these can contribute to or work against the overall music education of the student. Aspects of a musical phrase include melodic contour and pitch selection within certain tonal constraints. Some programs choose to use a database of prepared phrases, while others generate notes algorithmically. Neither is inherently better than the other, but a poor database choice can lead to predictable or already-known phrases, while overly simple algorithms, such as random selection, can result in counterintuitive musical examples. Similar comments can be made about generation of rhythm and harmonic examples.

Often in aural and musicianship examples, elements are isolated to focus student attention. This results, for example, in intervals played in isolation with static dynamics and timbre. While potentially useful in clarifying what students should attend to, this isolation is generally undesirable, and can limit transfer of learning from the computer to "real-world" music. Technical limitations of computer technology have historically reinforced this decontextualized approach because it was difficult to store long passages or use complex generative algorithms, but as media rich computer technology advances, more contextualized examples can be expected. One program that emphasizes the presentation of aural activities in their musical context is the Functional Ear Trainer application that provides musical preamble to pitch recognition tasks that clearly establish the key.

Audio quality of built-in sounds is improving also, and there is little excuse for programs to employ simple periodic waveforms. Most frequently applications use samples of acoustic instruments and provide of a variety of timbres and pitch ranges, for example, phrase playback. If software enables MIDI playback, then the audio quality of the synthesizer, physical or software, is an important choice. The ability for the user to substitute a software synthesizer plugin is a great advantage in customizing the aural training experience for particular students or situations.

Teaching considerations

As with all resources for music education, there are issues other than software functions to consider in the discussions about the choice and use of aural and musicianship software. One of the first considerations is deciding *who* will use the programs. If the use is compulsory for all students in all year levels, there will be different criteria for selection than if it is to be used for a selected number of students only. If a broad base of students are envisaged, then the breadth and depth of content is important such that it covers all the content requirements, also it is likely that customization options will be more important. Classroom management strategies for compulsory usage will likely require a significant number of computers thus making multiple-copy software license cost considerations critical.

When selecting aural and musicianship programs as part of a music course, the appropriateness of these programs to other elements of the curriculum should be considered. Relevance to the curriculum relates to the stylistic bias of the program, the types and complexity of the skills covered, and whether the software is more appropriate than other alternatives such as books, CDs and DVDs. For example, it may be more cost effective to purchase several portable CD players and training materials than several computers and software, unless the computers have more applications that justify their purchase.

One of the advantages often cited for the use of computer programs in aural training or musicianship is the ability for the computer to monitor student progress. Teachers wishing to make use of these facilities need to consider a number of factors. First, what is the program assessing? Some programs keep records of all student activity, others allow students to practice then do assessable activities, while others keep records of the highest score achievement only. Second, can the software individualize a program for a student in an appropriate way? A number of programs allow students to register so that on subsequent sessions they can continue on activities and levels they were previously at. Some also allow the teacher or student to set a pathway of activities along which to progress. Third, is customizing worth the effort? While a few of the aural programs allow sophisticated individualization the question remains as to who is going to take the trouble to use such features and keep track of student progress at a detailed level. There are a couple of solutions; the students could be instructed how to set their own task pathways thus freeing the teacher from setting all of them herself, or use assessment feedback to consistently reset short-term goals rather than attempting to plot a long-term path. Fourth, can you trust the computer assessment? What status will computer-based results play in the student's grade or feedback? Many educators prefer to use aural and musicianship programs as supportive of their curriculum and to trust their own judgment of the student's progress and achievements by individually examining each student, or setting their own tests. Some software applications allow teachers to set their own tests that are administered by the software when required.

For aural or musicianship training to be effective it cannot be ad hoc. Time needs to be allocated in the curriculum for work on aural and musicianship training for it to be effective. It has been found that regular short work sessions are more productive than extended sessions in these areas, thus the down time or rotational management strategies mentioned previously seem appropriate. Regular monitoring of student progress is required to keep students on task and to make sure the training time is well spent. This can include class charts of weekly progress or a series of skill hurdles set at regular intervals.

Simple programs are often required for younger students who cope less well with abstracted aural tasks and intricate naming conventions. The free online Music Essentials tools at the BBC Web site provide a useful starting place for basic musicianship tools, but they are not very extensive. The Music Ace and Theory Games software programs are aimed at younger students and include colorful on-screen

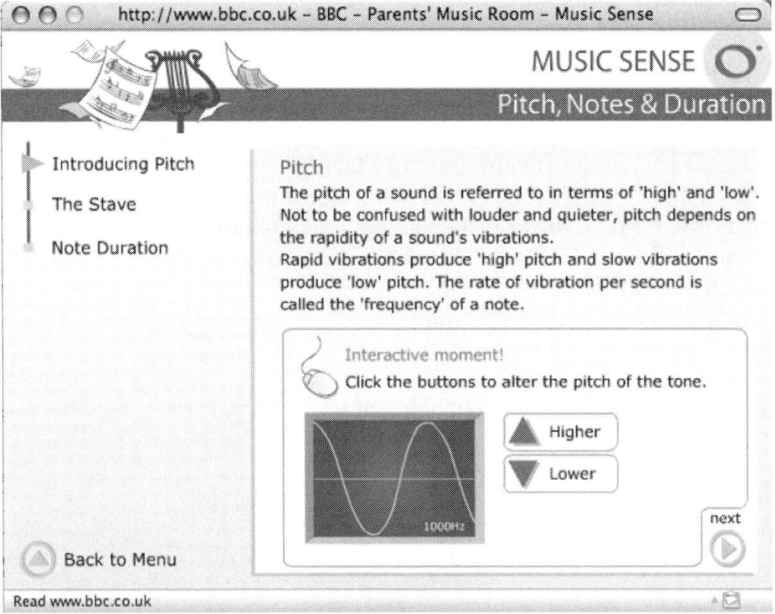

Figure 18.3   A screen from the Music Sense application from the BBC's Music Essentials Web site.

activities that involve the fundamentals of music theory and a section for creative activities. At the more open-ended, but fun, end of the musicianship continuum is Morton Subotnick's Hearing Music program that encourages aural development through progressive interaction and play with the software musical environment.

It is possible to use computers to prepare aural training and musicianship resources, rather than relying on the examples in one of the manual software packages. An audio recording or MIDI sequencing package can be used to prepare examples that can be delivered on CD in class or to students for private work. The processes of using these applications were covered in chapters 4 to 8 of this book. While preparing examples and tasks is somewhat time consuming, it does provide precise control over the materials and makes it easy to directly relate the examples to the repertoire or existing areas of study. For the more adventurous, simple drill and practice programs can be written in algorithmic music software environments such as Impromptu, jMusic, Max/MSP, Supercollider, Pure Data, and others covered in chapter 6. Indeed, many of the commercial applications, and most of the free or shareware ones, started life as projects by music teachers interested to provide some specific emphasis or angle on aural or musicianship training for their students.

Useful links

Information about many of the applications mentioned in this chapter can be found at the Web addresses below. These links include free, shareware, and commercial aural and theory training applications.

Aural training

Absolute Pitch (atonal pitch recognition)
http://www.silvawood.co.uk/pitch-intro.htm
Auralia (aural training software)
http://www.risingsoftware.com/auralia30/
Calma (software for aural training and listening exercises)
http://www.hud.ac.uk/mh/music/calma/calma.html
Functional Ear Trainer (software for pitch recognition in context)
http://www.miles.be/
Good-Ear Ear Trainer (online ear training)
http://www.good-ear.com/
Listen (aural training software)
http://www.imaja.com/listen/index.html
MacGAMUT, (ear training software)
http://www.macgamut.com/
Practica Musica (sight reading and aural training software)
http://www.ars-nova.com/practica.html

Musicianship

Hearing Music (software playground for musical sound exploration)
http://www.viva-media.com/products/hearingMusic/hearingMusic.html
Interactive Musician (musicianship software series)
http://www.alfred.com/sub_software/aim/aim.htm
MiBac Jazz (jazz musicianship tutorials)
http://www.mibac.com/Pages/jz.html
Music Ace (elementary level musicianship games)
http://www.harmonicvision.com/mafact.htm
Music Essentials (online musicianship games)
http://www.bbc.co.uk/music/parents/musicessentials/index.shtml
Musicianship Basics (simple software music theory quizzes)
http://users.dragnet.com.au/~donovan/mb/index.html
Music Lessons I & II (musicianship tutorial software)
http://www.mibac.com/Pages/ML.html
Muisctheory.net (online musicianship exercises)
http://www.musictheory.net/
Musition (music theory and musicianship software)
http://www.risingsoftware.com/musition2/
Sibelius Notes (musicianship teaching resource pack)
http://www.sibelius.com/products/notes/
Theory Games (early years musicianship software)
http://www.alfred.com/frameset.cfm?sub=software

Conclusion

Assisting students to perceive and understand the elements of music and how they operate together is fundamental to music education. An important part of acquiring these skills is the continued practice of listening, identifying, and performing exercises that reinforce the basic principles of these elements. Such repetitive tasks are well suited to the computer, and it is not surprising that a wide range of software applications have arisen to support aural and musicianship training. The challenge for music educators is to use these wisely, not to allow the tireless computer to exhaust the easily bored student, and to continually relate the abstract exercises and tasks typically found in drill and practice methods to real-world musical situations and activities. Used well, the computer can be a powerful ally in the teaching of aural and musicianship curricular. Used poorly, it can stifle enthusiasm and passion for music.

Reflection questions

1. The sonic features tested by aural training software include which musical elements?
2. What added skills and knowledge are suggested for contemporary musicianship?
3. What are the differences between task-based and case-based training applications?
4. Which interaction characteristics do video games and aural training software share?
5. What are some of the options for students to continue aural or musicianship training on their home computer?
6. Describe the difference between teaching musicianship through imitation and through application.
7. List three of the issues of access to computers raised in this chapter.
8. How might aural and musicianship applications take account of style and genre requirements?
9. What is meant by taking about the "musicality" of the aural or musicianship software?
10. How might the software features for younger and older students vary?

Teaching tips

1. Choose software that allows for self assessment at any time, especially prior to formal assessment gateways.
2. Focus on measurable competency outcomes and allow students to do more or less computer-based training as required to achieve those outcomes, rather than a set period of time weekly.

3. Ensure that musicianship study on computer is well augmented by composing, arranging, and performance applications of that knowledge.

4. Ensure that there is an opportunity for student out-of-hours access to aural or musicianship software, either at school or at home.

5. Utilize software that provides a range of interaction activities to ensure development of a range of abilities and to maintain student interest.

6. Have some computer-based sessions where students work in pairs so that they share problem-solving skills and develop some healthy competitive spirit.

7. Integrate aural and musicianship software into lessons by spending some time on the computer or reflecting with students on their results from recent tasks on the computer.

8. Have a computer available in the music room for students to use in "down time" between activities.

9. Make sure that the software used has a visual representation (stave, tablature, etc.) that is familiar to the student.

10. Students have different learning styles, and software has different ways of operating. It can be helpful to have more than one application and to allow students to pick the one they are most comfortable with.

Suggested tasks

1. Test your own aural abilities using a software package to assist you in moderating between the scores and feedback provided and your intuition about a known skill level (your own).

2. Take one curriculum as an example and match up the aural and musicianship requirements with software systems that meet those needs.

3. Use the fact that setting goals for use of aural software requires specification of outcomes to refine and revisit the aural skills components of you curriculum.

4. Take time to explore some of the more exploratory software packages, such as Hearing Music, rather than settling on a very didactic system as an easy choice.

5. When next you are composing or performing, take a moment to reflect on all the aural skills you are tacitly utilizing. Use this information to help your students learn.

Chapter summary

Acquiring the basic skills in musicianship and aural perception continues to be a core aspect of music education. The recognition of timbres, melodies, harmonies, rhythms, and other musical elements underpin aural perception, while understanding symbolic musical systems and developing social and historical contextual perspectives enrich musicianship. There is a vast array of software for aural and musicianship training and they come with a broad array of features and capabilities, it is critical to match these with the educational needs of a particular situation. When relying on a computer-based training regime for aural musicianship the question of access to computers and software needs to be addressed. Some helpful free online resources can assist students to continue these activities home. All music exists within a culture and this can be reflected in the musical phrases and timbres used in aural and musicianship tasks, as well as in the visual representations of music that are used to communicate questions and answers. Alignment between contextual needs and software features is important to the successful implementation of computers to support aural and musicianship training. A computer system can provide helpful one-on-one support to budding musicians in the area of aural and musicianship training, but such skill development needs to be used wisely so as to support, not dictate, music education activities and priorities. Skills are developed so they can be used, and computers can be a powerful aid to both musical skill development and musical skill usage.

Notes

1   Pratt, George, *Aural Awareness: Principles and Practice* (Buckingham: Open University Press, 1990).
2   Mozart — music sight-reading game, for Palm devices, http://www.rogame. com/pages/Mozart.html.

Chapter 19

Assessment

Assessment in music education is concerned with what students know and can do. This chapter focuses on how the computer can assist with the assessment of students' musical intelligence. So what is meant by assessment? David Elliot, in his book *Music Matters*, makes a distinction between evaluation and assessment. He understands assessment as "constructive feedback" and evaluation as "grading".[1] For the purposes of this chapter we will gloss over such semantics, however we will hold onto Elliot's main purpose for the distinction which is to draw attention to the fact that the primary purpose of assessment is to "articulate feedback to students about the quality of their growing musicianship"[2] with an ultimate aim that students develop the ability to competently self-assess their musical achievements.

Given that the overall purpose of assessment is to improve a student's learning, there are a number of more specific ways in which assessment contributes to music education stakeholders; teachers, parents, schooling authorities and community. Assessment is used to motivate the student to reach particular goals and achievements. To help students and teachers understand what areas of knowledge and skill to prioritize going forward. Assessment can assist teachers in monitoring the effectiveness of teaching practices and identifying where they might be improved. The results of assessment can inform stakeholders about the achievements and progress of an individual student or groups of students in reaching specified standards or targets.

What to assess

There is evidently, in human kind, a musical intelligence as labeled by Howard Gardner, manifest in a number of ways not least that almost every human culture on the planet has developed a musical practice, even if at time these were closely linked to dance, religion or some other cultural expression.[3] Understanding musical intelligence is a first step to knowing how to assess it, and Gardner provides a good overview which we will now summarize and discuss. First of all, musical intelligence involves musical thinking or imagination. The ability to hear music in one's head, and to identify and reproduce the most critical elements of music which, in Gardner's research, are pitch and rhythm followed closely by timbre and structure. The ways these elements are experienced through external musical input and expression pivot on a person's sonic imagination, being able to think in sound and envision sonic form and structure. Clearly, imagination is not directly accessible for assessment, but evidence of it through actions can be observed. This is not to say that music is simply a cognitive skill, it is much more direct than that. Music making is closer to action than thinking, it is gestural, and involves the body either directly in production or indirectly in imagination. Therefore, externalizing music through performance, composition and other modes of production are key elements in musical assessment. However, musical intelligence is not only about externalizing or representing music but also about interpreting, understanding, analyzing and appreciating music and sound.

It is also revealing to see what music is not, or which other ways of knowing it is similar to. Gardner suggests that there is evidence that music is not like language, even though it shares some semantic structural features, music is like dance and other bodily-kinesthetic intelligences in its gestural nature, music is like mathematics in its fascination with patterns and elegant organization but it not about abstract structures like mathematics rather only concerned with sonic organization as it leads to music, and music is somewhat related to geometry and spatial intelligences broadly. When conducting musical assessment it is important that when these other intelligences are involved, for example written tests that require linguistic skills or theory tests that require mathematical skills, that we are able to distinguish which intelligence is really being tested.

Musical intelligence also relates to aesthetics. Music is expressive and should have some emotional content that has an affect. Therefore, while exercises and test tasks may indicate some skill developments the ultimate test is how all these elements come together in complete music productions. Assessment can focus both the appreciation and the production of music with particular emotional or aesthetic qualities. These are critically bound by cultural and stylistic norms and conventions and having the knowledge and control to work within and beyond these is important measure of musical intelligence. The musical skills and abilities that are valued also vary between cultures and musical genres so curricular and assessment proprieties need to be sensitive to this.

Musical intelligence is a complex phenomena involving imagination, gesture and emotion. It is possible to develop criteria for these as aspects of musicianship, and also possible to develop tests to assess these individually, however, their interconnection means that assessment should largely involve demonstrations of complete musical activities and outcomes, rather than isolated tasks or exercises that are abstracted from a musical context. This use of realistic or complete tasks is sometimes called authentic assessment; where assessment is designed to test the essential nature of the skill or understanding in a realistic situation. There is, however, a danger to assuming that gesture understanding implies music performance. Given the wide acceptance that composing a score or analysis of a musical work also requires musical intelligence, it is clear that gestural understanding can be expressed in a nondirect way. This is important for computer music activities that involve a mixture of directed and indirect gestures in their production and may not involve any direct gestures in their presentation as recorded or rendered works. Similarly, musical intelligence can be articulated as computational algorithms, which, like notated scores, embed understanding in implied gestures and sounds yet to be rendered.

Finally, in this section we turn our attention to what data to use as evidence for assessment. Complete musical tasks can exist as performances, scores, recordings or media rich documents. Many of these forms can be stored digitally, with live performances being the most problematic in this regard. Video and audio documentation of performance can be used for moderation and revisiting during assessment. Music productions can be digitized as graphic, audio, or MIDI files. Media-rich documents are likely to be created in digital form in any case and are easily managed. As assessment proceeds data is generated and can include written comments and statements, digitized explanatory examples and numerical scores. In the next section, we will explore some details about how the computer can be used to generate and manage data and provide other assistance during music assessment.

Computers in assessment

Computers are often used at the end of the assessment chain to collate marks and grades and to write reports. In this section, we will examine how computers can also be used throughout the learning process to provide feedback and support. In particular, the computer is useful during production processes for reflecting on the state of a work and with facilitating communications between peers, team members, and teachers about progress and plans. The computer can store information about musical works in progress as files, documentation, and commentary that provides a data trail for reflection and assessment. The computer can even be used to make judgments about student competence in well-defined areas of knowledge or skill ranging from online music theory tests to automated performance measurements; the results of which can become part of the assessment data mix.

Production and response

Evaluation of work is an iterative and ongoing process, done throughout the development of a musical work. Given that computers can be used in these musical productions, as detailed in chapters 4 to 8, then the computer as a tool, medium, or instrument of music production is well placed to assist with assessment and evaluation. The most obvious use of computers in this regard is as an aid to reflection about or response to the state of the work in progress. The computer can at any time playback or otherwise present a sequence, score, recording or document. To improve reflection beyond the levels of unavoidable observation or chance occurrence, it is therefore necessary to encourage students to be deliberate about their reflections on their work and to provide them with a framework for making insightful judgments about the work. A good place to start with such frameworks are the elemental categories outlined by George Pratt,[4] the aesthetic criteria proposed by Bennet Reimer,[5] or the dimensions of musical assessment proposed by Keith Swanwick[6] (Figure 19.1).

As works are produced, it is quite important for assessment (and creative) purposes to keep copies of the work as it proceeds. Many expert composers do this as

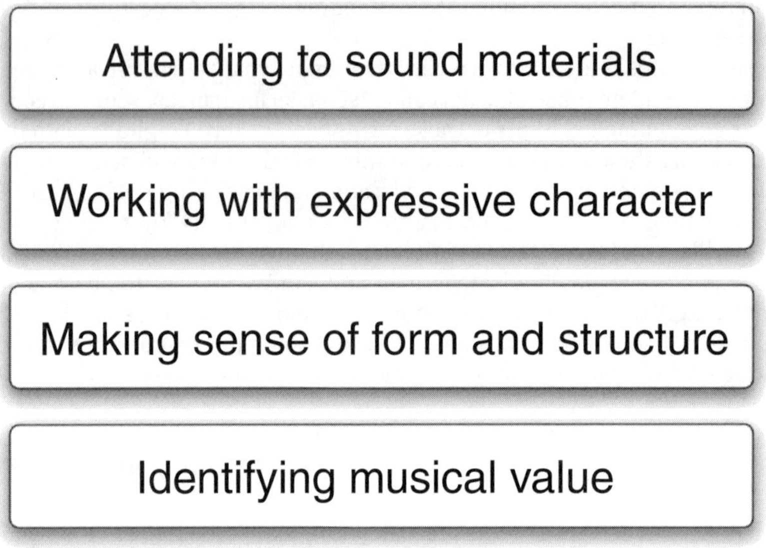

Figure 19.1 Assessment criteria based on Keith Swanwick's dimensions.

a matter of course so that if they take a development path that proves unproductive they can go back to a previous version and take another tangent. As an assessment tool, the ability to look back at the decisions made in the production of a musical work can reveal a lot about thought processes and musical decision making. This information can reveal where understandings are well developed or not and also how creative practices are effective or unproductive. The simple ability of most software to save a copy of a project file(s) at regular intervals can facilitate this and students need to be required or encouraged to do so until this practice becomes habitual as it is for many experienced computer musicians.

A final consideration when assessing work produced with computer music systems is to understand the potential and influence of the system itself. All technologies influence the activities done with them and computers can be powerfully so. For example, if a student uses Band In A Box or GarageBand to create an arrangement of a jazz standard, the teacher should be aware that these programs generate (or have available) patterns in various styles that can be recombined to form an arrangement. Different expectations are required when this arrangement is done using a publishing package such as Sibelius that has little in the way of prepared material for the student to use. More subtly, most sequencing programs can easily repeat material but it is less automatic to repeat material with variations or development of themes. It is important for an assessor to sort out the differences between the musical affordances provided by the software and the creative use of the leverage provided by the software. To assist in sorting out tool from technique, it can help to have students provide an explanation of their work, either written or verbal. It usually becomes clear in such reports to what extent they are in control of their processes and are making musical, rather than simply technical, decisions.

Communications

Computers are used often for communications including, e-mail, discussion forums, Web sites, and so on. The disseminating information about assessment can easily use these methods. Posting assessment requirements and criteria on a Web site makes them publicly accessible and easily updateable if required.

The Internet and e-mail can be used to gather information that can inform the production of or response to music, or that can help inform the value of a musical work through better understanding of the broader musical culture in which it fits. More details about the use of the Internet for music research can be found in chapter 16. In addition to seeking information on the Net, it can also provide access to other musical and experiences, such as audio recording, music videos, and reviews of works or performances. This enriches the musical environment in which the student works and can be a source of inspiration and influence on their work. Access to examples of other work can also aid in assessment by providing benchmarks and comparisons of work from different locations and times.

The potential of online forums for collaboration and feedback is enormous. In the same way that feedback and peer review are possible in music classes and ensembles, the use of discussion forums expands the range and access of views and opinions. Forums can be used to assist collaboration by being a focal point of discussions and posting of example and draft material. They enable participants to be spread over a wide geographical area or to work **asynchronously**. Forums can also be used for peer review where members of a group comment on each other's work and provide other musical material as examples to back up their statements. E-mail lists are often used in this way where questions or draft works are posted to the list for comment by any one on the list. Most forums store information in chronological order and in discussion threads that link related comments. This history of development can be reviewed as supporting evidence or for clarification when assessment is made about the resulting work.

Electronic communications can be used to increase interaction between students and staff by way of specific questions and answers, or exchange of draft versions of work for comment. The expert advice available to a student can be expanded through the use of other staff, senior students, or external experts as mentors.

Electronic submission of work or assessment results is possible where the work is suitable for storage in digital form. This is fine for scores, recordings, text documents, and the like, and can even be used for videos of performances in some cases. We will discuss electronic storage and management in more detail below.

Collaborations between assessors can be useful during formal assessments and moderation of results across several assessors. It is increasingly common for Internet video conferencing to be used for these purposes. These technologies are mostly used to facilitate discussions between people who are geographically distant and so it is most useful for connecting those in remote communities or for gathering together data across an entire state or country.

Information management

Music assessments, particularly those of work in digital form, can generate a significant amount of data and the organization of this is clearly a task computers are used for. At the heart of any computer-based information organization process is a database where information is stored and indexed. More formally this type of application is refered to as a content management system (CMS) and they typically have data stored on a server and a user interface accessed through the Web or as a stand along application. The model is to store information centrally and have access to it in many locations. The types of content that can be stored in a CMS should be any digital file, including audio files, videos, application documents, and so on. CMS systems can be added to, edited or viewed by any authorized person, and different levels of user privileges can be set. This allows, in a simplistic case, for students to add work, for teachers to edit, and for parents to view.

There are a wide variety of ways CMS systems can be used, but a few popular ones stand out. As a storage and reviewing area, CMS systems are commonly referred to as electronic or digital portfolios. With an ePortfolio students typically add and organize their work within the CMS and teachers, parents and other stakeholders can typically view and review the work. Music lends itself particularly well to ePortfolios because of their ability to store rich media assets, as outlined in "The Art of ePortfolios" by this author and Dillon and summarized below.[7] A variety of views can be created on the work in the CMS depending upon the use for assessment, exhibition, as a resume and so on. A chronological record of data stored in the CMS with a Web-enabled interface is often referred to as a discussion forum or a blog. Traditionally these applications have focused predominantly on text entries, but most support any media types as an entry or at least as an attachment to an entry (also called a post). As a data trail of student work, a chronological organization of entries is often quite sufficient. Forums usually allow many people to submit

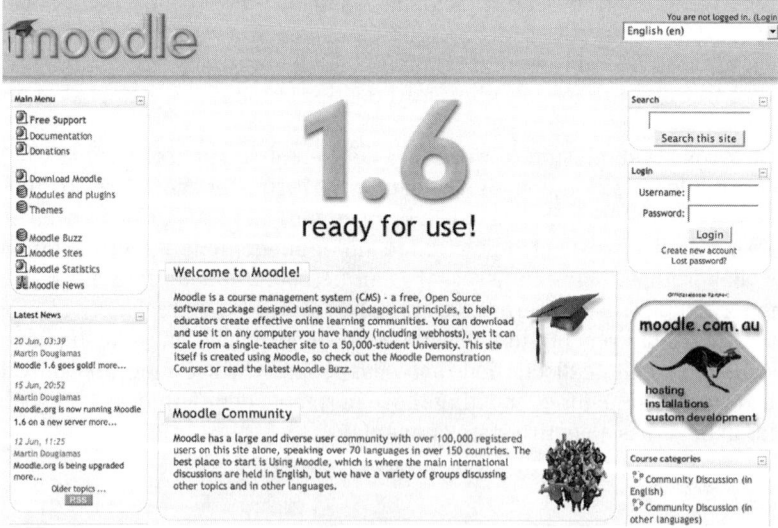

Figure 19.2   The home page of the Moodle CMS system.

an entry whereas blogs are typically designed for individual users. Both allow any many people add comments to an entry. Some CMS systems are tied to other database systems (i.e., school timetable scheduling and grade submission systems and then labeled as a Learning Management System). A popular CMS system for education is Moodle, which includes online lesson delivery, assignment submissions, forums and chat, and ePortfolio facilities (Figure 19.2). These are discussed in more detail in chapter 20, but are usually configured as systems for administrative rather than pedagogical support.

There are a number of advantages to using a digital portfolio system to accumulate and review student work. These include the ability to maintain a data trail from the statement of work requirement, through drafts and plans, to final artifact, reflections on it, and eventual evaluation or grade. The process of documentation enabled by a digital portfolio leads to accountability and reflection on the part of the student, and improves transparency of assessment processes for teachers. The ability to self-monitor progress is empowering for the student as it can lead to better self-evaluation and positive self-esteem through having concrete demonstrations of outcomes and achievements.

Ownership and access

Having assessment data, either raw information or comments and grades in databases, begs the question about governance of and access to the information. Assuming that the information is on a server controlled by a school or other educational authority, the question of maintenance and data backup is clearly with that authority. This would be part of any normal Information technology governance regime. If, however, a music teacher administers the database directly, then he or she would need to take responsibility for the safe keeping of that data, including backups and security arrangements, to prevent unwanted access. The simplest security from unwanted access is to not have the machine connected to the Internet, but this defeats the purpose of sharing that information with students and parents from their home machines and closes off opportunities for collaboration and input from those further a field. These issues are technically solvable, but they do need some close attention when computer assessment systems are established and from time to time thereafter to ensure reliability.

As well as technical concerns, there are policy decisions about access to online student materials. It is usual that students can access and edit their own materials, and that there be some way to enable students to make some works available for viewing by their peers. Teachers and parents often have rights to view student work and to add comments about it, and there may be a public Web site that features selected works and is usually is managed by teaching staff. Online governance regulations can be used to indicate the types of information that can be made publicly available and the needs for attribution and acknowledgment to students, staff and institution. These will need to align with regulations and laws that effect the institution. When it comes to assessment comments and grades in some centrally managed system, it is usual that teachers can add and edit these and that students and parents can access them. It is less common for student results to be publicly available, although many schooling systems aggregate student results and make these statistics available provided they do not identify individual students or particular work.

Automated assessment

The use of computers to measure and assess musical skills and knowledge is an umbrella for a wide variety of tools and pedagogical approaches, from what used to be called Computer-Assisted Instruction (CAI) where information was presented and student understanding tested through simple multiple-choice tests, to sophisticated artificial intelligence systems that measure performance deviations against statistical norms, benchmark performances, or even previous performances of the same musician.

Automated tests, ones where a computer makes assessments about a students' performance based on interactive tests the student does at the computer, are quite common in areas of the curriculum where correct and incorrect answers are available. In particular, they are frequently used for aural and musicianship testing, as for example in the Auralia, Musition, and Music Ace software packages. These types of tests became popular in the 1980s and 1990s and they are still quite common and in a few cases their techniques have become somewhat more sophisticated. The testing of simple correct or incorrect responses is quite trivial, even if effective, but systems that correct more contextual and complex tasks, such as the Music Theory Workbench that corrects counterpoint exercises, are becoming more widespread.[8]

Performance evaluations are provided by software systems such as InThe-Chair and SmartMusic. With these programs students play repertoire on their instruments while the computer provides accompaniment that follows the student. The programs can also provide feedback on the performance in terms of stability of tempo, number of wrong notes, and expressive deviation from other performances of the same work. Feedback from such systems can provide useful supplements to teacher feedback and progress in terms of statistics from these programs can be an additional external measure of progress for both students and assessor. In the early years of this century, there is much interest in the audio analysis techniques that make such systems viable, and further advances in music information retrieval research should see a rise in the effectiveness of computer-based assessment of compositions and performances during the twenty-first century.

Reporting

The computer is routinely used for reporting on student progress and achievement. Software tools for this task can be as general purpose as a word processor or as specific as a report template system in a school-wide learning management system. In between are simple tools such as Teachers Report Assistant and Smart School Report Writer that collate a selection of prepared phrases into a paragraph for use as a written component of a report (Figure 19.3). Various database and spreadsheet programs can be used to collate grades and/or comments. More details on the use of these administrative tools can be found in chapter 20.

Strategies to assist in the task of preparing reports include reviewing any CMS systems where student work is kept to develop or confirm assessment conclusions against criteria. Also, the maintenance of a computer-based journal throughout the term with "pages" for each student can spread the load of compiling report comments on student over time and also assist in reviewing progress and as a reminder of significant events or achievements that may have occurred.

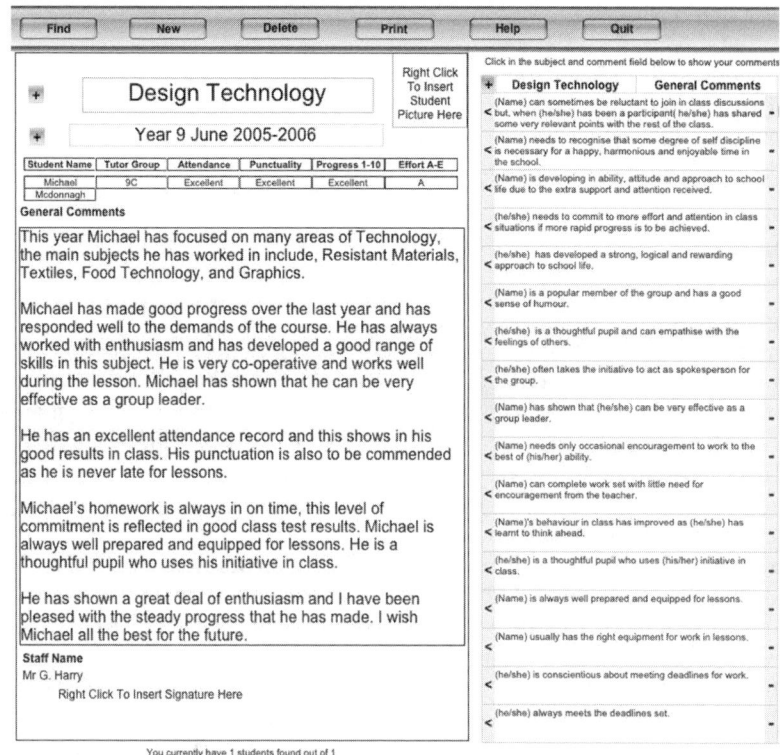

Figure 19.3   An example student report in Smart School Report Writer.

Useful links

Information about many of the applications mentioned in this chapter can be found at the Web addresses below. These links include tools to assist in assessing and reporting.

Tools for assessing

Auralia (aural training software) Figure 19.3. An example of a student report in
     Smart School Report Writer.
     http://www.risingsoftware.com/auralia30/
InTheChair (accompaniment and performance monitoring software)
     http://www.inthechair.com/
Musition (music theory and musicianship software)
     http://www.risingsoftware.com/musition2/
SmartMusic (auto accompaniment software)
     http://www.smartmusic.com/

Tools for reporting

Smart School Report Writer (report phrase compiler)
    http://www.report-writer.co.uk/
Teachers Report Assistant (report phrase compiler)
    http://www.rayslearning.com/report.htm

Conclusion

The computer has a role in the ongoing feedback to the student, the essence of assessment, especially when it is an active participant in music production and presentation activities. The function of the computer as a medium for the externalization of musical ideas and the documentation of musical outcomes makes it an ideal vehicle for the reflection and review of those activities. When the student is given control over those storage and reviewing processes they can learn to develop skills of self-assessment that will advance their musical intelligence. Because the computer stores and reproduces music in many different digital forms, from text to video, it can provide ongoing direct feedback to the user. As a medium for electronic communications, it can act as a link between students, teachers, parents, and community to connect the students' musical activities to those around them and to receive valuable advice, support, and encouragement. There are a number of practical software tools for directly supporting assessment including content management systems as portfolios and record keeping databases, automated testing, and measurement systems that can score student performance on various tasks, and word processors and result systems for compiling reports and grades. While the computer already plays a significant role in music educational assessment, it seems certain to increase as the systems of communication and knowledge management increasingly rely on the expanding network infrastructure.

Reflection questions

1. What is assessment in music education concerned with?
2. According to David Elliot, the primary purpose of assessment is to...
3. Who are mentioned as "stakeholders" in music educational assessment?
4. Who coined the term "musical intelligence"?
5. What is musical intelligence?
6. What type of data can be stored in a computer for review and assessment?
7. The works of which authors are suggested as helping to inform criteria for music assessment frameworks?
8. What is a CMS?
9. How can e-mail be used to improve feedback to students about their music work?
10. What types of skills can be measured through automated computer processes?

Teaching tips

1. Regular and ongoing assessment and feedback helps normalize these activities as part of the music leaning process and minimizes the likelihood of poor performance as a result of stress at times of summative assessment.
2. Set up group forums for students to discuss their music work with others.
3. Provide accessible audio and video recording facilities so that students can regularly record their work to share it and listen back to it.
4. Make sure that the aesthetic qualities and cultural value of music are routinely included as assessment criteria.
5. Encourage peer assessment as a way of providing more feedback to students and to help them develop their analytical and self-assessment abilities.
6. Make provision for storage and management of drafts of student work to capture process information.
7. Establish a music ePortfolio for each student that they can maintain during their time at the school.
8. Make sure all access to ePortfolios is password protected, but that students have access to the data from their home computers.
9. Provide exemplar works that students can use as benchmarks against their own work.
10. Continually revisit assessment criteria in discussions with students so that these are clear in their minds as they work.

Suggested tasks

1. Spend some time becoming more familiar with computer-based assessment software, such as a spreadsheet or CMS system, so that assessment processes can take maximum advantage of them.
2. Make sure you are familiar with the affordances (obvious features) of the software students are using so you can separate their contribution from the software's in music work.
3. Review some of the research in ePortfolios to see how they can best be used in your teaching.
4. Establish an electronic journal to make ongoing notes about student progress that can be collated at report writing time.
5. Evaluate some of the computer-based performance accompaniment systems for their ability to provide useful feedback to the student.

Chapter summary

Assessment is designed to improve student learning. To maximize the value of assessment it is necessary to be clear about what musical intelligence is and how we know when students are developing it. The use of music technologies for capturing and presenting student activities has resulted in changing student production activities and associated assessment practices. Students are now able to produce audio, video, and multimedia assessment items. These advances have resulted in changing the minds of teachers and curriculum developers about best assessment practice. For example, videoing a performance rather than holding central examinations is increasingly common as is the use of video conferencing for assessment moderation. These digital documentations and files can be stored in content management systems as an electronic portfolio allowing for rich media documents that make assessment activities more authentic, and for the process of student development to be more clearly traced. Computers can also be used to communicate feedback between students, staff, and parents and for the setting of computer-based tests and measurements of student progress, and they are routinely used for the preparation of student reports. It is clear that computers have a strong and potentially increasing role to play is music assessment.

Notes

1 Elliot, David, *Music Matters: A New Philosophy of Music Education* (New York: Oxford, 1995), 264.
2 Ibid.
3 Gardner, Howard, *Frames of Mind: The Theory of Multiple Intelligences* (London: Heinemann, 1983).
4 Pratt, George, *Aural Awareness: Principles and Practice* (Buckingham: Open University Press, 1990).
5 Reimer, Bennett, *A Philosophy of Music Education* (Englewood Cliffs, NJ Prentice Hall, 1970).
6 Swanwick, Keith, *Teaching Music Musically* (London: Routledge, 1999).
7 Dillon, Steve, and Andrew R. Brown, "The Art of ePortfolios: Insights from the Creative Arts Experience," in *Handbook of Research on ePortfolios*, eds. Ali Jafari and Catherine Jaufman. (Hershey, PA: Idea Group Publishing, 2006).
8 Taube, Heinrick, "Automatic Tonal Analysis: Toward the Implementation of a Music Theory Workbench." *Computer Music Journal* 23, no. 4 (1999), 18–32.

Chapter 20

Administration

In addition to its value for learning and production, the computer can help teachers and students manage information to make their daily work more effective. The use of the computer for administrative tasks may not be as exciting as using it for music production tasks, but it can make an important impact on the efficient running of a music program and is the area in which many teachers have their first or dominant contact with computing technologies. It is wise to take advantage of the opportunity to get better acquainted with how the computer operates in an area where it is almost impossible to avoid interfacing with it, the business and administration of music education.

There are a number of benefits and pitfalls in the use of computers for educational administration. Some of the benefits include the computer's ability to assist with managing data and information, tracking and organization of resources, timely tracking of student progress through assessment, assistance with reflection and planning of music programs, and as a tool for collating and reporting on activities. Some of the major pitfalls include the computer's ability to create too much detail and information, a tendency to direct the focus onto statistics and text rather than onto musical outcomes and social benefits, the lack of flexibility in some administrative systems that can make them frustrating to navigate, and the often rapid changes in systems that lead to a sense of serial stupidity because just as you start to feel comfortable with one process another seems to overtake it.

In this chapter we will explore some of the common applications and uses of the computer for music education administration. Hopefully, as we proceed, the benefits will become clearer, new opportunities for increasing efficiency will emerge, and a larger view of the underlying computing processes may make the surface-level changes in process seem less significant.

Document preparation

Like most other professionals, educators can spend a lot of time communicating via documents. These can include curriculum designs, grant funding applications, worksheets, written tests, student reports and so on. Given that this is such a significant part of the teacher's working life, it is well worth getting to know the computer-based tools that can assist in the preparation of these documents.

Word processing

Given that text is pervasive in documents, it is not surprising that word processors are the major application for preparing them. Throughout the history of computing, the humble text editor has been added to year after year to become an extensive and sophisticated application. Text editors were originally used to write computer code, and they continue to be used by programmers for this purpose. Text editors themselves have become much more sophisticated, but in different ways from their word processor cousins. Text editors focus mainly on illuminating program syntax and structure while adding tools to search and replace elements, and eventually auto-completion of keywords and other features. Word processors depart from text editors in their focus on preparation for a printed output. This usually means there is considerable attention paid to the appearance of the text including font types, sizes, formats (bold, italic, etc.), and layout options (i.e., page size, page margins, page numbering, paragraph justification, headers and footers, and so on). Word processors have added spell checking, insertion of graphic elements, and more to their list of potential features. It is usual that contemporary word processors, including Microsoft Word and the free OpenOffice Writer will do far more than is required by most educators, except those publishing their own books perhaps. Simpler programs are available, including Microsoft Works and Apple's iWorks, and may even be more appropriate and run more efficiently, but the larger office suites are almost standard. As well as general purpose word processors, specialized text editing programs are available for particular tasks (e.g., student report writing tools such as those reviewed in chapter 19).

The complexity of these large programs presents both a challenge and an opportunity to the music teacher or student using them. The challenge is to navigate around the program and not to be distracted by the array of menu options or unexpected behavior resulting from an accidental keystroke that happened to be a shortcut for an unknown function. The opportunity is that document preparation can be greatly assisted by mastering some of the word processing features. In particular, managing styles can help when updating the appearance of the document, managing text flow around images can be useful for imbedding notation examples in the document, and adding music words to the spelling dictionary can avoid special terms, such as serialism, being highlighted.

When sharing documents between people it is important to make sure that the files can be read by each person's word processor. The most widely readable format is a plain text file, usually denoted by a .txt extension to the filename. This format is universal but does not contain any formatting information, or any media other than text. If the file contains only text media then the rich text format can be used to maintain formatting and layout. These files typically have an .rtf extension. An alternative is the LaTeX format that also maintains formatting and is very popular in the scientific community. For documents that have media other than text alone, the OpenDocument format can be used. If a graphic representation of the file is sufficient (i.e., the file is for reading but not editing), then it can be saved to any common graphic format such as jpeg, png or PDF. As well as these file types, many word processors will read the native Microsoft Word format that usually has a .doc file extension.

Graphic design programs

While reports and grant applications may be acceptable as text-only documents, most others used for teaching, such as handouts, assignments, concert advertisements, and programs, CD booklets, and so on, will use graphics elements. These can be prepared using a wide variety of graphic applications, among the most popular of which are Adobe Photoshop and Illustrator. However, as with word processors, it is likely that these programs do far more than necessary for the music educator and any one of numerous simpler programs will usually suffice.

There are two main classes of graphic design applications, those that are pixel-based painting programs and those that are vector-based drawing programs. Pixel-based programs use a raster or bitmap image where the pixels (dots) on the screen are colored one by one. This is efficient from a computational perspective (it is fast) but the image does not easily scale. Pixel-based painting programs are useful for freehand illustrations or digital photos. Vector-based programs use geometric primates, such as points, lines, curves, and polygons to build up an image. The main advantage is that images can scale easily, and often the image description can be quite compact if the image is simple. Vector-based drawing programs are useful for designed images, particularly those with geometric shapes. Macromedia's Flash application is a widely used vector-based drawing and animation tool. When copying and pasting between applications (e.g., from a graphics program into a word processor), images may be converted to a raster-image even if they were originally vector-based. This can have implications if they are later rescaled in the document. An alternative is to save the vector-based images in a format (e.g., PDF) that can be imported into the word processor and inserted in the document without being converted.

Many graphic design programs come with libraries of clip art. These prepared images can provide a quick way to liven up a document or to prepare an illustration. A quick search of the Internet will reveal a number of music related clip art sites, such as Classroom Clipart, that have images freely available for use.

Desktop publishing

The ability to combine graphics and text in one document is now commonplace but emerged as part of desktop publishing. The use of a computer to lay out documents for publication was a revolution in the 1990s, when desktop publishing programs such as Adobe PageMaker and Quark Express were dominant. Since the turn of the century, these applications are used primarily by graphic professionals and most word processing packages provide enough layout functions to satisfy the needs of teachers and students. Desktop publishing features include typography control over characters, line and paragraph spacing, rotation of text, division of the document into columns, wrapping of text around graphic elements, arbitrary placement of text and image blocks on the page, and so on. Programs such as Apple's Pages, that deliberately combine word processing and page layout features, provide a good compromise for teachers and students preparing documents that combine text and image in equal amount, without having to navigate the serious desktop publishing applications.

Presentation programs

Making documents for screen-based presentation is an increasingly common task for educators, particularly as data projectors and larger screens are more commonly used in class rooms and lecture halls. Presentations can be given as part of a lesson, during seminars and conferences, at fund raising submissions, or staff meetings and public information sessions. Screen-based slides shows can include rich media such as text, images, video or audio and usually consist of a series of slides with information that summarizes or illustrates what is being discussed. Applications that can flip through media rich slide presentations include specialized programs such as Microsoft's PowerPoint, OpenOffice Impress and Apple's Keynote and more general purpose applications such as Adobe Reader for viewing PDF documents and any Web browser that can display HTML documents for this purpose. At the end of the day, any program that displays information on screen can be used as a presentational program. The useful features are the ability to include rich media elements and to move from one screen to another when required during the presentation.

Audiovisual documents

While documents are largely assumed to include text and image (including musical scores) that can be printed, documentation of musical activities often includes audio and vision. The management of audio and video files is addressed below, but the preparation of CDs and videos as listening materials for audition examination, as documented recordings for assessment and moderation, and as documentation to accompany reporting and accounting, and so on, are part of the administrative work load of the music educator. The preparation of these materials is covered in greater detail in chapters 8 and 12. In summary, there are a number of applications for audio recording on computer and for the editing of audio and video elements to CD and DVD. These audio and video documents and materials are en essential part in the operation and advocacy of a music education program.

Information management

Information for music educators can encompass class lists, student grades, equipment inventory, staffing allocations, class timetables, and more. Computers are often used to manage such data in systems that range from those that integrate schools, districts or states down to records maintained by individual teachers on personal machines. Managing this data typically conflates to issues of data entry, storage, manipulation and access, and the primary tools used are spreadsheets and databases.

Spreadsheet

Data that is primarily numerical and that requires calculation lends itself to manipulation by a spreadsheet. Tasks for the music educator in this category include calculating department expenditure, tracking lesson payments, accumulating grades and percentages, and maintaining attendance records. Spreadsheet programs are included with office suites including Microsoft Excel and OpenOffice Calc, and quite capable spreadsheets are in smaller software suites including Microsoft Works and Apple's iWork.

A spreadsheet consists of a two dimensional table, called a sheet, of cells. The sheet consists of columns named A, B, C, etc., and rows numbered 1, 2, 3, and so on. Cells are referenced by their coordinates. For example, cell B5 in Figure 20.1 contains "Josh." Cells can contain either text or numbers. The real magic of a spreadsheet is that cells can also contain formulae, as do the cells in the Percent and Grade columns in Figure 20.1. The results of the formula are usually shown. But when the cell is edited, the formula becomes apparent. The Percent column has the formula = $D2*0.4 + E2*0.3 + F2*0.3$ and like all spreadsheet formulae the equation begins with an equals sign and then math that may refer other cell values. In this example, the weighting of the first assignment is at 40 percent and the remaining assignments at 30 percent each. The Grade formula converts the percentage to a scale from 1 to 7, as required for this class. Cells with formulae update automatically when data changes in the cells they reference. Extrapolation on these principles can result in very sophisticated, and complex, spreadsheets, but these applications are also useful for speeding up simple calculations. Budgets are often done using a spreadsheet where items of income or expenditure can be summed, and budget forecasts and options can be easily compared.

Given that vast amounts of numerical data are not always easy to understand at a glance, most spreadsheet programs include the ability to generate charts from the data. Figure 20.2 shows the assessment data from Figure 20.1 with the distribution of percentages more clearly evident in the multiple bar graph.

One of the major advantages of spreadsheets is their ability to dynamically update the calculations. This makes it easy to create numerical models that simulate

◇	A	B	C	D	E	F	G
1							
2	SURNAME	NAME	Ass 1	Ass 2	Ass 3	Percent	Grade
3	COMERFORD	STEPHANIE	80	77	63	74	5
4	COOPER	BRIONY	90	67	77	79	5
5	CORFIELD	JOSH	70	73	90	77	5
6	ELLIOTT	ALEISHA	73	93	80	81	6
7	FULLER	DANIEL	73	77	80	76	5
8	GALLOWAY	TIMOTHY	70	73	70	71	4
9	GENOVA	AMANDA	70	73	63	69	4
10	GRADY	TRINA	80	80	70	77	5
11	GRIFFIN	MATTHEW	83	73	80	79	5
12	GRUNDY	KATE	73	48	73	66	4
13	HANSON	SHERRALEE	90	87	77	85	7
14	HO	LEE	73	83	73	76	5

Figure 20.1 Assessment calculations in the spreadsheet.

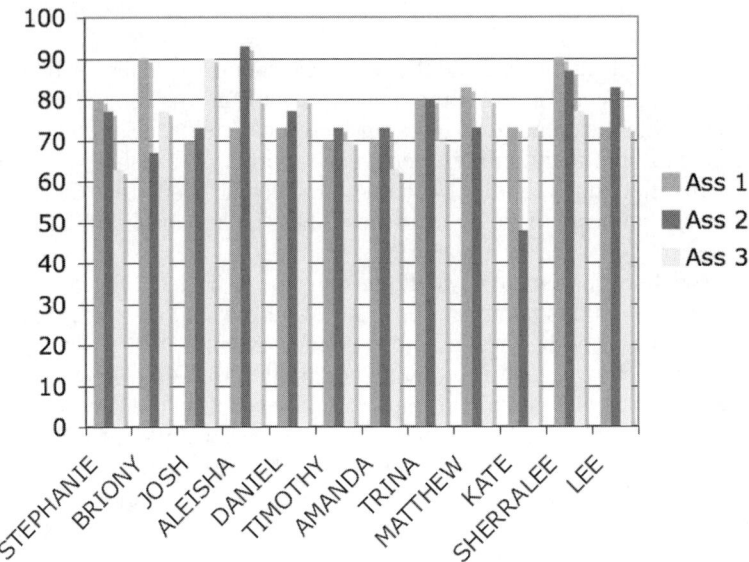

Figure 20.2   Graph of the assessment data.

situations and test hypotheses, for example, the effect of changing concert ticket fees or of purchasing additional instruments for a band can easily be explored.

Database

Wherever data needs to be stored, searched, and sorted on a large-scale, databases will be found doing the job. They are one of the most pervasive back-end computing tool. So long as the information can be digitized, a database can help manage it. Relatively easy to use database applications include Microsoft Access and FileMaker's *FileMaker Pro*. Databases that handle data across an entire school or district will more likely be based on one of the major database providers such as IBM, Oracle, SAP, or PeopleSoft. Databases are useful for storing student names and addresses, equipment inventories, for digital portfolios, and "friends of the music program" mailing lists. Databases consist of tables of data, where each row is a record and each column a field. The data layout may look similar to a spreadsheet, but the operations on the data are searching and matching rather than calculating. The table in Figure 20.3 shows a partial instrument inventory table where each instrument has its own record and the serial number field is a unique key identifying that record from others.

Database applications vary from simple "flat-file" databases such as electronic address books to "relational" databases that can be interrogated using the Structured Query Language (SQL). Flat file databases usually have a simple data structure that fits in a single table, whereas a relational database has a number of interrelated tables. For example, there may be a table of school musical instruments, and table of instrumental students, and table of teachers. The relationships between students, their teachers, and the instruments they hire could be constructed in the

Instrument	Serial #	Purchased	Location
Clarinet	34567	12/3/01	M217
Clarinet	42365	24/6/01	M217
Clarinet	13265	2/3/02	M114
Clarinet	86754	22/8/01	M114
Guitar	567-987	2/2/03	M114
Guitar	456-634	2/2/03	M114
Guitar	654-989	2/2/03	M114
Tuba	T45672	5/8/99	M217

Figure 20.3   A section from a database table of an instrument inventory.

database, while the tables of instruments, students and teachers can be modified independently.

Working with a database involves a process of querying, or searching it. Building up enquiries such as "How many clarinets, more than two years old, are in room M217?" are typical of the types of searches a database handles. We do, in fact, use databases quite often, a library catalogue is a database, and Goggle and Yahoo have databases of information available on the World Wide Web. We query these by searching for key words and use advanced searching interfaces to allow more focused or precise searches. Finding a phone number in an electronic address book is the same in principal as searching on Google for information about drum machines, however the amount of data to be searched is vastly different and so, therefore, is the computing power and storage space required by the database.

Web sites

An increasing number of Web sites are dynamic, meaning that the information they display is assembled from a database each time a request to view the page is made. There are a number of advantages to having a Web interface on the data, not least of which is that it can be accessed from any computer on the network without the need for special software, other than an Internet browser. Systems that include a database and Web interface are often referred to as a content management system (CMS) and are becoming increasingly common as a way of organizing and accessing information. They are also referred to as Web applications for managing Web sites and content. There are many freely available CMS systems including Drupal, WordPress, Pivot, Plone, and Bricolage.

CMSs can be used as an administrative tool because they can provide public or private access to information that can be added to or edited from any location on the network. CMSs are regularly used for online newsletters or blogs, digital portfolios, calendars of events, online tutorials, and collaborative document authoring. Setting up a CMS usually requires administrator access to a computer acting as a server. This typically means in a school that an IT coordinator may need to set up the system on the school server, after which it can be managed by anyone with administrator access. A CMS often results in a Web site that has public areas (e.g., posting events calendars and news notices) and private areas (e.g., student journal entries or group discussion forums). A CMS can assist in coordinating information in one system and act as a Web-based communication tool for notifications and discussions.

The ability to enable several people to edit the data can also distribute the workload amongst staff, or staff and students, and act as a coordinated hub for information about the music program.

Learning management systems

While a learning management system (LMS) may have traditionally focused on delivering online materials to students as a basis for eLearning, they have quickly accumulated record keeping and communication functions that can track student progress and facilitate discussion between students and staff. LMSs usually provide a Web interface to a database backend, so in this way share many features with content management systems. Some popular LMS systems include Manhattan Virtual Classroom, Moodle, OLAT, and The Sakai Project.

Many LMSs have evolved or combined administration functions beyond student grade-keeping to include time tabling, attendance, student records, and financial planning. Most of the larger LMSs are commercial products that provide solutions for entire institutions; examples include Blackboard, Learn.com, and WebCT.

Running a LMS is most likely to be an institution-wide project and the music educator may be able to utilize features of a system at their institution to assist with delivering materials, storing results, and communicating with their students.

Planning and scheduling

Managing time is another important aspect of teacher administration for which the computer can provide some assistance. Software applications for organizing classes and events, keeping track of to do lists, and managing projects, can assist in the planning and running of a music education program.

There are applications such as electronic diaries and calendars that can keep track of appointments and events. There are a number of software diaries; and most office suites or computer operating systems include a calendar program. There is a standard calendar data exchange format called iCalendar (or simply iCal) that allows transfer of calendar entries between software diaries. Software that supports this standard makes it much easier to distribute concert dates, assignment due dates, meeting dates and so on amongst staff and students. Online diary systems, as discussed in the section on CMS applications, can be used where many users need to access or edit the diary.

Project management software can assist in planning large events and projects including concert tours, musicals, or CD production. Project management software, such as Microsoft Project or Techno Grafik's iTaskX, will allow you to enter the tasks and timelines for a project and visualize the timeline as a Gantt chart, as shown in Figure 20.4, and track the progress as it proceeds.

A variety of timetabling software can manage small to large class scheduling tasks, including the organization of instrumental lessons. Applications include TimeTabler, Lesson Planner, Mimosa, and Lantiv Timetabler. Automatic timetabling is not a simple task and complex timetables can take quite some time to sort and achieve optimum organization. For smaller scheduling tasks, such as schedul-

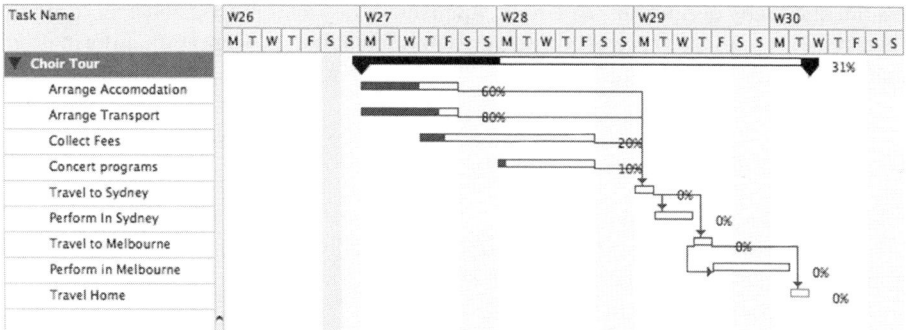

Figure 20.4 A Gantt chart displaying the timing and dependencies of project tasks.

ing instrumental lessons in one or two spaces, a calendar, and manual entry may be sufficient.

Data management

Having examined all the ways in which the computer can be used to manage information about the music education program, it is timely to talk about managing all the data itself. It can be a disaster if the computer data is lost or corrupted, so along with increased use of computers comes an increased vigilance about data management.

The most important consideration is to keep regular backups of files on a separate medium (e.g., an external hard drive or data CD/DVD). It is also best if there is a backup kept at a different location to the computer. Consider file or database size. It is usually more efficient to have several smaller files than one large one, unless cross references are made between them regularly. Smaller files are quicker to search and fragment the storage medium less often. One way of keeping data size manageable is to archive older data. For example, keep all the e-mail from last year in an archive file so that searches and sorting operations only deal with the most recent and relevant information. It is prudent to get into the habit of printing out summaries of data (e.g., student grades or project budgets); if the computer data is lost (or the power goes down), there is a physical backup. This need only be done occasionally and only the latest paper version need be maintained on file. Finally, make sure that you keep files and data well organized and clearly labeled so that you save frustration at not being able to find an important fact when the inevitable rush to locate it comes around. It is also useful to make the most of the alias or shortcut function of the file system that allows a link to a file or folder to exist in many places, which ensures that no matter which category you search under you will likely find the information.

Useful links

Information about many of the applications mentioned in this chapter can be found at the Web addresses below. There are many tools to assist with educational administration and many of them are free or inexpensive. They are categorized according to their relation to three areas of administration information presentation, information management or timetabling.

Documentation and presentation

Adobe Reader (a PDF reader)
  http://www.adobe.com/products/acrobat/readermain.html
AppleWorks (a simple office application suite)
  http://www.apple.com/appleworks/
Classroom Clipart (Web site with music and other images)
  http://classroomclipart.com/Music.htm
Flash (a vector-based drawing and animation application)
  http://www.macromedia.com/software/flash/
Impress (a screen presentation application)
  http://www.openoffice.org/product/impress.html
Keynote (a free screen presentation application)
  http://www.apple.com/iwork/keynote/
LaTeX (a document preparation system)
  http://www.latex-project.org/
Microsoft Office (a suite of office applications)
  http://office.microsoft.com/
Microsoft Works (a simple office application suite)
  http://www.microsoft.com/products/works/
OpenDocument (a rich media file format based on XML)
  http://www.oasis-open.org/committees/tc_home.php?wg_abbrev=office
OpenOffice (a free suite of office applications)
  http://www.openoffice.org/
Pages (a word processor with strong layout features)
  http://www.apple.com/iwork/pages/
PageMaker (a desktop publishing application)
  http://www.adobe.com/products/pagemaker/
PhotoShop and Illustrator (graphic design applications)
  http://www.adobe.com/
PowerPoint (screen presentation application)
  http://office.microsoft.com/

Information management

Blackboard (a learning management system) http://www.blackboard.com/
Bricolage (a content management system) http://www.bricolage.cc/
Drupal (a content management system) http://drupal.org/
Express (a desktop publishing application) http://www.quark.com/
Learn.com (a learning management system) http://www.learn.com/
Manhattan Virtual Classroom(a courseware and learning management system)
  http://manhattan.sourceforge.net/
Moodle (a learning management system) http://moodle.org/

OLAT (a learning management system)   http://www.olat.org/
Pivot (a content management system)   http://www.pivotlog.net/
Plone (a content management system)   http://plone.org/
WebCT (a learning management system)   http://www.webct.com/
WordPress (a content management system)   http://wordpress.org/

Scheduling

iTaskX (project management software)
    http://www.itaskx.com/software/en/
Lantiv Timetabler (a class scheduling application)
    http://www.lantiv.com/
Lesson Planner (a lesson organizing and scheduling application)
    http://www.lessonplanner.co.uk/
Microsoft Project (project management software)
    http://office.microsoft.com/
Mimosa (a timetabling application)
    http://www.mimosasoftware.com/
Sakai Project (a learning management system)
    http://www.sakaiproject.org/
TimeTabler (a class scheduling application)
    http://www.timetabler.com/

Conclusion

The computer can be a useful tool for assisting with the administrative tasks that inevitably proceed from professional music education. The areas in which the computer can be of assistance include documentation of plans and outcomes, budgets and financial planning and reporting, information management including student records and resource tracking, and the planning and management of projects and activities.

A wide variety of software applications can be utilized for these administrative tasks, and, up to a point, it is worth spending the time to use these efficiently to save time and frustration in the long run. It is also important to keep in mind that the music making is not only the important part of a student's music education, it is also the most important function of the computer in supporting the student's music education, therefore the effective role of the computer as an administrative tool does not diminish its important function as a musical medium and a musical instrument.

Reflection questions

1. What are the benefits of the computer as an administrative tool?
2. What are the pitfalls?
3. Describe the difference between a text editor and a word processor.
4. In graphic software, how is a vector image different from a raster image?

5. Imagine how can a Web browser be used for seminar presentations?
6. When might audio or video data be necessary for administrative purposes in a music education context?
7. What are the key differences between spreadsheets and databases?
8. What is a CMS and what is a LMS?
9. When might a Gantt chart be useful?
10. Why is it important to backup data?

Teaching tips

1. Save templates of forms and letters that are used regularly.
2. Have students help with preparing concert flyers and programs.
3. Get to know your software administration tools to the point where they assist rather than hinder your work.
4. Work out how to export and import data between your major administration applications so that each can be used for the tasks it is best at.
5. Make use of simple graphics programs and clip art to improve your documents.
6. Get into the habit of regularly capturing audio and video of student performances to assist in assessment and reporting.
7. Learn to use automated processes such as mail-merging form letters to save time.
8. Use CMS systems and blogs to help develop a sense of community amongst the music students and staff.
9. Take a laptop into lessons so that data can be entered on the spot rather than retyping from paper-based notes.
10. It is prudent to keep a paper copy of important data filed away, just in case.

Suggested tasks

1. See if a project management application might help organize your large projects.
2. Do a search for some useful clip art Web sites and bookmark them in your Web browser.
3. If your institution uses a LMS then learn how it can be made to assist your work.
4. Investigate the page layout functions that your word processor is capable of to make your documents look even more professional.
5. Compare data year on year to reveal longer-term trends in your teaching practice.

Chapter summary

The computer has made the most significant inroads in our society in the collecting and editing of information. The administrative uses of the computer are not all that interesting to the musician compared with music production or performance, however, efficient record keeping, preparation and dissemination of class materials, communication with peers and so on, are vital activities for the professional music educator. The main tools of the trade include e-mail, word processors, spreadsheets, databases, presentational packages, project management, and Web-based communication tools. It is no accident that these are also the most widespread business applications available for the computer, which guarantees that there is plenty of software choice in these areas. Effective use of these tools can make administration less of a chore and even assist with effective planning and development of a music education program.

Section V

IMPLEMENTATION

Chapter 21

Setting up a computer music system

For music educators, the purchase of music technology equipment is usually a love or hate affair. Some relish the task and enjoy delving into the details of the latest shiny thing. Others see the process as a chore or are overwhelmed by the jargon and just want something that works. Either way, choice of computing equipment is an important consideration for music education programs whose equipment budgets never seem adequate and for whom decisions must be lived with for a number of years to come. Along with the planning for purchases, come questions about physical location of equipment, how many systems, what additional infrastructure is required to install them, and so on. In this chapter we will discuss some guidelines to assist in the purchase and implementation of computer music equipment, including synthesizers, computer hardware and software, digital recording equipment, and the like. These guidelines, it is hoped, will provide a checklist and process of appropriate questions and considerations, which should instill some confidence in those who dislike choosing computer equipment and stimulation for further enquiry to those who enjoy it.

Task identification

By far the most critical step toward purchasing appropriate music technologies is defining what activities and tasks they are required to support. The need may be to print arrangements for bands, to scaffold the beginning composer, to record a CD of student ensembles, to provide resource materials for musicology assignments, or to assist in developing aural perception, to name a few. Often there will be a variety of tasks to achieve and each must be articulated and prioritized. The curricular needs should direct the prioritization process. At this stage, focus on outcomes more than processes, after which appropriate technologies to achieve those outcomes will become more evident. Be aware that, as discussed in chapter 20, the introduction of new technologies will open up new opportunities, so there will also be coupling between changes in technology and changes in curriculum; they will influence each other. For example, the current composition course may focus on popular songs in the "words and chords" tradition and may suggest that a music publishing system is required to generate lead sheets. However, if a digital-sampler or groove-box were purchased, the composition program might include a focus on the production of techno music and soundscapes and therefore publishing notated scores would be of little interest. Once the tasks have been identified and prioritized, it is time to select the most appropriate tools for those jobs.

Choosing equipment

What is the right computing tool for the musical job? This, of course, depends upon the musical needs and what equipment is available, with the decision processes following stages outlined in Figure 21.1. There are dedicated devices, such as synthesizers, that have quite well-defined functions, but the computer is a chameleon device. Its function can change with a substitution of software and perhaps some add-on hardware, such as a Musical Instrument Digital Interface (MIDI) keyboard or printer. Throughout this book, there have been detailed discussions about various classes of computer music technologies. Below is a summarized list of computer music tool categories defined by function.

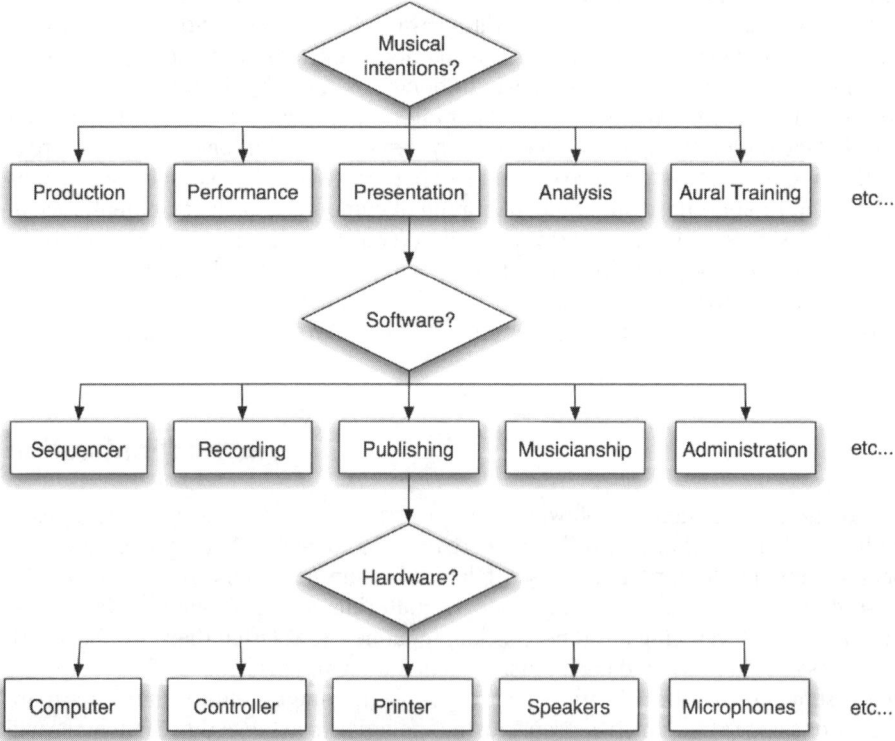

Figure 21.1 A decision-making process for choosing music technologies.

1. Synthesizers, virtual synthesizer plugins, samplers, and other sound generating devices. These include electronic keyboard-based synthesizers as well as stand-alone **sound modules** designed to be connected to existing keyboards and/or computers, and software-based versions of synthesizers and samplers that can work as stand-alone or plugin devices. Most computers come with a simple in-built synthesizer, often on a sound card and/or software synthesizer, but their sound quality can vary widely.

2. External controllers. Designed to control synthesizers or samplers, these usually emulate an acoustic instrument interface such as a keyboard, saxophone, drum, or guitar, but can also be control surfaces that feature varying arrays of knobs and sliders for direct parameter control. These usually connect using the MIDI protocol via USB connectors.

3. Digital recording and sequencing devices. Digital recording can include sequencing of MIDI data and recording and editing of audio data. Digital recording equipment can consist of stand-alone devices or computer-based hardware and software packages. Dedicated systems are often easy to use, portable, and provide removable data storage, while computer-based systems are usually less portable, but provide more sophisticated visual editing facilities. MIDI sequencers are a versatile and popular piece of music technology, which can often be connected to a keyboard synthesizer or MIDI controller to capture performance input.

4. Music publishing systems. These software applications are focused on printed outcome but include audio playback. Publishing systems comprise a software package running on computer and rely on high-quality visual displays and printers for best effect. They may utilize an external controller for note input.

5. Generative music software. While sequencers are widely used for composition where they act like mirrors that reflect back to the composer what was performed, there are some useful software packages that are designed as music generating and music processing systems. These assist the composer by assembling music from larger building blocks or algorithmically creating it. They fall into one of two classes; either simple tools for semi-automatic music creation in a building-block approach, widely used for primary school age children, or quite sophisticated tools that require some computer programming to assemble generative systems, often used in college or university programs.

6. Musicianship software. These software applications provide repetitive activities in areas of music theory and aural training. They range widely in complexity and cost, from simple tools focused on one task to entire systems that work across a range of skills and track student progress.

7. Musicology information systems. Software in the form of CD-ROMs or interactive Web sites can contain reference materials on all manner of musical subjects. Their multimedia nature makes them useful in the sonically-oriented music field. Some function much like enhanced books, others more like video games, and some employ drill and practice strategies to reinforce their topics.

After having made a decision about the tasks that are to be supported by the computer, music system, appropriate software from one or more of the categories above can be selected. There are many software packages listed in earlier chapters and the issues surrounding them are also discussed at length, so software applications will not be detailed here. Once the necessary software, or at least software category, has been identified, it is time to start making choices about the hardware that best supports those applications.

Digital musical appliances

One important issue is whether to purchase a dedicated device or a personal computer-based software solution. For music education uses, only a small subset of the capabilities of personal computer systems are required, but we are induced by marketing campaigns to acquire more features and more powerful computers just because we can. However, there are less complex and less highly featured dedicated devices available, such as MIDI-file players, keyboard workstations with built-in sequencers, digital multitrack mixer/recorders, even electronic tuners, metronomes, and drum machines. These devices are digital musical appliances. In them the "computer" is less overt; it is one component is an entire system. A detailed discussion of the usability differences between digital appliances and personal computers can be found in Donald Norman's book *The Invisible Computer*.[1]

Digital musical appliances start immediately, need little maintenance, are often portable, have more useful physical controls than a QWERTY keyboard and mouse (such as piano keyboards, sliders, play buttons, and so on), and usually do their specific job very efficiently. For example, the singer and songwriter Björk was shown in a documentary writing songs on a Yamaha QY20, which approximately the size of a VHS video cassette, while taking a walk in the countryside. In school settings, digital music appliances have other advantages too. The lack of configurability means they always present a consistent interface to the student, they rarely "crash," their smaller size means they can easily be moved from room to room or secured in a cupboard, and because they are good for little else but music, no other department wants to own, control, or borrow them. As another example, a digital recording system could use a personal computer with an audio interface and software such as a Digidesign's Mbox and Pro Tools, or similar functionality could be achieved with a Roland MV-8000 or the Yamaha AW16G for a similar cost. The ubiquity and popularity of personal computers may make this decision seem predetermined, but not everyone likes using personal computers and they can be prone to fail if not set up correctly or maintained. Another consideration in favor of a dedicated device is the time taken to start up and shut down a personal computer system. Compare the experience of setting up a guitar, where after a short tune-up it's ready to go, to starting up a personal computer then launching the application. The down side of dedicated devices is that they are rarely upgradeable and cannot be put to another task as priorities of use change. However, this is not a call to ban personal computers from the music classroom, but rather a call to consider how they might be more usable for music education. We need to seriously consider dedicated digital music appliances as an alternative to generic computers when they are used for specialized applications.

Selecting between alternatives

When choosing one tool over another, it is best to follow a process that matches your requirements with the tool that has the features most important for you. Features should be prioritized, or weighted, and not simply counted, because some features will be critical and others optional. As a parallel example with acoustic instruments, a soprano saxophone may be required to complete a saxophone quartet line up, however it might be suggested to buy a clarinet instead because it is much cheaper and there is more clarinet repertoire available to choose from, but that would not meet the main criteria of forming a saxophone quartet. When it comes to computer music systems, advice that is similarly off-track is too frequently given. As a precaution against such a situation, be clear about priorities and stick to them. For example, if a music publishing package that elegantly handles guitar tablature is required, don't be persuaded to purchase one which does not do this because there are twenty other functions it alone does, but that you are unlikely to use.

Another important aspect of choosing an appropriate tool is to select one of suitable complexity (or perhaps simplicity). Many music software packages are designed for professional musicians and may employ features and concepts that may be daunting, or simply confusing, to students. Many music software developers produce cut down or "lite" versions of their software, and these may well be sufficient for many educational purposes. On the other hand, be careful not to overly limit the potential of students with restricted software or to overly restrict the range of music that can be made by using overly specialized tools.

Regardless of the type of equipment that will be purchased, consider the following questions:

- Does it match the prioritized needs of the situation, curriculum, and institutional environment?
- Have all the available options been considered?
- Is it cost effective compared to other options?
- Is it compatible with any existing equipment?
- Is the equipment durable enough for the treatment it will receive from students?
- What is the amount of space available for positioning equipment?
- Does it need to be portable?
- Is the equipment safe to use in terms of electrical power, weight to be lifted, and so on?
- Does it suit the abilities and interests of staff and students?
- Has staff training on the equipment been arranged?

In addition, remember that many educators are likely to be searching for similar tools, so it is sensible to work together with others to share information and experiences about what looks promising and what has worked in similar circumstances. There are many Web sites and bulletin boards where teachers review and recommend applications for other teachers.

Finally, when selecting between alternatives, it is wise to prioritize the output quality of any system. This means, for example, in music publishing the quality of the printer, or for sequenced composition the sound quality of the synthesizer, for audio recording good audio converters on the audio interface, and for aural training the musicality of the computer generated exercise. As for all activities, the final output stage can easily ruin excellent preparation stages, just as a poor concert venue can ruin a well rehearsed performance, or a poor ensemble can make a mess of an elegant composition. One rule of thumb when budgeting for personal computer music systems is to spend one-third of the budget on the computer, one-third on software, and one-third on output equipment. For a computer-based digital recording set up this means that one-third of budget would be dedicated to the external audio interface and monitor speakers. For music publishing systems one third of the budget would be spent on the printer and a large visual display.

Ancillary equipment

Selecting the computer, keyboard, or production workstation is only a part of setting up a "studio" for music production. Extra equipment usually starts with a hardware audio interface to get high-quality audio signals to and from the computer. These connect to and from other equipment also, including microphones, mixing desks and audio monitors (loud speakers). There is not space in this chapter to detail these ancillary audio items in great detail, except to say that the quality of these components should match or exceed the computer system itself, because there is little point spending thousands of dollars on a computer for digital recording and then only tens of dollars on a microphone to capture the sound with. Likewise, the cost of a decent set of powered audio monitors may be close to half the price of the computer, and these are worth the money to be confident that they are accurately playing the music being made. Additional ancillary items will include cables, stands, table, chair, lamp, blank CDs, and other media. Each item, although not central, plays an important role in the chain of music production, Pay particular attention to those that impact the quality of the sonic result.

Physical set up

A core element of setting up computer music tools to use as part of a music program will always be the consideration of the physical location of the equipment and the number of students who need to use it. These considerations should inform all stages of the decision-making process rather than being an afterthought (despite the linear nature of this chapter requiring the placement of such discussion after other considerations). One of the first steps in dealing with the questions of space and organization of equipment is to establish which constraints are fixed and which are flexible. Most likely, room size will be relatively fixed, but make sure that the possibilities of distributing equipment in different rooms, or of making equipment portable, are considered as possibilities. Issues relating to student numbers are similarly open to creative solutions, and unlike physical restrictions are mostly constraints of habit and social expectation. For instance, the question of how many computers are required is a pedagogical one, not an economic one, and it is enlightening to examine existing equipment usage patterns and how they are applied to computers. In music education there are precedents for differing equipment usages. For example, recorders and most books are technologies that are reasonably priced

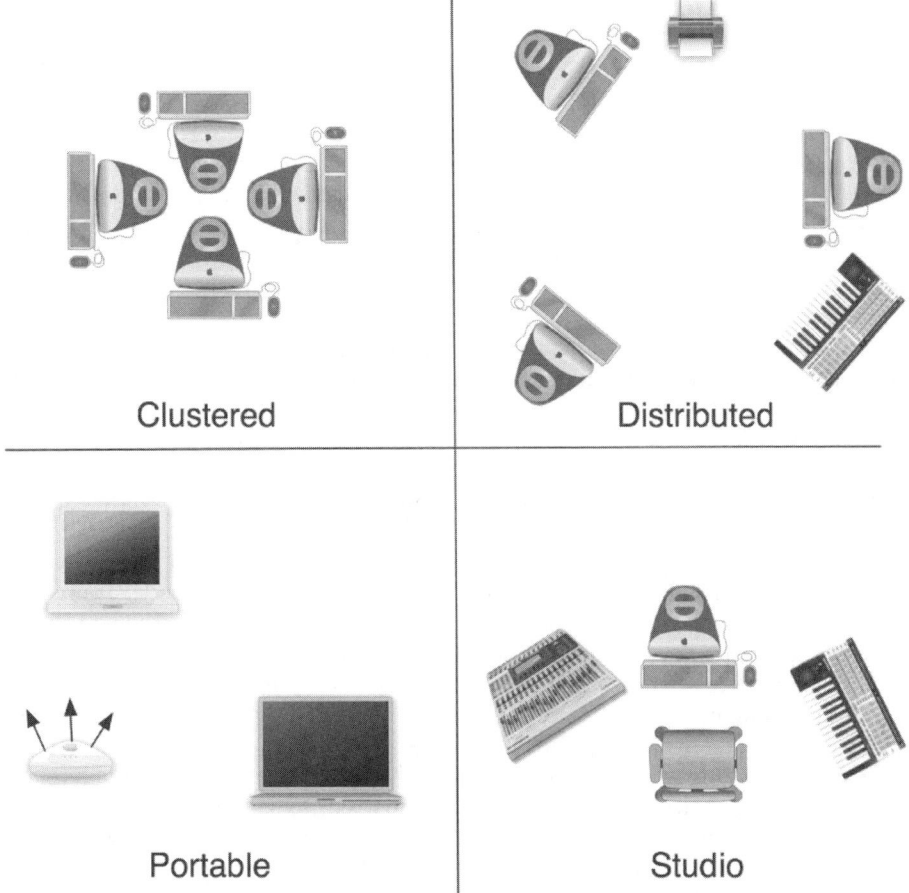

Figure 21.2 Some options for computer set-ups in educational institutions.

so that we usually have one per student in a class, while the school buys one or two copies of more expensive or specialized books or tenor recorders and shares them amongst the class. When teaching guitar in classes, it is not uncommon to have a limited number of instruments, perhaps half a dozen, and to rotate student groups between them and other activities; this model is also popular with computers in music classes (Figure 21.2). The use of pianos or drum kits is often more specialized and one or two students use them at a time; a single computer in a music classroom can be used successfully in the same manner, as explained by James Frankel in his article "The One-Computer Music Classroom."[2]

Very specialized instruments, such as bass clarinets, are often loaned to students who specialize in performance on them and thus contribute to the school's musical culture. A synthesizer, software package, or computer music system can easily be loaned out in the same way. It may be quite beneficial for a single student to reach a high standard by having such access, both for the student and for what they could then contribute to the school's musical activities.

Location and access

As computer-based equipment continues to miniaturize, the physical location of equipment becomes more flexible. Equipment such as synthesizers, digital recording systems, and even computers, are best viewed as portable (or luggable) items that can be moved between teaching rooms and to performance venues as required. Items that may need a more permanent location include printers, data projectors, and scanners. Ideally then, computer music equipment has a normal location either in the classroom, office, store room, or locker and is bookable to be used in other locations as required. The use of laptop or tablet computers makes this even more convenient.

With computing equipment becoming more ubiquitous, even to the stage where a growing number of students bring their own, the issue of students leaving music teaching spaces to access computing resources (most commonly in a school lab) should be almost extinct. Having to leave the normal music teaching spaces to "do" computer music making is both inefficient and disconnects computer music activities from other forms of music making, and should be avoided. It is often better to have a couple of computers in the music classroom with appropriate MIDI and audio hardware always set up than to have shared access to general purpose computing resources. Again, the metaphor of book usage is useful as a guide. There are some important books we expect students to purchase and bring with them to class, there are others we have in the teaching rooms for reference and regular access as required, and there are times when it is necessary to use the specialist resources of the library. Computer usage patterns should be increasingly similar to book usage patterns as the cost and size continue to shrink.

When deciding where and how to set up the new equipment, there is a human dimension to the choice of location based on who needs to have access to the equipment. If the equipment is in a staff room, what access do students have? If it is in a storeroom, who can access it and when? Do timetabled classes unduly block access to equipment? If it is in the library, how does it integrate with other musical instruments? How can it be utilized outside of scheduled classes, before and after hours for example? If it is bookable, how much time is it reasonable for one person to book? These, and other questions, are worth considering before the purchase is made so that appropriate equipment can be purchased to maximize effective use.

Consideration of the broader usage patterns might, for example, prompt a decision to purchase two smaller or cheaper units that would enable better access than the one planned for. Maybe a more robust and portable sampling keyboard could be made more widely available than a PC with an audio card. It might be that the purchase of a ten-pack of a sequencing software would allow each senior student to have a copy on their own computer at home, rather than spending the money on extra hardware set up that they would share at school. It is well worth considering how many people need to utilize the equipment, when they might have time and access, the places and times it would be most usefully employed, and how frequently and for what durations the access is likely. These issues of access, like the issues of task prioritization, will always require compromise to solve and, therefore, solutions found to the setting up of music technologies can vary widely.

Selecting the location of equipment has a lot to do with who will be the main users of it. If the main tasks are on-demand usage by staff for material preparation, then an office or workroom is an obvious location. If the main tasks involve regular student class activities, then locate equipment in the teaching spaces. If the main tasks are intensive usage by a select group of students, then a dedicated studio or practice room is an ideal space. Whatever the solution to location and access of computer music equipment, the solution should encourage usage and integration with other music activities. Computers may be clustered in small groups, set up individually in practice rooms, lined up in a row down one wall, spread around the classroom to act as small group hubs, or be of no fixed location but positioned wherever appropriate at the time. These choices have implications for teaching style and the types of student activity that become possible, and are also determined in part by the size and style of computer hardware that is purchased.

Computers should be networked where possible and there may be infrastructure costs to run network cables to the locations where the machines are used, although it is more flexible and cheaper to operate wireless networks in all areas. The networks allow students and staff to access school file servers, library databases, contribute to departmental discussion boards or blogs, and to communicate with others via e-mail or instant messaging. Collaborative music networks can be established between machines in the one location or across sites.

Ergonomics

With any increase in computing use in educational institutions comes a risk of common computer usage ailments including back pain, upper body muscle tension, eyestrain, and repetitive strain injuries. An important part of setting up computing equipment, therefore, is paying attention to ergonomic factors in its use. These issues include appropriate seating and equipment positioning, in particular the ability for seat height, monitor position and keyboard location to be adjustable to suit students, both tall and short. Long periods at the computer can also be problematic, and so computer usage patterns in classes should take account of this. Detailed advice on appropriate computer ergonomics and work practices can be found at occupation health and safety Web sites run by most state governments or educational authorities.

Security

After spending so much time selecting and installing computers into the music program, it is worth focusing on security so they are not lost or stolen. Desktop machines can be secured to the furniture with locking cables without any impediment to their use. Portable machines can be housed after use in lockers or storerooms. It is convenient if these have electrical power outlets to recharge batteries while the computer is stored.

Data security can be increased by taking precautions against viruses and other software invasions by using and updating virus protection software, using firewalls on machines connected to the Internet, and requiring users to log in. Data backups should be kept regularly and backups should be stored in a location different from the computer itself, in case of fire or other incident that may damage both.

Maintenance

An often-overlooked element of setting up computer music systems is the ongoing maintenance that will inevitably be required. This can include re-imaging of hard drives (reloading all the software back on) to keep them in a stable state, as students tend to shift, add, and delete items off the computer seemingly at random; regular updates to software and addition of security patches that are released from time to time; physical maintenance, including cleaning, fixing broken keyboards, and other minor repairs. Many larger institutions will have IT staff who can assist with these tasks, but smaller educational programs should plan and budget for ongoing maintenance. Many computer suppliers provide maintenance contracts as a service, although these tend to be quite expensive for most educational budgets.

Conclusion

Setting up computer music systems for music education is an activity that has implications in many facets of the music program and is, therefore, an important job worth some considerable attention. A range of equipment falls under the banner of a computer music studio. With the computer or some digital music appliance at the heart, there are also audio interfaces, MIDI keyboards, visual displays, audio monitors, printers, cables, mixers, and microphones; all potentially a part of setting up a computer music system. Despite the possible complexity of getting everything to work appropriately, setting up resources and seeing students use them effectively can be very rewarding. Educational success is most likely assured by keeping an eye on the tasks that need to be undertaken and molding the computer music systems to amplify abilities required for doing those tasks.

Reflection questions

1. Why is task identification a critical step in setting up a computer music system?
2. What are the seven categories of musical equipment mentioned in the chapter?
3. What are the arguments for and against using digital musical appliances?
4. Why should equipment features be prioritized?
5. What equipment, apart for the computer, makes up a typical computer music system?
6. What are the advantages of networking the computers?
7. What ailments can arise from extended or un-ergonomic computer usage?
8. Why should laptop lockers have electrical sockets in them?
9. What types of maintenance do computers require?
10. Why is the choice of appropriate computing equipment an important music education decision?

Teaching tips

1. Use interested students to help you keep up to date with trends in computing.
2. Keep musical tasks abstracted from any particular technology unless they are designed to train students specifically in the use that that equipment.
3. Make sure the software and hardware are updated to reflect contemporary musical practices.
4. If there are several computer music systems in a classroom, set them up to specialize on certain tasks (i.e., recording, publishing, net access, and research) rather than have them all the same.
5. Teach students to be able to select the appropriate software for the musical task they have to do.
6. Provide secure storage for students who bring their own laptops for use in the music program.
7. Emphasize safe and healthy computer usage with students.
8. Use a booking system for managing outside class use of computer music systems.
9. Utilize computer clusters to promote peer assistance.
10. Keep a file of student data CDs in the music room onto which students can regularly backup work.

Suggested tasks

1. Prioritize the activities you want the computer to help you with so you can better choose the features of the system appropriate for you.
2. Use the seven tool categories to reflect on the range of computer music software that you might be able to employ.
3. Locate and compare dedicated digital appliances against the software applications you use most to see how they shape up, and why there may be some who choose them.
4. Connect with other educators looking to use computers to compare experiences and knowledge.
5. Draw plans of four alternative computer system layouts to help stimulate nonobvious but interesting use of the equipment.

Chapter summary

Purchasing and placement of computer music equipment is not significantly different from other musical instrument purchase. Buying the instrument you need, within the budget you have, and always with an ear toward quality and a concern for the students' needs, is a recipe for successful computer instrument purchase also. Therefore, many of the suggestions about setting up a computer music system will seem familiar and many quite obvious, but there are also some new ways of considering priorities and special conditions, such as connecting to the Internet, that are particular for the computer. Because of the rate of change in computer-based technologies, each time you purchase new equipment it is wise to research and test the possibilities. Despite the rapid change in technologies, the processes required and questions to ask change much less frequently. Hence, as you gain experience in making computer purchases, that experience will accumulate. Issues typically relate to the tasks to be achieved with the equipment, selecting between alternatives, locating and accessing equipment, ergonomics, security, and ongoing maintenance. With these things in mind, effective and fun learning should be enabled through the use of computer music systems.

Notes

1 Norman, Donald A., *The Invisible Computer: Why Good Products Can Fail, the Personal Computer Is So Complex, and Information Appliances Are the Solution* (Cambridge, MA: MIT Press, 1998).
2 Frankel, James, "The One-Computer Music Classroom," *Music Education Technology* 2, no. 4 (2004): 10–14.

Chapter 22

Distance education and e-learning

The educational world is getting smaller. Information is available online from many providers across the world. E-learning involves the delivery of part or the whole of a study program electronically and the facilitation of communications between staff and students. The increasing utilization of Internet-based technologies to support learning away from the classroom has made e-learning a mainstream topic for all education in the twenty-first century. This chapter surveys the types of e-learning practices that are proving to be effective, assesses some of their limitations, and discusses significant issues relating to the teaching of creativity and performance skills at a distance where face-to-face contact is limited or absent.

Music education is problematic for distance education because of its reliance on embodied skills in many areas. Therefore, it is not surprising that distance education courses in music have chosen to focus on music appreciation, knowledge of music history and theory, and, occasionally, composition and arranging as their topics. Except in a few cases of necessity for remote students, the teaching of performance studies has usually been conducted face-to-face.

Mainstream education has not been particularly quick to include e-learning strategies because prior to the 1990s the infrastructure and economic drivers were not in place, and nor was there a compelling educational reason to do so. There were other technologies that delivered distance education prior to the Internet, and that still do, including radio and TV broadcasts, two way radio, postage of printed course materials, text books, CD-ROMs, video conferencing, and traveling teachers. There was a different pattern of e-learning uptake in large companies such as IBM that have been doing staff training via electronic networks for many years, because the cost efficiencies for their thousands of globally-distributed staff compared to on-site meetings and travel were significant. As network infrastructure and bandwidth has increased, so has the interest in e-learning strategies for on-campus students. It is widely recognized that the extra communications and access to information, for example, class discussion forums and reviewing audio taped lessons (podcasts), provides an enhanced learning environment for the students.

There is a lot of jargon surrounding e-learning and we will try to avoid it where possible, but some definitions of key terms are worth establishing. By "distance learning" we refer to situations where students and teachers are geographically separated and can rarely meet face-to-face. The term "flexible delivery" we will take to mean that students have choices about how and when they can access information; this usually refers to making resources available in different times or spaces, allowing students to undertake their study when it suits them rather when it suits someone else. The term "e-learning" refers to the use of electronic, typically Internet-based, technologies to deliver or support educational programs.

E-learning technologies

There are a range of e-learning technologies and new variations are appearing all the time. Since many of these technologies have been discussed in chapters 19, 20, and 21, we will assume some familiarity with them and seek to organize them according to the type of interaction or educational support they provide. The list below offers an overview of available tools and the types of functionality provided by e-learning technologies, a theory of interaction with creative practice outlined in more detail in chapter 23.

- Information distribution—extending the history of distributing audio tapes, videos, CD ROMs, and broadcasting TV (e.g., the UK's Open University), e-learning technologies make information available through Web sites, streaming content, file downloads including podcasting, and posting materials on various content management systems (CMS).
- Interactive software—as well as providing electronic versions of books and videos that are passively read by students, e-learning can also include interactive technologies such as simulations and learning games.
- Asynchronous communication—the Internet provides a variety of ways to send and leave messages for others in an e-learning environment. These include discussion forums, e-mail lists, online journals, and assignment submission systems.
- Asynchronous collaboration—making a distinction between the previous category where messages are left and one where projects are jointly developed but independently worked on, separates out applications, in particular wikis, for Web-based editing of documents and document repositories for exchange of documents for distributed editing.
- Synchronous collaboration—all the previous communication methods were out of time, but group learning collaborations also benefit from real-time discussions with tools such as Skype, iChat, and various instant messaging clients that allow immediate transmission of text, audio and video data between users.
- Web Content creation—as well as receiving information students also create information. Online tools for doing this include blogs for creating online journals, digital portfolios, Web page authoring tools such as Nvu, Frontpage, and Dreamweaver, and Web-based media content creation tools for creating visual images, music passages, character animations, and so on. These are often packaged into course creation systems, courseware, including those applications listed in the UNESCO free software portal[1] and by a range of commercial providers.

Mostly these resources are tools for more efficiently or conveniently achieving many tasks that are already a part of music education programs, such as peer group discussions, collaborative work groups, access to recordings and videos about music, and storage of work and ideas. The advantage, like most new technologies, is that e-learning tools extend the reach of these ideas to cover greater distances and to work across different time scales. The breaking down of barriers of time and space that electronic technologies offer provides the opportunity for a rethinking of how music education is delivered, including the scheduling of lessons, regularity of interaction, session durations, and the complexity of musical networks that can be managed. Perhaps most importantly, because all e-learning interactions are mediated by technologies, it prompts a reassessment of the role and importance of face-to-face interaction for learning music.

Learning at a distance

Distance learning can take advantage of e-learning technologies to augment traditional communication methods including posting materials, broadcast media, and telephone, or radio voice communications. In order to assess the ways in which distance learning can apply to music education, we can examine the types of learning activities that can be accessed at a distance through the lens of meaningful engagement.

Distance learning, even with synchronous Internet communications, can support the director, explorer and participant modes of engagement with music so long as the tasks and theoretical frameworks within which they are pursued are diverse enough to encompass these types of musical involvement. Distance education can lead to personal meaning, given that the process of music making can be intrinsically rewarding. However, distance education is limited in its ability to provide social and cultural meaning because of the diminished interpersonal relationships that result from a reduction in face-to-face communication.

Hubert Dreyfus discusses the impact of this reduction in face-to-face contact on learning in his book *On the Internet*.[2] Dreyfus outlines stages of education in which different skills are learned in specific ways and provides a critique of the impact of embodied or emotional knowledge at each of these stages. He argues that the semi-detached nature of distance education makes the transference of some advanced understandings difficult. Given the heavy reliance on physical involvement and emotional commitment in musical activities, Dreyfus' conclusions should inform the ways in which distance and e-learning are used to support music education. He suggests seven stages through which a student progresses to become an authority in the domain:

1. Novice—features and rules of the domain are provided for the person to acquire and follow.
2. Advanced Beginner—the person learns maxims that contextualize general rules in a specific context that they experience and based on a variety of examples.
3. Competence—the person develops plans or perspectives that make sense of and prioritize an otherwise overwhelming number of rules and maxims.

4. Proficiency—the person develops intuition through involvement that replaces reasoned responses.
5. Expertise—the person is able to make more subtle and refined discriminations allowing an immediate intuitive response and the development of style.
6. Mastery—the person develops his or her own style and innovative abilities.
7. Practical Wisdom—the person develops a sense of cultural style that allows them to act appropriately within their domain at any time.

Dreyfus argues that distance education alone can only hope to be successful in the first three stages, and that face-to-face interaction is required to advance the learning beyond these stages. Involvement, he suggests, is learned through modeling of intellectual and emotional engagement with the domain provided by the teacher or other mentors. Emotional engagement is developed in situations where the students take risks in situations that matter to them, such as in public performance and master classes with respected figures. Beyond stage three, Dreyfus suggests that some form of face-to-face apprenticeship model is required, within which the student will pick up ineffable clues about the domain and how to navigate through it in the complex of its real world situations. For stages six and seven he suggests that multiple apprenticeships with more than one teacher or mentor are required to gain sufficient diversity of perspective. While e-learning can provide many opportunities for enhanced interaction and access to information for students in music programs, it is worth keeping Dreyfus's comments about the disembodiment of mediated commutations in mind as we develop courses and materials.

E-learning design

Given that e-learning contexts often have to assist instruction and learning in the absence or reduction of face-to-face contact, then the design of e-learning materials needs to take account of the difference between traditional instruction and the mediated nature of electronic communications. A series of design elements for e-learning materials were developed by the author and Bradley Voltz with just such a context in mind; these design elements are presented below.[3] They arose after years of experience in creating and evaluating e-learning resources designed for a wide range of age levels and curriculum areas, with a particular emphasis on music education.

The critical step in developing e-learning materials is the design phase, where the planning of the e-learning resource occurs. Such educational design work combines elements of lesson planning, instructional design, creative writing, artistic visualization, and software specification. At the design stage, it is important to take account of the technologies of delivery, and the design strategy presented here requires consideration of the delivery platform, but good designs can be largely independent of the technology platform with which they are built or delivered.

There are six elements of an e-learning design that, we suggest, cover many of the issues involved with e-learning materials and keep the focus on effective learning outcomes: the activity, the scenario, feedback, delivery, context, and the impact of the resource. These design elements provide a framework within which designers of e-learning can work that assists them to create rigorous resources appropriate for education from primary through to tertiary levels. Paying attention to these design elements can minimize the gap between the educational goals and the experience of students using the e-learning resource.

Here is a brief overview of the six elements for effective e-learning design:

- Activity—the design should include tasks that will provide students with a rich experience and lead them to the desired educational outcomes.
- Scenario—a situation or story should be developed that situates the tasks in a meaningful relationship to each other and the real world.
- Feedback—it is important to include reaction or commentary on student actions that assists them to reflect on their work and turn experience into understanding.
- Delivery—the design should consider the opportunities and limitations of the technical means of production and interaction with the materials.
- Context—the design should accommodate other material and human resources that are likely to be available to the student undertaking the e-learning activity.
- Impact—designers should anticipate the likely effect of the activity on staff, students and the environment, including potential educational, psychological, cultural, ethical, and physical influences.

These elements of effective instructional design can be used within a number of design approaches, but a participatory design method is especially appropriate to education. In participatory design, the users, in this case students, are involved throughout the design process to inform decision making and offer critique as the design progresses.

When using these elements of effective design, it is important to remain aware that technology can amplify the strengths and weaknesses of activities and delivery systems. Because of this amplification tendency, the design phase is critical in ensuring that the student experiences the mix of ideas and interactions that are planned rather than those that are available. Managing the e-learning technologies in this way should allow the resources to have a positive impact on the student that, in turn, should result in an amplification of their musicality.

Conclusion

When used effectively, e-learning technologies should extend the reach of great educators and facilitate increased involvement by students. There are times when distance is so great that e-learning techniques are the primary method for students to access music education, but for most students e-learning resources should enrich face-to-face musical interactions. The benefits include the ability for students to review material and self-pace their learning, to encourage more discussion and collaboration between students and staff outside of class times, to provide a richer set of resources and information to the student, and to enable the use of media rich documents and resources. The challenges of e-learning include keeping the focus on developing musical intelligence and not letting increased access to and communication about music (quantity) replace the experience of making music (quality). The challenge of distance education, whether or not it includes e-learning technologies, is to ensure that students are not limited to entry-level musical skill development because of the lack of face-to-face interaction, through which they learn much more than we can tell.

Reflection questions

1. Why is e-learning a particular challenge for music education?
2. Why was big business an early adopter of e-learning?
3. List the six categories of e-learning technologies mentioned in this chapter.
4. What are the strengths of e-learning technologies?
5. List Hubert Dreyfus's seven stages of learning.
6. Why does Hubert Dreyfus think e-learning has limited educational prospects?
7. What are the six elements of effective e-learning design suggested by Brown and Voltz?
8. What is the difference between the scenario and context design elements?
9. How might peer communications be supported by e-learning technologies?
10. Why might e-learning challenge the traditional organization and structure of schooling?

Teaching tips

1. Use e-learning technologies to maximize lesson time on practical tasks and have theoretical tasks done online.
2. Student forums can be used to share knowledge amongst peers to encourage greater debate about topics.
3. Have students comment on each others' work on a class blog as a method of formative assessment and feedback.
4. Use rich media materials online to minimize the distancing effect of mediated communication.
5. Use a CMS system for students to store their digital work and as a repository for electronic submission of assignments.
6. Have interactive music game software available as an extension activity for students who finish other work early.
7. A wiki can be used for collaborative writing of ensemble activity reports.
8. Enhance the education of remote students by establishing links between them, or their schools, and other students in remote or urban locations.
9. Provide flexibility for student work loads by putting some tasks online for students and letting them set their own due dates for these tasks throughout the term.
10. Obtain some Web cameras so that instant messaging between students can include videoed demonstrations of musical techniques.

Suggested tasks

1. Do an audit of all the e-learning technologies you currently use.
2. List the skills you consider essential for musical expertise and mastery and see if you can imagine how they might be taught using e-learning technologies.
3. Use the e-learning design elements as a guide to creating a new e-learning resource.
4. Identify the way Web site technologies tend to distort the way information can be presented on them.
5. Read up about how to install and maintain a blog or wiki as a professional development exercise.

Chapter summary

One of the major impacts of Internet technologies on education is its use as a delivery platform for educational materials and as a communication device between staff and students. The use of electronic technologies, including the Internet, in educational delivery is called e-learning. Often these technologies are used for distance education where students are not able to attend regular music lessons or to support conventional teaching methods. Looking at it another way, all e-learning is distance learning, in the sense that it is mediated communication between people who are distanced from each other when communicating that way, and it is this disembodied nature of e-learning experiences that also imposes a limitation on what can be taught using them. Designing e-learning experiences for students needs to take this into account and effective e-learning designs consider the activities being undertaken, create scenarios within which those tasks make sense, make effective use of feedback to students, and take account of the delivery platforms and existing resources found within the learning context. Most of all, effective e-learning designers are deliberate about forecasting the impact of the e-learning on students, their communities and the environment. E-learning can assist learning but is not a panacea for either location-based or distance learning programs. For developing musical intelligence, which is a particularly experience-based endeavor, e-learning can provide rich media experiences and interactions which are an improvement over text-based materials, but are not a replacement for face-to-face musical encounters.

Notes

1   UNESCO free courseware listing, http://www.unesco.org/webworld/portal_freesoftware.
2   Dreyfus, Hubert L., *On the Internet* (New York: Routledge, 2001).
3   Brown, Andrew R., and Bradley Voltz, "Elements of Effective E-Learning Design." *International Review of Research in Open and Distance Learning* 6, no. 1 (2005): http://www.irrodl.org/content/v6.1/brown_voltz.html.

Chapter 23

Integrating new technologies

Implementation of new technologies into music education programs can have a positive effect on the learning and musical outcomes. However, the process of integrating new computing technologies can disrupt established practices and prompt reflection on aspects of the music program beyond the equipment and new activities surrounding it. When well managed, the integration of new technologies can be a stimulating process of renewal for the music program. If new technologies are ignored, the use of computers may be ineffective or even counterproductive.

Andrea DiSessa, who is very experienced in the use of computers in education, points to the fact that understanding the computer is becoming an increasingly essential general-purpose skill. DiSessa observes, "The gradual evolution to a computationally literate society guarantees we will experience changing circumstances that we would like to negotiate with skill."[1] The increasing importance of computers to all facets of contemporary life, including music making, places increasing pressure on the need to provide students with an understanding of how computing resources will enable them to realize their potential.

Ongoing concerns for music educators include, how to make sure that any introduction of new computer music making integrates with other music activities in the students' life, how the computers can be easily available to students, and how to ensure that staff maximize the opportunities afforded by computer music production. This chapter addresses these issues that, at the fundamental level, involve changing the attitudes of students, staff, and others so as to provide a supportive intellectual and physical environment for computer-based music activities.

Accepting that the role of music education is to enable students to increase their musical intelligence and that the computer can be an effective tool, medium, and instrument for music making, then it is the responsibility of educators to promote both access to and a positive attitude toward computer music systems.

Understanding and knowledge

Computer music systems carry with them musical understandings embedded, in particular, in the metaphors and functionality of the software. Educators choose one system over another based on those predispositions such that the students are exposed to those musical understandings and techniques and will learn to embody them. Therefore, computer systems for education are primarily epistemological but secondarily pedagogical. The ways in which they are used for musical activities teaches students about how musical activities are conducted, for example whether or not music is a private or social activity, individual or collaborative, interpretive or inventive, unimportant or important, and so on. The integration of computer music systems into the music program is, as with all other activities and resources, not simply about the provision of a tool or about the transference of ideas; it is about situating the student in a musical culture.[2]

To facilitate successful integration of computer music systems, it is important that they are comprehensible and that students are motivated to utilize them. A system will be comprehensible when the interface can be "read" easily, the complexity of material is appropriate, and the musical concepts being explored relate to and extend a student's existing knowledge. There is a wide range of hardware and software for music production; it should not be difficult to find a system at the appropriate level for students at almost any skill level or age. Computer music systems come in an ever-expanding array of shapes and sizes. Hardware include desktop and laptop computers, hand-held computers, mobile phones, and dedicated sequencers, recorders, and synthesizers, to name a few. Software systems cover the range presented throughout this book and many new interesting software packages are released each month. Picking the right combination of hardware and software involves consideration of many factors; most importantly, how a student will use them.

Computer music systems will be motivating when their relevance to the students' musical interests is clear to them, which implies that the styles of music used are ones they like, the type of activities are ones they perceive as productive, and the activities are ones that help them develop their skills and achieve outcomes new to them. Sometimes the relevance of the activity relates directly to the software, as in the case of audio file remixing software that will appeal to those interested in electronic music. At other times relevance is based around the task rather than the software, for example, a sequencer can be used to transcribe melodic dictations or to write a new pop song with clear differences in the likely motivation of students doing those tasks. Computer music systems can be made available without much difficulty, but their impact on learning depends on careful consideration of their utilization, which derives from approaching them with a positive attitude. Access without a positive attitude is a waste of resources, and enthusiasm without access leads to frustration.

Skills and techniques

Since the late 1990s, the use of computers for music making in Western societies has been quite explicit. Musicians in nightclubs perform on stage with laptops, images of recording studios prominently feature computer displays, and music stores are filled with a wide array of digital music equipment. In the early part of the twentieth century, portable music players, such as the iPod have become an increasingly important part of the computer music scene, not only for music consumption but also as sources of music for live DJing and mash-ups. Students are well aware that contemporary music making utilizes computer in its many forms and are keen to acquire the skills and techniques necessary to make the music they hear on the radio and TV, download over the Internet, and that they experience at concerts. Even instrumentalists performing traditional repertoire are conscious of the difference that good recording production techniques and processes can make to how music is received and judged. The integration of computer music systems introduces a new set of musicianship skills and a host of new performance or production techniques that need to be understood, practiced and mastered. These contemporary musicianship skills include a thorough understanding of acoustics, familiarity with amplitude and frequency representations of sound, as discussed in chapter 7, familiarity with techniques and works in electronic and computer music developed during the latter half of the twentieth century, an understanding of digital processes and computer architectures, and familiarity with sound synthesis and **digital signal processing** techniques.

Increasing student awareness of digital processes and computing systems has benefits beyond music education because it is increasingly recognized as a generic competency or a new literacy.[3] Similarly, a greater focus on the acoustics of sound and signal processing can inform acoustic instrumental performers about the operation of their instrument, and can inform composers and arrangers when making choices about orchestration and texture. These are some of the ways in which the integration of new technologies can have benefits across the music program through a renewed attention to skills and techniques necessary for effective computer music production that relate to other areas of the curriculum. When producing music with a computer, students are not only developing their musical intelligence, but they are gaining transferable technological skills and confidence.

Integration prompting change

Because new understandings and skills are implicated in the introduction of computer music systems, it is clear that music programs will be changed by their integration. Many music education programs are resistant to change because it can take time and effort to learn new skills or develop new teaching resources, changes can be seen as a threat to highly valued existing practices, and there is a risk that the results of change may not improve the lot of students or staff. Weighed against this are the implications of not embracing changes brought about by the integration of computer music making which include wasted time and effort in continuing to use processes that are labor intensive and tedious, marginalization or increased irrelevance of a music program that focuses on musical practices that have a decreasing audience or cultural value, and a risk for staff and students of not benefiting from new or improved outcomes.

There are, of course, many ways of integrating computer music activities while managing change processes, such that the integration is a development of the music program rather than a revolution and such that computer-based activities are additional activities rather than a replacement of previous ones.

Change as evolution

When we think of technological change we think of the rapid pace of information technology development during the twentieth century. This century also witnessed great changes in Western musical ideas, for example, the challenge to tonality through serialism and stochastic compositional methods, and the influence of non-Western musical styles, for example, African musical influences in jazz, rock, hip hop, and minimalism.

Technological development has also contributed to these changes. Tape recording technologies enabled musique concrète techniques while computing technologies assisted stochastic and algorithmic compositional techniques. Sound amplification technologies enabled softer voices to be heard over large ensembles facilitating "crooners" such as Bob Hope and Frank Sinatra. Audio recording altered access to music and ways of making music. The extent of these changes is immense and well beyond the scope of this chapter. However, it is important to understand that this parallel development of music and technology usually followed the path noted by McLuhan—a technology first imitates an older medium and then moves on to establish itself as a new media.[4] For example, hard disk recorders were based on tape recorder metaphors but now programs such as Sony's ACID and Ableton Live make a feature of nonlinear access to audio regions. Another example is music publishing systems based on the paper manuscript metaphor, and programs such as Sibelius and Finale now have playback and movie synchronization functions. It is clear that the evolution of music technologies, and particularly computer music technologies, begins with metaphoric imitation leading to innovative usage and then to establishment of new metaphors.

Music education programs have emerged, and can continue to evolve, alongside technological developments by embracing innovative musical practices, and evolving their curriculums and pedagogy to change those elements that can most obviously be improved by taking advantage of computing systems. As new metaphors are established and new techniques for music making are introduced, music education programs can teach from these perspectives as they develop from previous ones in an iterative process of renewal through modification.

Change as addition

Whilst much technological change is seen as developmental, not all is. Some technologies or musical practices are simply new. The use of the laptop computer as a live performance instrument is an example. This is not a development from another instrument even though it inherits features from synthesizers. Further, it is a new instrument, just as the saxophone was in the twentieth century even though it inherited features from other woodwind and brass instruments.

The pressure for regular additions to the music curriculum are not new, but the speed of advances during the twentieth century have meant that music curriculums have been under increased pressure to include more material, topics, and activities. In addition, educational theories have developed, perhaps most influentially with the ideas of John Dewey, who emphasized experience over observation, and such participatory learning requires time for activity and reflection.[5] Continual addition to the music program will crowd the curriculum to such an extent that depth and quality will be sacrificed—a process too often in evidence as educators endeavor to accommodate changing musical cultures, globalization, vocationalism, and other trends. At some point incremental curriculum bloat becomes too much and old conceptions of curriculum structure must be substituted with new ones; technological change often facilitates such shifts of mind in curriculum developers. This is because the implications of technological change are often far reaching, and usually unpredictable, therefore the full implications of changes—particularly the changes in students' understanding of music—need to be reconsidered. The integration of new technologies and musical practices associated with them into educational programs should be seen as an opportunity to reevaluate the learning objectives of the music program and to allow for the establishment of critical learning pathways that focus on musical intelligence rather than a mindless acquisition of musical skills and facts. This is often a challenging reassessment process as the difference between important and essential understandings is sorted out, and the recognition that musical intelligence is not equated with particular musical styles, culture, or privileged musical context, but rather with the development of intuitions and abilities situated in any authentic context.

Updating curriculum and pedagogy

The introduction of computing systems to music education will, as already indicated, have an impact on what is taught and the way it is taught. The rapid development of technologies and changes in the ways of making music that computers introduce require a new view of music education that allows the educational program to keep pace with the changing world without having to be in a constant cycle of updating curriculum documents. Such a view can be provided by focusing on the objectives of the music education program to provide meaningful engagement with music (using computers and/or other equipment) rather than specifying prescriptively the particular activities or tasks.[6] The rapid changes in technologies and expansion of musical genres and distribution methods also mean that it is unlikely that a teacher will be more knowledgeable than their students in all respects. Thus the role of the teacher and the relationship with students can be challenged by the integration of new technologies. A technology-rich environment encourages the teacher to act as a helper to the students, assisting and guiding their learning and behavior during the music lesson. An example of how computer activities have been designed to encourage the use of music technologies in primary schools is the work done at the Sir Robert Hitcham's Primary School in Suffolk, U.K. They have a Web site with examples of the projects and students' music work with the computer.[7] In this section we will discuss these curriculum and pedagogical implications in further detail.

A meaningful engagement with music

In recent times, music curriculum design has focused on balancing classes of musical activities as a way of ensuring a balanced music education. Typically, these activity classes have been listening, composing and performing (although the exact titles used may vary slightly). This taxonomy of musical behavior is deeply embedded in a nineteenth-century Western musical ontology, where there is a clear separation between the composer, performer and audience. The technological changes of the twentieth century severely test the validity of these divisions.[8] First of all, recording technologies enable activities like musique concrète where distinctions between composer and performer dissolve; these are challenged even further by sampling and improvisational remixing activities of electronica. Interactive techniques, such as those outlined in chapter 11, further confuse the boundaries of audience and creator. As a result, cultural practices driven by technological developments have made the historical divisions highly problematic.

A more appropriate framework is one that focuses on the relationship and experience the student has with and through music. It is these engagements with music that lead to the development of musical intuition and intelligence. For these engagements with music to have full educative power, they need to be meaningful to the student in ways that are enjoyable and enhance the student's self-conception as a musician (Figure 23.1). The view of music education design based on meaningful engagement with music derives from the research of the author[9] and Steve Dillon[10] and was discussed previously in chapter 2, but will be briefly reiterated here for convenience. Five modes of engagement are particularly important for music education; director, explorer, and participant.

These modes of engagement with music relate to the different ways in which a student may approach musical tasks.

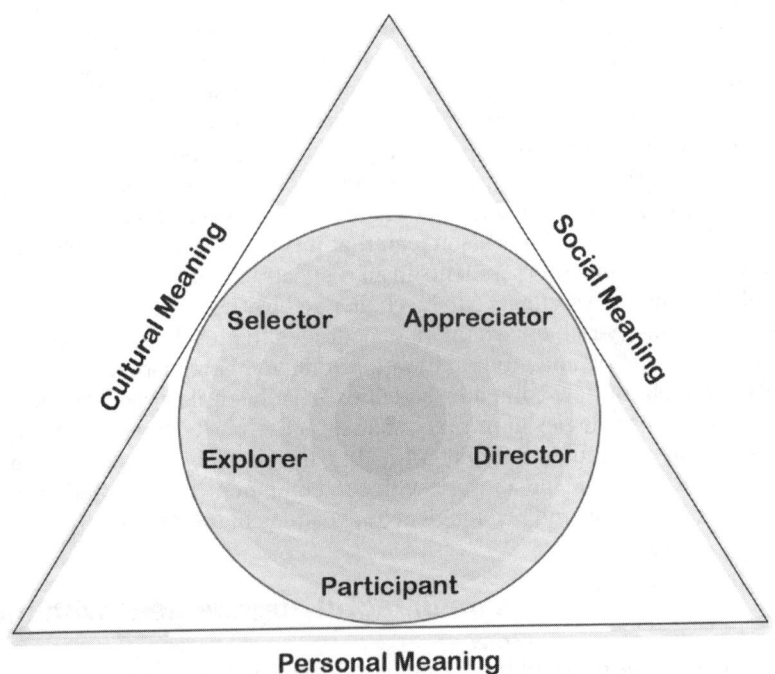

Figure 23.1   Meaningful engagement.

- As an appreciator, the student analyzes and listens carefully to musical productions, whether they are made by him- or herself or by others.
- As a director, the student has a clear vision about the musical result to be achieved and uses whatever resources they have to realize that vision. For example, the student may have a commission for a public multi-speaker sound installation and use sampling and algorithmic composition technologies to build it.
- As an explorer, the student has some musical territory or space they wish to investigate and uses different techniques to reveal possibilities. For example, the student may wonder if a useful new style of music will result from combining African drumming patterns and polyphonic writing for string quartets and so they undertake musical analysis of features from works in each style, then compose a series of syncretic exercises utilizing those features.
- As a participant, the student involves him- or herself in an intuitive musical exercise. For example, the student performs with others in an improvised sound track to an old silent film.
- As a selector, the student exercises aesthetic and cultural judgment to makes choices between musical options created by themselves, others or by machines. For example, the student selected the tracks and their order for the school's annual compilation CD.

There are three types of musical meaning that students can experience through musical activities; personal, social, and cultural.

- Personal meaning is derived from the satisfaction of making a good sound or completing a difficult task, or understanding a new musical concept. The student exploring the musical possibilities of combining African rhythms and polyphonic harmony is likely to achieve personal meaning from that self-directed task.
- Social meaning is derived from interacting musically with others. The student improvising with others to the silent film is likely to achieve social meaning from that activity.
- Cultural meaning is derived from receiving feedback from the community that your role as a musician is valued. The student who was commissioned to make a public sound sculpture is likely to receive cultural meaning from both the receiving of the commission and the responses of people at the exhibition of the work.

For the teacher designing curriculum and pedagogy with a view to maximizing the depth and breadth of meaningful engagement, the responsibility to be a content and equipment expert takes a back seat. The curriculum should focus on ensuring that meaningful engagement is maximized, enabling the teacher to act as a designer and facilitator of activities, to respond to student needs and to modify task specifications so as to assist each student in the development their musical intelligence. This approach encourages curricula to specify high-level outcomes rather than specific content to be assimilated, and encourages teachers to keep their eye on how each student maximizes those outcomes rather than simply checking off completion of set tasks, in effect policing a minimal outcome.

Teacher as helper

The integration of computer technology into the music program can enable students to work at the computer in a self-directed way, it can enable them to access information via the Internet from a wider pool of people and resources than previously, and it can provide tools that leverage their musicality to produce musical results more efficiently than otherwise. This potential is maximized when teachers facilitate rather than direct the learning activities and when students' work is more autonomous and small-group oriented, rather than teacher-directed and large-group oriented. The teacher in this situation has a role as a helper, who facilitates, encourages, mentors, advises and monitors student activities. At times, teachers become fellow travelers with students on the learning journey, as they uncover new features of the software, new artists, or new musical uses of the computer. Ian Brown defines the helper relationship with students as a healthy one for the teacher and as the approach most likely to lead to effective student outcomes. He summarizes his research into the way students respond to different teacher personalities as indicating that "students of the late 1990s believe they will most readily respond in terms of motivation or desire to learn, to a person who is 'caring,' 'considerate,' 'accepting,' 'empathetic,' 'thoughtful,' 'forgiving,' 'understanding,' and 'tactful'."[11] Being a supportive facilitator is not the only way that teachers can act in response to the integration of computers in music education, but it seems to be congruent with maximizing the capacities of the technology for student learning.

Organizing space and time

One of the major practical issues relating to the integration of new computing technologies in the music program is choosing and placing the computing and music hardware. Questions related to hardware include; what hardware to use, where to put it, when can it be accessed and by whom? Details and advice about establishing computers in classrooms were discussed in detail in chapter 22 so for now only some of the broader options relating to computer system choices, connectivity, ownership, and storage or housing will be addressed.

If the computer as an instrument, it would be ideally as accessible to staff and students as the guitar or electronic keyboard. If, whenever a question about the computer is raised, we substitute these instruments to arrive at an answer it will be mostly on track, although the computer does have some special requirements and options that don't apply to other instruments.

Hardware options

Computers come in all manner of shapes and sizes; they have been in different forms in the past and will certainly take on new forms in the future. With this in mind, the discussions about hardware usage will always be provisional and we will try to focus on principles rather than hard and fast rules where possible to cope with the inevitable change in circumstances.

In the 2000s, the most common form of the computer is the desktop, although the most useful form for music and education needs are laptop computers, which are increasingly common. Laptops are useful because of their portability, and portability of musical instruments is likely to always be a consideration as music making, and creativity more generally, can and should be able to happen at any time or place. Even more portable forms of computers include tablet PC's, personal digital assistants and mobile phones. These latter devices are generally fine for memo or idea capture, ear training, and music theory training. The small size of PDAs and phones makes detailed editing of data awkward with current graphical user interface conventions. For many music education purposes, a mobile phone would probably have the computing power required, but the lack of suitable software and the difficulties of interfacing with it make this impractical for now. There are some dedicated portable sequencing devices, such as the Yamaha QY series, and recording devices, such as Roland's R-1 and R-4 or recordable MP3 players from Apple, iRiver, or other providers that can be useful for the mobile musician where portability is more important than functionality. Desktop computers are popular for workstations in classrooms where the system rarely moves, and laptops are ideal for teachers and students that move from room to room and between institutions to home.

Connecting to and from the computing device via MIDI, USB, Firewire, audio, or other cable is typically handled reasonably by most computing devices, although wireless data communication is becoming increasingly common. External music keyboards or other control surfaces are quite popular for capturing performances or controlling parameters in real time and often communicate via the MIDI protocol connecting with a USB cable, and for professional quality audio input and output an external audio interface that connects via one of those data protocols will be required. We can assume the computer has a screen (the larger the better), keyboard, and mouse and, of course, that headphones or loudspeakers are necessary to monitor the audio output. A printer is useful for hard copies of scores and documents, and most computers include a CD or DVD burner for saving and distributing musical productions.

Connectivity

One of the ways in which computers can contribute to the social and cultural meaning for students is by enabling communication between people. The connectivity of the computer also relates to communication with other computing devices, including printers, servers and synchronizing with mobile devices. These communications can be local or global. A local area network (LAN) may be as simple as one computer and a printer, or slightly larger to include three or four computers in one classroom. Even such small networks can be useful for network jamming activities (discussed in chapter 11) or for using a shared external hard drive as a data storage space for student portfolios, ensuring that students can use any of the computers in the room and still access their files. Larger networks, often referred to as wide area networks (WAN), may cover an entire school or institution. WANs enable access to central databases from all locations and for discussion forums, instant messaging or e-mail between people within the institution. Usually these networks also have a connection beyond their walls to the Internet. The Internet, in turn, is simply everyone else's networks that have provided information for public consumption, much like most institutions will have.

Network connections between computers are typically wires or optic cables that carry the information between the machines. There are a variety of types of cables, but typically an Ethernet cable it used to connect the computer to the network. When directly connecting to a printer, another cable, such as USB, may be used. There is an increasing use of wireless networks where information is transmitted like a radio signal between machines. The most common wireless standard is Wi-Fi, or more formally the IEEE 802.11 wireless local area network standard. Many educational institutions are installing Wi-Fi zones, just like in shopping centers, around their campus and in class rooms. These provide much more freedom of mobility and flexibility about the number of machines connected to the network. Typically, a Wi-Fi network requires authentication when first connecting to prevent unauthorized access. Another popular wireless networking standard is Bluetooth, which operates over a much smaller range than Wi-Fi, typically around thirty feet as opposed to Wi-Fi's one hundred yards or so. Bluetooth is therefore more popular with devices that are in close proximity such as printers, or for low power devices like mobile phones, personal digital assistants, and MP3 players.

Ownership

Computers were once so expensive that only institutions or governments could afford to purchase them. Now each person may have several in their home, in devices such as microwaves, cars, phones, televisions, and so on. Personal computers and laptops that are typically used for computer music systems are not inexpensive, but when viewed as a musical instrument are about on par with many orchestral instruments or a good quality electronic guitar or drum kit. Ownership of computers for music programs can, like all other instruments, vest in the institution or the individual student based on outright purchase, hire or loan and so on. In most educational settings, there will be a balance of institutional and personal computers. Institutional computers can be set up permanently in music rooms, or other locations in the institution, or they can be available for hire or loan like other instruments are, especially for students that are specializing in computer music activities. Personal computers owned by students in some schools are widespread, and as such infrastructure for them is provided. In schools where student laptops are the exception rather the rule, the institution may be able to encourage these students to use their computers in music classes by providing spaces, wireless network hubs, audio interfaces, audio monitors, MIDI keyboards, and other auxiliary equipment.

Software costs are often a significant proportion of the outlay involved in owning a computer music system. The cost of a professional level sequencer, music notation package, and a few software synthesizers can almost equal the cost of the computer hardware. Less serious packages that are often adequate for educational use may not be as expensive and there are many free, shareware or open source applications that can reduce the cost of owning a computer music system. In order to have students use software on their own machines that is also being used at the institution it may be possible for the institution to own sufficient licenses that some can be installed on a student's machine for the duration of their study or as required. This will depend on the conditions of individual software licenses.

Storage and housing

The integration of computing systems into the music program will necessarily require some physical accommodation of the computers, even if they are laptops only temporarily in the music teaching space. Many computers are desk-bound and so require a tabletop, and usually a chair to sit at will be required too. In a classroom this is unlikely to be problematic but in an instrumental teaching room it may be more of an issue. Also required will be connections to electrical power, audio playback systems, and network connectivity. Storage of student laptops optimally involves lockers, like ones often provided for instruments, but with the addition of a power outlet to enable the machines to be recharged while stored. Lockers assist with laptop security as well as being convenient. The security of desktop institutional hardware can be assisted by locking the machines to the furniture with a security cable. Institutional laptops will normally need to be secured in a locked storeroom or cupboard when not in use.

Funding

Funding is always a barrier to resource innovation in educational settings, and even though computing equipment is increasingly more affordable it is not a trivial cost in the scheme of education budgets. Fortunately, there is reasonable support for the introduction of computing technologies into schools and so at least the argument for funding computers is not as difficult as it might be for other areas of arts funding.

Sources of funding can be both local and farther afield. Most music departments have an annual operational budget and so, with planning, it may be possible to acquire computer music resources as part of the normal operational budget, or via a special grant from the school or institution. It is quite likely that the school parent association will support technology and a proposal to them is well worthwhile. Most school districts, counties, or states have development grant programs. Often these are tied to specific strategic goals that the governing body has set, but it should not be difficult to find either a technology, pedagogical, or cultural angle that supports the deployment of computer music systems. Advertisements for these programs may appear in published newsletters or gazettes and often there will be a grants officer that you can call for advice about schemes and their requirements. There may be opportunities for philanthropic support from alumni or companies operating in the surrounding community, especially from technology-focused companies looking for a "feel good" cause. Be sure to follow up what assistance-computing companies can provide with educational discounts and other support programs.

When applying for funding, it is important to have good documentation that supports the educational merit and technical appropriateness of your project. Such evidence is often available from music associations, computer companies or from the state music curriculum support documents themselves.

Training and professional development

Educators' work commitments are usually quite demanding and their time highly scheduled, therefore a planned staff development program is critical as part of the integration of new music technologies. The purchase of equipment is just a splash that starts a ripple of cultural change throughout the music program and all connected with it, and a staff development program is critical to ensuring that the impact takes hold as a permanent improvement.

Changing technologies requires a process of training and support to enable changes of mind in the staff that will make use of them. These changes may include additional skills in using the equipment, revised teaching strategies to encourage best student use of the equipment, and workshops on curriculum revisions that incorporate some of the opportunities afforded by the new technologies. As with all learning, it is useful to reinforce the skills and knowledge by having a series of professional development sessions that start before and continue during the use of the integrated technologies.

Depending upon the significance of the music technology integration and on local circumstances, there can be a range of options for professional development. It may be possible for an existing staff member, alumni, or a student to assist staff with how to operate new software or hardware purchases. Staff of retail outlets from which equipment is purchased may agree to run a session covering installation and operation of the equipment. It may be possible for staff from outside the music department to offer their experiences in pedagogical approaches or to facilitate a workshop. A number of institutions run short courses in particular software applications or on music teaching ideas with computing technology that staff could attend. In the United States these include MENC, ProSchool, and TI:ME. In the United Kingdom courses can be found through the Sonic Arts Network and the Music Education Directory. In Australia the SoundHouse organization run short courses for staff and students in using music technologies. There are likely to be many similar associations and private training providers in these and other countries.

Conclusion

There are many considerations regarding the effective integration of new computing technologies into the music program; these include logistical issues of funding, location, connectivity and security, and educational issues such as modifications to curriculum and pedagogy supported by professional development. The benefits of integrating new technologies and associated musical practices are that they renew the music education program and force it to reassess and refine its mission and direction. The integration of the computer music systems and practices will enable a broader, more relevant, more inclusive and more efficient range of music making opportunities for both staff and students, the potential of which awaits their imagination and enthusiasm. While the pace of technological change is unlikely to slow down and the computational instruments yet to be invented are difficult to predict, one thing is certain: humans will continue to strive to express themselves though sound and to apply technologies to tasks in order to amplify their musicianship.

Reflection questions

1. What does DiSessa mean by "computationally literate"?
2. Why might it be that computer systems for education are primarily epistemological but secondarily pedagogical?
3. What are some examples of how the use of computers for music making has become more explicit in our societies?
4. What is the difference between technological change as evolution and as addition?
5. Name the six key words used to describe types of meaningful engagements with music?
6. Why is mobility of computing hardware important for musicians?
7. What is the difference between a LAN and WAN?
8. What are the advantages of music students owning their own portable computer?
9. List the sources for funding mentioned in the chapter.
10. What groups of people might be used to provide professional development assistance when integrating new music technologies?

Teaching tips

1. Use the computer's cachet to enhance the perceived relevance of the music program to students.
2. Focus assessment on general outcomes that allow students to use the computer as one vehicle for achieving those musical outcomes.
3. Many students find the immediate gratification of sound sampling and manipulation a motivation to pursue music further.
4. Be sure to use a range of software with appropriate interfaces and complexity for the different ages of students you teach.
5. Consider how increasing the helper or facilitator aspects of your teaching approach may lead to parallel increases in student motivation in music activities.
6. Use the ability of computers to provide access to producing contemporary music styles to broaden the musical genres covered in your program.
7. Use computer-based tools, such as notation programs and sequencers, to make student tasks more efficient for them.
8. Provide activities that maximize the depth and breadth of students' meaningful engagement with music through the computer.
9. Use mixed equipment resources in a single activity to enrich students' musical experience (e.g., include computers, guitars, percussion equipment, and electronic keyboards).
10. Encourage students to bring their laptops to class so that activities started in class can be continued at home.

> **Suggested tasks**
>
> 1. Examine your music teaching activities with a view to enhancing them with the increased use of computing technology.
> 2. Make a list of the options for funding in your area that could be used for the integration of computing technologies into a music program.
> 3. Locate organizations or individuals in your area that could provide professional development training in computer music.
> 4. Undertake a music technology training program to increase your skills in a relevant area.
> 5. Visit a music store with a good range of computer music equipment to keep up to date with what is available.

Chapter summary

The integration of computers and other music technologies can expand the horizon of opportunities for music production. However, as with any educational change such integration requires planning to be effectively implemented from an educational, technical and social perspective. The integration of new computer music technologies can maintain the relevance of the music program, but the effectiveness of the integration will depend on how the teaching that surrounds that technology responds to the change. The design of teaching programs that focus on maximizing a student's meaningful engagement with music is likely to use the technology effectively because they are not fixated on the equipment but on the student's experience when using it. The attitude of the teacher is also critical to successful implementation; a positive approach to the computer as a musical instrument and a helpful approach to the student are likely to be effective. Computing technology is changing so rapidly that expecting teachers to be experts in all aspects of this domain is unrealistic, and so it is appropriate that teachers focus on guiding students and tasks and sharing the learning journey about the opportunities of computer music systems. Providing staff with professional development opportunities will assist in making the changes associated with technology integration less disruptive. As with any new equipment, there are logistical considerations associated with the integration of computing technologies, including space requirements, power and networking connections, storage or security precautions, and not least securing funding to facilitate the integration.

Notes

1   DiSessa, Andrea, *Changing Minds: Computers, Learning, and Literacy* (Cambridge, MA: The MIT Press, 2000), 110.
2   Papert, Seymour, *Mindstorms: Children, Computers, and Powerful Ideas* (New York: Basic Books, 1980).

3   See DiSessa, 2000 and Fuertes, Christina. 2005. Music Education by Computer, RTEE project, http://www.xtec.es/rtee/eng/tutorial/index.htm (accessed October, 2005).

4   McLuhan, Marshall, *Understanding Media: The Extensions of Man* (London: Sphere Books, 1964).

5   Dewey, John, *Art as Experience* (New York: Putmans, 1934).

6   Brown, Andrew R., "Modes of Compositional Engagement." Paper presented at the Interfaces: The Australasian Computer Music Conference, Brisbane 2000.

7   Sir Robert Hitcham's Primary School, http://www.hitchams.suffolk.sch.uk/ictmusic/index.htm.

8   Cain, Tim, "Theory, Technology and the Music Curriculum." *British Journal of Music Education* 21, no. 2 (2004): 215–21.

9   Brown, "Modes of Compositional Engagement."

10 Dillon, Steve. "The Student as Maker: An Examination of the Meaning of Music to Students in a School and the Ways in Which We Give Access to Meaningful Music Education" (PhD thesis, La Trobe University, 2001).

11 Brown, Ian, *On Becoming a Teacher: The Teachers' Personality and the Students' Response* (Melbourne: North Essendon Therapy Center, 2002), 72.

Chapter 24

Possible futures for computers in music education

It is inevitable, given the pace of computer technology developments, that specific information in this book will become out of date, however, the principles and approaches should continue to be relevant for some time to come. An even more risky endeavor than describing past or current activity is to predict possible future directions, however, when planning the integration of computing technologies in music education contexts it can be useful to imagine where the future might head and hope that the investments and changes being made are in line with emerging trends. With these hazards in mind, this chapter includes speculation about some emerging technological trends and how they might have an impact on music education.

As computing power grows, smaller battery-powered devices will replace desktop computers. The student's mobile phone will be their main computing device. As the physical limitation of large boxes connected to power sockets disappears, computing devices will become almost as easily integrated into group work and ensembles as a flute. The need for some loudspeaker system will be the remaining physical limitation and so wireless in-ear monitoring will become widespread. The need for institutional infrastructure for shared loud speakers, printers, and screens/projectors will remain. Students and faculty will be in continual electronic communications with others through their computer-phone. Membership of social networks including ensembles, interest groups, tuition lessons, and homework groups will blur across physical geographic boundaries to include others within network geographies. This will enable both larger and more niche interest grouping and open up increased opportunities for learning about music beyond the expertise or resources of the local institution. Students will be able to share their music with a wider audience and teachers will be able to collaborate with colleagues near and far more readily. More fluid electronic communications will make the management of information and privacy a more critical issue for parents and educational institutions. The location, analysis, and tracking of digital music content will become more sophisticated and the use and reuse of materials for educational purposes will become more complex before it becomes more straightforward.

The remainder of the chapter will discuss the trends underlying this scenario.

Equipment

When looking to the future of computers in music education, one obvious place to begin is with the future of computers and associated equipment. It seems unlikely that there will be a relaxation in the steady increase in computing power even if one does not believe in Ray Kurzweil's predictions that by 2029 "human learning is primarily accomplished using virtual teachers and is enhanced by the widely available neural implants."[1] For musical uses of computers, the increase in processing power will have more impact in the mobility of computing devices and their analytical autonomy than in the ability to create sound, because since the turn of the century real-time digital audio has been common-place. Of course, musicians will always want more power to do more signal processing, but current systems are already quite capable.

A more noticeable effect of increased computing power will be that smaller and smaller computing devices will have sufficient computing capability for real-time music making. This means that mobile phones and portable music players, such as the Apple iPod, will become capable musical instruments within the next decade, able to do recording, signal processing, synthesis generation, and real-time control at least equivalent to today's laptops.

Solid-state memory, as used in digital cameras, will become the normal storage medium and of such capacity that enormous volumes of music files can be reliably carried at all times. Music students will commonly have a pocket-sized device with all the computing power required to support their music studies, and the resulting ubiquity of computing tools will shift discussions about the use of computers in music education toward a focus on how best to use them, rather then whether or not to use them; rather like current discussions about how to use recording technologies.

As computers get smaller, the issue of gestural control and interface will loom larger. How do you play a device the size of mobile phone as a musical instrument? Shake it? The use of interactive control surfaces for laptop music systems is currently expanding and we should expect even more activity in this area as the "computer" itself diminishes in size. In many cases the cost and size of the control surface will be much more significant than the computing power leading to more musical appliances, each with their own internal computer being coordinated by the musician's main device, the phone-computer. With this development of control surfaces, new performance opportunities will arise and older ones will be challenged. Music educators will need to continue to balance the embracing of these new practices as they emerge while letting go of other outmoded ones.

Cables will disappear. The use of wireless audio connections between devices, as seen in Bluetooth headsets for mobile phones, will make the tangle of leads a thing of the past, and few will shed a tear. Power cables notwithstanding (and smaller more efficient devices should allow batteries to last all day), classroom data communications should be seamless and live computer performances should be almost as easy to set up as a woodwind ensemble.

Connectivity

Apart from hardware developments, a second trend likely to impact on computer use for music (and other aspects of life) is the increased connectivity of people to the Internet. Many computers are already permanently connected to the world via the Internet, and with mobile networks and small portable computers, school environments are likely to become places where everyone is always connected to a network. People are social beings and music making is a very social activity, so we can expect increased networked connectivity to significantly effect music education. These systems will likely be used for network jamming, either in organized ensembles or as spontaneous improvisations, as well as coordinating real-world music making activities. Current patterns of mobile phone and SMS (Short Message Service) usage provide clues to the increase of networked music making as the cost and infrastructure provide more network access. The challenge for the music educator will be how to make these exchanges creative and constructive and not simply limited to rampant file sharing or unrelated chat.

Increased network access is seeing a significant rise in social computing, lead by sites that exploit the links that users make with other users and between information sources. The World Wide Web has always been about hyperlinks, but leading Web sites such as Amazon, Blogger, MySpace, Flickr, and del.icio.us rely on users to provide content and links. The educational implications of social computing include how to manage the collaborative information gathering that occurs at these sites and how to utilize these techniques to musical ends. If, for example, a class uses del.icio.us to bookmark Web sources about a study topic, then the research effort of collecting data is distributed amongst the class and the references located in one place. The focus for assessment might then place more emphasis on the appropriate interpretation of the material. Shared information spaces, like blogs, forums or site tagging, can also allow the live tracking of topic threads throughout the semester. This might change patterns of assessment from being assignment and deadline oriented, to topic and participation focused. Portfolio-style pedagogies are enabled by social Web applications where drafts of work can be posted for peer and staff review, and changes are tracked or logged such that learning style, as well as content, can be discussed.

Collaborative work can be made easier in a highly networked future (or present) with tools such as wiki's, especially SocialText[2] and JotSpotLive[3], enabling multiple users to work on the one document at the same time. While interaction and collaboration are enhanced with these tools, tracking individual contributions to group work may not be, and the way in which group work is approached and assessed may change as a result. However, increasingly these collaborative online sites track individual contributions in any case. The early text-centric nature of these collaborative sites will eventually give way to sites where the management of rich media materials, such as audio, will become common-place. It should not be too long before similar facilities enable synchronous co-writing of musical scores, MIDI sequences or audio soundscapes, are common place and real-time collaborative composing over the Internet will be a standard practice. Online collaboration tools could be used for student group work or staff curriculum design, both within local teams and with others beyond the normal geographic boundaries. In addition, student centered teaching notes could be contributed to and accessible by the classroom, instrumental, band teachers such that each knows what musical experiences the student has had. As these facilities for remote collaboration increase, the reasons for face-to-face interaction need to be highlighted, and the value of the physical school setting and how to best use face-to-face time may need to be refined.

Data mining

The data supporting social computing initiatives and search engines is often centrally stored. Companies like Google, Hotmail, and Yahoo! store massive amounts of data and the difficulty of mining that data for useful information increases in parallel. In order to manage the increased amount of information that the interconnected networks and centralized storage pools will expose us to, automated data analysis tools are used to summarize, evaluate, sort, filter, and locate information for us; the processes known as data mining. In the music world, this trend is mainly visible as *music information retrieval*, where features of score representations or audio signals can be analyzed to assist in music searches. For example, the MusArt[4] system allows a user to hum a portion of some music and the system compares that melody fragment to a database of music and returns either the name, score, or recording of it. This has direct implications for musicology studies and research assignments but the broader implications include the ability for composers and arrangers to locate complementary music or audio fragments as possible material for their work, and for online radio stations like Pandora[5] to automate their customizing of playlists to listener preferences. There are also implications for how musician's promote and distribute their work in ways that maximizes selection by musical data mining software and how interactive performances may utilize on-the-fly selection of accompaniment fragments in response to improvised performance input.

Information sharing

Content accumulation and aggregation are replacing large-scale publishing on the Internet—blogs are overtaking books. The promotion of music through the Web is facilitated by services such as MySpace[6] that allow the easy setup of Web sites or by using music blogging and podcasting tools such as Loudblog.[7] These augment peer to peer music sharing services including LimeWire[8] and BitTorrent.[9] Although popular, these provide little contextual information to support the music and often do not have the sophisticated social organizing features of Web services that assist users in locating music that they might like.

In an attempt to organize all the information being posted to Web sites and blogs, a number of tagging services are appearing. People can add tags (keywords) to their Web sites and blog posts enabling them to be aggregated by services such as Technorati.[10] Users can then search the tag sites for information on topics they are interested in. Students and teachers can use group authored blogs and tag-based aggregation services to follow global debate on topics. This process can enable the ongoing revisiting of important curriculum themes and thus assist changes in educational organization from serial topic organization to iterative reflection on parallel themes that are tracked over time.

In conjunction with the focus on just-in-time information retrieval that is driving the success of Google and other search providers, microcontent information delivery is expanding. "Microcontent" is a term to describe a shift to the posting of small amounts of information regularly within a Web page, rather than requiring the user to refresh the entire page when information is updated. Real-time data such as stock quotes, Web cams, and clocks are obvious candidates for microcontent applications, driven by technologies such as Ajax (Asynchronous JavaScript and XML) that are often called Web 2.0 features. This also means that information on a Web site can be provided by different suppliers, each contributing their specialized content section to the page. As with previous Internet innovations, time-based media content such as music and video, is lagging behind text and image in microcontent services, but early approaches to Web 2.0 audio such as AjaxAmp[11] show that these services are likely to emerge quickly. The use of microcontent in these Web 2.0 application platforms can provide opportunity for music students to aim at careers providing niche music and sound content and functionality that others can embed in their Web sites.

Stylistic diversity and syncretism

Another result of increased communications is greater exposure to musical styles from different cultures and times. Management of stylistic diversity will be an important challenge for music educators as their students are both exposed to a wider range of music and as their communities become increasingly multicultural. New music that incorporates influences from several styles is often called syncretic music. At present, Western musical processes, tuning and metric systems, and modes of interaction heavily influence most music software. At present, popular tools such as Sibelius, ProTools, Ableton Live and GarageBand are deeply imbedded in Western musical understandings and practices. It is likely, or necessary, that software systems become more accommodating of various musical practices and systems if they are to contribute positively to the world's increasingly multicultural circumstances.

Sampling software has played a strong role in these syncretic music process, at least since the release of music by Deep Forest in 1992. Sampling is a crude method of appropriation and integration, and involves a tangle of legal implications, and it is likely that computing systems that support a variety of musical styles at a more abstract level will be required. One of the outcomes of increased computational possessing power in the near future will be the development of more sophisticated methods for manipulating and integrating sampled material into new compositions and remixes, further blurring the boundaries of stylistic musical integration.

Legal frameworks

Given the increasing ease of music sampling and recording, copyright violations are easier to commit, even without intention. The 2000s saw a backlash and conservative lock-down in response to these activities. However, prohibition has rarely been a successful long-term strategy in social control and the identification of a way forward through schemes such as creative commons[12] licenses and open source software will need to be found to balance creative freedom and the protection of creative property. Technology is already implicated in the implementation of these legal frameworks through digital rights management schemes, and the way in which software systems integrate licensing and rights management will require increased attention. Educational uses of material have often been exempt or treated in a special way in copyright and related laws. As these legal frameworks are integrated into software services, such as music and movie downloads, the ability to make distinctions based on educational use may become harder to identify and enable. Educational associations and governments will need to be mindful of the impact on education of any changes in rights management.

Live computational processes

Early in the history of computer music activities, there was a strong focus on computational processes and algorithms for music making. Lejaren Hiller, Milton Babbit, Iannis Xenakis, and Max Mathews were among the musicians involved who had privileged access to computing resources and dedicated significant time to working with awkward technologies. In more recent times, the focus of tools that support creativity has been to simplify user interfaces, increase the features of software, with the result of consolidating on a small set of musical metaphors including electronic manuscript page, tape recorder/studio, portfolio, book, and training drill. With the ability for computers to process data in real time, there has been a renewed interest in musical and sonic processes or algorithms which previously would have been off-putting due to their difficult implementation. This trend is evident in the rise of modular synthesis software including Reason, to Reaktor, Max/MSP, Impromtu, and Supercollider. It is also evident in visual arts tools such as Processing and Node-Box.[13] Increased control over the computational processes will enable musicians to be more innovative in their music making and have greater control over processing material and approaches to creativity. The education implications include the curriculum modifications necessary to keep pace with these developments, the reassessing of notions of musicianship and what constitutes musical skills, and the reengagement with music theories and techniques which have often been put to the side in recent years in preference to more practically focused music programs. Computational processes can now be performed in real time (if required) and as a result the distinctions between practice and theory will increasingly blur.

Sonic expression

In the midst of all these discussions about the future and technological changes, it can be reassuring to remind ourselves there are some things that won't change; in particular our desire for personal and communal expression through music. The style of that music and the means of creation and distribution may vary over time, but the motivation to express and communicate will persist. The challenge for music educators is to identify and encourage sonic expression in themselves and their students, to see past the changes in musical aesthetics, instrumentation, and distribution so as to embrace whatever interests and musicality a student has and to fan those flames. The computer is the dominant technology of our age and is sure to play a significant role in music making and thus music education for some time to come. Whatever the evolution of computing technologies and their uses brings, the educational response should be to ensure that these contribute constructively to amplifying musicality.

Notes

1 Kurzweil, R., *The Age of Spiritual Machines*. (London: Pheonix, 1999),276.
2 Socialtext, a collaborative writing site, http://www.socialtext.com.
3 JotSpotLive, a collaborative writing site, http://jotspotlive.com.
4 MusArt, an audio-input melody search project, http://www.dlib.org/dlib/february02/birmingham/02birmingham.html.
5 Pandora, an online radio station that selects songs similar to ones you specify, http://www.pandora.com.
6 MySpace music, a free Web site facility that includes audio file playback, http://myspace.com.
7 LoudBlog, open source blogging software focusing on audio playback and podcasting, http://loudblog.de.
8 LimeWire, a peer to peer file sharing application, http://www.limewire.com/.
9 BitTorrent, a peer to peer file sharing application, http://www.bittorrent.com/.
10 Technorati, provides aggregation of blog posts based on user-defined tags, http://technrati.com
11 AjaxAmp, a music player library for using in Web 2.0 applications, http://ajaxamp.com/.
12 Creative Commons, a set of content licenses and services designed to allow more flexibility in sharing digital content, http://creativecommons.org.
13 NodeBox, an algorithmic graphic art program for MacOS X, http://nodebox.net/.

Glossary

This glossary contains definitions of word that are frequently used in music software and tutorials about music technology. The glossary is ordered alphabetically.

Acoustics   The study of the physics of sound.

Aftertouch   Pressure adjustments applied to a MIDI keyboard while the note is sounding.

Algorithm   A step-by-step procedure for problem solving.

Amplifier   A device the increases the magnitude of a voltage or current without distorting the wave form of the signal. An amplifier takes a weak signal from a line level or mike level source and provides the necessary power level to operate loudspeakers.

Amplitude   The value of the largest sample in a signal, and corresponds to perceived loudness.

Analogue signal   An electronic signal that varies along a continuous dimension.

Asynchronous   A type of communication between computers requiring no specific timing.

Attack   The beginning portion of a sound when the musical note begins. Antonym: Release.

Binary   Base two number system, typically using values 0 and 1 only.

Bit   The smallest unit of computer data, capable of being in one of two states, 0 or 1.

Blog   A method of Web-based publishing consisting of text and rich media entries, often listed in reverse chronological order. Sometimes called a weblog.

Buffer   A temporary storage area in memory.

Byte   A computer data amount equal to eight bits. A MIDI message is usually 3 bytes long, and a single audio sample is usually 2 bytes (16 bits) in size.

Clipping   Amplifier overload or signal processing increase above maximum level, resulting in a form of distortion.

Compression   Reduction of the effective gain of an amplifier at one level of signal with respect to the gain at another signal level.

Controller   A device allowing the user to enter or change events into a computer or other digital device. Examples include: synthesizer, wind controller, mouse, computer keyboard. A MIDI controller is a controller that "speaks" the MIDI language.

Continuous controller   Refers to non-note MIDI information where values change on a linear scale rather than simply have two states, on and off. For example, volume, pitch bending, and modulation (vibrato). These parameters can change continuously over time and allow electronically generated music to sound more expressive.

CPU   Acronym for Central Processing Unit, the chip which is the main 'brains' of your computer. Sometime used to refer to the computer's "box" in which the CPU is housed.

Digital signal processor (DSP)   Digital Signal Processors are devices, often chips, that have a special set of functions designed for speedy processing of video or audio data.

Distortion   A variation or transmutation of a sound or electronic signal, sometimes undesirable.

Cycle   One repetition of a periodic waveform.

Envelope   The changes in a sound over time (e.g., amplitude envelope is the change is loudness over the duration of a note—attack, sustain, decay, release).

Equalization   The selective adjustment of volume at a specific frequency.

Filter   A electronic device that permits certain frequencies to pass while stopping others.

Frequency Modulation (FM)   The altering of the pitch of one signal by the pitch of another; small amounts create vibrato, large amounts create new timbres.

Fourier transform   A procedure for changing a time domain representation (waveform) into a frequency domain representation (spectrum).

Frequency   The number of vibrations or oscillations per second. Measures in cycles or Hertz.

General MIDI   A standard that specifies (among other things) what types of sounds will be in synthesizer patch locations 1–127.

Glitch   Interruption in the audio stream, usually unwanted.

Grain   A very small sound fragment.

GUI   Graphical user interface.

Hard drive   A memory storage device common to all computers. Memory capacity is listed in megabytes (MB) or gigabytes (GB).

Microtonal   The use of notes closer than a semitone in pitch.

MIDI   An acronym for Musical Instrument Digital Interface. It is a standard language that let's instruments, devices, software, and hardware from different manufacturers communicate fluently.

Mixer   A device that adds different audio signals together.

Modulation   The effecting of one signal by another. For example, vibrato is caused by regular modulation (variation) of pitch.

Morphology   The study of forms and structure. In music, how audio spectra change over time and through space.

Musique concrète   A form of musical composition made from a collage of recorded sounds.

Mute A sequencer command to turn off specified tracks.

Network A collection of computing devices connected so that they can share information and peripherals.

Network Jamming Performing music using a computer with others via local or Internet connections.

Noise Unwanted sound.

Overtone A spectral component of a sound; by itself a sine wave of a particular frequency.

Oscillator A device for generating a periodic waveform.

Pad A long sustained "washy" chord with a lush texture often played on a synthesizer.

Panning Refers to moving an audio signal left or right in the stereo spectrum.

Partial A spectral component of a sound; by itself a sine wave of a particular frequency.

Patch/Preset A synthesizer sound or software setting stored in computer memory.

Plugin A computer program that can add functionality to another. In music software, plugins are often synthesizers and effects processors used by host music applications.

Podcast Refers to both the content and means of distributing multimedia files such as audio programs or videos over the Internet for playback on portable devices or personal computers.

Quantize A process of rounding values. Typically used in MIDI sequencers to "fix" rhythmic inaccuracies in a musical track. Quantizing "rounds off" musical notes to the nearest eighth note, sixteenth note, and such, as specified by the user.

RAM An acronym for Random Access Memory. This is computer memory that can be used over and over.

Real time Occurring so fast that a delay is imperceptible.

Reverb The reflecting and echoing of sounds in a space.

ROM Acronym for Read Only Memory. Computer memory or storage that cannot be erased and reused.

Sampler A type of synthesizer which derives it's sounds from recording actual sounds (instruments or nonmusical sounds).

Sample rate The speed (frequency) at which measurements of an audio signal are taken when converting to a digital waveform.

Sample resolution The degree of accuracy with which samples are measured when converting to a digital waveform.

Sequencer A piece of hardware or software which allows you to record multiple tracks of music one on top of the other while listening to what was recorded previously.

Signal A temporal phenomenon that carries information, such as an electrical current or digital stream of numbers.

Sound event A sonic occurrence that occurs in a particular place during a particular time interval.

Sound object An acoustical recording for human perception and not a synthesized sound. Treated as a phenomenological sound formation referentially independent of its source.

Sound module A sound making device (synthesizer) that does not have an integral controller and must be controlled remotely.

Soundscape The sonic environment. Either as actual environments or abstract sonic constructions/montages.

Spectrum The representation of a signal in terms of its frequency components.

Synthesis The generation of a sound from mathematical principles or electronic processes.

Synthesizer A programmable device that generates (synthesizes) sound.

Track Sequencers borrowed this term from multi-track recording studios, referring to tape tracks. A track is one of a number of locations where a musical part can be recorded and played back.

Velocity Velocity is the MIDI way of determining how hard a note is pressed on the keyboard controller.

Waveform A pattern of sound pressure variations over time, often represented as a series of digital sample values in a computer.

Wavetable An area of computer memory that stores waveform values.

WYSIWYG "What You See Is What You Get" (i.e., what is displayed on the computer monitor is what the printed output will look like).

Note: This glossary owes a debt to several resources including:

- Dodge, C., & Jerse, T. A. 1997. *Computer music.* New York: Schirmer Books.
- Schafer, R. M. 1977. *The soundscape: Our sonic environment and the tuning of the world.* New York: Knopf.
- http://vtg.org/cimonline/Glossary.html.
- http://www.portnet.k12.ny.us/port200s0/glossary.htm.

References

Webography

abc, music notation language, http://staffweb.cms.gre.ac.uk/~c.walshaw/abc/.

Absolute Pitch, atonal pitch recognition, http://www.silvawood.co.uk/pitch-intro. htm.

Adobe Reader, a PDF reader, http://www.adobe.com/products/acrobat/reader-main.html

Algorithmic Composer, a MIDI-based algorithmic visual programming environment, http://www.users.bigpond.com/angelo_f/AlgorithmicComposer/.

Allmusic, music information database and search engine, http://www.allmusic. com/.

Alsa Modular Synth, graphical synthesis toolkit, http://alsamodular.sourceforge. net/.

Amadeus II, audio editing software, http://www.hairersoft.com/Amadeus.html.

Amazon, online shop, http://amazon.com.

AppleWorks, simple office application suite, http://www.apple.com/appleworks/.

Archive.org, information repository, http://www.archive.org/text.

ArtistLaunch, Web music hosting and sales, http://www.artistlaunch.com/.

Audacity, audio editing software, http://audacity.sourceforge.net/.

Audacity, audio editing software, http://audacity.sourceforge.net/.

Audacity, free audio editor and recorder, http://audacity.sourceforge.net/.

AudioMulch, interactive music and sound environment, http://www.audiomulch. com.

AudioSculpt, audio editing and analysis software, http://www.ircam.fr.

AudioStreet, Web music hosting, http://www.audiostreet.net/.

Auralia, aural training software, http://www.risingsoftware.com/auralia30/.

Band In A Box, algorithmic software, http://www.pgmusic.com/.

Electronic Music Timeline, history of electronic music, http://www.intuitivemusic. com/techno-guide-time-line.html.

REFERENCES

Beatnik, digital audio technologies, http://www.beatnik.com/.

Bio2MIDI, algorithmic software, http://algoart.com/.

Blackboard, learning management system, http://www.blackboard.com/.

Bricolage, content management system, http://www.bricolage.cc/.

Calma, software for aural training and listening exercises, http://www.hud.ac.uk/ mh/music/calma/calma.html.

CD Baby, http://www.cdbaby.com.

CDnow, http://cdnow.com.

Center for Computer Assisted Research in the Humanities, Braun Music Center, Stanford University, http://ccrma-www.stanford.edu/CCARH.

Choral Wiki, http://www.cpdl.org/wiki/index.php/Main_Page.

Classical CD Exchange, http://classicalcdexchange.co.uk.

Classroom Clipart, Web site with music and other images, http://classroomclipart. com/Music.htm.

Cmix, text-based music synthesis environment, http://www.music.princeton.edu/ winham/cmix.html.

Common Lisp Music, sound synthesis language, http://ccrma.stanford.edu/ software/clm/.

Compose World, algorithmic software, http://acorn.cybervillage.co.uk/esp/cw2. htm.

Coverpop, searchable collages of items, http://www.coverpop.com.

Creative Commons, licenses for creative content, http://creativecommons.org/.

Csound, algorithmic sound processing software, http://www.csounds.com/.

Cubase, music sequencer, http://www.steinberg.net/.

Cyclops, video analysis and tracking for Max/MSP, http://www.cycling74.com/ products/cyclops.html.

Digidesign, audio production systems, http://www.digidesign.com/.

DMusic, Web music hosting, http://www.dmusic.com.

Drupal, content management system, http://drupal.org/.

eJay, interactive music creation software, http://www.ejay.com.

Electronic Music Foundation, experimental music organization and music distributor, http://www.emf.org.

EMusic, http://www.emusic.com.

Encyclopaedia Britannica Online, http://www.eb.com/.

Esellerate, e-commerce service provider, http://www.esellerate.net.

Express, desktop publishing application, http://www.quark.com/.

FileInfo, descriptions of audio file formats, http://www.fileinfo.net/filetypes/audio.

Finale, music publishing software, http://www.finalemusic.com/.

Flash, vector-based drawing and animation application, http://www.macromedia. com/software/flash/.

Functional Ear Trainer, software for pitch recognition in context, http://www.miles. be/.

GarageBand, music sequencing and audio production software, http://www.apple. com.

Good-Ear Ear Trainer, online ear training Web site, http://www.good-ear.com/.

Google, Internet search engine, http://www.google.com.

Grove Music Online, music encyclopedia, http://www.grovemusic.com/.

Hearing Music, software playground for musical sound exploration, http://www. viva-media.com/products/hearingMusic/hearingMusic.html.

HMSL, algorithmic music software, http://www.softsynth.com/hmsl/.

Home Concert, auto accompaniment software,. http://www.musiconmypc.co.uk/art_music_making_software.php.

Humdrum Toolkit, software tools for music research, http://www.humdrum.org/Humdrum/

Hyperinstruments, MIT Media Lab project, http://brainop.media.mit.edu/Archive/Hyperinstruments/.

iMovie, simple video editing software, http://www.apple.com.

Impress, screen presentation application, http://www.openoffice.org/product/impress.html.

Impromptu, computational arts software, http://impromptu.moso.com.au.

Inform: Music analysis system, http://www.ecsmedia.com/indivprods/inform.shtml.

Interactive Musician, musicianship software series, http://www.alfred.com/sub_software/aim/aim.htm.

Interactor, algorithmic software, http://www.troikaranch.org/interactor.html.

Internet Archive, educational resources page, http://www.archive.org/details/education.

Internet Music Resources, http://www.music.indiana.edu/music_resources/.

InTheChair, accompaniment and performance monitoring software, http://www.inthechair.com/.

iTaskX, project management software, http://www.itaskx.com/software/en/.

iTunes, http://www.apple.com/itunes/.

Jam2jam, network improvisation software, http://explodingart.com.au.

Jammer, algorithmic software, http://www.soundtrek.com/.

jMusic, Java-based algorithmic music library, http://jmusic.ci.qut.edu.au.

K-12 Resources for Music Teachers, http://www.isd77.k12.mn.us/resources/staff-pages/shirk/k12.music.html.

Keynote, a free screen presentation application, http://www.apple.com/iwork/keynote/.

Koan, algorithmic music software, http://www.sseyo.com/products/koanpro/index.html.

Kyma, graphical synthesis toolkit, http://www.symbolicsound.com/kyma.html.

Lantiv Timetabler, class scheduling application, http://www.lantiv.com/.

LaTeX, document preparation system, http://www.latex-project.org/.

Learn.com, learning management system, http://www.learn.com/.

Lesson Planner, lesson organizing and scheduling application, http://www.lesson-planner.co.uk/.

LilyPond, music publishing software, http://lilypond.org/.

Listen, aural training software, http://www.imaja.com/listen/index.html.

Logic, sequencer, http://www.emagic.de/.

M, intelligent composing and performing system, http://cycling74.com/products/m.html.

MacGAMUT, ear training software, http://www.macgamut.com/.

Making Tracks, simple online sequencing tools, http://www.bbc.co.uk/radio3/makingtracks/makeatune.shtml.

Manhattan Virtual Classroom, courseware and learning management system, http://manhattan.sourceforge.net/.

Max/MSP, algorithmic software, http://www.cycling74.com.

Max/MSP, graphical environment for music production, http://www.cycling74.com/products/maxmsp.html.

MENC, music education association, http://www.menc.org/.

MetaCrawler Internet, search engine, http://www.metacrawler.com/.

MetaSynth, music painting software, http://uisoftware.com/MetaSynth/.

MiBac Jazz, jazz musicianship tutorials, http://www.mibac.com/Pages/jz.html.

MICNet, musical Internet connections, http://collaboratory.nunet.net/micnet/.

Microsoft Office, a suite of office applications, http://office.microsoft.com/.

Microsoft Project, project management software, http://office.microsoft.com/.

Microsoft Works, simple office application suite, http://www.microsoft.com/products/works/.

Midi2Text, create a text file from MIDI file note data, http://jmusic.ci.qut.edu.au/applications.html#Midi2text.

Mimosa, a timetabling application, http://www.mimosasoftware.com/.

Moodle, learning management system, http://moodle.org/.

MSN Search, http://search.msn.com/.

Muisctheory.net, online musicianship exercise, http://www.musictheory.net/.

Music Ace, elementary level musicianship games, http://www.harmonicvision.com/mafact.htm.

Music Education by Computer, online music technology usage advice, http://www.xtec.es/rtee/eng/tutorial/index.htm.

Music Education Directory, list of U.K. music organizations, http://www.bpi-med.co.uk/search_courses.asp.

Music Essentials, online musicianship games, http://www.bbc.co.uk/music/parents/musicessentials/index.shtml.

Music Histogram, view statistical analysis of MIDI file, http://jmusic.ci.qut.edu.au/applications.html#histogram.

Music Lessons I & II, musicianship tutorial software, http://www.mibac.com/Pages/ML.html.

Music Mouse, algorithmic music software, http://retiary.org/ls/programs.html.

Musicianship Basics, simple software music theory quizzes, http://users.dragnet.com.au/~donovan/mb/index.html.

MusicKit, text-based music and synthesis environment, http://musickit.source-forge.net/.

MusicXML, musical score markup language, http://www.recordare.com/xml.html.

Musition, music theory and musicianship software, http://www.risingsoftware.com/musition2/.

Musolomo, software instrument, http://plasq.com/musolomo/.

NetNewsWire Lite, Mac OS RSS reader, http://ranchero.com/netnewswire/.

Niall's Pedal Board, dedicated plugin host, http://www.niallmoody.com/niallspedalboard.htm.

NIFF, notation interchange file format, http://www.musique.umontreal.ca/personnel/Belkin/NIFF.doc.html.

O-Generator, simple cyclic sequencer, http://www.o-music.tv/product.htm.

OLAT, learning management system, http://www.olat.org/.

OpenDocument, a rich media file format based on XML, http://www.oasis-open.org/committees/tc_home.php?wg_abbrev=office.

OpenMusic, algorithmic software, http://www.ircam.fr/equipes/repmus/OpenMusic/.

OpenOffice, free suite of office applications, http://www.openoffice.org/.

PageMaker, desktop publishing application, http://www.adobe.com/products/pagemaker/.

Pages, word processor with strong layout features, http://www.apple.com/iwork/pages/.

PayPal, e-commerce service providers, http://www.paypal.com.

PhotoShop and Illustrator, graphic design applications, http://www.adobe.com/.

PICS, content rating platform of the WWW consortium, http://www.w3.org/PICS/.

Pivot, content management systems, http://www.pivotlog.net/.

Plone, content management system, http://plone.org/.

Podcasting, explanation of podcasting, http://en.wikipedia.org/wiki/Podcasting.

PowerPoint, screen presentation application, http://office.microsoft.com/.

Practica Musica, sight reading and aural training softwarem, http://www.ars-nova.com/practica.html.

Pro Tools, hard disk recording system, http://www.digidesign.com/.

ProSchool, Digidesign training and education programs, http://training.digidesign.com/index.cfm?page=centers/preschool.

Pure Data (Pd), graphical music programming language, http://www-crca.ucsd.edu/~msp/Pd_documentation/.

Rax, dedicated plugin host, http://plasq.com/rax/.

Reaktor, graphical synthesis toolkit, http://www.native-instruments.com/.

Reason, modular virtual synthesizer and sequencing software, http://www.propellerheads.se/.

Recording Technology History, http://history.acusd.edu/gen/recording/notes.html.

Roland MV-8000, audio production workstation, http://www.roland.com/products/en.

Rollercoaster, the ABC's interactive games and music toys site, http://www.abc.net.au/rollercoaster/games/.

Sakai Project, learning management system, http://www.sakaiproject.org/.

Sequencza 21, new music wiki, http://netnewmusic.net/wiki/.

SharpReader, Windows RSS reade, http://www.sharpreader.net/.

Sibelius Notes, musicianship teaching resource pack, http://www.sibelius.com/products/notes/.

Sibelius, music publishing software, http://www.sibelius.com/cgi-bin/home/home.pl.

Sir Robert Hitcham's Primary School, examples of student music work with computers, http://www.hitchams.suffolk.sch.uk/ictmusic/index.htm.

SmartMusic, auto accompaniment software, http://www.smartmusic.com/.

SoftStep, algorithmic sequencer, http://algoart.com/softstep.htm.

Sonar, music sequencer, http://www.cakewalk.com/Products/SONAR/.

Sonic Arts Network, U.Kk-based computer music association, http://www.sonicartsnetwork.org/.

SoundHouse, music technology professional develop in Australia, http://www.soundhouse.com.au/.

Spongfork, software instrument, http://www.spongefork.com/.

STEIM, Center for Research & Development of Instruments & Tools, http://www.xs4all.nl/~steim/main.html.

SubEthaEdit, collaborative text editor, http://www.codingmonkeys.de/.

SuperCollider, algorithmic music software, http://www.audiosynth.com/.

Symbolic Composer, algorithmic software, http://www.symboliccomposer.com/.

The Continuator, details and video of the imitative software in action, http://www.csl.sony.fr/~pachet/continuator.html.

The Shape of Song, visualizing musical structure, http://www.turbulence.org/Works/song/.

Theory Games, early years musicianship software, http://www.alfred.com/frame-set.cfm?sub=software.

TI:ME, music education and technology organization, http://www.ti-me.org/.

TimeTabler, class scheduling application, http://www.timetabler.com/.

Überlabel.com, Web music hosting, http://www.uberlabel.com/.

vOICe, image sonfication applet, http://www.visualprosthesis.com/javoice.htm.

V-Stack, dedicated plugin host, http://www.steinberg.de/ProductPage_sbdff5.html.

VSTI Host, dedicated plugin host, http://www.defectiverecords.com/vstihost/index2.html.

WavePad, audio editing software, http://www.nch.com.au/wavepad/index.html.

WebCT, learning management system, http://www.webct.com/.

Wiki.org, information about wikis, http://wiki.org/.

Wikipedia, online encyclopedia, http://en.wikipedia.org/.

WordPress, content management system, http://wordpress.org/.

Yahoo, http://www.yahoo.com.

Yahoo! Musical Instrument Sites, http://dir.yahoo.com/Entertainment/music/instruments.

Yamaha AW16g, audio production workstation, http://www.aw4416.com/e/16g/.

Young Composers wiki, http://www.youngcomposers.com.

Books and Articles

Assayag, Gerard, and Carlos Agon. 1996. Open music architecture. Paper presented at the International Computer Music Conference, Hong Kong.

Barrett, William. 1978. *The illusion of technique: A search for meaning in a technological Civilization*. New York: Anchor Press, 1978.

Boulez, Pierre. 1986. Technology and the computer. In *The language of electroacoustic music*, ed. Simon Emmerson. London: Macmillan Press.

Brown, Andrew R. Teaching synthesizer performance: Issues for an instrumental music program for synthesizer. The University of Melbourne, 1994.

Brown, Andrew R. 2000. Modes of compositional engagement. Paper presented at the Interfaces: The Australasian Computer Music Conference, Brisbane.

Brown, Andrew R. 2003. Music composition and the computer: An examination of the work Practices of five experienced composers. PhD diss.,, The University of Queensland.

Brown, Andrew R., and Kevin Purcell. 1988. Music technology: A transparent integration. Paper presented at A world view of music education: The XVIII ISME International Conference, Canberra, Australia.

Brown, Andrew R., and Bradley Voltz. 2005. Elements of effective e-learning design. *International Review of Research in Open and Distance Learning* 6, no. 1, http://www.irrodl.org/content/v6.1/brown_voltz.html.

Brown, Ian. 2002. *On becoming a teacher: The teachers' personality and the students' response*. Melbourne: North Essendon Therapy Center.

Cain, Tim. 2004. Theory, technology and the music curriculum. *British Journal of Music Education* 21, no. 2: 215–21.

Chadabe, Joel. 1997. *Electric sound: The past and promise of electronic music.* Upper Saddle River, NJ: Prentice-Hall.

Cope, David. 1992. Computer modeling of musical intelligence in Emi. *Computer Music Journal* 16, no. 2: 69–83.

Cope, David. 1996. *Experiments in musical intelligence,* vol. 12. Madison, WI: A-R Editions, 1996.

Dewey, John. 1934. *Art as experience.* New York: Putmans.

Dillon, Steve. 1995. The student as maker: An examination of making in music education and the implications for contemporary curriculum development. Master of Education thesis. La Trobe University, Melbourne, Australia.

Dillon, Steve. 2001. The student as maker: An examination of the meaning of music to students in a school and the ways in which we give access to meaningful music education. PhD thesis. La Trobe University, Melbourne, Australia.

Dillon, Steve, and Andrew R. Brown .2006. The art of ePortfolios: Insights from the creative arts experience. In *Handbook of research on ePortfolios,* eds. Ali Jafari and Catherine Jaufman. Hershey, PA: Idea Group Publishing.

DiSessa, Andrea. 2000. *Changing minds: Computers, learning, and literacy.* Cambridge, MA: The MIT Press.

Doornbusch, Paul. 2005. *The music of CSIRAC: Australia's first computer music.* Melbourne: Common Ground.

Dreyfus, Hubert L 2001.. *On the internet.* New York: Routledge.

Elliot, David. 1995. *Music matters: A new philosophy of music education.* New York: Oxford. Forte, Allen, and Steven E Golbert. 1982. *Introduction to Shenkerian analysis.* New York: W. W. Norton.

Frankel, James. 2004. The one-computer music classroom. *Music Education Technology* 2, no.: 10–14.

Gardner, Howard. 1983. *Frames of mind: The theory of multiple intelligences.* London: Heinemann.

Hagen, Earle. 1971. *Scoring for films: A complete text.* Miami, FL: E D J Music.

Heidegger, Martin. 1977. *The question concerning technology and other essays.* Trans. William Lovitt. New York: Harper & Row.

Hiller, Lejaren, and Leonard Isaacson.1958. Musical composition with a high-speed digital computer. In *Machine Models of Music.* Cambridge, MA: MIT Press.

Kay, Alan. 2005.The dynabook revisited, interview by the Book & the Computer. http://www.honco.net/os/print_kay.html (accessed December, 2005).

Lerdahl, Fred, and Ray Jackendoff. 1983. *A generative theory of tonal music.* Cambridge, MA: MIT Press.

Levenson, Thomas. 1994. *Measure for measure: A musical history of science.* New York: Touchstone.

Lohner, Henning.1986. The UPIC system: A user's report. *Computer Music Journal* 10, no. 4: 42-49.

McIlwain, Peter. 2002. A survey of software designs from the Sonic Art Group. In *The Australasian computer music conference,* ed. Paul Doornbusch, 81–90. Melbourne: ACMA.

McLuhan, Marshall. 1964. *Understanding media: The extensions of man.* London: Sphere Books.

REFERENCES

Miranda, Eduardo Reck. 2001. Evolving cellular automata music: From sound synthesis to composition. Paper presented at the Annual Congress of the Brazilian Computer Science Society (SBC) - SBCM, Universidade Federal do Ceara.

Norman, Donald A. 1998. *The invisible computer: Why good products can fail, the personal computer is so complex, and information appliances are the solution.* Cambridge, MA: MIT Press.

Papert, Seymour. 1980. *Mindstorms: Children, computers, and powerful ideas.* New York: Basic Books.

Papert, Seymour. 1993. *The children's machine: Rethinking school in the age of the computer.* New York: Basic Books.

Paynter, John.1992. *Sound & atructure.* New York: Cambridge University Press.

Pool, Otto Ede. 1996. The Apollo project: Software for musical analysis using DARMS. In *Computing in musicology: An international directory of applications,* vol 10, eds. Walter B Hewlett and Eleanor Selfridge-Field, 123–30. Stanford, CA: CCARH.

Postman, Neil. 1992. *Technopoly: The surrender of culture to technology.* New York: Vintage Books.

Pratt, George. 1990. *Aural awareness: Principles and practice.* Buckingham: Open University Press.

Prendergast, Mark. 2003. *The ambient century: From Mahler to Moby - the evolution of sound in the electronic age.* London: Bloomsbury,.

Reimer, Bennett. 1970, *A philosophy of music education.* Englewood Cliffs, N.J: Prentice Hall. Rowe, Robert. 1993. *Interactive music systems: Machine listening and composing.* Cambridge, MA: MIT Press.

Schaeffer, Pierre. 1977. *Traité des objects musicaux,* 2d ed. Paris: Éditions du Seuil.

Schafer, R. Murray. 1977. *The soundscape: Our sonic environment and the tuning of the world.* New York: Knopf.

Selfridge-Field, Eleanor. 1997. *Beyond MIDI: The handbook of musical codes.* Cambridge, MA: MIT Press.

Sohne, B. Schotts. 1993. Mozart dice game. In *Machine models of music,* eds. Stephan M Schwanauer and David A Levitt, 533–38. Cambridge, MA: The MIT Press.

Swanwick, Keith. 1979. *A basis for music education.* London: Routledge.

Swanwick, Keith. 1999. *Teaching music musically.* London: Routledge.

Taube, Heinrick. 1999. Automatic tonal analysis: Toward the implementation of a music theory workbench. *Computer Music Journal* 23, no. 4: 18–32.

Towsey, Michael, Andrew R. Brown, Susan Wright, and Joachim Diederich. 2000. Towards melodic extension using genetic algorithms. Paper presented at the Interfaces: The Australasian Computer Music Conference, Brisbane.

Truax, Barry. 1973. The computer composition: Sound synthesis programs Pod4, Pod5 and Pod6. In *Sonological Reports, No. 2.* Utrecht, The Netherlands: Utrecht State University, Institute of Sonology.

Xenakis, Iannis. 1971. *Formalized music: Thought and mathematics in composition.* Bloomington: Indiana University Press.

Index

808 State 126

AAC 46, 147–148, 183
abc (music language) 153–154
Ableton Live 46, 79, 128, 137, 168, 298, 315
Absolute Pitch 242, 323
access
    to computing resources 14, 209–215,
       235–238, 282, 302
    to information 251–253, 265, 287–289
Access Virus 126
Acousmatic 123, 131
affordance 10, 18, 77, 169, 257, 306
AIFF 45, 147, 148, 157, 183
Akai 127, 136
Alesis 50. 126. 127
Algorithmic Composer 140, 185, 323
algorithmic composition 84–87, 90–92,
    117, 182, 298, 301
aliasing 10
Allmusic.com 209, 323
Amazon 193, 200, 202, 313
amplifier 6, 34, 35, 47, 49, 101, 114, 117,
    122, 190, 298, 319
amplifying musicality xxii, 6, 11–18, 29,
    284, 291, 306, 317
analogue 10, 21, 37, 44, 72–73, 79, 97–103,
    119, 126, 146
analysis
    aural analysis 28, 233–245
    of music 71, 78, 87, 88, 152, 218,
       221–231

    research 314, 324
Anderson, Laurie 125, 134
Aphex Twin 126, 172, 175
applications; *see* software
Arp 126
arranging music 23, 60, 62, 69, 71, 76, 80,
    117, 128–129, 150, 244, 287
ArtistLaunch xvii, 198–200, 323
assessment xvii, 54, 55, 56, 156, 161, 178,
    184, 234, 240, 247–270, 292, 307, 313
Audacity 51, 58, 148, 229, 323
audio
    editing 46, 103, 106, 148, 167, 182, 229
    files 20, 23, 45, 128, 147–160, 182,
       192,–196
    recording xxi, 4, 38, 51–57, 71, 81,
       146–151, 216, 231, 235, 241, 280
    rendering vii, 60, 65, 76, 77, 146
AudioMulch 104, 105, 117, 137, 140, 142,
    182, 186
aural training xxii, 7, 24, 69, 131, 158,
    233–243, 255, 277, 280
Auralia xviii, 7, 234, 242, 254, 255
Autechre 126
auto-accompaniment x, 87,140, 142, 255
automated music vi, 31–33, 38, 139, 209

balance (amplitude) 78, 151
Band In A Box 186, 82, 87, 90–92, 250
Barrett, William 188, 328
Beatnik 214, 324
Behringer 127

Biles, Al 136, 143
binary xvii, 3, 8, 44, 319
Blackboard 266, 268
blog xvii, 20, 177, 197–202, 210, 213, 252, 270, 313–319
Boulez, Pierre 111, 113, 118, 120
bricolage 146, 159
Bricolage (CMS) 265
Brown, Ian 302
Buchla, Donald 137

Cage, John 32, 33, 85, 92, 93, 124, 169
Cahill, Thaddeus 34, 122
Calma 239, 242
Carlos, Wendy 124, 131
Cary, Tristam 124
Casio 126
ccMixter xviii, 192
CD Baby 194, 200, 324
CD, see compact disc
CDnow 193, 200
censorship 208, 212
Chadabe, Joel 132, 134
Chafe, Chris 136
Chowning, John 99
clipping 47, 319
Cmix 90, 104, 324
Coldcut 126
collaborate 11, 124, 139, 169, 187, 311
compact disc 51, 179
composing 7, 11, 18, 25, 32–39, 54, 57, 62, 77–94, 114–117, 123, 136, 164–175, 182, 191, 222–229, 249, 277, 298–301, 315
computational 10, 20, 33, 130, 148, 175–179, 248, 261, 306, 307, 315, 316
computer 3, 4, 10, 20, 276
  as instrument 10, 18–20, 111, 122–125, 130
  as medium 8, 10, 14, 16–18, 37, 159
  as musical partner 4, 11–15, 81, 138–141, 169, 217
  as tool 7, 13, 77–81, 103–107, 155, 185, 227–231, 260, 279, 313–316
conducting 23, 137, 248
connectionist 87–89, 92
content management system 252, 256, 265–269, 288
context
  cultural 17, 59
  educational 29, 270, 311

historical 31, 37, 40, 244
  physical 20, 170
  social 20, 27, 117, 222, 233
controller(s) 7, 36, 71, 90, 112–119, 126–138, 140–143, 277, 320, 322
convergence 156, 159, 160, 177, 209
Cope, David 34, 87, 226, 227
  Experiments in musical intelligence 34, 40, 84, 87, 226
copyright; see rights
CPN; see notation
creative commons; see rights
criticism 55, 202
Croquet 179, 185
Cross, Burnett 123
Crystal River Engineering 180
Csikszentmihalyi, Mihalyi 24, 29
CSIRAC 33, 40
Cubase 71, 90, 91
Cunningham, Merce 169, 174
curriculum 3–6, 22–25, 146, 178, 184–188, 240, 298–301, 314
Cycling 74 19, 90, 104, 137

dance 130, 163, 169, 170, 17
dance music, see electronic dance music
Dannenberg, Roger 134
DARMS 154, 224, 231
database 34, 178, 207–209, 218, 235–239, 252–256, 262–267, 271, 303, 314
Dean, Roger 134
delay 33, 47, 53, 54, 103, 113, 134, 137, 170, 180, 211
desktop publishing 36, 261, 262, 268
Dewey, John 18, 23, 29, 298
Digital rights management (DRM) 193, 201, 202, 316
digital video disc 50–52, 145, 147, 156–161, 168, 174, 179, 182, 188, 193, 202, 240, 262, 267, 303
digital
  audio 39, 47, 50, 71, 147, 178–182, 188, 192, 231, 312
  data 49, 146
  image 163, 171
  media 4, 21, 145, 159, 160, 171, 177, 185–188
  video 51, 80, 156, 159, 179, 209
Dillon, Steven 26, 29, 184, 188, 252
director 7, 25, 26, 134, 166, 300
DiSessa, Andrea 295

distance education 287–291
DJ Spooky 134
DMusic 198, 200
Download 23, 158, 189, 190–202, 209, 288, 297
Dreamweaver 180, 185, 288
Dreyfus, Hubert 289–293
drum machine 121, 126–131, 137, 265, 278
Drupal 265, 268
Duckworth, William 139
Duran Duran 125
DVD, see digital video disc
DX7 36

eBay 193
eCommerce 193, 199, 200
Edison, Thomas 34
education 54, 81, 114, 217;
    contexts 29, 50, 52, 63, 158, 196, 305
    programs of xxii, 111, 262, 266, 275, 289, 295–299, 306
    resources 156, 180, 200, 293, 317
effects, audio 44, 78, 104, 111, 114, 137, 165–167, 174, 180–184, 321
eJay 23,141
e-learning 266, 287–293, 328
electroacoustic 10, 22, 28, 115, 130, 132, 229
electronic dance music 97, 106, 115, 123–127, 131
electronic music 11, 23, 31–36, 55, 71, 79, 96, 103, 112–132, 190, 296
Electronic Music Foundation (EMF) 194, 200
Elliot, David 247, 256, 258
Eminem 8
Emmerson, Keith 119, 125
Emu Systems 124, 126
Emulator 124
Engagement
    creative 25, 26
    meaningful xxii, 27, 299–301, 307
    modes of xxii, 25, 28, 289, 200;
Eno, Brian 86, 125, 202
ensemble 28, 114, 70, 174
    electronic 119, 125
    synthesizer 116, 118
Ensoniq 124, 126
envelope xvii, 21, 47, 96, 101–106, 113–115
Enya 125
equalizer 37, 47, 52, 76, 111, 180

equipment, musical 13, 66, 197, 275, 280–286, 297, 308
ergonomics 66, 283–286
Errante, Gerard 133
Eurithmics 125
evolution 89, 136, 298, 317
exhibition 163, 166, 171–175, 252, 301
experimental 79, 116, 121–126, 129, 132–137, 169, 194
explorer 10, 25, 289, 300, 301

Fairlight CMI 35, 36, 124, 126
FairPlay 195
Fatboy Slim 126
FileMaker Pro 264
film music 115, 125, 163, 166,168, 174
filter 10, 47, 99, 102–106, 113, 136
Finale 7, 62, 70, 298
FL Studio; Fruity Loops 71, 79, 128
FLAC 46, 148, 159
Flash 147, 155, 180, 235, 261
font, music 63, 154, 159
fourier
    analysis 224, 229
    transform 7, 151, 172, 228, 320
FFT 151
Frankel, James 281, 286
frequency
    modulation (FM) xviii, 37, 99, 100, 106, 113
    pitch 47, 95, 151, 152
    spectra 86, 135, 151, 152, 228
Functional Ear Trainer 239, 242
Furse, Tony 35, 124

GarageBand xviii, 71, 73, 165, 250, 315
general MIDI 35, 36, 44, 112, 118, 152, 182
generative 84, 86, 135, 141, 239, 277
genetic algorithm 89, 94, 136, 143
GenJam 136, 143
gesture 5, 11, 59, 67, 71–73, 81, 119, 129–141, 170, 217, 248
Glass, Philip 124
Good-Ear 235
Goldsmith, Jerry 166
GoLive 180
Google 191, 208, 265, 314
Grainger, Percy 34, 123
graphic score 228, 230
graphical user interface 20, 303, 320

Green, Lucy 20
GTTM 34, 40, 227

hammond organ 34, 97
hard disk
    drive 67, 190
    recording xvii, 36, 43, 48–51, 73, 104,
        179, 231
hardware, *see* equipment
Hartman 126
headphones 67, 113, 119, 129, 173, 303
Hearing Music 241–244
Heidegger, Martin 18, 29
Henry, Kevin 32, 180
Henry, Pierre 123
Herman, Bernard 166
Hill, Geoff 33
Hillier, Lejaren 33, 85, 86, 94
Horner, James 166
HTML 145, 154, 157, 215
Humdrum Toolkit 227, 229
Huron, David 180, 227

iChat 288
Illustrator 261, 268
Impromptu xvii, 84, 90, 91, 104, 117, 182,
    241
improvisation 11, 23, 26, 91, 124, 130–143,
    170, 210
    networked 23, 87, 139, 141
Instrument, *see* computer as instrument
intention 9, 17, 23–25, 47, 77, 84, 222, 315
interactive
    computer 28, 134, 139–142
    music xxi, 94, 133, 136–143, 292, 323
    performance 18, 54, 86, 117, 133–142,
        178, 314
Interactive Musician 235
Internet
    connection 139, 189, 194, 213, 321
    distribution 191, 194, 201
    research 208, 213
    search 211, 217
InTheChair 134, 140
invisibility 17–19, 27–29
iPod 43, 78, 148, 158, 189, 195–197, 297,
    312
Isaacon, Leonard 33, 85, 94
iTaskX 266, 269
iTunes 46, 148, 195, 200–202
Iwai, Toshio xviii, 171

iWork 263

Jackendoff, Ray 34, 40, 231
Jam2jam 23, 86–92, 139–143, 210
Jarre, Jean-Michel 125
jMusic 90, 140, 182, 241
Jones, Howard 125

Kahootz 179
Kay, Allan 9, 10
Kern 224, 227
Keynote 262, 268
Koan 86, 90, 154
Korg 103, 126–128
Korngold, Eric 166
Kurtzweil, Ray 312
Kurzweil (synthesizer) 126
Kyma 90, 104, 139, 172, 325

Lake Technology 180
Lansky, Paul 11, 15
learning
    environment xxii, 20, 287, 290, 293
    experience 20 134 213 293
    strategy 22, 26, 55, 249, 287
learning management system 253,
    266–269
Lerdahl, Fred 34
Levenson, Thomas 32
licence; *see* rights
LilyPond 62
Linn 127
Lippe, Cort 134
Listen 238
Logic 71, 90, 117
loops, musical xviii, 54–56, 71–80, 126,
    129, 137, 141, 168, 172, 182
LoudBlog 314
Lucier, Alvin 124

M 137, 141
MacGammut 7, 239
Machover, Todd 134
maintenance 21, 253, 254, 278, 284
Markov 33, 85, 89, 136
Massive Attack 126
Mathews, Max 134, 316
Max/MSP 19, 85, 88, 90, 104, 117, 128,
    137, 142, 182, 241, 316
McIlwain, Peter 172
McLuhan, Marshall 7, 9, 18, 209

meaning xxi, 26, 29, 31, 38, 40
meaningful engagement xxii, 27, 299–301, 307, 308
medium, see computer as medium
memory
  card 49, 52, 213
  computer 43, 48, 73, 190, 213, 321
MENC 306, 326
metaphor 4–6, 14, 20–22, 28, 73, 81, 87, 114, 179, 221, 224, 238, 282, 298, 316
MetaSynth 172, 175
MiBac Jazz 239
Microcontent 315
Microsoft Access 264
Microsoft Office
  Excel 263
  PowerPoint 145, 157, 262, 268
  Project 266
  Word 157, 261
MIDI xviii, 4, 7, 19, 32–36, 39, 71–73, 104, 137–143, 224–232, 319–320
  controller; see controller
  file 62, 63, 78–81, 134, 152, 157, 182–184, 214
  sequencing; see sequencer
mini disc 51
Mirage 124
mixing desk 47, 53, 123, 127, 131, 280
Moodle 252, 266
Moog 35, 124, 126
Moraz, Patrick 125
Morrill, Dexter 136
mp3
  file format 46, 147–148, 157, 159, 183, 193–201, 214
  players 51, 148, 194, 303
MPEG 147, 148, 156
Mumma, Gordon 124
MusArt 314, 317
Music Ace 240, 254
music information retrieval 254, 314
music performance; see performance
music production; see production
music publishing; see publishing
Music Sense xviii, 241
music theory 33, 62, 154, 241, 249, 277, 303
Music Theory Workbench 254, 258
musicianship 13, 17, 22, 28, 80, 164, 231–248, 254, 297, 316
  amplifier 6, 13, 306

Musictheory.net 235
MusicXML 154
musique concrète 5, 21, 35–39, 43, 46, 57, 122–124, 131, 145, 228, 298, 300, 320
Musition 234, 254
MySpace 198, 313, 314, 317

Nelson, Gary Lee 136
NetNewsWire 198, 200
network 20, 201, 256, 265, 283, 287, 304
  improvisation 23, 139, 141
  jamming 200, 210, 303, 313, 321
neural 88, 89
neutral, see invisble
NodeBox 317
Nord 126
Norman, Donald 19, 278
notation 59–69, 160;
  CPN 8, 9, 69, 72, 77, 79, 131, 153, 155, 221, 224;
  piano roll 33, 79, 153, 174, 225, 230
Numark 127
Nvu 157, 180, 187, 288

Oberheim 126
O-Generator 71, 81
ogg vorbis 148, 159
Oliveros, Pauline 124
Ondes Martenot 122, 123
OpenMusic 86, 90, 91
OpenOffice 260–263
Orff, Carl 111, 118
oscillator 8, 34, 97–107, 122, 123, 132
oscilloscope 149–151, 159, 160
overtone 47, 97, 99, 102, 228, 321

Pachet, François 136
Pages 261
Pandora 314
Papert, Seymor 12, 15, 146, 159
Pärt, Arvo 87, 92
participant 25, 26, 213, 256, 289, 300, 301
partnership 4, 12, 14, 138, 141, 269
PatchWork 86
pattern matching 221–227, 231
Pawla, Rick 180
Paynter, John 115, 120
PCM 147
PDA, see personal digital assistant
PDF 62, 155, 158, 185, 260, 262
Pearcy, Trevor 33

pedagogy 118, 145, 254, 280, 298–301, 306, 313
performance
  computer 6, 11, 312
  music 21, 32, 111, 121, 129, 132, 135, 191, 202, 248
  persistence 9, 37
  personal digital assistant 237, 303
Pet Shop Boys 125
phone
  mobile 86,, 145, 183, 296, 303, 311–313
  ringtone 196
PhotoShop 261
Piaget, Jean 23, 146
Pioneer DJ CD player 127
pitch shifting 46
pitch to MIDI conversion 137 141
Pivot 265
plugin 20, 48, 57, 65, 78, 101–107, 157, 215, 239, 277, 321
Pocaro, Steve 119, 125
podcast 39, 57, 158, 195, 288, 314
Pollak, Linsey 134
portfolio 54, 159, 197, 252–264, 303, 313
Postman, Neil 18
Practica Musica 236
practice, training 7, 14, 24, 114, 187, 202, 229 234, 235, 243, 250, 283
Pratt, George 233, 249
presentation 145, 157–161, 218, 262, 271
Pressing, Jeff 116
Pro Tools 36
probabilistic 33, 87, 298
Processing 316
production
  media 165, 184
  music xxii, 32, 54, 128, 140, 164–166, 216, 248–249, 256, 271, 280, 296, 308
  sound xxii, 79, 324, 327
professional development; see training
programming 22, 83, 88, 90, 93, 104, 116–119, 130, 140, 183–186, 277
promotion; marketing 119, 198–202, 314
Prophet V 36
publishing
  desktop 36, 261, 268
  music 5, 18, 36, 59–77, 62, 66, 81, 159, 180, 226, 276–280
Pure Data 90, 104, 117, 140, 182, 241, 327
Pythagoras 32

quantize 9, 10, 44, 136, 167
Quasar 35

radio
  Internet 183, 196, 201, 218, 314, 317
  program 39, 158, 196
Reaktor 104, 128, 316
RealAudio 147, 157, 183, 215
Reason 140
recording
  digital 21, 37, 58, 104, 145, 179, 202, 224, 275, 280
  sound 3,4, 8, 31, 37–60, 81, 126, 147, 168, 191, 214, 289, 298, 312
  tape 19, 33, 37–60
  video 14, 55, 257
reflection xxii, 28, 50, 55, 207, 215, 249, 259, 314
rehearsal 60, 65, 69, 76, 164
Reimer, Bennet 249
Report Writer xviii, 254
reporting 254–256, 270
representation
  digital 8, 10, 44, 173, 233
  graphical 79, 146, 155, 244, 260, 320, 322
  musical 14, 22, 68, 72, 131, 160, 230, 238
reverb 30, 47–49, 53, 57, 104, 113, 117, 170, 180
rich media 14, 160, 177–188, 207, 215–217, 234, 249, 252, 262, 291–293
rights
  copyright 191, 201, 208, 213, 218, 315;
  creative commons 191, 192, 200–202, 209, 213, 218;
  licence 148, 196, 235, 316
ringtones 196
Rising Software 234
Risset, Jean-Claude 8, 134
Rockmore, Carla 123
Roland 36, 126, 127, 137, 278, 303
Rowe, Robert 87, 134, 224
RSS 198–200
rule-based 33, 87, 89
Rundgren, Todd 125
Ryrie, Kim 35
sample 22, 43–48, 56, 72, 98–102, 126, 147, 239;
  editing; see audio editing
  rate 22, 44, 147;

resolution 44, 147

sampler 35, 46, 66, 121, 126, 131, 134, 276, 277

SARA 226, 227

scaffolding 17, 22, 23, 28, 29, 80, 134, 141, 275

Schaeffer, Pierre 15, 29, 35, 123, 125, 228, 232

Schafer, R. Murray 15, 115

scheduling 55, 62, 253, 266, 269, 289

Schenker, Heinrich 222, 227

Schultz, Klaus 125

Score Writer 62

security 253, 283, 286, 305–308

selector 25, 26, 90, 301

sequencer 4, 7,18–20, 36, 71–83, 90, 113, 127, 165, 168, 277, 321–325

Sequential Circuits 36, 126

serialism 33, 86, 123, 136, 260, 298

Sibelius 7, 61, 180, 226, 298
  Notes 181, 242

signal flow 48, 49, 57, 90

simulation 7, 23, 45, 102, 179, 288

Singer, Eric 137

Skype 288

Smart School Report Writer 254–256

SmartMusic 134, 141, 254

Smith, Dave 36

social computing 134, 313

Sonar 71, 90

Sonic Arts Network 306, 327

sonogram, see spectrogram

Sony ACID 46, 71, 128, 298

sound design 18, 113, 135, 168, 173–188, 209

SoundHouse 306

spatialization 53, 116, 124, 168, 179, 222

spectra 5, 10, 21, 78, 86, 152, 229, 231

spectrogram 149–152

spectrum analyser 150, 151, 160

Spiegel, Laurie 134

Spongefork 134

spreadsheet 221, 227, 254, 257, 262–264, 271

Stanton FinalScratch 128

STEIM 36

Stelarc 134

step-time 72, 79 80

stochastic; *see* probabilistic

Stockhausen, Karlheinz 32, 35, 107, 123–125

streaming audio 147, 157, 183, 190, 193, 196, 214–218; video 166

structure
  musical 32, 69, 85, 87, 89, 122–124, 152, 182, 226, 248
  organizational 215, 299

Subotnick, Morton 241

Supercollider 85, 91, 104, 137, 241, 316

Swanwick, Keith 20, 25, 249, 250, 258

Sylivian, David 125

synchronize 77, 80, 123, 128, 164, 167, 170, 298

synchronization rights 191

Synclavier 35, 124

synthesis 18, 33, 36, 78, 95–122, 212, 297, 312
  additive 97, 113, 172
  FM 99, 107
  granular 101, 102, 106
  physical modelling 102, 103, 113
  ring modulation 99, 100, 106

subtractive 98, 106, 107
  waveshaping 100, 101

synthesizer 11, 21, 31, 34–39, 44–48, 56, 65–73, 78, 90, 97, 100–107, 111–127, 136, 140, 152, 182, 239, 277
  virtual 65, 78, 103, 107, 113, 140, 277

TAB; *see* notation

Teachers Report Assistant 254, 256

Technics SL-1200 127

technologiess
  changing 3, 4, 13, 15, 21, 184, 306
  recording 3, 34, 54, 56–58, 298, 312

Technorati 314, 317

Teharmonium 34, 122

Teitelbaum, Richard 134

television 37, 166, 191, 304

Telharmonium 34, 122

Temporal 78, 79, 146, 156, 172, 183

The Chemical Brothers 126, 212

The Human League 125

The League of Automated Music Composers 139

The Orb 126

The Prodigy 126

Theremin 34, 39, 122, 123, 130, 131

Thérémin, Leon 34, 122

TI:ME 306, 328

time stretching 10, 167

TimeTabler 266
Tomita, Isao 124
tone 84
    control 47
    generator 104, 106
    timbre 9, 52, 55, 122, 123
tool, *see* computer as tool
toolkit,
    analysis 227, 230
    media 185
    synthesis 103–107
Torque 180
training
    aural 7, 24, 69, 131, 158, 233–243, 277,
        280
    computer–based 235, 243, 245
    musicianship 236, 240–245
    theory 241, 303
transparent; *see* invisible
Truax, Barry 85
Tudor, David 124
turntable 3, 11, 79, 111, 121–134
TV, *see* television

Underworld 126
UPIC 85, 155

Vangelis 125, 175
Varèse, Edgard 107, 122
Vercoe, Barry 134
Very Nervous System 137
video
    digital 51, 80, 156, 159, 179, 209
    music 146, 195, 251

vinyl 39, 127, 192
virtual instrument; *see* synthesizer virtual
virtual reality 179
visualization 74, 75, 111, 149–154, 160,
        207, 221–228, 290
Vogel, Peter 35

Wakeman, Rick 125
Walshaw, Chris 153
Wattenberg, Martin 154, 226
wav 147, 148, 159, 183, 196
waveform 34, 44, 75, 79, 97–105, 149–152,
        228–231
WebCT 266, 269
weblog; *see* blog
Wessel, David 134
Wikipedia 121, 132, 196, 200–203, 208
Williams, John 166
Winkler, Todd 134
word processor 156, 157, 254, 260, 261,
        270
WordPress 265
world wide web, *see* Internet

Xeankis, Iannis 8, 32, 33, 85, 101, 155

Yahoo! 208, 265, 314
Yamaha 36, 99, 103, 126, 127, 136, 278,
        303
Yazoo 125
Yello 125
YouTube 189

Zeta 136